Trusting the River

Jean Aspen

Epicenter Press

Epicenter Press is a regional press publishing nonfiction books about the arts, history, environment, and diverse cultures and lifestyles of Alaska and the Pacific Northwest. For more information, visit www.EpicenterPress.com

Text and images copyright © 2016 by Jean Aspen
Lyrics from *Across the Great Divide* © Kate Wolf. Used with permission.
Lyrics from *American Rivers* © Tom Russell. Used with permission.
Original poem *Supernova* © Ela Harrison. Used with permission.

Cover photo and author photo: credit to Tom Irons
Editor: Tricia Brown
Cover and interior design: Aubrey Anderson

All rights reserved. No part of this publication may be reproduced, stored in a retrieval system, or transmitted in any form by any means, electronic, mechanical, photocopying, recording, or otherwise, without the prior written permission of the publisher. Permission is given for brief excerpts to be published with book reviews in newspaper, magazines, newsletters, catalogs, and online publications.

ISBN: 978-1-935347-69-9
Library of Congress Control Number: 2017936862

10 9 8 7 6 5 4 3 2 1

Trusting the River

By Jean Aspen

Epicenter Press

Flattop watches over the River.

DEDICATION

I am grateful to my many teachers, especially:
Our gracious planet, mother of all life,
Winifred Chittenden, who gave me roots into this blessed Earth,
Janet and Bert Cutler, who taught me the joy of simplicity,
Connie Helmericks for the wings of her dreams,
Annie Helmericks, deeper than sister,
And "Rude" Amerud, who rides with the raven upon my left shoulder.
Phil Gordon and Laurie Schacht accompanied Tom on his journey into darkness,
While countless others tended our flames.
Above all, I am grateful to my husband, Tom Irons, for paddling with me across three magical decades,
And to our luminous son, Lucas Foster Irons,
Whose name means Light, Keeper of the Forest.

Contents

Dedication 5
Contents 6
Acknowledgments 9
Preface | Whorls in the River 11
Chapter 1 | Quest 15
Chapter 2 | Legacy 25
Chapter 3 | Eddies 39
Chapter 4 | The Edge 49
Chapter 5 | Kernwood Homecoming 57
Chapter 6 | Changing Course 67
Chapter 7 | Crossing America 79
Chapter 8 | Land's End 89
Chapter 9 | Echoes of the Past 97
Chapter 10 | Another North 105
Chapter 11 | Wild Goose Dreams 115
Chapter 12 | Winged Migration 125
Chapter 13 | Harvest 133
Chapter 14 | Winds of Change 141
Chapter 15 | Backpacking to the Stars 151
Chapter 16 | Fairbank, Arizona 165
Chapter 17 | Tributaries 175

Chapter 18 | California Gold 187

Chapter 19 | A Pretty Face 199

Chapter 20 | Sacred Ground 211

Chapter 21 | North to Alaska 219

Chapter 22 | Arctic Refuge 233

Chapter 23 | Divided Dreams 249

Chapter 24 | Distant Rapids 261

Chapter 25 | Little Red Truck 273

Chapter 26 | Lost and Found in America 285

Chapter 27 | Olympia 297

Chapter 28 | Uncommon Ground 307

Chapter 29 | Moments of Grace 317

Chapter 30 | Playing at Life 327

Chapter 31 | Homer Bound 337

Chapter 32 | Neverland 349

Chapter 33 | Meanders 363

Chapter 34 | Song of Friendship 379

Chapter 35 | Straight on 'til Morning 393

Chapter 36 | Across the Great Divide 407

Supernova 419

Other Works by Jean Aspen 420

Acknowledgments

Although much of my life has been lived in remote wilderness, I could never have traveled far without friends who championed my journey. The names of those whom I owe would fill a book in itself. I am deeply grateful for candles in the window and the unexpected hand from the darkness. I am also beholden to elders whose books glimmer down the years, assuring me that awakening to our human purpose is worth the effort. I have been blessed with spacious nights and dawns drenched in wonder. When I lost my way, I discovered notes left in bottles and hieroglyphs among the stones. I am not alone! I am awed by this vast, evolving Cosmos. Our sacred Earth, of which I am a cherished member, has provided my every breath. The more-than-human world has graced me with silent forgiveness. I am, after all, just a human, a member of a new species struggling to find its way.

In telling my story, I have endeavored to be truthful and fair, though events are filtered through my personal lens and memory. To those who find my descriptions unjust or who recall a different story, I apologize. I never intended to damage anyone. I am deeply grateful to each who have shared the remarkable adventure of my life.

Friends who generously gave their time reading and making suggestions for this book: Anne Davies, Barbara Burnham, my cousin Bert Cutler III, Leslie Garrison, Jody Henry, author Nan Leslie, Alaskan author Stephen Reynolds, Terry Smith, and Denise Wartes. I am deeply grateful to my beloved husband, Tom Irons, and to Laurie Anne Schacht, companion of many adventures. Finally, I am indebted to the wise and concise editing of Carol Sturgulewski, Tricia Brown, and Aubrey Anderson whose knowledge and integrity held me to a higher standard.

In deep appreciation,
Jeanie Aspen
Kernwood Cabin, Brooks Range, Alaska
August 2016

Kernwood Cabin

Preface

WHORLS IN THE RIVER

It takes two logs to keep a fire burning. Most of this book was written at our cabin in the remote arctic wilderness, two logs at a time. While my husband, Tom Irons, picked blueberries of a summer afternoon, I sorted memories like familiar old clothes, holding each to the slanted light before before releasing it into the fire with the next log. Curious as an ermine, I followed emerging patterns in and out of time. Occasionally I would climb onto our sod roof to rotate the solar panel that powered my laptop toward the low arch of sunlight twinkling through stunted trees. From my perch on our homemade ladder, I could see the river and hear its song of nameless mountains. For more than forty years, this wild valley has cradled my dreams. It has nearly taken my life many times—and yet I owe it everything.

What began as a series of letters to our son, Lucas, when Tom and I set out to search for a different future, evolved over the seasons into this fourth snapshot of my life. My mother, who also loved northern wilderness, caught glimpses of me as a wild girl of fourteen in her seventh book when she, my little sister, and I paddled across Canada. I wrote my first book while wandering arctic mountains at age twenty-two, and another when I returned two decades later with a family of my own. Now at sixty-six, I close the circle—only to discover familiar footprints in the snow. Life sometimes takes such unexpected and violent twists that it can appear frighteningly arbitrary, and yet seen from this distance of years, it glimmers with underlying motifs. All those seemingly random threads have woven the tapestry of my mostly completed journey home.

Each person who crossed my path left a gift—some obvious and others only visible in retrospect. In truth, the shore I arrived upon is very different from the one I set out to find. Life is much deeper than it is wide, and while the power of choice cannot determine outcome, it creates who we become along the way. Thus I choose to keep my mother's dreams, but not her fears; Aunt Janet's whimsy, while releasing her debility; Rude's keen alertness, and let go of the fighter who battered like a moth against life. Even my father left me something of value, though he never intended it.

Wilderness is the matrix of my life, for which I am grateful to my parents. Because of them, I've spent perhaps a third of my years remote from the complex issues of our times. Nevertheless, the struggle to integrate these two worlds and come to peace with our culture has been the driving force of my quests. Despite my adventurous choices, I am not intrinsically brave, and I have often listened with apprehension for the sound of rapids. I have also deeply grieved for our wounded planet and lost children. If life's purpose (as I believe) is to evolve and express at ever-higher levels, a safe and uneventful course may not serve. In any case, I have repeatedly chosen the more difficult channel—and for that I am not sorry. The miles have humbled me and I have learned compassion by smashing into boulders. Life is a journey into mystery. No matter the careful preparation, we wander a starry night on an unknown course. Yet if one can surrender to the grace and magic of each shifting moment, this dance is everything—exquisite and profound.

It was perhaps inevitable that Tom and I would end up in Alaska. I was drawn inexorably as a salmon back to my natal landscape, while gentle Tom would have followed me anywhere. I have not been an easy partner. My questing carried us at last into a quiet backwater, our travels reduced to seasonal migration. When ice claims the Northland, we are snug in a little Alaskan town, watching December light spill over the glaciers and pool on the breaking surf. I work at the small hospital, welcoming neighborhood children onto the planet and easing the departure of their grandparents. Tom creates the art of daily living and builds community. Each spring we migrate with the birds a thousand miles north to our cabin in the Brooks Range.

I've spent so much of my life trying to direct its flow that it's a relief to simply pay attention. Like a flower content to wilt in an autumn field, I return to the ground after a season of bloom. I watch the young ones set out on their own grand adventures and wish them joy. For me, it is good to be aging and mostly at peace. Could it really be this simple after all my searching? Celebrate the day that arrives.

Rosy dawn brushes the glacier across the bay and I imagine myself walking that far ridge, crystals shimmering into the sky with each step. Someday I will follow them, slipping from this planet as strangely as I fell onto it. I sip my coffee and watch the sun blaze suddenly from behind a peak, turning the horizon to molten gold. It is good to rest in the moment, my feet tucked warm beneath me on the sofa. I smile and think of our sleeping cabin—hip-deep in whispering snow—and of the frozen river, where next summer's birds and I will celebrate the sound of running water.

Jean Aspen and Tom Irons in 1982.

Chapter 1

QUEST

October 2003

Wynken, Blynken, and Nod one night
Sailed off in a wooden shoe —
Sailed on a river of crystal light,
Into a sea of dew.
"Where are you going, and what do you wish?"
The old moon asked the three.
"We have come to fish for the herring fish
That live in this beautiful sea;
Nets of silver and gold have we!"
Said Wynken, Blynken, and Nod.

—Eugene Field (1850–1895)

As the current of life swept us into our final decades, I asked my husband to jettison the business, home, and possessions accumulated in our quarter-century together, and take to the road with me in a used Honda. Over the years we had sometimes glanced up from routine and, like aging children, set out for adventure, but convention seemed to dictate caution at this stage. Nevertheless, I found myself again yearning for the freshness of uncertainty and for a gentler landscape than the twenty-first century.

This journey had been incubating in my heart along with a growing unease about the American Southwest. Tom would happily have remained in the art-glass studio home he had built with his hands on our five natural acres. For over two decades we had lived open to the desert and surrounded by our own art. Once we could have named the people who built within a mile of us. Those had been good years, with little money and much beauty, but while our land evolved into an oasis, Tucson was swallowing the thirsty valley below. The Arizona of my childhood lay submerged beneath shopping malls, while skies—once as blue as forever—were smudged and vague. An unsettling dream had finally triggered my decision. I dreamed of climbing Wasson Peak, highest of the Tucson Mountains, at sunset. Below me, city lights blazed to the horizon on every side. The Sonoran desert was forgotten; the kit fox and tortoise were ghosts upon the dry wind. I had awakened in tears.

"We need to leave here," I told him the next evening.

We were seated by our backyard campfire, cooking salmon over mesquite. I stared into the fire and listened for his response. The Sonoran Desert lay hushed beneath an expanse of sunset sky, mountains shading into autumn dusk where Wasson Peak loomed in silhouette, dark and mysterious.

"I think we should sell our place when Luke transfers to the University of Arizona," I continued.

Tom listened quietly, knowing my many voices. The fearful one had yet to speak. My colorful mother, dead sixteen years, would be lurking in the shadows, thrilled at the prospect of adventure but edgy as a racehorse. "Don't flap, Mother!" my sister and I used to admonish. Don't make a big deal of it. Now I heard our son, Luke, saying those words to me. *What is this tension between stillness and movement, security and enthusiasm?* I wondered. After the uncertainty of my youth, I had longed for safety, yet having created this haven, I was again seeking change. Then there was the deeper pull of my other home—Alaska.

I breathed in the evening and gazed across the darkening valley. Tom leaned forward on his bench and turned the salmon. Grizzled chest hair curled from the neck of his T-shirt, and his dark beard was streaked with white. Behind him the ancient saguaros stood black against a fading lemon sky where rafts of clouds flamed coral and then pearled to gray. Through the stained glass of our nearby kitchen door, a shaft of light spilled across the ground. I could hear the twitter of quail bedding down in the vines along the wall and a sudden scuffle of javelina near the fishpond. Lucy, our old Corgi-mongrel, muttered. Life seemed suspended in that moment, precious and ephemeral as a flower. It was all so heartbreakingly dear.

"I miss the old neighborhood," Tom said at length. "It was fun when families helped each other build. All you needed for a work party was a case of beer. These new houses are so remote and sterile," he waved vaguely towards lights speckling the nearby hills. "I don't know many people anymore, and they don't want to know me. I'd like to be part of a community again."

"Remember when it was dark at night?" I asked. We had slept on the roof, wrapped in starry mystery or lit by a waxing moon. It seemed that the few molecules of air separating us from Orion could not keep us from floating off between the stars. "I miss the darkness… and the silence."

"The newcomers are afraid of the dark and the animals," Tom said.

As if on cue, a coyote barked from the nearby wash. Another answered to the west and Lucy growled. I relaxed into the evening sounds of desert and fire, yet even here I caught the grumble of traffic carried for miles up from the flatlands. The city never slept. I could feel it rising like a slow flood. Then I remembered how the desiccated Santa Cruz River could awaken in summer rains, scouring away bridges and stores. It was heartening to think that humans might not have the final word. *We aren't wise enough for that*, I thought. *The world we work so hard to craft will not be good for us.*

An autumn breeze rattled the leaves. Winds of change were beginning to stir through my life as well. I shivered recalling how opportunities for growth often appear as whispers, becoming progressively more strident until my fingers are pried loose with a cataclysmic roar. It seemed prudent to take to the river voluntarily, nevertheless I was afraid. *Security is an illusion*, I reminded myself. *Time is our only currency. To waste it is to squander life.* How often I have tucked my fears beneath my arm and leapt.

Tom was mulling over my idea. His face, as familiar as my own, was lined. Hazel eyes, wise as an aging otter, crinkled behind thick lenses. Though nearly sixty, he was strong and agile, often winning gold in senior Olympic volleyball. He was only a couple of inches taller than my sturdy five-foot-six, and we could trade shoes. His compact hands, nails always clean, were powerful. His skin was lighter than mine and dusted with freckles. The top of his head was almost naked with a wispy island of hair in the front, while the back and sides grew collar-length chestnut hair threaded with gray.

"So where would we go?" he finally asked.

I sighed and pushed a stick into the coals, watching it flare. My elbows were propped on tanned knees. "I don't know. Away from the Southwest, maybe a small community where we can grow food and not feel guilty about using water. I want to simplify our lives. I'm tired of caring for five acres and all that we've built. I want less."

"How will we move everything?" Tom blurted. "What about my woodshop? Our glass studio? Portfolios, slides, your mother's films, my mother's quilts, books—there must be a truckload of books!"

"I think it's time we gave up making glass art... at least for now." I was twisting my fingers. "I work hard at the hospital and come home to design glass projects. It's just not fun anymore. Maybe someday... but right now I'm tired."

Tom watched me, nodding. He was a master craftsman; his hands had always known what to do with glass. He said it must have come from another lifetime. I was the artist. For twenty years we had created original work in leaded, beveled, etched, and painted-and-fired glass for clients throughout the Southwest.

"Okay," he nodded. It was that easy.

I let out my breath and glanced up. "Maybe we can find an old house to renovate down near the university for Luke," I continued. "He could rent rooms to other students to help pay for college while we use travel-nursing to look for a new home."

"Selling this place won't be easy," Tom said. "Those people," he waved at the hillside, "want big and modern, not artistic."

The fire had died to glowing coals. Dusk under a spreading sky smelled of creosote bushes and settling dew. Stars were appearing in the deepening turquoise where a trace of yellow lingered against the black mystery of Wasson Peak. "Things always work out once we align," I said softly.

Tom looked thoughtful. I initiated most of our adventures, but he threw himself into them like a dog invited for a walk. Oddly, it was I who resisted. Until I was ready, we both knew we weren't going anywhere.

"Life has become too frenetic," I continued. "I wonder if there still is an America where people sit on porches and talk. I'd like to know the babies I help deliver and watch them grow up." I'd gotten my nursing degree after Tom almost died of pneumonia one year when our family was alone in the Arctic. I tried to prepare for everything, but instead of allaying my fears, nursing had educated me about new perils. Now that I worked at the hospital, we had a steady income, but I was managing two careers. *That's the way it is with answers,* I thought, *they run their course.*

We paused to listen as a car came up Sunset Road and topped the hill a quarter-mile away. Our teenage son was out with friends and I pushed back concern. Luke had been rear-ended by an uninsured motorist and walked away from the wreck of my old Honda. We'd bought another used Civic and he was out trying his wings again. We heard the car slow at the corner of our property and the adolescent boom of a radio as it turned into the driveway. Headlights flared momentarily in the trees, disturbing the quail. Silence, then the slam of a door.

When Luke rounded the flowerbed, I felt his presence like a warm glow in my chest. At seventeen he looked to be in his twenties, a head taller than either of us, with Tom's glossy dark hair and mustache and my tanned skin. Seeing him shadowy there by the wall, I recalled a vision that had surprised me several times during my pregnancy—a dark-haired youth passing just beyond the window.

"Any salmon left?" he asked, voice soft and deep. Luke dropped onto the bench beside me, his amber eyes smiling. His frame was lanky and strong with the unconscious ease of youth. He had my high cheekbones and square chin with a cleft—undeniable mark of my remote father. He was dressed in T-shirt and shorts; his muscular legs were peppered with dark hairs, as were the backs of his large hands.

"Yes, and salad too," I rose and handed him a plate. "I picked the first winter lettuce and spinach. How are John and Kevin?" Our home offered the desert and marshmallows around a fire, but his friends had Nintendo at their homes. The guys rarely chose our place.

"We ended up just hangin' at John's and playing a new game." Luke gave me a gentle hug as he accepted the plate. He was unabashedly affectionate, holding my hand in public and walking with an arm around his father. Until this fall he had attended Greenfields, a private school of mixed ages, where he made friends with young children as well as teachers. He sometimes bought teddy bears with his own money to leave anonymously on the desks of kids who were having a rough time. It tickled him that no one knew who gave them. After his junior year, Luke had tested out of freshman subjects at the community college where he was now enrolled as a sophomore.

"Do you miss high school?" I asked.

He shook his head and a cowlick feathered across his brow. "They all envy my freedom. I'm glad I got on with my life."

"What about graduating with your friends?" I persisted.

"Naw. Graduation's overrated. I really like my classes this semester. I've been thinking about going into nursing. I wanna work with handicapped kids… well, who knows? Maybe in ER or as a flight nurse."

Tom spoke up. "Your mother and I are talking about buying a house for you near the university. We'd sell this place and use travel-nursing to find another home."

"Where it rains," I added, "and we can grow a real garden."

Luke glanced from one to the other. "It'd save on driving into town and I'd like to live on my own. It's kind of dull out here on the desert with you guys." He gave me a wicked grin.

I felt a pang. Our only child had arrived late, after I had almost given up hope. He'd been a light these short years and I wasn't ready to let go. Yet something had been set in motion—a subtle upwelling of deep water. I could feel the current shifting and sense the thunder of rapids somewhere ahead. I chewed my lip and tried to trust the river, to sense when to paddle and when to be still. Certainly, one must choose a direction, or life chooses—and usually not what you desire. On the other hand, floundering about is no answer. It's a balancing act, this dance with the river.

THE METAPHOR SERVES ME WELL, for rivers have played a profound role in my life. Often have I set my canoe upon the shoulders of some great waterway—those living arteries of our planet. My parents, Constance and Bud Helmericks, were Alaskan adventurers who filmed early documentaries for national lecture tours. My mother wrote eight published books. As a toddler, I traveled with them by canoe, small plane, and dogsled, while my little sister Annie was left with paternal grandparents in Colorado.

I was twenty-two when Alaska called me back with my first husband, Phil Beisel. My book, *Arctic Daughter: A Wilderness Journey*, recounts how Phil and I naïvely set forth, without even a map, on the mighty Yukon River in the spring of 1972. We were scantily equipped for a year of living alone off the land in the remote Brooks Range, that massive group of mountains that extend across the northern third of the state. We carried only the supplies that would fit into a nineteen-foot canoe. With a few dried staples, axes, sleeping bags, pup tent, rifles, folding Yukon stove and pipe, small plexiglass window panes, and a few tools, we paddled downstream from the end of the road at Circle, Alaska. Reaching a tributary, we ascended on foot, pulling our craft north into the mountains. When autumn overtook us, we set to work building a log cabin and hunting food to see us through the cold and dark of arctic winter. Ultimately, we would spend close to four years walking that great and unpeopled wilderness.

Two decades later, I repeated this adventure with Tom, six-year-old Luke, and Laurie Schacht, a young woman who had never camped. It was spring of 1992 when the four of us were flown into the Brooks Range and left fifty miles upstream from my old cabin. My second book, *Arctic Son: Fulfilling the Dream*, tells of building another log home and living for a year remote from other humans. When spring again released the river, we embarked on a six-hundred mile canoe voyage back to that other world, a treacherous journey of more than three weeks. We filmed our fourteen months alone, and two decades later Tom and I produced a documentary, companion to the book.

Arctic wilderness remained integral to our family throughout the years, beckoning us back repeatedly, including another fifteen months alone at our cabin with Laurie and Luke when he was thirteen and fourteen. These pivotal years of immersion in nature guided our choices in ways that diverged from those of our more domestic friends. The river also coached me about taking my fear along, for the current knows where it's going even when I don't. Still, there is no a guarantee that evening will find me warm and dry on some welcoming shore. This I understood, but could not deeply accept.

AFTER OUR CAMPFIRE DISCUSSION, TOM shifted gears. I was still toying with the idea of change—dipping my toes into possibilities—when he launched us into midstream. There was no turning back. Before I knew it, he had cleaned out our glass studio, sold the equipment, and located a rundown, three-bedroom house close to the university. It was on Sylvia Street, which seemed propitious, for my mother had named our first dog Sylvia. "It means 'She of the Forest,'" she had told my little sister, Annie, and me. Sylvia had been a sleek, black beast with smiling eyes and snowy chest—our guardian throughout an uncertain childhood. My mother, of course, was the real forest creature.

The "Sylvia House," as we soon called it, was built in 1948 and randomly enlarged by a man who had grown old there and died. The walls were yellowed with tobacco smoke and avocado shag carpet festered over layers of linoleum. Roaches skittered out of dark closets. The tiny evaporative cooler wasn't ducted into the hodgepodge of rooms and the gas furnace was a menace. The plumbing was dank, the rooms cramped and dingy, and the electrical wiring dangerous. The house squatted on a large barren lot that was enclosed in back by an unfinished block wall. It would certainly engage Tom's energy.

When we showed the ugly little house to Lucas—he now preferred that name to Luke, though a lifetime of habit wasn't easy to shift, and we would continue to use both names—he looked ready to cry. "If you really think you can make something of this…" his voice trailed off and he turned to his father. "I'll trust you, but it looks hopeless to me."

Using an equity loan on our Sunset property, we bought the Sylvia House for cash. I worked extra shifts at the hospital, but money drained through our fingers as Tom dug into major renovations. He spent that winter of 2003–04 in town, coming home filthy and complaining about faulty wiring and makeshift construction. Whenever we could, Lucas and I joined him in the cold house. We stripped the floors to the cement slab and removed superfluous walls, old steel-frame windows, furnace, toilets, sinks, appliances, shelves, and crumbling Spackle. In went ceramic tile, carpet, a new heating and cooling system, ductwork, modern wiring, underground 200-amp service, insulated windows, new appliances, lights, and fresh paint. As spring advanced, even Lucas began to see the possibilities. With growing excitement, he started to look for roommates.

Spring of 2004 blushed the Sonoran desert, when—just before his eighteenth birthday—our son moved out, taking his old dog, much of our furniture, and my green Honda. Tom and I were suddenly alone in the vacant studio sharing his old four-cylinder Toyota pickup, bought when Luke was born.

Now there were two properties to support on one income and our family lived divided. Against my growing disquiet, plans for another year in the wilderness had crept into the mix and the clock was ticking down. To survive arctic winter, we would need the brief summer to prepare. Two friends (who had yet to meet one another) planned to join us for fourteen months at our cabin. Tim ("my friends call me Rude") Amerud was a kindred spirit and a man of wild spaces. Tom, Rude, and I were tested wilderness companions— all Aries, lined up like close siblings. Heather, on the other hand, was an unknown. Twenty-five years younger, she had a childlike openness and a variety of piercings. Like Laurie, she had little outdoor experience or money, but was excited and willing to commit. She was working as a student editor on our documentary and pleaded to be included. As foster parents, Tom and I have taken many young people under our wings throughout the years, finding enthusiasm to be a powerful indicator.

As the season advanced, I became increasingly uneasy. There's a fine line between challenges that are part of an adventure and the signposts of impending disaster. Tom and I had learned that a major obstacle need not stop you, but when a second one appears, you should pay attention. The river speaks in symbols. By the time a third large problem emerges, it is time to back-paddle. The dance between boldness and retreat is subtle and it is the wise adventurer who lives to plan another trip.

We had intended to sell our Sunset property and pay off the Sylvia House, but, no buyer arrived, and without our glass studio my earnings were our only income. Strike two was Lucas: he had yet to find roommates and although he was excited about flying solo, I wasn't sure he was ready. As I worked those extra shifts at the hospital, a ton of dried food in five-gallon buckets, totes of arctic clothing, and various supplies were accumulating along the empty studio walls. Preparation for a year in remote wilderness is a complex task and choosing an attractive mix of nutritious food that will keep without refrigeration requires good planning. With our limited funds, ingenuity and foresight were paramount.

In Minnesota, Rude was also spending money and making items for the trip. He had commissioned a new stovepipe oven built to my design for baking bread and roasting meat. Sleeping little, he worked to enclose the home he was building on forty acres of woodland. He had shut down his plumbing business and found a caretaker to live at his place and feed his team of seventeen sled dogs. Heather had arranged her life and assembled clothing for the coming winter. Tom and I bought her ticket to Alaska.

The sun climbed above the Sonoran desert, flowers wilted, and temperatures rose into the 90s. I was feeling drained and anxious, poised on the edge of a precipice. I was afraid to move ahead, but couldn't face the disappointment of my friends by calling it off. The rapids were sounding louder and dread took root in my stomach. I didn't feel adventuresome anymore; I just wanted my predictable life back.

My parents, Bud and Connie Helmericks, travel the Arctic coast by dogsled about 1948.

My father paddles me on Takahula Lake, 1952.

Chapter 2

LEGACY

It was my romantic mother who inspired me to dream large, though she gave me few tools. She had scant practical skill and no stomach for conflict—an odd combination for an "author and arctic explorer," as she defined herself. Words and imagination were her gift and escape was her main device.

In early childhood, Connie fled her nannies, slipping away from her powerful and abusive father to ramble the woods of upstate New York. Her younger and more docile sister Janet told of my seven-year-old mother climbing out their second-story bedroom window and down a tree to sleep beneath the stars. Janet learned to appease their father, while Connie rebelled. When the two girls and their mother summered at the family cottage on Quaker Lake, my mother often spent the night alone, adrift on the lake in her canoe. In nature she discovered freedom from the rigid female roles of her day and in Emerson, Wordsworth, Longfellow, Whitman, and Thoreau, she found a model for life. Touching that ideal and manifesting it, however, were different stories.

Born Constance Chittenden on January 4, 1918, my gentle mother was named for a lake in Switzerland and she loved wild country beyond all else. Although she spent only a dozen years in Alaskan wilderness, they measured the rest of her life and in some ways imprisoned her. She met my father while a student at the University of Arizona in the fall of 1939. America was awakening from the Great Depression and another World War grumbled like a bank of clouds along the horizon. My parents were introduced at a dance: he in old sneakers and corduroy pants, she with her gown and dance card. Connie was studying sociology when Bud enrolled in engineering.

Connie was a slender girl of average height with a fetching bosom.

She had dainty feet and ankles, which, she told me, had been tightly laced in childhood for that purpose, and her delicate wedding band fits my little finger. She had wavy light brown hair worn off the collar and parted on the left. Her translucent skin was lightly freckled, and her generous mouth flashed in a bright and hopeful smile. Even in the wilderness, she wore red lipstick. She had gray-green eyes with fine lashes. Over them, she penciled her brows in high arcs. A sketch of Connie at age fourteen portrays her in trousers and boots—very much the tomboy. Early photographs also show her coquettish in summery frocks. These two faces—the educated young lady from an upper class family and the wild romantic—were her continuing dichotomy.

My father was the eldest of three boys and a girl. He was christened Harmon Robert Helmericks, but everyone called him "Bud." From the beginning there are mysteries and his stories do not add up; little can be taken at face value. In her books, Connie states that they were the same age, though she told me she thought he was a year older. According to his birth certificate, Bud was born January 18, 1917, a year after his young parents were married. His conscription papers, however, place his birth in 1918, but the date has been written over.

My grandfather Clarence was only nineteen when Bud was born; his wife Abby was twenty-one. Clarence worked as a farm laborer near Elliott, Illinois, for thirty dollars a month and the use of a house, milk cow, a dozen hens, and a garden patch. He had been on his own since the age of twelve—driven out by a new stepfather. Grandpa was as solid as a brick, with powerful arms and a thick neck. I recall him always in overalls. About the time Clarence made a down payment on a farm of his own, his three sons left home to seek their fortunes elsewhere. Within a few years, my grandparents gave up farming and moved to Colorado, where Clarence opened a gun shop.

I have only one memory of my paternal grandmother. Abby was a small woman who seemed faded like a cut flower too long in a vase. She arrived in Tucson on the train one afternoon when I was about five. I remember her carrying a box suitcase up the walk of our little back-alley rental. She spent the night with Annie and me playing with teddy bears in our bunk beds. In the early morning, she held our hands on a walk to the neighborhood park. Our mother awoke to a quiet house and the sudden fear that Bud's mother might have taken us back to Colorado. Mama looked scared when we returned for breakfast. Not long afterward, Abby died.

Early pictures of my father capture a boyish charm. He had blond hair, golden skin, rosy cheeks, steel-blue eyes, and a square jaw split by that severe cleft—a softer version of which dimpled my own chin and my son's. At six-foot-one, Bud towered over Connie, appearing confident and relaxed in pictures—a man entitled. He was strong, bright, and nimble with excellent vision, a host of practical skills, and the desire to shoot things—an urge that he never outgrew. He arrived in Tucson with little beyond ambition and entered the University of Arizona, taking a room with three other students who all shared a motorcycle. His younger brother John had agreed to help put him through college with the promise that Bud would return the favor.

Connie and Janet lived with my grandmother Winnie in her modest two-bedroom home across from Tucson High School. My parents' two-year courtship consisted mainly of hunting rabbits and javelina in the Sonoran Desert, which in those days surrounded the university campus. One of their first dates was a hike out to Sabino Canyon. Connie pointed out a colorful hummingbird and much to her distress, Bud shot it for her. My mother was sentimental and tenderhearted and it is hard to imagine her shooting anything. Nevertheless, adventure was in her blood and she had found a man to share her wild dreams.

They were married in Winnie's living room in front of the rose-colored brick mantel early in May 1941. Connie wore a beige traveling dress with a lace collar, a stylish hat, and white gloves; my handsome father wore his old sneakers and corduroy trousers. Within an hour, they caught the train to Seattle and then boarded a steamer for Alaska. Winnie paid my mother's passage. "We were twenty-three," Connie wrote in her first book, *We Live in Alaska*. She had just completed her junior year. Bud was a sophomore. He didn't return to college, and his brother John was never able to go. Connie told me that it was years before Uncle John forgave her for luring Bud north.

Although Bud later accused Connie of marrying him to get to Alaska, I don't believe that was the whole story. She deeply loved him and saw him in poetic terms: her handsome wilderness partner. Even in youth my father enlarged his life—as if he could never be enough. Connie, the romantic, was swept up in his glamorous (if spurious) tales of South America, Cuba, and Alaska. Perhaps he felt deficient: he was a farm boy from a meat-and-potatoes family; she was cultured and articulate. Connie loved the superlative and even as his stories unraveled, she forgave his inconsistencies and wrote him into a hero. I never heard his side. The closest he came to speaking of her in later years was "that woman."

"Your father was very jealous," Connie once said. "Not just of men. When I joined a women's sewing circle during the war, knitting socks and mittens for the soldiers, he accompanied me so that I wouldn't get close to anyone."

Their first year in Alaska was spent in Anchorage, whose muddy streets were swollen with newcomers and haphazard construction as Alaska prepared for war. My father found work as a day laborer toting bags of cement for the construction of an airfield, and then as a sheet metal worker making $75 a week. Connie cooked, washed clothes, and carried buckets of water to their rented log hovel while a dreary winter pulled down. It was remote from both the natural beauty she sought and the intellectual conversations to which she was accustomed.

In December 1941, America entered World War II in a clap of thunder that rolled across Alaska. The remote Territory was vulnerable and strategically located. Over seven thousand planes were flown across the Bering Sea to keep Russia in the fight. The rapid buildup of military forces dramatically shifted demographics. Alaska fell under military rule and in May 1942, my parents were sent to the army camp of Fort Raymond near Seward—then Alaska's main port. Seward perches on the Kenai Peninsula amid dense spruce forest soaked in 115 inches of precipitation each year.

In early June 1942, the Japanese bombed the U.S. naval base at Alaska's Dutch Harbor and invaded the islands of Attu and Kiska: Americans were fighting on home soil. In the panic that followed this invasion, martial law was declared for the Territory. Every able-bodied man was conscripted or set to work in the war effort. Later that month, my father obtained materials and built a nineteen-foot canoe from two layers of thin canvas and hand-cut planks. He had never seen a canoe and used Connie's descriptions along with a borrowed catalogue. When he was given permission for a month's holiday, my parents shipped the *Queen Beaver* by rail to Fairbanks. Amid hordes of mosquitoes, they embarked on their first real adventure, paddling down the Tanana under the midnight sun and onto the great Yukon River. It was after freeze-up, five months later, when they caught a flight back from the Bering Sea. That winter in Seward, my mother wrote her first book.

With the military directing all activities, civilians unnecessary for the war were being evacuated, so Connie got a job in the base laundry. In the spring of 1944, my father constructed a second canoe, the *Little Willow*, fourteen and a half feet long and very beamy. This time, my parents disappeared into the wilderness on an odyssey of epic proportions. Twenty-eight months later they emerged on the Arctic coast of Canada at the delta of the Mackenzie River. They had traveled hundreds of miles by canoe, foot, and dogsled, living off the land for two winters and three summers. The war was over.

The trilogy of books Connie wrote of this adventure catapulted my parents into national acclaim. Initially Bud had dismissed her writing, but as success mounted, he wanted his name on the cover. She acquiesced and put him as co-author on her subsequent works. After all, they were a team; she would do what it took to keep peace. Connie saw everyone, including herself, as characters and willingly played foil to Bud's prowess. His life hunting polar bears with Iñupiat men seemed more dramatic than hers writing cross-legged in a tent, so she even adopted his voice at times. It was the story that mattered. She also ghosted his three children's books, never imagining he would claim it all. One has only to read my father's letters to know the truth: Connie's writing is complex and engaging, while his is as stolid as a grocery list.

Connie's books topped the New York Times Best Seller List for weeks, and the American public was entranced. I am still contacted by people who say they came to Alaska, moved from the city, or were inspired as children by her words. She wrote hundreds of letters in a meticulous hand that were cherished by friends for half a century. It's strange that I held on to so few. Perhaps I never imagined they would stop arriving. She was also a tireless promoter, and opportunities poured in: cameras, rifles, and a Cessna 140 airplane—the first *Arctic Tern*. Her fifth book, *Flight of the Arctic Tern* opens as they set off to film their wilderness haunts by Bush plane. My photogenic parents sold their story to *LIFE Magazine*, including the cover and pages of color photos, and began filming documentaries. Bud was probably the major photographer and his work is impeccable—especially under the conditions. On national lecture tour, it was Connie who narrated. Soon they traded up airplanes.

At some point, the rift in their basic values began to widen. While both loved adventure and fame, Bud was a conqueror and builder of empire; Connie, the intellectual and naturalist, was happier watching a grizzly than skinning it. He was secretive and controlling; she was as open and as friendly as a puppy.

I arrived in the spring of 1950, followed a short eighteen months later by Annie. I'm not sure if either of our parents considered how children would alter their lives. I have a collection of letters that Bud wrote to Connie while she awaited my birth with Winnie in Tucson. Reluctantly, he had embarked alone on their scheduled lecture circuit. He voiced concern that the baby not spoil their adventures. They would leave "him" with friends and continue on as before. Repeatedly, he urged her to write more of "our books," and warned her to not listen to her mother or women friends. Most people, he cautioned, were "hares," while the two of them were "beavers."

"When people think of Alaska," he wrote, "they think of Helmericks." Africa would be next, he told her. The world was theirs, if only she would keep writing and guard her thinking from the hares.

I turned out to be the perfect prop for continuing the Helmericks saga—a golden toddler to star in their next documentary, *Jeanie of Alaska*. Again they were featured in *LIFE Magazine*—idyllic color pages of me nestled between my charismatic parents at our snug wilderness cabin on beautiful Takahula Lake. It looks too perfect to be true. Meanwhile, my invisible baby sister remained in Montrose, Colorado, with Bud's parents. Grandpa propped little Annie between sacks of mail on the front seat of his green Ford pickup as he drove the high mountain passes, supplementing the income from his gun shop where Uncle John worked.

The curtain came down on our family's very public fairy tale in March of 1953. At Bud's insistence, they had settled in Montrose and were constructing a home near his parents. It was to be magnificent, with an artificial lake and swans. Bud was in his element, talking guns in his father's shop, but for Connie it was the final link in domestication. "He would sit me down at the typewriter and tell me to write," she said. "His mother was to care for the children while I produced books."

It must have taken great courage for her to leave. "It had gotten so I couldn't walk across the street without him," she told me. "He supervised everything I did." She packed up her babies (one of whom she barely knew) and returned to Tucson on the train. I recall that trip—a toddler's view of legs and leather shoes, as we waited interminably on the metal platform. Connie had never driven before, but Winnie soon persuaded her to return to Colorado for their car. My mother taught herself to drive on her way back to Arizona. That black-and-white Ford, her book copyrights, and her children were all she salvaged from twelve years of marriage.

"Your father convinced me that we would save money by using the same lawyer," she later said. "He had banked everything under his name and I never knew how much."

Bud soon flew the final *Arctic Tern*, a Cessna 170, back to Alaska with the seeds of his new family: Martha and her eight-year-old son, Jim. They had run in the same circles in Montrose. Connie once told me that Bud's shift in interest allowed her to escape the relationship. Nevertheless, it wasn't until May 3, 1956, that she granted him a divorce. She held out for half-interest in that five-acre homestead on Takahula Lake, which Bud had registered under his name. It was not a pragmatic decision—money would have served us better. She said she wanted it for her girls, and perhaps she couldn't release wilderness she would never see again.

My father remarried and edited Connie and her daughters from the official version of his life. This was a curious sleight of hand for a public figure, but such was the force of his personality that few questioned it. Bud retained the money and the fame, but what he lacked was Connie's gift with words. For years he tried to write, often alluding to "the books," but it was a dry well—a secret he somehow concealed even from his family.

My mother disappeared into obscurity, from which she never recovered. No longer the famous arctic explorer dressed in furs and smiling from the cover of magazines, Connie was penniless with two small children—a "divorcee" without social status in the 1950s world of Betty Crocker moms. She didn't have to answer to Bud anymore and was free to write with candor, but no one was listening.

Connie brought her babies to the only refuge she had: Winnie's modest home across the street from Tucson High. It had a small lawn of thirsty Bermuda grass, white-and-pink flowering oleander bushes, a privet hedge, and a porch enclosed by heavy pillars. These were bracketed with two orange trees whose fruit was inedible. Winnie had planted "artificial oranges" to keep the high school kids out of her trees, but the street was often littered with squashed fruit. Beyond the hedge, a wild arroyo dove beneath the traffic in two square concrete tunnels, each large enough to drive a car through. I well recall the dank blackness, where unsupervised small children could explore for miles in a maze beneath the city. During summer monsoons, these arteries throbbed with a muddy torrent. It was a fascinating and perilous place.

I was not quite three when we arrived in Tucson, and yet wilderness had already carved a deep belonging in my soul. The flaming colors of dwarf birch against burgundy peaks laced with the first snows have never left me. The scent of spruce and Labrador tea lingers always in the back of my mind. In the sterile chaos of the operating room, I will suddenly hear the song of a white-crowned sparrow and fill my lungs with remembered mountain air. Then my toes grow into the Earth like roots, and I recall who I am and why I have chosen to be here.

My sister and I spent much of our childhood in a tiny cottage on Bean Alley within walking distance of Winnie's house. Our grandmother was well into her seventies by then. There were also numerous foster placements as our mother struggled to resurrect her writing and lecturing career, for Connie never relinquished her dream of untrammeled wilderness. Someday, she told us, we would be liberated from pettiness, drudgery, and public schools—free to wander a vast and beautiful landscape. There were wild rivers, she promised as we sat on the little porch in the heat of a summer evening, and we would explore them.

In my childhood memories, my mother wears colorful skirts with a flared hem at mid-calf, cotton blouses that showed off her bosom, and wide belts accentuating a slender waist. She painted her nails, went barelegged in hot weather, and was pleased with her tan. I recall a gold lamé bathing suit, a dove-gray evening dress with layers of fringe, and a large black hat with artificial fruit that I used to chew. I loved to play in the closet among her shoes. She had an evening stole of white foxes that she had trapped, with a clamp where the mouth used to be, but she seldom got to wear it. She dyed her thick hair red in imitation of my father's second wife, who reminded her, she said, of "a little red fox."

I had just turned fourteen and Annie was twelve the spring our mother secured an advance for her seventh book, *Down the Wild River North*, from her old publisher, Little, Brown and Company. It was an audacious undertaking: a canoe voyage spanning two summers and three thousand miles that would traverse northern Canada on the Peace, Slave, and Mackenzie Rivers to the Arctic Ocean. Connie was in her mid-forties and packing an extra twenty pounds. Annie and I had never seen a river. Still, we three set out on the mighty Peace during the worst flood in thirty years. Even getting there was an adventure, for much of Montana and Alberta was underwater in the spring of 1964.

I recall our first mosquito-infested camp in the shadow of the bridge at Taylor Crossing, Alberta. After the Hudson Bay man deposited our outfit, Connie stood frightened and unsure, staring at that roiling brown current. "Remember this, girls," she told us, "for you are living history. They will dam the Peace and kill its spirit." There was a catch in her voice. "Never again will there be this wild and free river."

We hesitated for several days on that muddy shore. Curious locals and tourists stopped on the bridge to stare down at the strange woman and her two daughters with their twenty-foot plank canoe, poorly pitched canvas-wall tent, and mounds of gear. Caught between the realities of an ugly torrent that uprooted forests and piled them like matchsticks and her commitment for the seven thousand-dollar advance (now partially spent), Connie finally garnered the courage to shove off. It was a foolish and heroic act—tackling that river with her two inexperienced daughters—and it changed my life.

Legacy

For all her spirit and dreams, our mother was woefully impractical. She had relied upon our pragmatic father, and soon came to lean heavily on her children for the muscle and ingenuity behind our "expedition." We could easily have disappeared—bodies never found—but instead, the days brought forth strength. An adventurous life is not safe or easy, but it is the most interesting passage between birth and death. When you think about it, that's all we really have—those finite miles along an uncharted river. Double or nothing—why not? In the end the chips are taken away. It's only play money but the Journey is real. And what a journey it turned out to be!

I recall the night Connie burned down our canvas wall tent. It was after midnight in the endless twilight of northern summer and we were exhausted. We had camped high on a bluff, the only dry land in a long and weary day on that bloated river where stands of trees emerged like islands from a moving landscape. Our canoe was tied a hundred feet below, mired in sucking mud. After my little sister and I fell asleep, our mother clambered down the steep bank for a bucket of turbid water, leaving the door of the little woodstove open to smoke out mosquitoes. I can only imagine her horror when she saw the flames erupt high above. I recall Annie rolling from the tent like a worm. She had tied her sleeping bag and head net around her neck to keep out the probing mass of mosquitos. I saved the camera and rifle as the structure collapsed. I have a photo of Annie in dirty pajamas barefooted in the wild roses, her face swollen with bites and smudged in soot, blonde hair tangled with dawn. She is staring out over the expanse of river as day creeps back from the edge of the world. It is an image out of the Pleistocene, the face of elemental human life in a vast and unstructured world.

It took us two summers to arrive at Inuvik on the Arctic Ocean. I had written to my father, a man I couldn't remember, from a small town along the lower Mackenzie River, asking if I could to come to live with him in Alaska. After traversing much of Canada by canoe, I felt worthy of reclaiming my past. Connie was supportive, thinking perhaps of her early years. I was deliriously happy when I opened his hesitant reply. When Connie and Annie returned to Arizona at the end of our journey, I climbed aboard a DC-3 and continued north by a series of small planes to meet my mythical Bush pilot father and his new family.

It was a rainy autumn day when the *Arctic Tern* settled noisily onto the Koyukuk River and taxied toward the Hughes trading post. I was standing anxiously on the shore as the tall man with light brown hair and hip waders swung onto the floats. His movements were graceful and his hands were sure as he rotated the little plane, lifted the rudders, and tethered it. It was all strangely familiar. A pinched smile was fixed to his rosy face, but the blue eyes were intense and guarded as he greeted me.

"Well now, Jeanie," Bud said, "I see you've been feeding well." His voice was strangely high and weak for such a large man. No hug, not even a handshake, just the apprising look of a man who would rather have one hundred seventy-five pounds of supplies than an awkward teenage daughter.

Caught up in fantasies of life with my glamorous father, I was unprepared for this critical man or the prison of his remote world. I was suddenly aware of my heavy body, long greasy hair, and adolescent skin. I was wearing black stretch pants with a hole worn in the right knee and a blue plaid shirt, stained and frayed. Rubber boots over musty wool socks completed my outfit, for I had frugally saved the money my mother had given to buy new clothes on my layover in Fairbanks. Now there were no stores. *Well*, I decided, *I will earn my keep and his affection.*

"I just canoed three thousand miles," I told him shyly.

He shook his head sadly. "Jeanie, there's nothing special about that. We live that way every day. Go on up to the store and start carrying down the supplies."

I later asked my mother why she hadn't warned me.

"I hoped he would be different with you, his firstborn. I didn't want to prejudice you against your own father." Then she looked at me with a glint of humor. "You wouldn't have listened anyway."

It was drizzling as I hauled five-gallon cans of gas to the river and Bud talked with the trader, Will James. Soon my father and I were aloft, headed for his new cabin and family on Walker Lake. I was airsick as we bumped through the gray sky. Close beneath the wing, autumn colors scrolled by, gold and russet. At last, I was coming home! Walker Lake appeared ahead, seventeen miles long and cradled like an emerald between snowy peaks. We circled a small island with an iconic cabin and then settled noisily onto the clearest water I could remember. It reminded me of dreams where I swam among beautiful fish—like flying through teal-green sky—and I realized they came from my childhood.

My father and Martha with their two little boys were a showcase family for the wealthy client and his wife, who were there for the fall hunt. At seven, my half-brother Mark was guileless. He had green eyes, light brown hair, our father's cleft, his mother's dimples, and an infectious giggle. Four-year-old Jeffrey Todd had eyes as blue as the lake, rosy skin, and hair like spun gold. The two boys played happily together while their slender mother—her hair now dark brown—baked bread on the wood-burning stove. Each day my father and his quiet, older client flew out to hunt a variety of game: sheep, moose, bear. The hunter's pleasant wife remained with Martha. As she went about playing the hostess and the homely chores, my stepmother seemed as chatty and bright as a bird.

It appeared idyllic and yet tension squeezed my chest, making it hard to breathe. There was something scripted and deeply secretive here, unspoken rules that I transgressed without ever knowing. Try as I might, I felt like an embarrassment in this careful, picture-book story. Often I slipped away to circle the small island on foot. I would build a tiny fire down in some hollow overlooking the azure waters, but it was rainy and cold and I couldn't stay out forever. In any case, my absence seemed as awkward as my presence.

After hunting season, my father flew the hunter and his wife back to Fairbanks and then took our family north to the Arctic coast for the annual run of fish. Packed with the final load, I peered out at snowy crags as we crossed the Continental Divide and descended toward the ocean. Beyond the mountain ranges, we landed briefly on a tundra pond where my father kept a cache of fuel. Caribou dotted the clear expanse, which undulated treeless to the horizon. It looked deceptively open, yet one could hide entire herds in the gentle contours of this land. On closer inspection, I saw that the ground was cut into polygons by a labyrinth of watery veins. It was a tawny and subdued landscape where the wind never rested.

The anemic sun hung low by the time the Cessna 170 flared over a freshwater lake in the middle of a large island on the Colville River delta. The land here rose only a few feet above the muddy river and was incised with a network of connected ponds. My father's two-story frame house was visible for miles. I shivered in the icy breeze as I clambered awkwardly from the plane onto a float.

"Jeanie, you are so clumsy," my father observed. "Didn't anyone teach you anything?"

My stepbrother Jim met us. Silently, he tied off the plane and began hauling supplies toward the buildings. At twenty-one, Jim was quiet and we rarely spoke to one another. He had Martha's brown hair and dark blue eyes in an angular face. He was about my height, but wiry and immensely strong from a life of brute labor. One of his jobs was digging ice cellars thirty feet down into the permafrost, using a jackhammer to chisel tunnels for storage of frozen meat and fish.

"The family" consisted of my father, Martha, and their two young sons.

They lived in the heated upstairs, which was carpeted and furnished. It had large triple-glazed windows, a fireplace, electricity, two bedrooms, a full kitchen, and a cozy living room with comfortable sofa and chairs. Outbuildings, one of which was the "greenhouse" housing the power generator, were connected by raised wooden walks. Jim lived with the generator until winter set in, when he moved to his room downstairs. I rarely saw him except when he came in for meals. I believe he was kept busy with various construction projects and keeping "the family" comfortable by pumping water, hauling out trash, and emptying the toilet bucket.

I was shown to an unheated downstairs storeroom and given an insulated cot and sleeping bag. "The cave," as I came to think of it, was filled with bags of cement, nails, plywood and sawdust. It was destined to become a laundry room. I swept the floor and covered the pallets with tarps to make it seem homey. As winter descended, frost grew down the walls and temperatures fell below zero. It was harder for me to stay invisible at the Colville, for eventually the cold drove me upstairs.

The first job beyond dishes that my father assigned me was gathering driftwood. Although the Arctic coast is treeless, ocean currents bring wood from the Mackenzie River. Bud liked to rise early and build a fire for his small sons, a special "family time" that I was not supposed to interrupt. There were many such implied rules. If I missed the nuance he would tell me in a disappointed tone, "Everyone knows these things." I would come upstairs for breakfast, wash the dishes, and then go out to collect wood. It was a relief to be outside alone, and I pulled driftwood from the freezing mud along the riverbank in my old rubber boots until forced inside by winter. In the rapidly waning days, ice as clear as glass grew across the dark potholes and dusted with frost-flowers and the first snows. Ptarmigan turned white and flocked up, cackling when they flew in groups of fifty and more. Days were gray and indistinct. Sometimes Mark, Jeffrey, and I played outside, sliding together on the potholes. We could see down about four feet through the windowpane of ice. I loved my little brothers and felt at home on the changing tundra.

Coming inside was another story. "See how nice Mother looks," my father would point out as I washed dishes. "Just because you live in the wilderness doesn't mean you have to be slovenly. You should try harder."

I hung my head, seeing the black pants with the hole. To make matters worse, I had become a sneak eater, and was miserably growing ever fatter in my tattered outfit. My life seemed over. *If only I could disappear without a trace,* I thought. *Maybe I could walk out on the tundra and just keep going.*

"You were such a precious little thing, Jeanie," my father said. "I took such good care of you. One time when you couldn't sleep without your blanket, I walked a mile back to the plane to get it."

It was a story he often repeated, the apparent culmination of our relationship—and I didn't even remember it.

"If I had gotten you when you were little, I could have trained you," he said with the sad disappointment of a cook whose cake has fallen, "but now your ears are hard." He pinched the upper curl of my ear then reached down to stroke Jeff's tender lobe. "See? His ears are soft."

In truth, I have suffered from hard ears all of my life, but at fifteen I had no idea how to heal them. I gazed out the windows at the advancing twilight of arctic winter, feeling lost beyond hope. I doubted anyone would ever find me.

Winter 1972 when my first husband, Phil Beisel, and I walked into the Arctic and built a cabin.

My sister, Ann Helmericks and Phil Beisel 1975. Phil took Annie under his wing as a sister.

Chapter 3

EDDIES

Spunky little Annie may have saved my life that winter. Although my father forbade me to write to "the enemy camp," my sister came looking for me. When she didn't hear from me, Annie persuaded our mother to put her on a plane and found her way to Hughes, Alaska, just before her fourteenth birthday. Bud was furious when he got the radio message that his youngest daughter was waiting for him. Had Martha not pleaded Annie's case, he would have shipped her back to Tucson unseen.

Our father had a quick and cutting humor, but Annie seemed immune. Where I wilted under his derision, it cascaded off her bonnie head like water from an otter. When he placed a mop over his head and stood swaybacked at the sink, pretending to wash dishes in caricature of her slow progress, she laughed; but if he ventured to make light of me, she was fierce as a mink. This was loyalty I probably did not deserve—for I had not always been kind to my little sister—but it also speaks to the solidarity of kids who need one another.

The Colville River had frozen over by then. My father set out a line of gill nets, threading them under the new ice with a long hooked pole. The ends were tied to sticks frozen into the surface. Six mornings a week I walked half a mile in the shifting dawn to pull fishnets. Once the ropes were chiseled free, the long nets could be hauled from beneath the ice with their struggling load. Two related species of foot-long fish were running in October. Arctic cisco, with emerald backs and bellies as luminescent as the moon, would be eaten by the Iñupiat people of Barrow and Barter Island. Raw, frozen strips whittled from the fish tasted of buttery nutmeg. Silvery common cisco were sold for dog feed.

Bud had flown in two Athabascan men for this commercial fishing.

The elder, Little Joe, was shorter than I and had a round beaming face. He laughed with me, making a game of hauling the nets from beneath the ice and plucking the freezing fish. The younger man, whose name I don't recall, seemed a brooding and silent presence. I believe he walked with one stiff leg from a snowmobile accident. About midmorning we would see Annie coming through the pastel mist, drifting between sky and snow as she gradually drew near. She was my height, but had our mother's delicate frame and translucent skin and our father's blue-gray eyes with his small mouth. Despite her slim agility, Annie was never very strong. Accustomed to being second best, she was not motivated to compete by Bud's disapproval.

One subzero day in November, a C-46 arrived for the thousands of frozen fish that were stacked in hundred-pound gunnysacks along the runway. The sky above was clear, but ice fog swam along the ground like syrup. We could hear the plane swing by repeatedly overhead, and even glimpse it passing through the blue, but it finally returned to Fairbanks with its precious supplies. A few days later it came back and Jim spent the day heaving gunnysacks of fish seven feet up into the belly of the plane.

Light rapidly bled from the arctic sky until all that remained of day was a delicate reflection on the clouds from below the horizon. I thought we had settled in for the dark of winter, when I was told to pack my few things one morning.

"We're leaving?" I stammered.

"If you paid attention, you would know," my father said.

Martha had ordered clothes for me from the Sears catalogue, but I felt as awkward as a pig in knit pastels and girdle when we suddenly moved to town. The family rented an apartment in Fairbanks, where Annie and I at last had a room. Abruptly we were back in school just before Christmas. My memory of that time is starkly written: black night, biting cold, ice fog, and fluorescent classrooms. The new year was young when my father shipped me back to Tucson alone.

"I'll try harder," I pleaded when he told me, though I wasn't clear exactly what that entailed.

"Don't you see, Jeanie," he said reasonably, "you will never be one of the family."

"I'll write," I promised as the two of us stood alone in the airport a few days later. Annie and the boys had been sent to school as usual. Apparently my departure was of little import, for I don't recall it being more than mentioned at breakfast.

My father shook his head. "A clean break is better. No point in dragging it out."

"But I want to stay in touch with Annie and my brothers!"

"Mark and Jeff are too young to understand these things. I can't have you intruding on their lives. I think Annie will do better without you dragging her down."

Thus, despite all my efforts, I was set free. Away from my father's disapproval, my body returned to a healthy weight and I remembered how to laugh. A few months later, Annie trailed me back to Tucson.

I was seventeen when our mother set out with Annie and me for a year of driving around outback Australia and walking across Tasmania. Our fifty-thousand-mile odyssey would culminate in Connie's eighth book, *Australian Adventure*. I had managed to enroll my sister and myself in the all-male auto mechanics class at school before we left. This served us well as we traveled far from the beaten path, red dust thick on our sweating bodies under a broiling sun. We followed faint ruts through eucalyptus forests, where range fires flared to either side and wild cattle rushed. There were dense jungles too and crocodiles in mysterious billabongs, with flocks of parrots loud across the sky. On the Cape York Peninsula, we forded a shallow river by winching our vehicle through the current and up a cutbank. Each night when we pitched camp, Connie would scratch an arrow into the dirt to indicate the direction we were traveling. I was invincible and young in those days and laughed at her concerns.

Although Connie had written hundreds of letters to orchestrate our "expedition," she soon abdicated control to her teenage daughters. She never learned to drive a stick shift or on the "wrong" side of the road, and so resigned herself to our capricious charge. While Annie and I gained confidence, our mother took a backseat—often quite literally. Once we changed directions on a whim after picking up a young couple who were hitchhiking to Alice Springs. After her years of careful planning, we turned north out of Adelaide. This meant we had to rush through Darwin, where the impending "wet" might bog us down for weeks. Our mother argued feebly, but eventually was railroaded into whatever the two of us wanted.

Our year of driving was transected by an odd side trip. One of Connie's promotional letters had netted a freighter voyage to Southeast Asia, and she chose to give it to me. While my mother and sister continued along the dusty back roads through Queensland and New South Wales, I flew to Perth and boarded a Norwegian ship. Dressed in a miniskirt, sandals, and a naïve smile,

I set out alone for two months of exploring Singapore, Hong Kong, Malaysia, and Manila. I am lucky to be alive.

I realize now that Connie had hoped to find love and a new life in Australia, but traveling with her lovely teenage daughters only reinforced feelings that life's river had left her stranded and aging. Originally, she planned to remain in Australia, but when I returned to Perth, she and Annie had already flown back to Tucson. She left me a list of chores, and I shuttled about the continent shipping and selling our belongings before following my family in the fall of 1969.

I WAS NINETEEN WITH ONLY two and a half years of high school and no desire to go back, so I took the entrance exam and applied to the University of Arizona. With a partial scholarship and a job on campus washing chemistry glassware that paid $1.35 an hour, I bought a used motorcycle, put my little sister back in high school, and looked for a place to live. Connie was still paying most of our bills, but she had withdrawn quietly into depression, a change I hardly noticed in my focus on independence. Annie and I moved into a rented apartment, abandoning the maternal nest if not her pocketbook.

I soon picked up with my old sweetheart, Phil Beisel. We had met in Southern Arizona Search and Rescue when I was fifteen and he was sixteen. Our courtship consisted mainly of late night scrambles into the Catalina Mountains after injured hikers. Phil was remarkably male: a new energy for our family. At just under six feet tall, he was muscular and agile. He wrestled in high school and had an outgoing can-do attitude. His olive skin was smooth except for a modest triangle of chest hair, heavy two-day beard, and dark hair on his lower arms and legs. He had a chiseled face with a hawk nose, short brown hair, and a single, dense brow over limpid, green eyes as large and fringed as any girl's.

Youngest of three boys, Phil came from a career military family that epitomized the stiff-upper-lip. He had early joined the National Guard, where he managed to skip many exercises to work on their trucks. His mother was a tiny, cheerful, and determined woman of Pennsylvania Dutch heritage. His good-natured father was a warrant officer and, I think, a dreamer. Phil was a natural leader—tough, charismatic, and resourceful. He knew how to handle the physical world. While our household boasted a ball-peen hammer and flathead screwdriver, Phil had a shop full of tools and the skill to use them. Connie—master at safety-pin repairs—had taught us how to get by with broken equipment; from Phil, I learned that things could be fixed or even crafted. He took Annie under his wing as a little sister, providing us both with stability, for despite our bravado, the Helmericks girls had received little mentoring in life.

Phil and I went together throughout the next three years. Many of our hiking friends also attended the university and a group was usually gathered at one of the tables in the student union. This provided me (and soon Annie) an easy transition into college. Nevertheless, as my final undergraduate year loomed, I again dreamed of wilderness and, like my mother, quit college to lure my mate north for an arctic adventure: fourteen months alone in Alaska's Brooks Range.

Connie was our champion and resource. In a remote land where the sun doesn't rise for more than two months and temperatures plummet to sixty below, two short summers with their connecting winter is a logical timeframe. Even today with satellite phones, conditions make it difficult to enter or leave this land in deep winter. Shrinking from my father's judgment, I did not contact him when Phil and I drove through Fairbanks on our way to the town of Circle on the Yukon River in the spring of 1972.

Soon after Phil and I disappeared into the Alaskan wilds, Annie married a charismatic young man who was remarkably like our father. Steve Boice was Annie's height, but muscular and broad. He had blond hair, steel blue eyes, and an aggressive, take-charge masculinity. Heir to a legacy in cattle ranching, Steve had nevertheless been given little guidance by his aloof father. Annie sewed her own wedding gown and walked down the aisle of Tucson's prestigious Saint Philip's Church on the arm of an old friend. A scattering sat on the bride's side, while the groom's pews were packed with the elite of Arizona cattle families. Neither Bud nor Connie came for fear of seeing the other.

The newlyweds moved to the old Empire Ranch, southeast of Tucson. Established in 1860, the Empire had grown into the largest ranch in southern Arizona with a million acres of juniper-grassland. It still supported a thousand cows and their calves, but was in limbo. Sold to a developer, it had passed to Anamax Mining for water rights. Enormous cottonwood trees shaded the old adobe homestead. One could almost hear the clatter of hooves in the passageway between the great house and the bunkhouse where stagecoaches were once driven in to keep them safe from Indians. Annie went to work making a home of the cavernous twenty-two-room structure: sewing curtains, painting walls, and baking bread.

Phil and I paddled out of the mountains in the summer of 1973 and were married in Fort Yukon. We spent most of the next three years wandering arctic wilds, and between excursions joined Annie and Steve working the ranch. When Steve's father crashed his plane over the red-rock mesa of Four Corners, Steve's remaining legacy fell apart. We helped him, pregnant Annie, and their young daughter move to a ramshackle property south of Tucson, and settled into the little adobe guesthouse on their seven desolate acres. I returned to college and Phil—who was by then certified as an airplane mechanic—went to work at the airport.

It was here that my marriage abruptly dissolved. Abiding friendship and shared love for wilderness could not carry us through the complexities of settled life. Still, I had seen the cost of acrimony in my parents and when Phil left me, I kept only his Case knife, my sleeping bag, the camera, and our 35 mm slides. He took our three huskies, canoe, and his sleeping bag. Despite the financial needs of his new family, Phil helped me finish my last semester in biology and apply to medical school. I had taken several semesters of scientific illustration, and I spent that summer copying all our slides to give to him. It was a brutally painful time, but I have always been grateful that we treated one another fairly. Adding bitterness to hurt does not heal it.

I was twenty-eight, back in Tucson, and rudderless. Phil and his new wife had returned to Alaska to await the birth of their first son. My pragmatic father ensconced them in his Fairbanks basement to use Phil's mechanical skills. My future, which had stretched so clearly before of me, lay tumbled. *Another punctuation, another opportunity*—but I didn't see it that way. Caroline Myss writes of "sacred flaws," events beyond our control whose purpose is to change us. Life does not unfold according to our script, and these pivotal moments are portals for surrender and rebirth. I couldn't imagine finding another mate to share my love of wilderness and I wasn't ready for surrender. My life seemed to be turning into an uncomfortable rerun of my mother's.

I stalled in the little adobe guesthouse, helping to raise my niece Faith and new nephew Ben—waiting on the medical school alternate list for a call that did not come. I took a position in research at University Medical Center and completed a fifth year in college with honors in English, but again failed to gain one of the fifty coveted places. For three years I treaded water, afraid to strike out for an unknown shore.

IN THE SPRING OF 1981, I quit medical research and got a job driving an airport limo. At least it was outdoors. That October, my cousin Bert drove from

Phoenix to see me. He was the son of Janet—my mother's only sister—seven years and three days my senior. Janet and Bert, Connie and Bud had paired in college, explored the desert together, and dreamed around Winnie's table in the little house across from Tucson High. Our grandmother's complex and candid voice echoed down the generations, gifting each of us with interesting lives. Like his father of the same name, "Bert-Son," as his mother called him, was tall with dark hair, olive skin, and features that spoke of Native American. He had Janet's crowded teeth and Winnie's gray-green eyes. Born with clubbed feet, he had endured numerous childhood surgeries—another shared trait, for my feet had also required surgical correction.

Bert-Son and I often served as catalysts for one another's growth. By asking the hard questions and standing witness, we held each other to a high standard of integrity. I knew he had come for more than a social visit when he seated me knee-to-knee in Annie's living room and skewered me with that direct gaze.

"What are you planning to do with your life?"

I squirmed. "I don't know."

"You can't drive a cab forever."

"I couldn't stay in medical research—dead human lungs and animals in basement cages," I said with defiance. "I was dying there. I didn't get into medical school… Phil's gone… I just don't know."

He continued to study me. "You're avoiding the question."

"I could get another degree. Maybe law?" I gazed out the window and chewed my lip. Dust drifted across the empty acres where broken and rusted equipment were the only legacy Steve had salvaged from the Empire Ranch.

"What can you do that doesn't require more education?" he pressed, unwilling to buy into my helplessness.

"I can draw," I felt a sneer lift my lip. I had never seriously considered art. Apart from scientific illustration and drafting, I had no training. I was supposed to become a doctor—like my mother's father. The silence grew into a weight. *Okay, so I can draw.* "I will be an artist," I finally stated.

"Can you make a living at it?" His studied me intently.

"I can also draft and make business cards. Yeah… maybe."

"When?" he pressed.

I took a deep breath and raised my eyes to his, making a powerful declaration. "By November I will quit my job driving and be an artist."

It was as if my soul had been waiting for me to choose a direction. My words broke the spell. I glanced around as one awakened from a long sleep.

This was not my life. It was time I cast off. *We use the power of our Word so casually*, I thought. *The world is an out-picturing of our expectations. Why do I forget?*

～

ON NOVEMBER 17, 1981, I drove out a dirt track into the Tucson Mountains looking for Sunset Bevels, the only hand-beveling studio in Southern Arizona. In my new career as artist, I had sandblasted a dolphin into quarter-inch plate glass that needed the edge beveled for a stained glass panel Annie and I were building. She had taken a class, and although neither of us were skilled, our artwork was whimsical and intriguing.

I was thirty-one years old with close-cropped honey-colored hair. At 145 pounds, I was as strong and beautiful as a quarter horse—only I didn't know it. In photos it is easy to see the resolute slant of my jaw and a look of disappointment in my gray-green eyes.

I downshifted into first gear to cross a rutted wash and then eased my red Honda up a steep hill. The wintry sun felt warm as I stopped in a cloud of dust before an unpainted block structure. *It's too far,* I remember thinking. *I won't use bevels again.* There was no front entrance, so I walked around the building, calling. Native desert stretched up the hillsides, silent except for the whistle of a curve-billed thrasher. I could see only one other house, half a mile away.

Dressed only in boots, straw hat, and ragged cutoffs, Tom Irons was stacking cement blocks east of the building. He was not a large man, but rugged and quick. He looked happy, like someone who had chosen his life rather than settled for it. I remember his powerful hands. His skin was tanned from work in the sun; his limbs and chest were covered in soft, dark hair. He had a stubble of beard and his chestnut hair was trimmed short.

Did I feel a sense of destiny? It's hard to tell from this distance. Tom led me through the crude wooden door into a tiny living space. The studio beyond was spacious and cool. There were worktables and great stone wheels where his buddy Jack was beveling a mirror. Tom was born an Ohio farm boy and had spent nine years in the navy. He had abandoned the fast lane of Californian aerospace to live on his own schedule, close to the land and without indoor plumbing. We talked late into the afternoon. There was a chicken in the Crock-Pot and a good bottle of wine in the refrigerator. We ended the day on his roof watching stars emerge over the inky mountains. I never left. We were married two years and a day later. My artistic ability and Tom's craftsmanship became the backbone of Aspen-Irons Studio—our livelihood for the next two decades.

There are events that divide life into "before" and "after." The birth of our son, Lucas Foster Irons, in February 1986 became our yardstick. Luke was fourteen months old when I finally got Tom to Alaska. After my mother died, Tom asked me to give my father another chance and I agreed to summer with Bud and Martha on Walker Lake.

"He can't be as bad as you remember," Tom said. He had lost his own father at the age of eleven and was looking for deep connections.

That summer on Bud's turf was far from idyllic, for my father was still adept at dominating others and making them look foolish, yet wilderness opened a deep communion for Tom as he fell in love with the Brooks Range. On one of the few days we were not assigned work, we paddled a canoe along the shoreline, dipping into reflected peaks as emerald waters slid below. I picked blueberries on a sunny bank while Luke crawled through the low bushes like a bear cub, happily stuffing his mouth. He rode contentedly through the alders on Tom's back and bathed in a bucket near the fire as I brushed away mosquitoes. I don't recall my father being particularly interested in his grandson beyond a pat on the head, but Martha was kind.

Our son was four when our family again went north. After canoeing the upper Koyukuk River from the Dalton Highway down to Bettles, we called Annie and invited her to join us for the summer. A day later a chartered floatplane took the four of us high into the mountains. We spent five leisurely weeks camping and paddling downstream past my old cabin. While Tom and I propelled the small craft through rapids, Luke nestled happily between my knees taking it all in.

My sister was thirty-five that summer and back in college after a divorce, waiting tables at night as she raised her two children alone. Like Connie, she had landed in poverty and without marketable skills. Annie had also developed rheumatoid arthritis and we sometimes needed to haul her ashore from her cold seat in the bottom of the canoe. She spent our camp-over days painting the land, engrossed in a deep and personal exploration. It was a pivotal summer for each of us. Annie was studying accounting, yet in the song of the river she found courage to change her major to art. Then one gentle evening we camped by a creek that whispered to Tom and me, sparking an audacious plan to return and build a cabin. Do we listen to our fears or follow our hearts? Possibility hangs upon our dreams.

Connie's last camp, Madera Canyon, 1986. She holds grandson Lucas Foster Irons.

Luke and I play at building a cabin, Walker Lake, 1987.

Chapter 4

THE EDGE

May 2004

I was again stalled on the brink of a dream, straddling a growing chasm across which Tom and I needed to leap or retreat. Only this time my heart wasn't engaged, I just hated to let my friends down. That was my clue: for the heart speaks truth.

"Well, do I go?" Tom took a sip from his old coffee mug as we gazed from the doorway.

The day was already hot. Trumpet vines covering our Tucson Mountain home were heavy with yellow blossoms where hummingbirds buzzed in fierce competition. A new dual-axle trailer stood in the driveway, weighted with three thousand pounds of supplies for a year in Alaska secured under a blue tarp. Tom's old one-ton, four-cylinder pickup was gamely hitched to this load. A friend's borrowed vehicle squatted nearby for me.

I had dreaded this day, with Lucas too soon fledged and our home unsold. Alarms were going off in my body. My face in the mirror that morning looked grim. Graying honey-blonde hair, pinned back with a barrette, curled down my back. The troubled gray-green eyes, high cheekbones, full lips, even teeth, and strong jaw with that cleft chin were a perfect blend of my parents. The anxiety was my mother's too. There was no way of getting around it.

"Heather and Rude have their tickets and we have that," I nodded toward the trailer.

"I'll have a satellite phone this time so we can keep in touch," Tom said. He would buy the two thousand-dollar phone in Fairbanks—a lifeline anywhere in the world. He pushed his ball cap back and wiped sweat with the kerchief that banded his forehead. "If you don't feel good about this, we should cut our losses now."

He was leaving it up to me, but his face looked eager. I eased under his arm as we regarded the trailer.

"I can't join you if the house doesn't sell. You three will be on your own."

"If you don't charter in, I won't stay all winter."

"You can't leave them alone out there," I said. "I'll be okay, but I can't quit my job until this place sells. We'd lose everything." On prior trips, we had leased our home (dog and all), but with the added expense of Sylvia House, that wouldn't be enough.

"Well, you always say that commitment opens doors."

I nodded. It was a balance. There are times when it's better to retreat, and this felt like one of them. "Okay," I finally said. "I've got my plane ticket to Fairbanks. I hope to see you in six weeks. Be safe on the road." I pictured the long and dangerous journey ahead for Tom with that heavy load.

We held one another, gently caressing familiar curves, and then Tom boarded his red truck and slowly pulled onto Sunset Road. It was paved now, a dark ribbon through the drying land. I watched him make the corner and climb resolutely over the hill, then I went inside and listened to the frightened beat of my heart in the empty silence.

I climbed into Luke's old play loft and sat on the thick carpet hugging my knees. Large windows protruded into the pines like a treehouse. Below me, a cottontail rabbit pressed into the damp earth where quail were fluffing hollows in the dust. Numerous small birds decked the branches and I spotted four young screech owls—motionless as statues—watching me at eye level. A bobcat lay stretched in the dappled shade by the fishpond. A big rattlesnake would be arched under the cool lip of the sunken bathtub. All were sheltering from the heat.

The bobcat twitched one ear at a dragonfly. *Who will steward this oasis?* Memories whispered through the empty building, but there came no answers. I thought of friends who had arrived for a weekend or month to rest in this quiet eddy. Jenny-Wren's bare feet had pattered down the stairs of the guest cottage Tom built over his shop. She would slip through our unlocked front door to start morning coffee. Germaine had learned to garden here before creating her own desert home. Foster children had played in this loft—and of course our beloved son. I missed that boy—my three-year-old Luke, and Luke at seven, and at twelve—all gone down the river of time and yet part of the evolving young man. Each birth requires a death of what has been. How had I ever taken a single day for granted?

Ten days later Tom had safely driven forty-five hundred miles into Fairbanks. Rude and Heather arrived and were eyeing one another like different species. They were all staying with our Fairbanks family, Mark and Denise Wartes, before heading to the cabin.

The phone rang and I raced through the echoing studio to pick it up.

"Mom...?" Lucas's voice broke. "I've been in an accident! A car turned right in front of me at the light and I plowed into it! I was so concerned that someone was hurt I didn't even think about myself... They're fine, but the ambulance took them to the hospital. I'm covered with glass and my neck hurts and they say they don't have an ambulance for me... please come..."

"Where are you?" I steadied myself.

"I'm sitting on the curb at Swan and Speedway," he was crying now. "The other driver told the police it was my fault and they believed him! Their big SUV is hardly scratched, but Mom... I'm so sorry... your car... ," his voice trailed off.

"I'll be there in forty minutes," I calculated. "Stay put." I wished I had a cell phone and was glad Lucas had insisted on getting one, paying for it himself.

Another omen, I thought as my borrowed gas-guzzler sputtered to life. At least I was still in Arizona. The odds against our year in the wilderness were stacking up. I arrived at the accident in time to see my second used Honda hoisted onto a truck—a total loss. Lucas was sitting alone on the curb. He had a seatbelt bruise across his chest and sparkles of glass in his sweaty hair. His face was frightened and dazed. After months of dithering, my priorities came suddenly into sharp focus: *I am not leaving my son.*

When the emergency room had cleared him, I took Lucas out for lunch. He was quiet and a little withdrawn, but his foot rested against mine under the table as if to draw comfort.

"Don't worry about me," he said. "I move through things faster than most kids, like I don't have time to waste. Remember how shy I was in seventh grade? When I returned from the cabin, I was so disappointed to find that my friends were shallow, but it was a breakthrough, too, because I stopped trying to impress them."

"Won't you come home and let your old mom spoil you today?"

He shook his head and looked down at his big hands. They were neat like his father's, beautiful hands—strong and masculine. I thought of his large feet, his ankles sturdy as tree trucks, of his frayed shoes.

"Can I buy you a new pair of shoes? You may be walking for a while."

"I'll manage," he said in a tone that ended the discussion. He was silent, eating his salad, and then in a soft voice he said, "Mom, I'm really sorry about your car."

That evening I was surprised to get a call from Tom. I had thought they were gone. "We had to cancel the charter," he told me. "Small planes can't fly because of smoke from forest fires. I don't know how long we'll be delayed."

"Come home," I said softly. "Let's cut our losses." Then I told him of Lucas's accident.

"What about Heather and Rude?"

"I'm sorry," I said. "We aren't supposed to go this way. Nothing good will come of pushing it."

Tom's voice was quiet. "I was thinking the same thing." Relief and disappointment were mingled in his tone. "I'll buy Heather a ticket home, and maybe Rude and I can tour Alaska. What should I do with the trailer and all our stuff?"

"Park it in the Wartses' backyard." The support of Mark and Denise made our wilderness life possible. "In three weeks I'll fly up and we can figure it out, then drive back together." I suddenly laughed. "They'll be delighted at the hospital that I'm not quitting, and I'll have a vacation." It was ironic that I had plenty of paid time off, but could never be spared.

I felt a sudden lightness in my chest. "You can spend next winter renovating Sunset House. Most people want closets and an inside laundry." *And I can keep my family together one more year.* It was the first full breath I had drawn in months.

By the following spring Lucas had been through a series of roommates and was getting his feet under him. At nineteen, he was working for a major resort escorting guests around Tucson, and he had been accepted for the fall semester in the University of Arizona's College of Nursing. Meanwhile, Tom transformed our studio into an artistic approximation of a conventional home: finishing the walls, building closets and laundry room, and putting in carpet. We sold our desert home to a gentle young man and gave him our remaining furniture. Tom moved his tools and our few personal belongings into an attached shed at Sylvia House.

Tom and I were again headed for our cabin in May of 2005. We held a last family gathering on the desert, setting up a table by the campfire. Quail were nesting in the raised planter along the west wall where trumpet vines and hollyhocks competed for the late afternoon sunlight. Aunt Janet and her lifetime mate Uncle Bert drove from Scottsdale to bid us goodbye. Annie's beautiful daughter Faith was also present. Now in her late twenties, Faith had taken the hard road to adulthood, but arrived on her own terms. She managed a large company and was putting herself through college. She had Annie's thick blonde hair, dark blue eyes, and innate sense of fashion, but her rugged frame and tanned skin were reminiscent of me.

Lucas was driving another used Honda, bought with the insurance money from my car plus two thousand dollars he had earned doing field research for U.S. Fish and Wildlife the summer he was sixteen. Steaks were just coming off the campfire when we heard his expensive stereo on Sunset Road. He was bringing a friend from class, a woman ten years older than he, with a seven-year-old daughter. Lucas had never dated, so I was curious about Eve. They had become friends at Pima College, where she was doing prerequisites for the associate degree nursing program.

We heard them laughing before they rounded the hollyhocks. Lucas held each by a hand and the little girl was smiling up at him. His steps were confident, his smile shy and proud. Eve could have passed for his older sister. She was tall and voluptuous with amused dark eyes and heavy chestnut hair loose about her shoulders. She returned his complex wit like a skilled tennis partner—a flashback of Laurie, whose presence in our wilderness family helped form his personality. The child was big for her age and unusually self-possessed. Megan's large dark eyes and glossy brown hair reminded me of Luke at that age. She was wearing a skirt and her tanned coltish legs promised size, like a puppy's large paws. She soon warmed to me and nestled against my side as the family talked easily around the table and the sun lowered behind the Tucson Mountains. A nimbus of light fanned across the sky.

"So what are your plans?" my uncle's voice rumbled.

Bert Cutler was a big man with the John Wayne personality born of World War II and the Depression. As a civil engineer, he had traveled the globe and he spoke with the measured strength of a man whose word was his bond. At eighty-three, he had long black hair threaded with silver worn in a trailing ponytail and his beard was iron gray. His big shoulders hunched forward as he leaned on elbows across from me.

"We don't really know," I admitted. "We're prepared to stay a year, but with just the two of us, we're not certain. We have more than enough supplies stored in Fairbanks. We can use our new satellite phone to call in a plane if we decide to leave."

"Only when a plane can get in," Tom added. "They can't land in midwinter when it's dark and really cold or when the river ice isn't solid."

"Where will you go after that?" Bert asked.

Tom shrugged and grinned. "Jeanie wants to do travel-nursing. She'll sign with a company that will supply housing during thirteen-week assignments all over the United States. That will give us a way to explore the country while we look for a place to settle."

"We're hoping to find a small community where we can live gently on the land," I said. "I want to use less of the world's resources and grow some of our food."

"Why not stay in Fairbanks?" Bert wondered.

"It's a harsh climate for old age," I explained. "Driving to work in the dark at forty below isn't the same as living at our cabin. Besides it takes a lot of oil to keep warm."

Tom turned to Lucas, "Your Mom never wants to let go. She's working right up to the last minute, so I'll drive up alone. I've been thinking, maybe you'd like to go with me? Once you start nursing college, you'll be in harness."

"For years," I added, helpfully.

All eyes turned toward Lucas. He didn't respond immediately, but seemed to be gazing into the future. Then he smiled hugely. "I'd love to if we can afford it."

"It's only money, Son," Tom grinned back. "We've had some wonderful trips through the years, have we not? From the time you were in diapers."

"I wouldn't have missed the time you invited me to drive north," Bert stated. "Trip of a lifetime." Tom usually became restless each spring, yearning to go north even when we didn't plan a wilderness sojourn. Sometimes he got a job in Alaska for the summer; others, he turned around at the Arctic Ocean and came home. Mostly, I just kept working in Tucson.

"It's all been so good!" Janet said. Like me, she seemed to be savoring this moment with an almost painful happiness. In her gray-green eyes, I sensed a joy born of the impermanence of all things and the sweetness of ordinary days.

Janet sat with her leg touching Bert's. She was hard of hearing now and walked with difficulty. Her ash-gray hair was shoulder-length and held back with a child's pink headband. When she laughed, which was often, her eyes almost disappeared in wrinkles, and she displayed large teeth without embarrassment. Where once she had looked me in the eye, her body was now shriveled and twisted under the weight of years. She seemed to watch it with a kind of surprised curiosity, as if observing frost on the leaves. I thought of my mother's fierce battle with age and how death had overtaken her like a predator amidst struggle and fear. By contrast, Janet had a quiet glow as if some interior light shown more brightly through fading cloth.

She reached across the table and drew my strong hand into her two frail ones, then beamed her generous smile. "Oh, joy!" she declared, and her face illuminated each of us at the table—a benediction. As her gaze came to me she said, "Jeanie, at times you remind me so much of Connie. You know, I miss her every day. And I love you so!" Tears glistened in her eyes.

A WEEK LATER, TOM AND Lucas set out in Little Red for a wavering forty-five-hundred-mile drive to Alaska. They had a goal, but like a couple of otters, they would explore and play along the way: visiting Laurie in Washington, taking excursions, even seeing a theater production. I smiled as they pulled away from Sylvia House, where we were staying. If I was envious, it was not of their fun—for in that I more than delighted—but of their carefree ability to enjoy life. I told myself that I worked and organized so that others could play, but the truth was far more complex. Somehow, early in childhood I had decided that if I were not vigilant, my world might crumble.

Through the magic of modern air travel, Lucas and I traded places in Fairbanks two weeks later. Tom was his gentle self when I arrived trailing my last-minute lists. Our ton and a half of supplies had overwintered in my father's airplane hangar beside his old Cessna 180, the *Helmericks*, which sat unused and dusty on flat tires. My nephew, Derek Helmericks—grown son of my stepbrother, Jim—offered to truck us north up the Dalton Highway to Grayling Lake, where a chartered plane on floats would meet us the next morning for three shuttles into the mountains. Usually called the "Haul Road," the Dalton had been pushed through wilderness with the Trans-Alaska Pipeline in the 1970s, face of a rapidly changing land.

"Who was Connie?" Derek asked as he maneuvered his big pickup and the trailer with our supplies around a pothole. By the casual way he asked, I guessed that it was an important question. Each of my nephews and brothers had ventured it. Many had copies of her books—books never seen in our father's house.

My mother, the invisible woman.

"She was complex," I began, "a free spirit who loved the Earth. She was kindhearted and easily moved to tears... bright and creative. She loved me deeply, and yet was not very motherly..." I paused, not knowing how to sum up my years with this remarkable human. *Annie and I hold crucial pieces*, I thought. *When we die, Connie will vanish. Who was she? Did anyone really know?*

Tom cradles Luke, age four, in camp the first summer we canoed the river, 1990.

Luke was at home traveling wild lands for months at a time.

Chapter 5

KERNWOOD HOMECOMING

June 2005

Though early in the season, mosquitoes were abundant at Grayling Lake. Derek helped us unload onto the dirt pullout and then shared a late lunch before heading back to Fairbanks. We secured tarps over the mound of supplies and pitched our tent on the sloping gravel. There was little firewood, so Tom and I crawled in, out of the bugs for an evening of soft rain. Familiar birdsong soothed me into a fitful sleep, broken by the occasional semi-truck thundering past us a few yards away. Traffic ceased and the sun slid briefly behind a peak about midnight.

It never gets dark in arctic summer, but the weather has a rhythm. Morning came, clear and calm. Grayling dimpled the lake's mirrored reflection of a nearby mountain where patches of old snow sheltered below the greening ridge line. I sorted our possessions into three loads—roughly eleven hundred pounds each. It was late morning (and several calls on the satellite phone) before the pilot showed up. A de Havilland Beaver came rushing over the dirt highway, so close that a passing van startled like a deer. The noisy plane dropped onto the pond in a rooster-tail of spray, slowed and then taxied about and idled up to shore. Tom and I wallowed out through the shallow water and mud, lugging supplies and handing them into the plane where the pilot waited. Last aboard was our seventeen-foot canoe, turned over and lashed to the floats.

After Tom and the first load had departed, I squatted in the sun with the remaining supplies. I hoped the river was high enough to land near our cabin. Steve Ruff always worked to get us close, but this was a different pilot. Sitting on a five-gallon bucket of powdered milk, I emptied muddy water from my knee-high rubber boots and wrung out my socks. It had been five years since we'd seen the cabin and there was no telling how it had fared. Our family had overwintered again at the millennium, the year Luke turned fourteen. I paced the gravel, swatted mosquitoes, and rearranged the next two loads as the hours ticked by. Finally, the growl of the approaching Beaver carried on the breeze.

"Did you land near the cabin?" I asked eagerly when the pilot cut the engine and opened the door.

"Nope. I put him down on that lake just north of you."

We'll deal with it, I thought. I plunged back into the water, hauling the second half-ton of totes out and lifting them onto the float. Soon the plane lumbered into the sky, where afternoon clouds were gathering. I wrung my socks and then dug dried fruit from a bucket and ate it while awaiting the final trip.

It was late and I was tired by the time the plane returned for the last load. With relief, I lugged the final thousand pounds through the shallow water and then climbed aboard. As the lake fell behind, I breathed a sigh. Whatever lay ahead, Tom and I would face it together—two old friends. We had all summer to carry supplies home.

About an hour later, the Beaver banked north around Horseshoe Lake. Swinging over the muddy river, the plane dropped onto the shallow pond and glided to a stop at the southern end in a whisper of sedges and cottongrass. We had named this lake (and almost every feature in the valley), for there were few on any map. Often whimsical, sometimes descriptive, our words—like our structures and those of the early peoples—were transitory and did not claim this land.

When the propeller clattered to a stop, I swung my door open and dropped stiffly onto the pontoon. In the sudden hush, the song of a hermit thrush carried on the breeze. I lifted my eyes to the familiar mountains. Sun splashed the disturbed pond in a million diamonds. Tom had our tent up between the stunted spruce and a small fire going. Supplies were piled colorfully in the slanted light. Taking the trailing rope, I lowered myself into cold water over my knees. Air burped up from my submerged boots.

"You stay on shore," Tom said. His voice had a quiet edge. "I'll unload."

"You sure?" I asked, but the look in his eye told me he was.

"Most people don't make it out here," the pilot commented as he stood on the floats, tipping supplies into Tom's arms.

"Uh-huh," Tom grunted. He was mired thigh-deep in muck and waving sedges.

"Careful with that!" the pilot warned, dropping the 128-pound cast-iron stove into Tom's arms. Tom sank to his waist, turned slowly, and waded toward shore.

"Just last week I flew some guy out of the Bush," the pilot continued. "He quit. They mostly quit."

When the plane taxied out from shore and roared into the sky, we looked at one another and then at the great mound of supplies. "I thought the river looked fine," Tom said a bit wistfully. "I don't think he ever intended to land near the cabin."

"It's going to be a long trek home," I said. "Is it my imagination or did he enjoy watching you struggle with the mud?"

Tom sat in the damp moss by our fire and poured water from his boots. He smiled up at me. "Maybe he wishes he had a summer to himself. He gets a glimpse of this world, but can't slow down to enjoy it. We live here."

I smiled back. "It's just us now, and there's no rush."

EARLY LIGHT GLIMMERS OFF HORSESHOE Lake as Tom and I heft awkward packs and set out for our cabin, which lies a mile away through stunted taiga forest and across Luke's Creek. This is a soft land, yielding. Ankle-deep moss, blueberry bushes, Labrador tea, and lupine spring back as our steps rouse clouds of torpid mosquitos. Cold mist snags in the reeds along the far shoreline where a pair of trumpeter swans float on their reflections—white against green. The thrush is still singing, sylvan tones mingling with the minor key of a golden-crown sparrow. To our west, much of Annie's Peak is scorched from last year's wildfire and beyond the pond we enter a band of blackened trees. Willows are erupting from the cinders and a thin fuzz of moss glistens the sooty hummocks. Dew soaks our legs as we again enter living forest, land untouched by the hopscotch of flames.

"It's just as well we weren't here last summer," I say. Tom is leading, his packframe ponderous with a five-gallon bucket and the stovepipe oven. In one hand he carries the chainsaw. "I hope the cabin's okay." We weave between gnarled spruce trees through chest-high Arctic birch. Tom's legs, steady as a clock, choose the way. I can't see his head. Mosquitoes ride on his packframe and trail out in a mist behind him.

We hear the creek before we see it, and then emerge above a broad gravel swath. The water is low enough to ford, rushing clear as glass over colored stones as we wade. With growing anticipation, we ascend a cutbank and enter the dappled shadows of Kernwood Forest, picking up our familiar home trail. Crossing the three-log bridge over Trickle Creek, we mount our sunny bench where the cabin emerges—bright and solid—among spruce. Below us, Luke's Creek joins the river in a quarter-mile of sandy delta. Across the river, Mount Laurie and Flattop anchor the edges of home. I have returned here a thousand times and yet it always surprises me: this woodcutter's cottage out of a fairytale—so welcoming it almost seems to smile.

We had removed the windows and door, so the grizzlies have done little damage. Despite these empty holes, the cabin looks snug beneath its blooming sod roof. Naturally shed antlers—picked up in our wanderings—protrude from the flowers. We grin and help one another pull off our odd loads. An old porcupine stands pensively in the doorway. One front toe is deformed and the nail hooks in a half circle. As we enter the dark interior, he moves into the yard and begins to gnaw a caribou antler. He has nibbled it into a lace doily, leaving a translucent shell.

Tom uses a homemade ladder to climb into the sleeping loft for his toolbox. He pulls the remaining boards from the windows and tacks in mosquito netting while I sweep the hand-hewn floor. It's dry and in good shape. Clumps of blond fur are stuck under the counter and on the door jam, signature of Goldilocks. For six years we have respectfully shared the valley with this large golden grizzly. White streaks on the windowsill speak of spruce chickens roosting; a squirrel has nested in the loft.

There are two rooms of peeled logs, joined by an arched doorway, with eleven double-paned windows. Each element is a conscious work of art: the logs are hand-doweled, and the sleeping loft extends the length of the main fifteen-by-fifteen-foot expanse. I raise two ladders made of poles and turn the homemade table upright while Tom hangs the door. It represents weeks of his patient work—thick slabs cut from dead spruce, planed and pegged, inset with two long, double-paned windows and a carved handle. He sets the bolt made of wood and a spring.

A few yards away, the log storehouse is also intact. Tom, Luke, Laurie, and I built it as insurance against fire when we overwintered again in 1999–2000. If you lose your cabin at fifty below, you don't survive. The upper story, a closed cache with trapdoor, is cool and inviolate, securing buckets of flour, rice, beans, and powdered eggs. Tom hangs the storehouse door and we stash our loads safely inside. In front of the cabin, I untie Luke's old swing, which was secured up to protect moose from becoming entangled. I watch it sway between the trees.

Tom steps behind and encircles me with his arms. "It's been a good life," he says quietly, resting his chin on my shoulder.

I nod, watching the empty swing. "We played a lot, didn't we?"

It takes nine days—one hundred and two miles of trudging—to get everything home. We make four trips each day, sleeping nights at the lake. Early spring lingers in snowy crevices atop Mount Laurie. We sip coffee by our small fire in the chill of morning and watch a young bull moose wade like a phantom through the mist, feeding in the shallows along the far shore. Ducks paddle companionably around him, tipping in the stirred vegetation. Swans wrinkle the reflection of Annie's Peak, which turns rosy with fireweed blossoms as the season advances. Arctic terns and a pair of marsh hawks skim the lake. After breakfast we help each other up from the damp tundra and into our packs.

Early summer is spent replacing much of the sod roof, damaged in a chimney fire the winter of 2000. We cut and pull off heavy squares of sod, carry them down the pole ladder on our shoulders, remove dirt, lay down black plastic sheeting, and install a new stovepipe with a homemade insulated collar. Gently, we replace the living sod and the antlers. The flowers and grass don't seem to mind. I mend the sphagnum-moss chinking in the walls. The logs are small and twisted—one could as well call it a "moss cabin." Each holds a memory of Tom, six-year-old Luke, Laurie, and me searching for dead trees, cutting and hauling them with slings over our shoulders, rafting them downriver, and then skinning and doweling them into place. Of twisting the hand auger down through the layers and cleaning out the jammed chips. How challenging and rewarding it had been to build this haven.

Returning to Kernwood, as we call our cabin, is a fulfillment of Tom's dream more than mine. While I appreciate time away from the stress of hospital nursing, I miss community and our son. This is our first big adventure without Lucas and although we keep in touch through weekly satellite phone calls (at a dollar a minute), Tom and I seem an impoverished tribe. Lucas anticipates our brief conversations and I realize that our roles are gradually shifting: he is as concerned about his aging parents alone in the wilderness as we are for him.

"It's good for him to be on his own," Tom reassures me. "Trusting him to be okay is the greatest gift we can give."

Still I worry. Tom and I take turns calling, standing together in the yard as we wait for satellites to align. We hold the phone so that both can hear. There is that delay which makes conversation stilted and frustrating, and it frequently drops out. I value this tenuous connection and yet touching our son's world kindles anxiety.

"You call," I say. "You're always so calm and you won't nag him. I don't want him to know that I worry. I just need to hear that he's okay."

"He's nineteen," Tom says. "I was in the navy at that age. He needs to gain his own strength and test his wings."

"I know, it's just me. It's hard to let go."

I recall how Tom had fallen ill with pneumonia our first winter in the wilderness and had come close to dying, while I carried fear in my stomach for eight months. This later propelled me into a bachelor's degree in nursing, but it hadn't healed my fear. Avoiding pain through hard work and planning requires eternal vigilance. *It's a balance,* I decide. *Going unprepared is a recipe for disaster, but living with apprehension is no fun.*

Days melt into weeks with the timeless patience of flowers maturing, fruiting, leaves beginning to rust along the edge. "It's a neighborhood," I point out as we sit by our morning fire in front of the cabin. "The osprey nesting over on Cassidy Park, the ravens here all these years. The gray jays. Goldilocks. It takes time to hear that conversation. People might say, 'Cut down those trees so you can see the view,' and never realize that it's a neighborhood."

Nevertheless, change creeps undeniably upon the wilderness. It is melting and drying out, lakes receding with scary momentum. Muskegs are dry and crackling underfoot. Smoke from forest fires often blots out the mountains, turning the sun to a red ball and the river to molten bronze. When the smoke becomes too dense, we retreat into our cabin where moss chinking helps to filter the air.

Desert and Arctic are places of delicate balance, landscapes that foster resourcefulness and reverence. Each supports a limited number of species: tough plants and animals adapted to severe conditions, yet vulnerable to change. Birds arrive here underweight, having used even their muscles to fuel the flight north. They gamble their lives that the insect population will bloom and the lakes will be open. For many it's a one-way trip. By the time the young are fledged, busy parents are often in poor condition, but if they have accomplished their mission, the species will continue.

My interior landscape resonates with this natural world, where my muscles accomplish much of the work of living. Someone born in Pennsylvania might find the desert or tundra bleak, while I feel oppressed by high buildings and even dense forests. The repetitive geometric patterns of human colonization make me uneasy. In such a fashion does the terrain of childhood imprint itself on inner vision. Each area of the planet carries a unique fingerprint. If we are paying attention, we can find our way home by the slant of sunlight and the smell of familiar plants. *Yet where is home to a mobile people living in identical boxes? Who are we without this sense of belonging?*

Ancient peoples were keen observers—they had to be. Lacking scientific method they made shrewd guesses about life, coming perhaps closer to the truth than we who are biased by those methods. *Labeling and counting obscures more than it illuminates.* I had believed that college would give me keys to understanding life. Two degrees later, I am listening for the conversation of trees. It's a language you can't learn with your head. When the planet is viewed as real estate, we no longer see magic in the falling rain. In a forest of concrete buildings, the Creative becomes abstract. Our food bears little resemblance to anything alive, and saying grace is more a formality than a communion. We are nevertheless children of this natural world and very dependent upon it. Today's humans, like ospreys and bears, are a sacred link between yesterday and tomorrow.

FOR THREE MONTHS TOM AND I live quietly. On days when the wind shifts from the north and clears the valley of smoke, we take long hikes. Much of early summer is also spent cutting several cords of firewood—dragging dead spruce to the river and floating log rafts down to the cabin. Removing the beetle-killed trees helps the forest and we notice seedlings thriving where we logged in past years. We cook over an open fire in the yard and wash clothes in a large tub after we bathe. Most evenings, though, we bathe in a basin on the bench near the woodstove. Simplicity opens a well of inner stillness… and yet I feel lonely.

Tom hauls water from a spring near the river in five-gallon buckets. He picks berries and sometimes catches a grayling or two for dinner. I edit my novel *Child of Air* by hand and bake bread in Rude's stovepipe oven. Tom reads aloud while I cook. Despite a variety of dried staples, meals for two are staid. Not that we aren't good company, but we are subdued. There's no banter and little laughter. It just isn't the same as living in a clan.

I recall the winter Luke was thirteen—his happy joking with Laurie as they dragged firewood across the frozen river, our picnics at thirty below, breaking trail to Cassidy Park just to slide down the hill. Images of Annie painting and four-year-old Luke playing in the mud rise before me as I look out on the delta. I think of the summer of 1995 with nine-year old Luke and another young friend, Julia Beckley. The four of us had flown to a lake in the mountains with our nineteen-foot canoe and food for the summer. We lugged everything a mile to the river and then paddled the overloaded craft down to our cabin, which we found trashed by bears. Our futile attempts to keep grizzlies out were laughable in retrospect. We had salvaged and cleaned what we could and then spent a few weeks exploring the surrounding mountains before paddling downriver to the bridge. A sense of community had made it all play.

Autumn descends and the peaks blush to burgundy, scarlet, and gold. Tom and I take pictures and create art on driftwood and naturally shed caribou antlers. The summer continues dry; the river sinks lower and turns emerald-clear. I can see the bottom and there are places I could probably wade across. Berries peak early and grizzlies return to grubbing for Eskimo potatoes—their scat ropy with twisted fibers. Hungry bears do not make good neighbors.

In mid-August, the stars return and the daylight we have taken for granted begins to fade. Auroras dance in the lingering twilight. Wildlife, accustomed to our benign presence, seems strangely drawn into our yard. A pair of young weasels scamper over our feet and play like puppies as they follow us on walks. Their mother is more cautious. Gray jays land on our shoulders and eat from our hands. A pair of great gray owls float silently overhead, big as bombers, to land nearby. Their giant chick looks like Einstein in its new feathers as they feed it lemmings a few feet away. The only spruce chickens within miles have gathered in our yard where they drum and strut. Even our ancient and haughty raven family, the Blackhearts, edge closer. They have watched us from an aloof distance for almost two decades. When one lives harmlessly in nature, the land knows.

OUR WORLD CHANGES ABRUPTLY WITH hunting season. Wilderness as commodity has reached even here. For decades we have lived in seclusion, but this September brings a startling influx of wealthy hunters. The sky echoes with small planes and our sanctuary is suddenly flooded with hearty men decked in matching Cabela's and toting expensive rifles. They are astonished when we step from the forest in our Goodwill Levi's and woolen shirts.

One evening we watch from the bluff as the young bull moose, who has become accustomed to our presence, drifts down the river bar. He is careless in his new antlers and the timeless message of rut. We hear him grunting softly into the twilight. Moments later a barrage of shots smashes the stillness.

The next moose is shot on our side of the river.

"I got my moose," the man calls to us from across the emerald current. "Can we borrow your canoe? He's upstream over on your side."

It's late afternoon and we stand on the bluff, drawn by the concussion of shots.

"I'll take it over," Tom says to me. "You stay here."

"Look downstream," I point.

In the low sunlight White Wolf stands out sharply against the dark spruce. He is heading toward us along the bank.

"Be careful, White Wolf," I hear Tom say under his breath.

Animals gamble with death on a daily basis and learn rapidly. Before the hunters are across, White Wolf has beaten them to the carcass and ripped a hole in the side. Once shy and retiring, Goldilocks is also lured into this dangerous game. Each night the great bear now visits our cabin, pressing his nose into mosquito netting that separates us from the night. Tom threads a piece of fishing line across the path and hangs cans to alert us, yet even in the dark Goldie senses it. A grizzly that could dismantle our cabin approaches the line, digs in the sawdust on the other side, and leaves us in peace. He is not so benign with the hunters and hauls off some of the choicer pieces of moose to the nighttime echo of shouts and rifle shots.

CHAOS LASTS TWO WEEKS AND then—as quickly as the men came—they are gone, leaving boned hulks of moose like burned-out ships rotting in the sluggish river. They take only a Super Cub's worth of meat from the two-year-old bull dropped on our side. We snag the carcass from the icy water and pull it up where bear, wolf, jay, and raven can fatten. The sky-men return to a land of stores and freezers, while arctic animals pace themselves for the long dark and cold.

Tom and I play cards by lantern light as the kettle simmers on the woodstove. Our game is comfortable, but not much sport, for Tom invariably wins. He lays out his hand and scoops up the pile of M&M's used as poker chips.

"We don't have as many books as I thought," he states. "I've read most of mine."

The Coleman lantern makes a hissing noise, and a log thumps down in the stove. Plexiglass has replaced mosquito screen in the window frames. Beyond them, falling night rings clear with a breeze gusting from the north. Cirrus clouds smudge the full moon, circling it with a pale rainbow—a "snow moon," my mother would have said—as it rides the spine of Mount Laurie. Jupiter's refection glimmers in the slowing river as twilight fades.

"Winter will be here any day," I say. "Once it snows, we're stuck until the river ice is strong enough to hold a plane on skis. If it's not solid before the sun disappears in November, we can't get out until March." Bush planes use three types of landing gear: floats on river or lake, skis on snow, and "tundra tires" on a sandbar. In former years, winter owned this land by the end of September, but it is almost October and still no ice. The unnatural Indian summer has drawn on for three weeks—beautiful sunny days, too warm to keep a moose had we shot one.

"Wouldn't we have more fun finishing the renovation at Sylvia House?" I suggest. "I could fatten up my 401k."

"Do you want to leave?" Tom's eyes are gentle, searching. Across the river a wolf howls, low and musical. We listen for an answer. Downriver a great gray owl is booming out his deep song.

"Yes," I nod. "I think we've had the best of it."

Tom smiles his assent.

Chapter 6

CHANGING COURSE

September 2005

The next day broke gray and drizzling. Autumn colors were gone; the somber land was painted in sepia beneath a sky the color of ash. Winter was at last gathering force. Using the satellite phone, we reached Dirk Nickisch, a Bush pilot the state trooper had mentioned. Dirk flew on tundra tires during the summer from Coldfoot, an outpost on the Dalton Highway north of Grayling Lake.

It took all day to close up: we lugged food into the storehouse and up the ladder, pulled the windows from the cabin and doors from both buildings, stashed the canoe on the roof, and put books and dishes into our sleeping loft. The following morning we packed a few things, bundled bedding and clothes in the cabin loft, and waited. The cabin was cold and dark with the windows boarded up. Even the stove and tiny sink were dismantled and wedged under the counter out of Goldie's way. Sleet whipped down the exposed delta, rattling the bare poplar leaves like old bones. Several times we called Dirk on the satellite phone as we waited for a break in the clouds.

By late afternoon the sky lifted enough for the trip. Threading his way through the mountains under a heavy ceiling, Dirk emerged in a sudden gust of noise: the unmistakable cement-mixer voice of a de Havilland Beaver. The plane circled our cabin and then settled onto a strip we had prepared on an exposed river bar north of Luke's Creek. We carried our few belongings across the swollen creek and shook hands. Dirk was around forty, a quick and wiry man of Tom's height with observant blue eyes, sandy hair, and an unkempt, reddish beard. After our experience with expensive camouflage, his canvas pants, leather boots, and stained red-and-yellow jacket were a comforting sight.

"I was getting ready to close up for the season when you called. You're my last flight."

Dirk was quick and strong, helping us carry gear and stowing it aboard. Within minutes we climbed onto the thirty-six-inch tires and buckled into the scuffed blue-and-white plane. Recalling how I get airsick, Tom insisted that I ride in front. The big engine roared to life as the pilot drove the plane down the bar with practiced skill, easing it into the wind like a big kite. I felt my eyes well with tears as our cabin slipped from view. I wondered if we would ever come back.

"How are you getting to Fairbanks?" Dirk's voice sounded loud in my headset.

I started to answer, realized that I couldn't hear myself, and adjusted the microphone. "We thought to catch the shuttle," I repeated, "or maybe hitchhike."

"Shuttle is down for the season and you won't see many tourists this time of year. Truckers aren't supposed to pick people up."

Light was rapidly fading and the cold sky was spitting when we landed on the airstrip in Coldfoot. Dirk unloaded our belongings onto the wet gravel and then said, "If you don't mind waiting, you can ride to town with my son and me. My wife and daughter drove in yesterday."

It took him an hour to load his big pickup and lock up. His young son cheerfully hauled a car seat out and climbed aboard. Dirk hitched on a trailer loaded with trash to which we added our small bucket. Tom secured a tarp over our possessions in the truck bed, and we climbed happily onto the bench seat behind the driver. Sleet was blowing as the four of us set off into gathering darkness. Often the truck crept along the muddy road as Dirk picked his way through fog. We shared the sandwiches I had packed while the slow miles passed.

Dirk never implied that he made that nighttime drive because of us, but I believe he did. Dawn was not far off when he deposited us in the Wartses' front yard. Their door was unlocked and a clean bed awaited us. It felt good to be home for the moment—whatever that meant.

CATCHING UP ON WORLD AFFAIRS the next morning, we read of the Katrina disaster. Serendipitously, we had also just read aloud the scholarly tome *Rising*

Tide on the history of flood control and the Mississippi River.

"We have no set schedule," I said to Tom over our usual breakfast of raw oatmeal, nuts and granola. "With your building skills and my nursing credentials we have a lot to offer. Most people are tied to a job. Want to volunteer?"

He looked up from back issues of the paper and nodded. "Why not call FEMA and see if they can use us?"

"We can't take just anybody," the woman on the phone told me.

"I'm licensed and can fax my credentials," I assured her. "I've been fingerprinted and had several background checks. My husband volunteers with hospice and has credentials as well. He's worked in hospice. We've been state-certified foster parents, too. It'll be easy for you to verify."

"We are not taking volunteers," she said with finality and hung up.

The drive back to Arizona proved a serene reentry into the twenty-first century. This was a blessing, for crashing headlong into the noise and chaos of modern life can be a shock after months of gentle silence. Winter's first snows chased us thousands of miles along the ribbon of highway that snakes through the Canadian Rockies, hemmed on the west by the great Coastal Range. Tom's little five-speed pickup climbed gamely into a lacy white world and descended back into autumn dozens of times. The Alaska–Canada Highway—the Alcan—was almost empty, and we paused to let streams of migrating caribou cross. Grizzlies ignored us as they dug for roots along the verge and wood bison sunned on the apron of the road.

We crossed into the United States and wandered through the Pacific Northwest, stopping at "intentional communities" to explore alternative living arrangements. I wasn't sure what I was seeking. Intentional communities are created by people with common values. Some are loosely organized—a parcel of land subdivided among families—others hold ground in trust and use common buildings, gardens, and equipment. There are communities committed to growing food and cooking together; others are built around home schooling or religious ideals. There are even elders who pool resources to care for one another. However, none that we visited appeared to be thriving or balanced. It seemed to be an incipient movement, people like us who were exploring new directions and had yet to formulate a strong course.

We arrived in Tucson to discover a clan awaiting us. Though we had planned to rent an apartment while Tom completed the exterior renovation on Sylvia House, Lucas insisted we move into his back bedroom. We soon realized that Eve and Megan spent most of their time there as well and within a month had officially moved in. We were swept up in daily life: picking Megan up from school and sharing chores. It was messy and noisy after our austere sojourn in the wilderness, yet engaging, too. Families take all forms when one cultivates an open heart.

I had called University Medical Center from Fairbanks and been promised reinstatement—for they badly needed a certified obstetrical nurse—but when I arrived, I was given "part time" work with no benefits on my old unit. With Lucas and Eve in school, my job was the family mainstay and I averaged sixty hours a week. I hadn't planned to support five of us, but life does not keep score. It did seem ironic, however, that my patients (who were often not citizens) had free health care, while I could not afford insurance.

That winter, Sylvia House metamorphosed under Tom's indefatigable hands. He enclosed the front yard in a graceful block wall that arched over the walk, creating a lighted patio with a fountain. We set a table under mesquite trees that I had planted the year before along with flowering desert shrubs fed by drip irrigation. Tom and Lucas poured a cement pad for the carport, chip-sealed the driveway, and laid curving walks. Tom built awnings over the windows and extended the roofline. He crafted large front and back porches where we could sit with our morning coffee and watch the birds. Finally, the whole house was insulated, stuccoed, and painted in adobe tones. Neighbors stopped by to admire the transformation and we found ourselves enjoying the city—a novel thought for a couple of old hermits.

As spring of 2006 crept over the desert, I noticed that Tom and I had wandered off course somewhere. I was working overtime to support a household we owned, but did not run: it was finally time for travel-nursing. I completed the mass of forms necessary to register with a travel-nurse company. There were a quarter-million nursing positions open and my obstetrical certification was a ticket to almost anywhere.

"Let's go east," I said. "I doubt if we'll settle there, but we may as well look." Tom had a map of the United States spread across the kitchen table. Beyond the screen door, mesquite trees were leafing out and doves were cooing. The evening air was balmy with a whisper of coming heat. Eve and Megan were doing homework on the sofa, while Lucas hunched over the stove sautéing tofu and vegetables with a great deal of flame and splatter. His hair was short for nursing school and the mustache was gone.

"Why not just go back to the cabin?" Tom suggested hopefully.

I shook my head. "Not this year. I want to explore places we might settle. Eventually. When we get old. I'm prejudiced against the East, but I really don't know much about it." I had similar opinions of the South, of which I was even more ignorant. My eastern travels were a road trip to visit Tom's brother in Maine before our marriage and a summer in New York with my cousin Chickie when I was nine. "I think we'd like the Pacific Northwest. We could head there by way of Florida. Annie and John are housesitting in Naples this summer." My sister had married a thoughtful man who shared her passion for visual exploration. They both taught art at the University of Missouri in Warrensburg.

"We have to be here at the end of May for your award," Tom stated.

"I really don't care," I shrugged. "It's dinner and people talking. I hate to build our plans around that."

"It isn't just about you. The medical students nominated you as the nurse who contributed most to their education. You need to go for them."

"I'm not even certain they'll be there. It might just be the OB residents. I'll be the only non-doctor—in my Goodwill clothes. They said I could bring a date…"

"Me?" Tom's eyes widened. "In a suit and tie? Oh, no! I don't even own one. Take Faith. She'll help you dress."

"I want to come, too," Lucas stated. "I'm very proud of you." He was dressed in cutoff shorts and a faded T-shirt riddled with holes with a picture of a wolf. Our family had always been fashion-challenged. He had put on twenty pounds in the stress of nursing school and no longer fit into the suit we bought for his junior prom.

I wavered. "We could take a swing up to Colorado to see my relatives, then come back before heading for Florida."

"I think it's worth it," Tom insisted. They all nodded.

With a flourish Lucas pulled the map from the table and slapped down plates piled with food from the smoking cast-iron skillet. There was a scraping of chairs as we gathered at the table.

Lucas pushed his dark hair back and looked earnest. "I want to put you on my cell phone plan. I know you hate to learn anything technical," he held up one hand to forestall my protest, "but I'll teach you. Then you can call me any time for free."

"All those little buttons and icons with multiple-use menus… arrgh!"

"Yes, I know," he patted me soothingly. "I'll get you a basic phone."

Megan was extracting bell peppers and dropping them on her mother's plate. She edged off her chair into my lap. "I don't want you to go."

"I know," I brushed the hair away from her eyes, "but we need to find a new town. Tucson is just too big and dry. Do you know there are places that have wonderful trees and oceans? It can be fun to choose a different life. Besides, you guys need a bit more space. You have to admit it's crowded with all of us here."

Megan wrinkled her nose. "I don't think so."

Compared to sleeping four people in a tent, Sylvia House was luxurious, but by most standards we were tight. "I'll send you postcards from the places we visit," I said. "We'll put a map on the wall and you can follow our trip."

She laid her head on my shoulder and sighed. "I'll miss our special mornings." Megan usually joined me on the sofa at dawn. It was our "special time" when she asked me about life and I told her stories, as my grandmother Winnie had done with me.

"Should I make some jerky to eat on the road?" Tom asked suddenly. He was practically wagging at the thought of a trip.

"We're not going into the Arctic. There'll be grocery stores," I assured him.

"What about our music CDs?"

I shook my head. "We need to fit our lives into a Honda." I had invested in another used Civic, oddly the same teal color as the last one.

The current was again lifting us. I felt like a grounded boat on the incoming tide. It was exciting and scary to let go of the shore, but this time it felt right.

CIRCUMVENTING THE DANGEROUS AND BORING interstate, Tom and I headed north out of Tucson along the backside of the Catalina Mountains. To our right, blue peaks erupted from the desert floor to above nine thousand feet. These "sky islands" were populated with pine, fir, black bears, and tree squirrels marooned after the last ice age. Until humans divided the valley, animals made the perilous journey between ranges to keep genetic diversity. A tortoise was tracked on a two-year transit from the Rincon Mountains to the Santa Ritas, where she spent a year before starting back. She was stopped by railroad tracks until scientists lifted her across. *How many others of this vanishing species are still out there following endless rails?*

For some miles the desert lay buried beneath cement, but gradually traffic thinned and we found ourselves amid tawny grasslands punctuated with yucca. Hawks watched from electric poles. I imagined oceans lapping the foot of those blue-gray peaks and thought of the miles I had walked. I'd been four years old the first time I hiked down the backside of Mount Lemmon to the little town of

Oracle with my mother. I recall Douglas fir and ponderosa shifting to scrub oak and finally to palo verde and cholla at a footpace and rainy nights wrapped in a wool blanket by our campfires. We had no tent or expensive gear. "More walk, less talk," she would say. I learned to move through wild country before I could read.

The tawdry outgrowth of Phoenix greeted us, hot and uniform: minimalls, billboards, and housing developments. We were swept into a network of freeways with traffic pushing us along at an increasing pace as we plunged into the city. Tom gripped the steering wheel and we rode the current through the merging and diverging lanes onto the Black Canyon Freeway and out toward Flagstaff. Phoenix dropped behind and the road climbed onto a high desert plateau where overgrazed hills looked as desolate as Mars. Eventually, we turned off I-17 toward Prescott and a welcoming night with friends. Once a sleepy town amid juniper and pinion, Prescott had broken out like hives onto the surrounding grasslands. The old center of town was less changed. It had been built along Granite Creek, shaded by large deciduous trees, where historic buildings still lent an air of community.

Stan Brown had been minister of the Catalina United Methodist Church in Tucson when we created their chapel windows two decades before. Now retired, Stan and Ruthie had chosen a smaller town in which to age. They were as merry as elves when they collected us at the front desk of their posh assisted-living complex. They'd been together since high school and looked more alike than ever: small and silver-haired with dancing blue eyes behind bifocals. Their God was an old friend and our names were mentioned regularly in conversations with Him.

Their elegant apartment was spotless and furnished with a lifetime of personal memories. The facility provided formal dining, gym, laundry, hair salon, and even a communal garden plot. I could see the advantages of this pleasant and safe environment where aging Americans needn't feel isolated. Our friends looked fit and happy; they volunteered with their church and Stan continued to write sermons, books, and articles.

"We planned to move into assisted living when we reached eighty," Ruthie said. She was curled in a chair wearing white shorts, her bare feet tucked under her like a girl. "Then we thought, 'Why wait?' We don't want our kids to worry about us. We've made many friends here and it's a relief not to care for a house. If we ever need it, we can move across the road to the nursing facility."

From their balcony we watched sunset smolder along the hill. Three floors below, the garden waded into shadow. "We're so fortunate," Stan said—a favorite phrase. "I always loved my work with people and now I can do it at my own pace."

"So where are you two headed?" Ruthie asked as she refilled our glasses with lemonade. The smell of pot roast drifted from the tidy kitchen. Stan leaned forward listening intently. He wore hearing aids now and his fingers were drifting with arthritis.

"Colorado first," Tom announced, "and then we circle back to Tucson for a few days before heading east. After that… we don't know. We want to connect with friends that we haven't seen in decades. When we run out of money or friends, Jeanie will take a job somewhere."

"What's in Colorado?" Stan asked.

"Most of my paternal cousins and my Uncle John, one of my father's two brothers," I said. "I'm not certain what I'm looking for, but being unclaimed by my father left me feeling unwanted by that half of my family. It turns out I'm not alone in this, for we share strange dynamics. Bud's other brother, Uncle Jim, once tried to bring the cousins together in a spirit of reconciliation after he left his children and remarried, but then he disowned them for sticking by the one who died of AIDS."

"Sad," Ruthie said.

Yes, sad. I had been angry with Uncle Jim, as if my judgment could heal his. His God wasn't the friendly sort you could ask for advice. I wondered how each of us would have fared had Grandpa been raised by a kindly stepdad instead of being kicked out as a child. What if my father had learned compassion rather than competition? We who are not yet wise pass down the crimes committed against us. *What if we could break this heritage and create a new dream?*

STAN AND RUTHIE WERE SMILING, arms looped around one another as Tom and I drove away the next morning. "They seem happy," I said. "Do you see us somewhere like that?"

Tom was concentrating on traffic. "It's okay, but you couldn't pound a nail in the wall. I need a shop."

"It might look like a community," I decided, "but it's commerce. If they outlive their funds, they'll be shown the door. The friendly staff isn't there out of love."

"There's that. Spending down your equity."

I sighed. "It would be comforting to believe in a benevolent deity who cares about me. Then I remember the Yukon River devouring thousands of acres and the calf moose we found drowned. I think of the babies I've seen born without brains. I don't believe that God 'cares' in a personal sense." I glanced over at Tom and continued. "Life is boundless and everything is sacred. It's all One: river, moose, trees, and me. Life keeps expressing in a kaleidoscope of patterns and the form doesn't matter. That's what Life knows, and I keep trying to learn."

Tom was used to my soliloquies and said nothing. The car twisted along Oak Creek Canyon until the road climbed to a stunning vista of red cliffs where juniper gave way to ponderosa pine. Beyond Flagstaff, we followed a side road into the quiet parking lot at the Walnut Canyon. Luke and I had discovered it on one of our summer trips when he was about ten, and I wanted to share it with Tom. We walked a mile of paved trail down into the gorge where prehistoric Indians had sheltered in natural hollows sculpted by wind and water in the rock walls.

It takes so little for a meaningful human life, I thought. *Monuments are not the measure of consciousness.* I tried to imagine raising babies here. These people had climbed down hundreds of feet for water and up to the canyon rim to grow dry-land crops. How had they teased enough food from this arid land to feed themselves? I've lived as a hunter-gatherer and know how much it takes. What about firewood? Where did they all poop? They probably didn't stay here year-round, I decided. Early humans owned little and moved with the seasons. They didn't try to control the planet, but adapted to it.

Continuing our drive north and east, we entered the Painted Desert and Navajo Indian Reservation, a poor country of windswept red sand. Thin horses cropped the scanty grass and an occasional desolate house stood surrounded by broken vehicles. Great monoliths of weathered sandstone rose from the flat landscape, and somewhere out of sight lay deep fissures and sunless canyons that I had hiked as a young person.

Spring draped the Rockies in new green and we stopped often the next day to explore upland meadows. Colorado would have been high on my list of places to settle twenty years before, but although the painted mountains were budding out, signs of drought lingered. Snowmelt was down to a fraction of normal and fires were a growing menace. As we transected the state visiting my paternal cousins, most of whom I had not seen in decades, I continued to ask the questions: *What seeds had their lineage planted in their varied lives? What did they value? How were they preparing for old age?*

Uncle Jim, my father's youngest brother, had become an engineer and a real estate millionaire. In religious zeal, he had rejected all four of his children— three boys and a girl. My father Bud set his sons against one another, a legacy that continues to bear sour fruit. My Aunt Lilly, the only sister, died young of cancer. She had become a nurse after her husband left her alone with three boys to raise. I have a picture of Lillie in her white cap and gown that could be me.

Lillie's sons told me they felt like poor relations to the only family they knew. My cousin Ralph used to call us sometimes, drunk and crazy, from West Texas where he lived with his dog and sheep. "Uncle Jim said he'd been awarded the Congressional Medal of Honor," he told me. "I thought, 'If I could just win the Medal of Honor like Uncle Jim, I'd be somebody.' I kept signing up for secret missions behind enemy lines in Nam. The one time that I should have gotten it, I was the only American left alive."

Ralph finally got too crazy for even the Special Forces. He tried to return to civilian life until he came close to killing someone, and then moved out to the desert alone where he could do the least harm. On his last visit to Arizona, he brought us two knives: a large folding Buck that he once used to cut his way out of a downed helicopter, and a Bowie knife in a handmade case. On the tarnished five-inch blade was inscribed RVN 8/65-8-70 and five notches were filed along the top. A shadow lay upon that knife, something dark. I didn't even want to touch it.

"Take them to Alaska," Ralph had said. "I need them out of my life. They should skin a moose."

I had placed them on the studio floor, surrounded by candles and prayers for the night. It wasn't long after that the calls stopped coming. Ralph's brother, John Robert, cared for him during the final stages of neurological decline, probably due to Agent Orange assisted by alcohol. Ralph died in Grand Junction a year or two later. The knives were still at our cabin and had skinned moose.

"Your Uncle Jim was never awarded the Medal of Honor," Tom told me as we drove toward Grand Junction. "Very few living men get it and they're all listed. You can check it out online."

I wondered if Ralph ever found out. Lies, perhaps meant only to make you look bigger, can have profound consequences. As we visited around the state, I began to see that I wasn't alone with my family legacy. What Adyashanti refers to as "generational suffering," an emotional tone we ingest with our mother's milk, can set the course of our lives. Some of my cousins were like trees that had spent a lifetime leaning into a harsh wind, yet others had shrugged off neglect or judgment to create close and loving families. *There is always a choice once we realize it*, I decided.

Our last stop was to see my Uncle John. We found him in a tired single-wide trailer near Austin, Colorado—satellite town to Grand Junction. When

Bud and Jim set out to make their fortunes, John, the middle son, had gone to work with their father. He was old now and stooped, his hands shaking a bit. His hair had thinned and he was hard of hearing. When he opened the door, I realized with a shock that I would have known him anywhere: those intense Helmericks blue eyes and the stubborn set of the jaw. He was dignified as he welcomed us in from the heat. His second wife, Angie, was a kindly woman who made us feel at home.

Compared with his flamboyant brothers, John had led a singularly modest life. He stayed in the town of Montrose working in his father's gun shop and remained married to the same woman until her death. They raised two children, a boy and girl, and then adopted two boys after their son was killed as a teenager. When Grandpa died without a will, John was forced to mortgage (and then lose) his home to buy back the business he and Grandpa had built. It was one more stone in a wall of family pain and discord.

"How do you feel about the way your brothers treated you?" I asked Uncle John. We were eating dinner in the trailer. It was hot inside, for the evaporative cooler had been turned off at sunset to conserve electricity.

He bent over his plate, seeming to focus on gathering potato salad onto his fork, his hands unsteady. For a moment I thought he hadn't heard me. Then I wondered if he would answer. Finally, he looked up and smiled gently, fixing me with those familiar eyes.

"I had the happier life," was all he would say on the subject.

The low evening light seemed to brighten momentarily in the stuffy little room. I felt as if a quiet depth were expanding in my chest the way a breeze heralds the dawn. These were words I had traveled to hear: *There is always a choice.* To go to war, or to see beyond appearances—and call them good.

Tom, Laurie Schacht, and Luke at age six building Kernwood.

Laurie, Luke, and me outside our new cabin, fall 1992.

Chapter 7

CROSSING AMERICA

June 2006

Back at Sylvia House for the award dinner, I climbed into Faith's Jeep for a whirlwind day of shopping. Like her mother, she wanted her old Aunt Jeanie to shine. She insisted on paying for everything, even having my nails done and hair styled—I who had always cut my own hair. It was a shifting of roles.

"You must have something elegant to wear for your award," she insisted. Faith was thirty-one now and, except for her self-confidence, looked very much like I did at that age.

"Make me young and beautiful," I joked to the youthful beautician, whose multicolor tresses appeared to have been styled with a weedwhacker. The girl stared blankly at me, shears poised, then plucked the barrette from my scalp like a bug and dropped it onto the counter.

"I've never felt old enough to wear makeup or drink alcohol," I confided to the two of them. "Now maybe I'm too old."

"You can do without either," Faith stated in her usual blunt tone. She took charge, pointing while the girl snipped obediently. "You need to feel really classy when you walk in there tonight."

Connie would've said the same thing. I could change a tire, saddle a skittish horse, or pick up your extra shift at work—but dressing up made me feel vulnerable. *Could my father still make me feel small after all these years?* I studied myself in the mirror: healthy color, strong features, clear eyes. I looked far less than my fifty-six years. As my fine locks fell away, the wavy hair lifted into a sassy, off-the-collar style. I tilted my head and admired the length of my throat and clean lines of my clavicles.

Faith directed a few last touches then nodded in satisfaction. "Now for the dress. A little black something."

I followed her docilely, recalling her grit as a small child. Repeated disappointments had only toughened Faith. When her father punished her harshly for failing some trivial test, she never repented. Before she reached school age, she had learned how to capture the dangerous horses that wandered between trash and bulldozers on their seven dusty acres. Using only a string, she managed to mount a stallion and gallop him into the fence, breaking her arm—yet nothing deterred her. She had found her way back into the cattle-and-horse circle, bringing her aging father along, and was now one of only two women on the Rodeo Parade Committee.

Faith and Lucas both accompanied me that night. As I proudly accepted the acknowledgment of the graduating medical school class of 2006, my two dates were perfectly at home among the throng of doctors. I was filled with pride for them: blonde Faith with her classic Greek profile and clean, golden limbs; Lucas, tall and darkly handsome in slacks and dress shirt. It had been worth the drive back.

NEXT MORNING TOM AND I cast off with everything needed for an indefinite future stuffed into my old car. I was looking forward to the trip, curious to see the choices our friends had made and to hear their plans for aging. My ninety-year-old father and his wife were now imprisoned on the dilapidated ground floor of their Fairbanks home. Instead of renovating the little place they bought in the 1970s, they had stacked on two gaudy floors—now beyond their reach—overhanging their neighbors.

"I never thought it would happen to me," my father had once said in a tone of bewilderment. He and I had worn the harsh edges off of our relationship over the years, but there was little depth to our interactions.

Well, I'm not going to fool myself about eternal youth, I decided as I watched the changing scene beyond the car window. *Better to make wise choices while we can.* The temperature was over a hundred as we sped east out of Tucson on Interstate 10. To our left, the Rincon Mountains climbed, smudged and remote, into a dirty sky. As usual, Tom was driving.

"Let's find a small town where it rains and the soil is rich," I said, "an intact community where relationships count. It should have a college, a small hospital, and bike paths. We need a simple home that's well insulated and environmentally sound. Maybe we can even build off the grid. We don't need much."

"Where the fish are safe to eat." That was Tom's major requirement. It excluded most of the United States where coal-fired generators rained pollution into streams and lakes.

I kicked off my sandals and rested one bare foot on the dashboard. At sixty miles per hour, our little car got excellent mileage, but traffic pushed us close to eighty. Out my window, I could see identical houses—seeded from the city like tumbleweeds. The Santa Rita landfill seemed to have ballooned up several hundred feet. Clanking yellow machines were grading it and I wondered if people would soon live on a mountain of trash. *Beauty*, I decided, adding that to my list. *Natural beauty is as important to my soul as food.*

"Welcome, stranger," Barbara said, rising from a stump and walking toward us through the uncut grass. We had arrived in rural Arkansas. The little hard-rock farm looked just as Tom had described it when he and Luke visited in 1991. I hadn't seen Barb in a quarter-century. She was thinner now: gray hair, mid-sixties, sandals, T-shirt, and worn shorts. The familiar cigarette was still in her fingers.

"You can stay with us," she had told me when I phoned the month before, "but I'll warn you, it's very primitive."

"We're the people who live in the Arctic," I reminded her.

"Well," she had replied with characteristic honesty, "our place is probably more primitive than your cabin and a good deal dirtier."

Barbara had left the fast lane two decades earlier to join her wild friend David on the land. She was a thoughtful and educated woman. During the seventies, she did my taxes in return for whatever I could pay, including yard work. Even then, she was in retreat from California, where she had served as a college dean. For thirty years she kept in touch with articulate letters in a neat hand. In return, I had printed missives off my computer—not really a fair exchange. Barb was a holdout from the electronic age.

Tom carried our single small bag into the house. Barb hadn't exaggerated about their rustic lives. The front door didn't shut and screens had long since disintegrated from open windows. Dauber wasps were covering the kitchen walls with mud.

"You can sleep here," she said, leading us to the only bedroom. I felt a qualm when I realized they were putting us in their bed. The sheets had been freshly laundered. "No," she waved off my protests, "I like sleeping on the sofa, and—well, David keeps his own schedule."

We joined them on stumps in the yard, where they spent much of the summer under huge trees. "We've given up farming," Barb told us, "but we feed a lot of wildlife. The only animals we have now are five elderly peafowl and cats."

"A coon hound showed up yesterday," David put in. He was a big man, bright and quirky, with a gentle face and soft voice. "They get so involved following a scent that they get lost. He's pretty skinny and I'm feedin' him up. I'll keep him in the pen 'til he gets used to us and learns not to chase the critters."

"How do you heat this place in the winter?" I wondered aloud.

"She hunkers next to the stove and I bring in loads of firewood," David said in a broad accent. He was well-read and possessed an amazing knowledge of birds—recognizing them by sound. Often he stopped our conversation to point one out. Although a recluse since Vietnam, he spoke proudly of Barbara's place in the community. "Folks 'round here really love her. She volunteers on the election board and writes letters. Lotsa hill folk don't read or write."

We sipped cold tea and talked until the sun slanted into the woods. Light radiated in spokes through the forest and across the empty field. It gathered in dusty beams in the long grass and rose in swirling columns of insects. I perched in their one rickety chair, keeping my feet tucked up away from chiggers. No traffic passed on the dirt road. Golden light fingered an elderly peacock with his lavish train extended as he paced, judging the distance to a huge branch that threatened the house.

"Sometimes I have to help them up into the trees," Barbara said. "Especially after a rain when those tails get heavy."

With a flap, the showy bird sailed onto a branch twenty feet from the ground and crowed his triumph. He called loudly again before leaping to the next level. Soon he was out of sight way above us. Barbara suddenly rose and disappeared around the edge of the house.

She was back a few minutes later. "I wanted to follow that peahen to her eggs. They sneak off and make nests on the ground and then the raccoons kill them. I only have two hens left."

Twilight pooled between the trees, and David descended into the clearing with a bucket of grain in each hand. We could hear his quiet voice speaking to the shadowy forms of deer and feral pigs that melted and reformed like smoke about him.

"We spend more on animal feed than on our own," Barbara said fondly. They didn't seem to eat at all. Their refrigerator was mysterious and very dark, seeming to hold little except milk. The four of us picked at the few items that we contributed from our little ice chest.

Tom, Barb, and I were quiet watching the scene below. I could make out half a dozen deer and fawns, and a great sow with four piglets in the gloaming. There were smaller animals as well, a family of raccoons, I thought, and perhaps two skunks. Fireflies were beginning to twinkle in the growing dusk.

"If you've given up raising cattle, how do you make ends meet?" I asked.

"Well, I'm still doing taxes. The IRS hates me because I refuse to use computers. As long as I never submit an electronic form, they can't make me. I charge eight dollars and sometimes get paid in eggs. The hill folk can't pay much. David gets a small pension. We live close to the bone. If I ever get sick with something I can't cure myself—and let's face it, with smoking I'm not going to last that long—I'll just die. That's what most people in this world do."

"Dying isn't the hard part," I said quietly. "It's the process."

She nodded thoughtfully. "Yes, there's that."

I thought about their tenuous support of the hill people and the wildlife. There was a web of community that ran deep in this land. I could feel it. There might be no doctors, but I could imagine chicken soup and split firewood appearing on their doorstep.

David returned to his stump and our talk turned to politics and land use. They were surprisingly well-informed and, unlike many we were to visit, lived their beliefs. With no children of her own, Barbara argued that leaving an intact world for future generations was the most important thing any of us can do.

"Things are changing, even here in the mountains," she told us. "If you drive north you'll see the land is being subdivided for 'McMansions.' Soon the hill people won't be able to afford the taxes and they'll be forced to sell."

"What's the local economic base?" I asked.

"It's very sketchy. You've seen the abandoned chicken sheds? Raising chickens used to be a cottage industry and then Tyson came in. They own the chicks and dictate all the terms to farmers—including sale of the feed and the finished price. Most small farmers went under, some lost their land."

"You make lumber by hand up at your cabin?" David asked Tom. "I bet you'd enjoy seeing my sawmill."

"He does some beautiful work," Barb told me as the two men set off for the barn. Stars were beginning to appear and bats fluttered against the rosy sky.

"Couldn't he use his skill to shore up your house?" I asked bluntly.

She laughed easily. "Well, it's just not his way." I could see that living with David was similar to the wildlife: on its own terms. Somehow, Barb was at peace with it. *Maybe that's the real accomplishment*, I thought. *Cherish what you get.*

The evening wound to a close and Barbara went to sleep on the sofa while David walked down to the barn, saying that he had work to do. Under the great trees, the house was completely dark. Forest sounds crawled through the empty window holes and sometime during the night I awakened to the smell of skunk permeating the bedroom. There came a light pressure on my feet and I wondered what kind of animal it was.

"WE COULD BUY PART OF that farm and build," I told Tom as we bumped onto the dirt road and turned south through a winding arch of trees. Barbara and David were again seated on their stumps in the morning sunlight, companionable as a pair of cats.

"They're good people," he agreed, "and David is quite an artist. You should see his lumber! He cuts hardwoods from the farm into beautiful boards and finishes them by hand. I don't think he has any plans for them, he just loves the process. He knows where each board came from and the use of every tree." He was quiet a moment, considering my suggestion. "That's a bit more primitive than I want for my old age," he admitted. "There comes a time when you can't cut firewood. What then?"

We climbed onto a paved state highway and turned south through rural Arkansas. The land unfolded in nameless shades of green on green. The road tunneled between trees, snaking along ravines and up steep hills past picturesque small farms. We stopped for fuel at the little town of Ozark. A teenage girl, blonde hair styled from the sixties, stood behind a counter stocked with pickled eggs and chewing tobacco.

"How long does it take to get to Pine Bluff?" I asked, pointing on our map.

She smiled shyly. "Well, I haven't been out of Arkansas..." she hesitated. "Really, I haven't been out of Ozark."

As we journeyed south, the country became more level and prosperous. Small farms gave way to vast lawns and well-kept homes interspersed with manicured patches of trees. I wondered aloud why anyone would mow instead of growing a garden. All that grass seemed a waste. I thought of a Japanese friend who told me how her mother tended four tomato plants in a window box. It was her sanctuary, her touch with the living Earth. *We are so fortunate*, I heard Stan Brown say again.

It was still very hot when we stopped for the evening in Pine Bluff, Arkansas. My new hairstyle had swollen with the unaccustomed humidity and stuck out in horizontal waves like a hat. I watered it down before we set out on foot to look for a local restaurant. We usually made salads in our motel, but trying local food, I argued, would help us experience the land. Walking seemed a good way to view the community and get a bit of exercise. There was, however, no sidewalk, and traffic roared by as we edged along the roadway.

"Did I mention that our new town must be friendly to pedestrians?" I yelled at Tom above the rumble of large trucks. "I am not having fun here."

"What about that place across the street? It's not local color, but it's food."

I nodded. Tom grabbed my hand and sprinted me between the speeding vehicles. The chain restaurant turned out to be everything odious in American food: salty, greasy, overcooked, and all-you-can-swallow. As we entered, a boy of about twelve held the glass door open for us.

"Thank you, Son," Tom said kindly.

The child nodded and dropped his gaze. He was morbidly obese, his young body swollen to grotesque proportions, hopeless blue eyes pinched between rolls of fat. The rest of his ponderous family had already bellied up to the buffet. I watched the boy out of the corner of my eye as I picked among the fried fare for something resembling a vegetable. With an air of resignation, he set to work mounding two plates with the congealed glop. Then he sat heavily on a bench, dropped his head between his shoulders, and started shoveling it into his mouth.

I smiled at the big child at the table across from us, blessing him, but he did not look up. I wished he could have a year playing in wilderness. *Growing up is hard*, I thought. I remembered Luke trying to hide his weight in seventh grade. With his permission, I quote from his journal:

> *My name is Luke and I am 14. I have brown hair and I am 6 feet tall, with dashing brown eyes and a wise smile. I am a man of kindness, love, and immense wealth that comes from who I am. But who I am would never have come to light had I not been given a gift.*
>
> *I have always been the "weird" kid. I don't mind now, but I used*

to resent it. Everyone has problems growing up, but I was able to escape most of the pain and confusion of puberty in the quiet of the wilderness. I don't understand how so many people survive it.

I was chubby all the way through 5th, 6th, and 7th grades. In middle school I could hide my vulnerability by hanging out with kids who acted silly and crazy. Then I didn't have to worry about being teased, because I could blow it all off. Seventh grade was different. I had moved to a small private school, and there wasn't a "weird" clique for me. I was honestly trying to get rid of my old image. There was also a girl who meant the world to me, but I never had the courage to speak to her. No matter what I did, I continued to shift back into the old mode of being silly. It was one of those things that one doesn't really understand.

I was feeling lovesick, hot and bored. The Tucson sun was beginning to warm up. Like all other kids, I had just gotten out of school, but unlike them, I was heading for Alaska. I now understand that it takes strength to disregard the teachings of culture. You must be willing to be criticized and even ostracized. Others may not understand your dreams, but people who truly love you will do their best to support you even if they don't understand.

THE AIR BECAME OPPRESSIVELY HOT and smoggy as we journeyed. The American South was a lot more beautiful than I had anticipated and much more rural. It reminded me of the summer Lucas and I had volunteered in Guatemala, only more prosperous. The highway was bordered to either side with immense trees that formed an almost impenetrable dark mass arching over swamps and black mud. As we crossed into the Deep South, kudzu buried the forests beneath a surreal blanket of vines, the disastrous result of a transplanted species. In Louisiana we began to see storm damage, which became more dramatic as we neared the coast. We discussed going through New Orleans, but the thought of gridlock in that desolate and sweltering city was depressing and a bit frightening—so many ghosts. Why should we gawk if we had nothing to offer?

"Strange to rebuild a graveyard city below sea level—between one of the world's great rivers, a lake, and the ocean—in a time of increasing hurricanes," I said, studying the map. "Every drop of water that falls from Montana to

Pennsylvania is headed for New Orleans. I'd snatch up my babies and head for higher ground, even if I lost everything." *But then I was raised with the belief in choice.* Many cultures accept fate with a bowed head. I'd tried to teach girls who became pregnant repeatedly, and their boyfriends who seemed resigned to short and violent lives, that they could choose another future. For them, it was not an easy concept. Perception is everything: without a new idea, it's impossible to change behavior. *Words and ideas can imprison or set us free.*

We crossed Big Muddy at Vicksburg and entered the state of Mississippi under a rebel flag. One could feel the unresolved issues, even after all these years. We stopped to ponder the old battlefield and read the plaques before continuing eastward. I wondered if I could see beyond my preconceptions. Someone who knew this landscape intimately would articulate it in far subtler shades than an outsider, no matter how well-informed. I recalled a black friend telling me he preferred the South, for boundaries here were unambiguous.

We spent the night in a Motel 6 in Meridian, a city with an ugly civil-rights history. The clerk was a lumpy young woman with skin the color of uncooked dough, bleached hair growing dark at the roots, and watchful eyes. This wouldn't be the place to take more than one bucket of ice from the machine. After checking in, we drove to a grocery store to buy produce for dinner. The market was eerily quiet—even children seemed tense and watchful. The employees were black, the customers all white. I had never before been so conscious of my skin. Tom and I often joke with strangers, but not in Meridian. The cashier counted out change without once looking up.

Back in our room, I made salads while Tom switched on the news. A group of angry-looking young black men were playing car stereos loudly just beyond our curtained window. I wondered if our tires would still be there in the morning. On the bathroom door hung a sign: "Welcome to Mississippi." There followed the law about pilfering from motels that threatened a year in prison for a theft under $25. *This is the karma of control*, I thought. *Once force is used, only fear secures the peace. How do we heal it?* The local news had a brief recital of an accident we had seen on the freeway. The driver of a loaded gravel truck had suffered a blowout and been killed plunging over a bridge. I wondered if he were black or white and why it would matter.

Dawn revealed our car intact. It had 130,000 miles and assorted dents when I bought it—not the sort of vehicle likely to attract envy. With relief, we put Meridian behind us that morning and then skipped across the bottom of Alabama and into Florida, where we entered a different world.

*In the fall of 1993 we returned to our
Sunset home on the Arizona desert.*

Luke with his beloved dog, Lucy, in 1994.

Chapter 8

LAND'S END

June 2006

Florida turned out to be very flat and humid—the highest point being only a few feet above the ocean. A long finger pointing out to sea, it was scrubbed of smog that blanketed the middle and eastern United States by winds that hit from either side during hurricane season. The freeway, crowded with big pickups towing enormous boats, was designed for the flood of aging and wealthy tourists. Traffic moved as efficiently as on a conveyer belt, hauling wallets deep into the state. Expensive vehicles loaded with gray-hairs were off to see our country, leaving American youth hitched to college debts and the corporate wheel.

"Our generation's sense of entitlement is staggering," I commented, as our little car struggled along in the herd. "Weren't we the children of the sixties who wanted to change the world?"

Tom, driving as always, glanced at me out of the corner of his eye and smiled.

Dark forest slid by, inaccessible and hidden behind giant billboards. There were emergency call boxes at one-mile intervals and rest stops every twenty-five miles—regular as a metronome. I wondered how Florida had captured such a lion's share of federal highway funds compared to... say, Mississippi. Rest stops were lavish and staffed by smiling officials who dispensed samples of orange juice and information. Armed guards were on duty. *Armed guards?* Was I missing something?

"Maybe America's love affair with large vehicles has to do with large butts," I commented as we pulled away from a rest stop. "Most of these people wouldn't fit in a Honda." It seemed the further east we drove, the larger people grew. Crippled with weight, they limped from their oversized SUVs and waddled painfully to the bathrooms. It all made me sad. *What is happening to us? Domestication exacts a heavy toll.*

A few blocks from Florida's western coastline, we pulled up to a modest home in Naples under a white afternoon sun. Annie's husband John welcomed us inside where a ceiling fan stirred the air and a dog's tail thumped briefly on the tile. My sister, John told us, was napping. He was dressed in shorts and a faded shirt stained with oil paints. A man of moderate height with a slight stoop, John had an open face and inquisitive brown eyes behind glasses. He was a professor now, clean-shaven with graying brown hair curling over his ears. Though interested in almost everything, John's complexity was hidden in his art—a depth he did not readily share beyond an amused eyebrow. When I once asked how he maintained such a dependably sunny nature, he had replied, "My mother said I was a happy baby."

What about those who aren't congenitally pacific? I wondered. After supporting some three thousand births, I can say that we are different from the beginning.

Annie was sprawled under a revolving fan in the master bedroom. She patted the mattress, inviting me to join her. She was lightly clothed in shorts and halter revealing pink skin. Her bangs were pushed off a damp forehead and her blue eyes, reddened from the sun, were circled with fine creases. She had put on a few pounds and I could see Connie—the way our mother used to lay in the afternoon heat at Bean Alley. I remember Connie reading the classics to us, how she would get choked up during parts that held special meaning for her. I thought of how Lucas appreciated that trait in me.

"You're lucky to be here off-season," Annie said as I flopped down beside her on the high bed. "We'll have the beaches mostly to ourselves. Wait until you see the birds and fish! John has fallen in love with fishing and spends most of each day out there with his bucket and pole while I paint. We have manatee here, too."

That evening the four of us walked around the neighborhood with the borrowed old dog that came with the house. They had left their own pets with John's teenage son at home in Missouri. This area of Naples was in transition, new mansions under construction and smaller homes being demolished to scale up.

"Our friends tell us their house is appreciating at a thousand dollars a month," Annie told me as we sauntered, hand in hand. Frogs were singing in the twilight and the air smelled lush and tropical. "It's their retirement fund. The house isn't anything special—it's the land."

"I hope they haven't missed their window," I said. Most of the houses were closed for the summer and several had "For Sale" signs in their driveways. "With the increase in hurricanes, I'd think twice before buying."

She smiled at my naiveté.

At dawn the next morning, Annie and I paddled their two kayaks along shadowy channels that wound between mangrove trees where cranes and herons vied for fish. Seen from behind, Annie's long blonde hair made her look girlish. The day was already hot and with her encouragement, I, too, was clad in a sports bra and shorts.

"Old ladies don't bare this much skin in public," I had protested.

"They do here," she grinned, "even in the stores."

The network of brackish sloughs meandered through buttressed tree roots. "Look over there!" Annie whispered, pointing to a trace of ripples. "Manatee. They are quiet folk. I bet very few people ever notice them." I could understand how motorboats roared right over them. "Sometimes we see dolphins feeding here as well."

Our progress was leisurely. Herons watched us from the twisted roots. An osprey skimmed the dark surface. Rounding a bend in the estuary, we suddenly emerged on an expanse of pale green ocean and a white beach dotted with egrets and pelicans. Here a series of little roads and picnic benches were tastefully situated beneath trees. John was standing waist-deep in the warm ocean holding his pole while Tom rested nearby in the shade. A cool breeze blew creamy froth against the shore, where schools of small fish flowed with the gentle surf in myriad shades of pale green.

I felt the sudden current of tide as we entered the ocean and paddled to shore. Annie set up her easel and a big umbrella, disappearing into her own thoughts. Day by day she explored the same sky and waves, seeing new elements with each painting, totally content in the moment. I looked through her sheaf of watercolors, dappled and vague. She had little interest in the particulars of bird or human subject, but was engrossed in what I thought of as "the background." Her small mouth, reminiscent of our father's, twitched in amusement as I studied the work.

"I am learning the vocabulary of a new landscape," she said. "It's like doing musical scales. These are a conversation with the quality of light. They're about the essence behind what you think you see..." Her brush never stopped as she spoke. She had poured most of her limited drinking water into a jar and was painting with it.

I recalled Annie painting along the river on our canoe journey that summer Luke was four. She had always been in love with the play of light. It seems we become more ourselves as we age. At least that is the possibility—to enter deeper and more complex levels of who we have always been. I am fond of saying that art is not something you "do," but a way of being; Annie was telling me it was also about communicating personal reality. Yet I wondered if that were possible. Each sees the world through a unique lens and unless someone resonates at a close harmonic, the experience you evoke probably differs from your intention.

I studied the horizon, trying to see it through her paintings. Tall buildings seemed to float above the curved sea. The sky arced high to the west with tropical clouds towering into the stratosphere: *a conversation with the light*. I thought of a friend who saw no reason to preserve ecosystems. In her reality, Jesus would take all the deserving people to a better place, so this world didn't matter. Yet we both raised our children on this beautiful island adrift in space.

"FLORIDA'S AIR SMELLS LIKE DOG breath," I said as Tom jockeyed in the herd of giant vehicles into Orlando. The city stood in strange contrast to rural Arkansas with all kinds of unreality. It seemed a larger-than-necessary copy of southern California, often with the same street names. Disney World covered miles. We saw giant billboards advertising a "Biblical Theme Park"—hard to imagine that. Robotic Moses delivering the Ten Commandments every hour? *Commerce and absolutism.*

Dean and Emmy greeted us at the door of their elegant home and showed us to a private wing. The sheets were 600-count and the towels were as fluffy as pillows. Everything matched. Our friends lived in a gated community where deer and sandhill cranes stalked across the golf course between groomed patches of pine trees. We joined them for cold drinks on the patio beside their screened-in swimming pool. Beyond the garden of tropical plants, a tempting path led into the distant green. A few hundred yards away we could see an occasional golf cart.

Dean was tall with graying blond hair and reflective blue eyes. Now retired, he had sent us glass restoration work over the years—hundreds of antique panels that Tom had repaired. Emmy had been a nurse. She was petite, fair, and attractive. It was a second marriage for both.

"Can we go for a walk after it cools down?" I asked, pointing to the alluring path. "We spend too much time in the car."

"It doesn't really cool down," Emmy hesitated. "I'm afraid pedestrians aren't allowed on the golf course, but we can walk around the compound."

"Not even the golfers?" I asked.

"Carts are required," Dean assured me. "They have computer chips to keep golfers on schedule."

I snorted. "Wasn't it Mark Twain who called golf 'a good walk spoiled'? Now we don't even get that." I opened my mouth to expound on the theft of the commons and turning public resources into profit, but Tom shot me a warning look.

WE STAYED WITH OUR FRIENDS for two days and were treated to perfect candlelit dinners against a backdrop of sunset woods. Dean grilled giant prawns and thick, tender steaks. Emmy tossed beautiful salads and served them with crusted French bread. We talked into the night and found that here, too, we had much in common. Mornings began with a variety of fresh fruit and berries, English muffins, and cereal. I felt honored and pampered sipping freshly ground coffee in the velvet dawn by the pool and watching the deer.

"I could use elements of that life," I told Tom as we headed for Georgia, "but not on that scale. I want a solid home that's easy to clean. I don't need a linen closet full of bedding, but I'd like two sets of expensive sheets and good pillows." I thought a moment and then continued, "I really don't want to retire either. I just want off the treadmill."

The Fourth of July found us in the forested hills of North Carolina. It rained intermittently as we climbed and descended. At Greensboro we turned off the interstate onto winding back roads through some of the loveliest country yet. The air was still dirty, but small farms looked alive, and the valleys were planted in a Norman Rockwell patchwork of fields. We followed instructions written in Bruce's wandering hand. He had been one of the "neighborhood guys" from the Tucson Mountains, a geology professor who'd built a home with scraps salvaged from the dump. Paulina was a nurse still working in the rural area where they had settled.

Bruce opened the door looking just as I remembered him: a bear of a man with shaggy mane and dancing blue eyes beneath craggy brows, his logjam of a beard now twisted with white. Paulina seemed rooted and balanced—attractive without effort, competent without ego. They showed us to a separate cottage hidden in deep forest and tight as a sailboat. A fluid and innovative use of space welcomed us into the presence of trees, while banks of windows made it feel like living outside. Bruce had renovated the original house and built two others, including this one, using mostly salvaged materials. Each was a living work of art that seemed to grow from the steep hillside.

Within minutes of our arrival, Paulina pulled a blueberry pie from the oven and laid it in a wicker basket along with other homemade foods. We piled into their rickety car and drove a few miles up the valley to where an art school was hosting a July 4th celebration. Several hundred people, many from a local intentional community, were greeting one another and settling onto the lawn for a parade and fireworks. We spread a tarp on the grass and laid out a banquet. Paulina introduced me to children she had delivered—some now grown and pregnant with babies of their own. Happy kids ran and played and several women nursed babies as they chatted and ate. I found myself speaking of childbirth with Paulina and another midwife, while Tom, whose passion was hospice, explored the other end of life.

"I still grieve the loss of my husband," a woman with long, snowy hair and strong brown limbs was telling him, "but the community has been so kind. They've really gathered around me." She was dressed in a calf-length skirt and sleeveless blouse, bare feet were tucked easily under her on a blanket. Her face wore seventy years with grace.

I looked about and smiled at nothing in particular. My body sighed and relaxed. After the hype of Florida, this evening in the hills of North Carolina refreshed like a drink of pure water. Here were people whose choices were not governed by the stick and carrot, who lived authentically and seemed not to hunger for "more."

"Do you notice," I whispered to Tom, "no one is fat?" Young and old they looked healthy, the result of homegrown food and an active lifestyle.

A sudden clapping drew my eyes toward the winding lane below, where a parade was coming through the trees. Students of the art college had formed in imaginative and playful procession. Spectators cheered or threw water balloons. Twilight deepened into purple and the fireworks began. Perhaps it was the front-row seat—we could see a group of young men setting them up in the field across the road—but it was one of the most spectacular displays I have ever witnessed. *How Lucas would enjoy this!* I thought.

We lay back on blankets and exclaimed together as brilliant colors bloomed like flowers over us. Despite the vivid lights and loud explosions, none of the children cried. I like to think it was because they felt loved by everyone. It was the kind of childhood we all deserve.

I could live here, I thought, *but it's a long way from Alaska.*

Luke was protective of his foster sister, Brittany.

We returned for another fourteen months at Kernwood in 1999.

Chapter 9

ECHOES OF THE PAST

July 2006

As we motored slowly northwest through the verdant hills and small towns of Tennessee and Kentucky, Tom was looking more relaxed and even I was settling into the journey. We were vaguely headed toward Blanchester, Ohio, the small town where Tom had grown up and much of his family remained. After a lifetime away, he still referred to Blan as "home."

Though I had visited the Midwest, it was novel to me—lush and picturesque in a Hallmark-card sort of way with small farms, orchards, little creeks, and old buildings. Freeway medians were neatly mowed or planted in flowers. Soon we veered onto back roads that had no shoulder and bent at right angles around the ends of unfenced soybean fields. For a country with so much grass, we saw few cows. We slowed through little towns that flew so many American flags, it always looked like the Fourth of July. Here lived the generous and patriotic folk who fed their youth into the Iraq war, believing steadfastly in the wisdom and benevolence of our leaders. They didn't race through traffic, build ever-larger houses, or make the evening news. "Salt of the Earth," Tom called them, backbone of the land. It was also an area where young people had few vocational choices. Main Streets were boarded up; towns had big and old graveyards with more headstones than living people.

"Why do people retire to Florida instead of Ohio?" I pondered as we slowed through yet another dying village. "Ohio is temperate and fertile, folks here are neighborly and ethical."

"Climate?" Tom offered. "I remember Ohio winters and I imagine others do, too."

"No worse than Florida summers," I countered. "I think it's tax breaks. If you want old people and their money, you don't ask them to support schools."

"I take it Florida is off your list of places to settle?" He glanced at me, eyes twinkling.

~

"Howdy, stranger," Tom's widowed sister Frances greeted as we climbed stone steps embossed with fossils.

Like their sister Alice (who lived a short distance away), Frances had dwelt in the same home most of her life. Her house was built into a hill, and the driveway descended from the street into a basement carport. We parked in the submerged drive and hauled our belongings into the basement where a double bed shared space with a woodshop that Frances and her late husband Don built together. The shop looked unused and damp. I remembered Don as a gentle man with a sweet smile. They had been high school sweethearts—he tall and thin to her short and round, the lake of quiet into which the current of her words flowed. Her reciprocal half. They had been headed into retirement when he collapsed suddenly and died in her arms. Her lifetime of medical training and taking command could not save him.

Tom was the youngest of five—or six, counting his half-brother—by many years. Frances had been twelve when Tom was born, and she had thought of him as her baby. She had silver hair cut in a shiny bowl, and brown eyes darkly ringed in a pale face, eyes that did not always smile with her mouth. A retired obstetrical nurse, Frances was accustomed to leadership—bossy, some would say—but now spent much of each day in a recliner. I could see it irked her to be losing stamina.

Over the next few days we visited Tom's friends and family—the wandering son returned. Blanchester had changed little over the years, though bedroom communities were creeping out from Cincinnati. We spent one casual afternoon looking at property and the prospect of spending our final years here. There was comfort in the thought of aging among connected generations. Tom drove me out to the old Irons family farm. His Uncle Everett had inherited it, and his father had started over. Tom would have been a farmer had his dad not died prematurely. The farm's current owners now boarded horses for wealthy suburban youngsters. We toured their imposing barn and then searched the hillside for the old family graveyard. We had located it on a cross-country drive in 1982, but it had since vanished beneath alders.

On our third evening, tornado warnings sent us to the basement as torrential rain whipped the trees. Water began to drip, then pour, through the sealed windows of the basement, down the walls, and onto the carpet.

"Have you thought of moving to a smaller place?" I asked Frances after the storm abated and we pitched in to clean up. Tom was using the shop vacuum to suck up buckets of musty water. The smell of mold told me this wasn't the first flood.

"I don't want to move," she stated.

"You could sell it and build a guest house at one of your kids' places," I persisted.

"This is my home," she declared with finality.

"Most of us end our journey alone," Aunt Janet had told us two decades before. "No matter how carefully you plan, life can throw you a curve."

It was 1985 and I was pregnant with Luke. I had wanted an indoor bathroom, so Janet and Bert—then in their sixties—drove from Phoenix for a weekend of pouring the foundation with us. We four shared a deep enjoyment in the process of working together, a satisfaction beyond the task accomplished. Now we were relaxing around our backyard fire, enjoying the good ache that comes from a day of physical labor and the contentment of full bellies. Sky arced turquoise above the dark bowl of the Tucson Mountains where Venus hung near the ridge.

Janet smiled fondly across the blaze. She was dressed in jeans and a faded cotton shirt over her slight bosom and wide hips. She was still coloring her shoulder-length hair then—the light brown of her youth. Behind bifocals, her eyes glinted with mirth and she often threw her head back to heehaw freely when she laughed.

"Our old friends are dying off," Uncle Bert put in. "We're learning that you have to keep making new ones or you'll end up by yourself."

"If you lose your mate, you also lose their skills and the activities you shared," Janet added. "Bert and I have started teaching one another. I'm teaching him to cook and do laundry and he's showing me how to maintain the car and manage our finances. We've also given each other permission to die or to remarry."

"These are important issues that many people don't want to look at," Bert said. "I'll probably die first," he continued, "but you never know." The outcroppings of his predatory nose and weathered face were lit like granite by the flames. His hair was long and still black, but his olive skin already showed years spent under the sun and below the reassuring rumble of his voice whispered a legacy of youthful smoking—a slight wheeze on the exhale. His vision remained perfect, as were strong white teeth. His thoughts were solid and complex.

Janet and Bert grew up in Tucson during the Depression. Tom and I appreciated their insight and wealth of thoughtful stories, including ones about my young parents. They in turn valued us. They had married in college in June of 1942, a year after Connie and Bud left for Alaska and just before Bert was called up for World War II. Bert trained as an officer and taught recruits until he was sent to the Pacific. He returned with little money in April 1946 to his wife and a son with clubbed feet to finish his engineering degree on the GI Bill.

The family lived in a village of Quonset huts built on the University of Arizona campus to house returning veterans. It was a close community, he recalled. When my parents breezed through Tucson on national tour with Connie's first book, Bert and Janet hosted a party, packing the little hut. Bud, they told me, had strutted success, flashing hundred-dollar bills and baiting Bert about living in "a rabbit hutch" and wasting his time in school. But Bert, quietly understated, had persevered to become a consultant on international projects and taken his family all over the world. Life in remote villages of Colombia, Iran, and Turkey taught them humor, flexibility, and the dance of good communication.

As Tom and I drove away from Blanchester, we stopped a last time at the nursing home to visit his mother. Mary Eva Irons was ninety-two, a tiny woman with thick snowy hair and nimble fingers. She had been artistic and hardworking, a woman who could feed farm hands, drive a tractor, and make clothes for five children. Until recently, she had beat most of her family at cards and word games. Mary Eva loved practical jokes and there was a calculating gleam behind her angelic smile. Youth spent in a Shaker orphanage had left her uncomfortable with affection and though she would invite you in with generosity, there could be daggers in her tongue. Tom got his competitive spirit and quick humor from his mother as well as his love for books.

"Did she ever tell you she loved you?" I once asked him.

"Not until after I was grown. Oh, she would sign her letters, 'Love, Mother,' but I always thought it just a salutation."

"Did it matter? Just the two of you alone after your father died."

"I didn't think about it. She did her best by me. She taught me to balance my finances. She gave me freedom to explore—even when she didn't approve. She wanted me to go to college, but accepted it when I quit and joined the navy. The year after Dad died, she gave me a hammer for Father's Day, saying that I was now the 'man of the house.' I tried to live up to that."

"You were eleven," I said.

"She showed her love in ways I didn't understand," he said thoughtfully. "Maybe she couldn't say it. She encouraged me to get out of Blanchester when it would have been easy to keep me there with guilt. She wanted me to be my own person and move into a larger world."

Mary Eva was sitting in a wheelchair beside a small window that overlooked a lawn she could no longer see. Never five feet tall, she was now tiny and light as a sparrow. Her memory was undependable and her hearing poor, but the fire had not left her impish blue eyes. Her room, like her person, was meticulous and clean. One of the many quilts she had made—without a machine stitch—adorned her twin bed.

She looked up and smiled as we approached. "Oh, Tom!" she cried, everything in those two words.

"We've come to say goodbye," Tom said, raising his voice. She stubbornly refused to consider hearing aids. He stooped to gently hug the small figure.

"Do you really have to go?" Her eyes filled with sudden tears. "I do miss you so when you're gone. They're good to me here and feed me well, but the days seem so long." Her face wrinkled and she removed her glasses. I handed her a tissue and she wiped her eyes.

We spent an awkward half-hour trying to shout loving things and listening for the affection behind her words.

"Frances tells me that the doctors can fix your cataracts," Tom said as we rose to go. "I think you should let them do the operation. Then you can read my letters."

A shadow of determination crossed her face, the old war for independence. If Frances wanted her to do it, she would resist. "I miss you," she repeated as Tom knelt to hug her one last time.

THERE WERE MORE TORNADO WARNINGS as we turned the car east across southern Ohio farmland and through scattered villages. The sky hung brooding, and a fine mist descended. It clung like sweat when we pulled over at a small store to refill our cooler with vegetables, bread, and cheese. As we neared the Ohio River, the land buckled into hills and we crossed a bridge into the jutting finger of West Virginia. Here towns grew like fungus along the river bank, sooty and moldering. There were weird tendrils of inharmonious pipes and rusting machinery. For a while we followed the mighty Ohio River, but it was a sad and tarnished scene.

"Rivers should be places of our deepest reverence," I said. I sang a line from Tom Russell's *American Rivers*, "…jigsawed old arteries, so clogged and defiled…"

"You want to head cross-country?" Tom asked.

I nodded. "This just makes me sad."

The air grew ever thicker as we slid eastward. At first glance, Pennsylvania seemed rural, with winding narrow roads that wandered through stop-and-go villages. Here were immense old mansions of an earlier era. Foliage hid everything a few feet from the road, but the map revealed a spiderweb of highways. In frustration, we finally pulled onto a toll road to bypass the constant traffic.

After visiting old friends outside Philadelphia, we headed for Binghamton, New York, where my mother was born. From the elevated toll road, the rolling and forested land obscured habitation. As we approached the small town of Vestal, there were signs of record flooding. The old Susquehanna River had rampaged through town, and Vestal was still digging out.

Here my cousin, Mary Alice "Chickie" Chittenden, welcomed us with open arms. Her little home was a scene from my childhood, the place she was born and raised and where Annie and I had spent a summer I was nine, while our mother recovered from cancer surgery on her foot. As a child, Connie had been burned with the new X-rays when her father treated her for a fungus infection.

Chickie was my age, the only and late child of my mother's older half-brother Joe and his wife Jane. She was about my height and stout, with short chocolate hair and direct brown eyes. I was drawn to her assertive voice and free laugh—so reminiscent of her father. Abandoned by his American doctor father and high-society mother, my Uncle Joe had spent his childhood running the streets of France during World War I. When Winnie married Arthur, she had insisted that he bring his son home. Young Joe was wild, and my mother said it was some years before anyone knew if he would be a cop or a robber. He had become a detective.

I recalled this home during the summer of 1959. The feral Helmericks girls—wary and unconventional—had been quite an education for our sheltered cousin. I remember Chickie as a timid child with a round face and soft body. Joe and Jane had rented a cottage on Spenser Lake in upstate New York for part of our visit. Whatever their sedate plans, Annie and I blew free of supervision to explore the woods. We taught Chickie to swim and introduced her to the "facts of life." Sex was an open conversation in our home. Chickie had looked appalled and then said, "Yuck!"

Chickie treated Tom and me like celebrities, introducing us proudly to her town, friends, and local foods. She recounted my life to her friends as a fabulous story, her generous flamboyance reminiscent of Connie. She chauffeured me to Binghamton to see the twenty-eight-room home (now an office) where Connie and Janet had lived, and to Quaker Lake—a pond now chest-deep in summer homes—where my mother spent pivotal months of her childhood. We explored the old graveyard where bones of our grandfather, Dr. Arthur Chittenden, and others of our tribe nourished mature trees. Unaccustomed as I was to thinking of myself as part of a clan (beyond Janet and Bert), I added this new dimension to my interior landscape.

Chickie spoke freely of her father's death from cancer in 1969 and the years spent with her mother. Jane had lived into advanced old age and dementia. "I kept Ma at home until she died," Chickie said in her flat, upstate New York accent. We were sharing a dinner of spaghetti in her well-planned kitchen.

"Tell me about it," I said.

"Oh, the last two years were very hard," she stated, "but I'm proud I did it. Ma was healthy as a horse and active right up to the end. For a long time she continued volunteering at the nursing home, playing piano, but I had to watch her every minute. I hired friends to stay with her while I taught school, but she'd be up all night."

Another aging strategy: reliance on a devoted child. Chickie had never married, but instead developed a life rich in friendships. I didn't sense any sadness. In many ways, Jane had been Chickie's life-partner, a companion who shared chores and travel.

"I have no regrets," she said, as if reading my thoughts. "Ma and I were great friends. I miss her every day."

I studied my cousin, thinking how she had chosen to be happy with each day, while I was continually looking ahead to chart a safe course through life.

"What are your plans for your old age?" I asked.

"After Ma died, I had the place completely renovated. I don't want to deal with problems later. I went through all this with Ma and I want to be prepared."

Nights in Vestal were unusually hot and we sweated in modest twin beds beneath the canted roof of Chickie's childhood bedroom. She had moved into her parent's old room a few feet away. One evening we watched a Tom Brokaw television special on global warming.

"Have you ever heard of this 'carbon footprint' thing?" Chickie asked.

My head swiveled. "You haven't heard of climate change?"

"Well… yeah… but that doesn't really affect me."

"You don't think this heat wave and the recent flooding might be part of a larger picture?" I persisted.

"I guess I never thought about it," she said honestly.

Chapter 10

A<u>NOTHER</u> N<u>ORTH</u>

August 2006

The capital of Vermont seemed a quaint village. Parks and public works of art were prominent in the streets of Montpelier and historical pride was evident in its buildings. In contrast to the threats and rules of Mississippi, signs in the hotel library encouraged us to read or exchange books and to use their computer. Instead of threatening notices about stealing, there were posted tips on recycling.

New Hampshire was another alluring state. We tarried on back roads and stopped often, imagining our lives here. The clean rest stops were almost empty except for volunteers who gave away coffee and offered advice about routes. Although conditions might well merit the use of big pickups, most people drove small cars, often with a pair of kayaks latched to the roof. Folks were friendly, yet under-spoken, athletic and healthy. Local newspapers carried thoughtful discussions on environmental concerns.

"We're running out of states and friends," Tom said as we crossed into Maine where his brother Fred and his wife Sally awaited us in the little town of Orono.

Eldest of Tom's full siblings, Fred was brilliant and self-deprecating. After a childhood of farm labor, he had put himself through college, receiving his Ph.D. in engineering from MIT. Having outlived his critical father by half a century, Fred was nevertheless driven to achieve by the memory of a man he could never quite please. Retired now from teaching at the University of Maine,

Fred still had an office on campus and continued to write books. He also headed the high school chess club, volunteered with his church, and took trumpet and art lessons. Older than Tom by thirteen years, he was cut from a different cloth. Where Tom didn't own a tie, Fred never wore blue jeans. His thinning hair was meticulously trimmed, pink face cleanly shaven, and clothing neatly pressed. He had their mother's mischievous blue eyes and persistence. Like me, Fred was driven to turning over rocks to dig below appearances. If I had one word to describe this complex man, it would be "integrity."

"What do you want to see?" Fred asked, his voice hearty and loud. We were in their formal dining room eating pot roast, salad, and buttered bread. "You might want to settle here."

They launched into a lively debate about which part of Maine we would most enjoy. Married since college, Fred and Sally looked like bookends, but their temperaments were very different. Short with a round pink face, glasses, and clipped gray hair, Sally had been born in New England and wore an amused smile like a sweater—a hedge against bad weather. One could sense in her the quiet determination of generations who survived the Atlantic coast with skepticism and viewed good times as the lull between gales. To Fred's inquisitive probing, Sally rested quietly at anchor and watched the tides.

Over the next few days they drove us through the uniformly dark forests of Maine on winding state roads. These were punctuated with picturesque little towns sporting parks that invited one to rest and talk. People were picnicking along the roadway. Traffic was polite and sparse.

"So what's your next step?" Fred asked as we sat on the pier at Bar Harbor eating fresh lobster and clam chowder above the swinging gray Atlantic.

"I should probably get a job," I said. "We're running out of relatives."

Fred threw his head back and barked his dry laugh. "Well, that could be a problem, though you haven't completely worn out your welcome here. How do you go about getting a job?"

"I'm registered with a travel company and I'll call my recruiter. It could take a few weeks, so I might as well get started." As we neared the end of our journey, I was beginning to feel uneasy. I spoke of trusting life, but never let go of the reins long enough to see if it worked.

"Just anywhere?" Fred asked.

"We thought maybe the Pacific Northwest," Tom said. "It's close to Alaska."

"Maine is a lot like Alaska, if you like long winters," Fred offered.

"It's beautiful," I admitted, "but we're not through looking. I have the feeling you'd have to be born here to be considered an insider."

Sally's blue eyes glinted humorously. "That really isn't enough. Your parents would have had to be born here, too."

Northern Maine lacked cell-phone coverage, so I used their landline to call Florida. When I finally got through, my recruiter Kelly told me that day positions in obstetrics were limited. "I have positions in New Mexico, Reno, and Milwaukee."

"Submit my application for New Mexico and Milwaukee," I decided.

While technically in the Eastern time zone, Maine—like Alaska—is remote in real time, a fact people rarely consider. That night the phone rang twice, waking up the household with prolonged interviews. I called Kelly the next morning to tell her I had accepted the position in Wisconsin.

"I'll fax you the contract and an employment package. You'll need to go online and do a series of competency tests and I'll FedEx the paperwork for drug-testing. You'll have to do that within twenty-four hours of receiving it. You need to send us a two hundred and fifty-dollar housing deposit…" her voice was fast and urgent as she ticked off the list.

"I wasn't thinking of starting right now. I'm not close to anywhere." I was feeling suddenly rushed.

"Hospitals want you yesterday. If you don't nail it down, it'll be gone."

Of course her job is to get me into harness, I thought. "I'm on the road without a fax machine or an address. My cell phone doesn't work here, and I am headed into Canada."

"Well, they're very sticky about these things. They'll only hold the position a day without paperwork," she sounded exasperated.

"I'll see if I can find a fax machine. You can send the drug testing and other paperwork to our friends in Wisconsin. We should be there in a week. As for competencies, I did all that." I was becoming irritated. I'd spent weeks doing online tests, copying everything from my driver's license to shot records, being fingerprinted, and paying for a physical and blood tests to prove my immunity to diseases.

"You can only do so much before you're hired!"

"You have reams of paperwork from me," I whined. "I'm credentialed in Basic Life Support, Neonatal Resuscitation, Advanced Cardiac Life Support, STABLE, and Advanced Fetal Monitoring. I'm certified in obstetrical nursing! What more could they want?"

"Each hospital has their own requirements, Jean." The way she said my name, drawing out the "eee," reminded me of a disapproving teacher. "You just have to do it! Luckily, Wisconsin is a Compact State and will accept your

Arizona license." Seventeen states honored one another's nursing licenses; the rest required a new one.

I could feel the river of my life suddenly picking up speed. Our peaceful days of floating were coming to an end.

IT WAS LATE IN THE afternoon the next day when we departed Orono. With the contract finally signed and faxed, Tom and I headed for Wisconsin by a route that would take us around the Great Lakes on the Canadian side. Sunlight shafted low between the trees along the two-lane highway as we drove north. Soon we checked into the lone motel in the village of Bingham, Maine. Deciding to try the local food, we set out on foot. The small restaurant was empty when we arrived, but gradually quiet families filtered in. The pace of life here felt like stepping back into the 1950s.

It was dawn the next morning when I set out for a walk. Occasional logging trucks sliced through the fog along the roadway. Beyond the verge, a modest river whispered through a forest anchored in ferns, mist, and wet flowers. It had rained during the night and familiar northern birds called sweetly as the fog began to lift. Turning onto a dirt road, I came upon a campground where families were awakening around small fires. There were no recreational vehicles or generators. On my return walk, I stopped at a little store across from our motel for hot coffee to take back to Tom. The owner refused my money and wished me a good morning.

Although northern Maine is sparsely populated and considered cold by most Americans, the other side of the border serves as Canada's tropics. Crossing into Quebec, we found a land of prosperous farms, smog, power lines, and industrial activity that became more congested as we drove westward. Quebec seemed a place of strange tension. While the rest of Canada had signs in two languages, here there was only French. Even the river that divides the capital, Ottawa, had different names on the Ontario and Quebec sides. My high school French was less than a memory, and I thought of the line from *My Fair Lady*, "The French don't care what they do, actually, as long as they pronounce it properly." It seemed best to keep my mouth shut.

"I wanted to see Niagara Falls from the Canadian side," I told Tom the next morning as we studied our wrinkled map, "but a glimpse of running water isn't worth hours of hellish driving through Toronto and back. Those little lines on the map are very different in real life." We were in Ontario now, and at least the signs were in English.

"I have to agree. Yesterday wasn't fun and I think it will only get worse."

"North," I decided. "We always like north."

"Let's follow the Ottawa River and then swing north around Lake Huron," Tom's finger traced the route. "We can cross back into the U.S. at the Upper Peninsula of Michigan along the southern shore of Lake Superior. I think we'll have more fun."

Three days later we arrived in northern Wisconsin, where we planned to visit an old friend. I'd known Matthew since he was a teenage Air Force recruit from a small farm not far from where he still lived. Tom referred to him as "Jeanie's old boyfriend," but he had dated my sister and (much to our surprise) listened attentively to our mother's visions of freedom and a larger world.

Matthew's directions carried us over a series of dirt roads to his forty acres. Pulling into the driveway, Tom switched off the engine. Silence flowed through our open windows and settled like the dust about our shoulders. There wasn't a hint of breeze or a cloud. Matthew came out to greet us, face split with a welcoming grin.

"Sorry, Jane is at her folks' cabin," he said. "She'll be disappointed to miss you."

Matthew was tall and spare, a man of unconscious physical strength and broad interests. His straight brown hair was chopped above the ears and beginning to thin at the temples. The angular face sprouted a two-day growth of heavy beard and there were crow's feet around his lively blue eyes. His big frame was draped in Salvation Army clothes, worn into threads. He gave me a bear hug, towering over me like one of his pine trees. He looked embarrassed when Tom came around the car and hugged him, too.

"Well, gosh, I suppose that's how they do it." He patted Tom on the shoulder.

Matthew was already talking as he carried our bag up the steps. He was a biologist, passionate about environmental issues and social justice. "I want to show you where I'm seeding native grasses for prairie restoration," he said. "Here, this came for you." He handed me an official-looking package.

I ripped open the thick packet and thumbed through the forms from my new employer. "Let me get settled first," I temporized. "Boy, it's hot here!"

"Yeah," he admitted. "We've never had anything like it. Nobody has air-conditioning around here, and the radio says it'll reach 103 today! You can sleep on the hideaway in the spare room or the bunk beds in the basement. It's cooler down there."

We chose the basement, an improvement of twenty degrees on the rest of the house. Even with the dehumidifier running, the space was damp and redolent of mold. I invited Matthew to join us in the basement, but he slept in their second-floor bedroom. He and his petite wife had spent their first years in a shanty, now moldering in the brush a hundred yards away. She was a teacher and he worked at a hatchery, but conveniences remained a point of contention between them. She wanted clean clothes and warm showers; he considered them a waste of fossil fuel. I think, too, he was uncomfortable with anything resembling self-indulgence.

The kitchen table was set into a bay window overlooking a large vegetable garden. Jane's homey touches were evident in curtains and garden art. In the yard were also enormous piles of oak and sheds of split wood for feeding the basement stove in winter. Tom had his elbows on the table, trying to identify birds at the feeder through Matthew's binoculars.

"Where do you plan to spend your old age?" I asked. Matthew and Jane frequently volunteered in rural communities in Central America and both spoke Spanish. They had helped Luke and me arrange a summer doing medical outreach in Guatemala. Retiring south of the border seemed reasonable for them.

"I'm staying here," Matthew replied. He seemed surprised by the question.

"You won't be able to split eight cords of firewood or feed a basement furnace forever. I don't see you going down those steep steps when you're eighty."

"I noticed the wind took down a big oak over by the information center," he said, changing the subject. "I'm going to ask if I can remove it."

"I'll help you once I finish my paperwork," I offered. "Cutting firewood makes me feel wealthy."

He looked at me oddly.

"Doesn't it give you a feeling of satisfaction?" I prompted between bites of the cucumber and cheese he had laid out for us.

"No. It just has to get done." He was hunched over his plate, resolutely feeding his body like the basement furnace—a job that needed doing.

"Matthew," I grinned fondly and laid a hand on his solid shoulder. "It's okay to enjoy life. I get pleasure out of the smallest things—a warm bath, a good meal. If you're going to cut firewood, why not enjoy it?"

He shifted uncomfortably, a man accustomed to shouldering into chores.

The next morning we loaded bags of homegrown cucumbers and squash into our car. Matthew hugged me lightly, then faced Tom for an awkward moment before gently hugging him, too, patting.

"Come back when it's cooler," he said. "This wasn't a good example." I knew the visit had been a disappointment. For years he had encouraged us to move to Wisconsin.

The day was already warming; the sky remained a calloused blue. Matthew bent to look through my car window and handed me a neat packet of brochures with photocopied articles about his state, with places of interest annotated in red. It reminded me of Connie, words underlined and explanations penciled into the margins. I touched his hand, and then waved as Tom backed between the trees. Matthew stood, long arms at his sides, watching us disappear in dust.

WE JOURNEYED WESTWARD INTO MINNESOTA where the Land of Ten Thousand Lakes languished under deepening drought. Although wild rice and cattails lined the narrow roads, the corn was only hip-high and brown in the heat and the oat crop had been harvested early as hay. Farmers, we heard, were buying summer feed for their cattle.

I thought of Rude, whom we planned to visit next. After our attempt to overwinter with him at our cabin in 2004, he had wandered back to Minnesota, but hadn't resumed his business or installed a phone. Our letters had gone unanswered.

Rude had arrived in our lives early in the summer of 2000 when Tom, Luke—then fourteen—and I had spent another year and a half alone at our cabin. Laurie again accompanied us, but had chartered a small plane on skis out to civilization when sunlight returned to the Arctic in early spring. With her had gone a letter of invitation. We hoped to find someone to help paddle our two canoes several hundred miles downriver to the lone bridge that crossed the Yukon River. A friend sent it on to Rude.

It had been July when a Cessna 180 broke our silence. Circling downstream, it flared toward us and touched the muddy current in a rooster-tail of spray. Our first image of Rude was his joyful brown face pressed against the window—alert as a fox. Native American was written in the angle of his smoothly shaven cheeks and the long silver hair that flowed from beneath a good felt hat. He was my height, but wiry and quick, his movements graceful and precise. Gripping his knapsack in one hand, Rude had dropped lightly onto the floats and leapt ashore.

He entered our family with uncommon awareness, stepping smoothly into the dance as if he had always been part of our lives: hauling water, doing dishes, splitting wood, packing up, and noticing all the quirky traditions that had evolved through our years together. He was attentive to each of us.

Luke had matured that year into a slender youth already six feet tall with dark mustache and chestnut hair to his shoulders. He was quiet and self-possessed—a different person than the awkward lad who had flown into the wilds the summer before. Rude treated him with respect, following his lead as the two set off to explore. With Tom, Rude fell easily into step, closing up the cabin and preparing for our departure. He was careful with tools and always conscious in his movements. Toward me he was considerate, bringing buckets of water and the right-sized wood when I cooked over the outdoor fire.

Nevertheless, Rude remained wild and cautious, flinching from affection. He had survived a childhood with little nurturing, hiding in the woods and trusting his own fists and legs. I soon learned not to encroach on him. If I got too close, his lip would twitch with a low growl. Like his shy sled dogs, it said more than words, "I don't want to bite, but I can."

By the time we embarked on the three-week voyage, the four of us had forged a powerful team. In his own words, Rude was a "good man to ride the river," totally at home in wilderness. Several bears came through camp that summer: in the mountains they were grizzlies and then as we wandered onto the Yukon Flats, black bears. We would be talking quietly around the evening fire when a glance would flicker between the two men—both coiled and listening. In the tent, Rude never seemed to sleep. He needed to be near the door, with Tom next, then me, and finally Luke curled into the far wall. I would awaken in the twilight to some imagined noise to see Rude's alert eyes. Tom and I were both light sleepers, but Rude was better than a guard dog.

Each day, Luke and I scouted the river ahead in the smaller canoe, while Tom and Rude followed with the ladened nineteen-foot Grumman. When occasionally the river quieted between rapids, Luke and I would let our craft drift abreast the freight canoe. As we took hold to their gunwale, Rude would intone in the deep voice of a Hollywood Indian, "Seen any buffalo?" and we would laugh.

Not far below the old cabin that Phil and I had built when I was twenty-two, a great rock I call "The Monolith" splits the clear river like a ship. Here the valley hangs in the shadow of steep mountains, and the current is peppered and lively. Luke and I paddled ashore in the sandy lee while Tom and Rude beached below us. A family of ravens took wing from the lichen-covered cliffs overhead, calling in complex repertoire as they danced down the wind. Ravens are long-lived and intelligent. Like humans, they can be reduced to eating from dumpsters, but in the wild they are proud and wary. I had stooped to pick up a single black feather that eddied against the cliff, and handed it to Rude. He ran his fingers along the shaft before placing it in the band of his hat.

Gradually we had left the mountains behind, and our river changed from a fierce and clear stream into a turbid beast that coiled across the flats in numerous fingers to be swallowed one at a time by the mighty Yukon. Just before entering the big river, we paddled up one of its sloughs to Martin Creek in hopes of catching dinner. There was something mysterious and a little frightening about the reedy depths that fell away in blackness where the clear water curled into the murky Yukon. Standing beneath the trees, Luke cast with his little collapsible pole. He had just reeled the lure clear of the water when a primordial monster erupted—a pike the length of his leg. Luke staggered back as the giant fish lunged upward, snapping like an alligator.

Before I could move, Rude was at Luke's side coaching quietly. We had no net and the chance of landing such a fish was slim. Luke maneuvered it close to the overhanging bank and Rude knelt, holding to a branch as he leaned over the water. The fish jumped, head as wide as my hand, shaking the lure, and Rude's small hand snaked out. His fingers sank into the eye sockets and he jerked the monster ashore. It was an astounding act, but what impressed me came next.

I saw Rude flinch as he ran his knife into the small brain of the thrashing fish. "I'm sorry," he whispered. Then he returned the moment to Luke, patiently guiding him through the process of filleting and skinning his first big fish.

At age thirteen, Luke shows that he can now carry his mother.

Luke, Laurie and Tom pack moose meat home for our winter food.

Chapter 11
WILD GOOSE DREAMS

August 2006

We had visited Rude's Minnesota home only once, several years before, yet Tom followed a scent of memory along the spiderweb of back roads. I trusted his recall—and Lucas's—over my own, for they organized information photographically, while I wove it into a fluid pattern of nuance. Our different strengths made us good partners.

"Do you think he'll want to see us?" I asked. It had been two summers since we bailed on our plans for a wilderness year.

"He was hurt when things fell through," Tom acknowledged. "I wanted to tour Alaska with him, but he wouldn't even talk. Maybe you could've brought him around, but you know about masculine energy. He would've bit like a badger if I had tried to hold him."

"It takes a long time to gain his trust. I'm not sure he'll give us a second chance."

That's part of living with something wild, I thought. It was easy to forget when you met the master plumber, loving father, and grandfather that fierce independence lay just below Rude's surface. After his three children fledged, he had moved out to live alone in the woods. Although still married and friends, he and Marge pursued different lives. *Like living with a raven.*

Rude was outside as we pulled up to his "shack" in the woods. "Well, look what the cat dragged in!" He grabbed each of us fiercely by the shoulders as his face split in a grin. "Gosh, I only get company once in a long while, and here my kids drove out to visit today, too! Come on in and we'll get you something to eat. There's kabobs on the grill."

Tom deepened his voice and intoned, "Seen any buffalo?"

Rude laughed happily. "Boy, it's great to see you! You're lookin' good, eh?" He stepped back and swept us in keen appraisal. Then he held Tom's eye and delivered two thumps with his fist above his own heart: the gift of two beats. Friendship.

Leading us inside, Rude carefully introduced each person. When he came to his grandchildren, he squatted and spoke quietly, explaining who we were and how he knew us. I smiled, wanting to wriggle with gladness like a puppy at the sight of him. My gaze rested contentedly in the smooth line of his jaw and the familiar hazel eyes that shifted with the light. Silver hair flowed like silk from beneath the old felt hat and drifted about his hard little shoulders.

Rude's "shack" was a massive, two-story garage supported by twenty-inch peeled logs, each selected and cut to fit a particular spot. His work was creative, precise, and "hell for stout." As he showed us about, I tried to imagine the tough little rooster hoisting those beams into place. A few yards away, the hexagonal home he was building was a work of art. He had designed it in his head and there were no blueprints. It was constructed of great poplar logs, beaver-killed from the pond that stretched below. He followed natural flaws in the grain and hollowed out complex spaces as he built. There was a storyline that only he could read, a fresco along the inside wall built of carved wooden "stones," each in memory of some person or event. Apart from its unique beauty, his home would rigorously comply to code and even had heated floors.

From the expanse of wooden deck, I could see Rude's sled dogs below, watching from their houses in the trees. On our last visit, there had been seventeen; now I counted six. They never barked, but attended to his slightest gesture with the clarity of wolves. Rude communicated with his intense gaze, soft voice, and hand signals. "Before their eyes open, I carry them in my shirt next to my skin," he once told me. "I breathe into their noses and handle them until they come to trust me like their mother."

"It looks like you have only a few dogs," I commented.

"Yeah, they're mostly too old to run now. I can't kill 'em. Not after all we've been through. Some of them dogs have saved my life, dragged me out when the sled went through the ice. I keep thinkin' about getting another team together, but that's a huge commitment—keeping 'em all 'til they die."

"I hate to see anything chained," I said. "It makes me sad."

"Yeah, I know. But you can't have sled dogs running lose. Somebody would shoot 'em. And it's all they know. They're happy."

Wild Goose Dreams

It was an old argument. He had wanted to bring three sled dogs to the Arctic. I didn't want dogs chained outside in the cold.

"Well, you can't keep sled dogs in the house," he had replied, exasperated.

As evening softened the forest, Rude's family departed. We settled comfortably together on his deck as if the intervening years had never occurred. The next morning, Rude led us out into his sacred space, the forty acres he knew so intimately. I felt like a child as we followed him between the trees. He shifted in and out of shadows with grace and economy of movement, almost disappearing before my eyes. Nothing he did was accidental or thoughtless. I knew his body had been broken repeatedly, that he had pulled a bicep free from the bone at the end our trip in 2000, but I could detect no trace of pain in his movements.

We rested there for two days, sharing coffee on his deck in quiet harmony while pastel dawn misted the wetlands below. Rude would hand me his binoculars and point to a pair of pileated woodpeckers or a young buck. I would look and then pass the binoculars to Tom. Sandhill cranes fed in the reeds and a blue heron watched from a snag. Beavers trailed Vs through the still water or dove with a slap of their tails. Rude had been advised to trap the beavers "before they kill all your trees," but he shrugged. "They took the poplar and are into the white oak, but they were here first."

"Why don't you kids move in here?" Rude broke the silence. "You can have the house. I don't need it. I'm used to my shack."

"Ticks," I intoned, lowering my voice. Wood ticks were part of summer for Rude, but the thought of them gave me the creeps.

"It's a wonderful offer," Tom said, "but we're still exploring options."

"What are you doing for your old age?" I asked my standard question.

"This house will be completely handicap accessible. All the doors are wide enough for a wheelchair. The tub and shower will have rails. Even if I end up selling it, those are valuable assets."

I looked at him curiously. Rude was full of surprises. I had figured him for crawling off in the woods to die alone, yet of our many friends, he had designed his house for aging. Now he was inviting us to join him.

"We are family," I said.

He looked at me quizzically. "You said that before, Jeanie. Explain to me, please."

I shook my head. "I don't know exactly. There's a soul connection that transcends time and place."

He studied me a long moment and nodded. "I don't know what I believe."

We were back to our running conversation: Rude the "recovering Catholic" (as I phrased it), deeply angered at early mistreatment by the church yet unable to shake the devil off his back, and me the seeker.

I grinned. "Ask your heart. Your head will get you into trouble. I think about the three of us playing in the woods like gray-haired children and it just feels right."

The next morning we packed the old Honda for our final leg into Milwaukee and my new job. Rude loaded us as for an expedition with gifts of home-canned corn and venison, wild rice, and deer sausage.

"We can't get any more in the car," I pleaded. I was beginning to think of the Midwest as the "feed-me states." Rarely did we depart a home without gifts of food.

He gripped each of us by the forearms and gazed long into our faces. Then using his right hand he gave his heart two thumps and nodded. "For Luke," he said. "Tell him."

"WHAT DO YOU KNOW ABOUT Milwaukee?" I asked Tom as we drove east on a narrow state road. "I think of it in black-and white. Remember *The Untouchables*, that 1950s cop show, and 'Schlitz, the beer that made Milwaukee famous'? I always think of a stark city haunted by men in fedoras and women with dark lipstick who get shot."

"They get some pretty severe weather off Lake Michigan," he offered. "I was there one winter in the navy. But we'll be gone before winter. Your contract is only for thirteen weeks." That was to become our mantra: *Why not? It's only thirteen weeks.*

For three days we loitered eastward past small farms interspersed with woodlands, and then south along the shore of Lake Michigan. This was some of the healthiest farmland we had seen: picturesque fields, tidy houses, and big red barns. The sky looked clean, though warnings about *E. coli* were posted along the beaches.

Our entry into Milwaukee was cushioned by Jennifer and her husband Matt. Jen was a nurse I had worked with in Tucson. She had gotten her Ph.D. and returned to Wisconsin to teach. She invited us to stay with them until we got housing.

"I feel odd staying with someone I've never met and you know only professionally," Tom confessed as I directed him along the winding, tree-lined streets that fronted Lake Michigan.

"She wouldn't have invited us if she hadn't meant it."

The attractive two-story house stood a block from the lake. Though Jennifer and Matt were a generation younger, they felt like peers and our relationship proved to be easy. Jen handed me sheets to make up the bed in their airy basement. Tom and I bought groceries and cooked the evening meal. After dinner, the guys went off to play tennis, while Jen and I walked with their four-year-old daughter to a park. The sidewalk was shaded by oaks in full leaf and buckled by their great roots. The park shouldered onto the bluff above an expanse of blue, and the cool breeze smelled of open water. A handful of children were engaged in polite play on swings and monkey bars.

"I like the way the races mix here," I commented as we ambled home in the dusk, "the way the children cooperated." For weeks we had only seen white people, but Milwaukee had a large African-American population.

Jennifer glanced sideways at me, blue eyes penetrating. Her skin was tanned, her face lean and angular, and she moved with the grace of an athlete. "Don't let appearances fool you. Racism isn't overt here, but some streets are literally white on one side and black on the other."

"I haven't detected any racial tension at all. People seem to disregard color. They seem more Midwestern than anything."

"It's different here," she nodded, "more subtle. There's something called 'Minnesota nice.' People are polite on the surface, but hold expectations they won't tell you—you're just supposed to know."

Tom and I spent the next few days exploring Milwaukee. I had been prepared for dingy brick buildings (and there were some), but we also found large parks, charming residential areas, and a living city heart. The population seemed older, more polite and quieter than in Tucson. Young people were included in activities, and there was a noticeable lack of rebellion. I saw no tattoos, gang signs, baggy pants, or graffiti. We heard no piped-in "music" in stores or loud radios playing along streets.

On the Friday before my first week at the hospital, we moved into a sparsely furnished condo provided by my company. It was located in the town of Brown Deer, a scary half-hour freeway commute from work. Our sliding patio door fronted an expanse of lawn and a small artificial lake. We spent Saturday shopping for dishes, sheets, and supplies, and bought the first season of an old television series, *Northern Exposure*, to view on the reconditioned laptop Lucas had chosen for us.

Our second-floor bedroom extended into the trees where gray squirrels were harvesting acorns and crabapples while Canada geese grazed the shoreline.

The weather remained balmy, and we kept our windows open. The place was surprisingly quiet except for the clamor of geese, ducks, terns, and gulls. We rarely heard voices beyond the afternoon sound of children at play. Our neighbors were predominately black working-class families. Most were long-term residents who personalized their homes with flowers and deck furniture. No patio walls divided the expansive commons.

The nonprofit hospital where I worked was beautiful and new. The Women's Pavilion, offering services from infertility to chemotherapy, was airy with little cafés, fireplaces, and gardens. Operating rooms were spacious, and the sixteen labor-and-delivery suites were larger than many dwellings, featuring ceramic-tiled bathrooms, Jacuzzis, colored towels, sofas, bay windows, and custom vinyl floors. Technology was tastefully hidden in cupboards. Directly above the labor floor, private postpartum rooms had carpets and queen-sized beds. Most patients had insurance, spoke English, and were married. Many couples were biracial.

The focus here was "frugal" rather than "defensive" medicine—meaning tests were performed only when warranted. There was little intervention in the natural process of labor and at least half the women chose not to have an epidural, often spending labor in the Jacuzzi. My training was to "manage" labor as a scary, medical condition—and this was new to me. Here was a supportive environment for giving birth. I wondered why we didn't provide this for all women. Perhaps Milwaukee's stable population contributed, as did Midwestern moderation, but the biggest drain on healthcare today are profit-making corporations. Community hospitals care for the poor as well as those who can pay; when forced to compete with companies that specialize in care of the rich, they inevitably have to reduce services. Community hospitals build strength in neighborhoods, while hospitals that are run for profit are driven by... well... profit—neither health nor care. That's the elephant in the room.

Hospitals hire "travelers" when their staffing is critically inadequate. In this case, another hospital had closed. Had I been hired as core staff, I would have received several weeks of orientation, but as a pinch-hitter I needed to learn on the run. Almost every piece of equipment (and all the computer programs) was new to me, as were all the staff, door codes, logistics and protocols. My face reddened as I fumbled with novel IV catheters and tubing. My heart pounded when the inevitable emergency arose and I didn't know who to call or how to use the equipment. I wasn't at all sure I was cut out for travel-nursing with my learning curve penciled against newborn lives.

Three days a week I departed at six in the morning to negotiate freeway detours for work at seven. On the drive, I prayed for guidance. *May I be a blessing* became my mantra. I would return home around eight-thirty each night, so exhausted I could hardly get out of the car. Tom served me beautifully prepared dinners and rubbed my feet while we watched *Northern Exposure* on our laptop. Then I climbed the stairs for bed.

Hardships do not arrive without a gift. I could no longer afford the whiny voice in my head that said it wasn't fair, or that I couldn't possibly manage everything. When all hell broke loose, a stronger voice surfaced: *Deal with it*. It pushed me into a higher level of functioning. *I know how to care for a woman in labor and her infant*, I reminded myself. *I could deliver this baby in a car. Patients before paperwork.* The saving grace was Midwestern kindness. Not once do I recall a coworker making me wrong. They jumped in to help whenever they saw me struggling.

On my days off, Tom and I explored Wisconsin on a grid of little roads. Here was America's holdout family farm—with seventy-five cows and a big, red barn. Tall corn was the richest green imaginable and each little town had acres of neatly mown lawns. Homes looked in good repair, and everywhere was tidy attention to detail. It seemed a land of moderation with a noticeable lack of poverty or displays of wealth. Milwaukee was articulated with parks and bike trails (which we had mostly to ourselves) including a path that clung to the base of skyscrapers above the tamed Milwaukee River. The city was not all parks and culture, however, for there was an industrial wasteland not featured in Matthew's brochures, of smoking stacks and unidentifiable tubes coiling for miles along the freeway. A gray smudge obscured the sky much of the time and the idyllic streams were posted with signs warning not to eat the fish or bathe in the water.

Despite the stress of my job, wildness seeped into my dreams on the song of the geese. Canada geese are light sleepers and twenty-six of them spent restless nights beneath our open windows. I felt a kinship with the great birds—wild creatures adapting to an artificial world that did not welcome them. The Milwaukee "Geese Police" came regularly with kayaks and dogs to "addle" their eggs and harass them into moving elsewhere. It was a not-in-my-backyard game, shifting the flock around the neighborhood. These birds may have descended from hunting decoys or perhaps, like pigeons, were attracted to urban life. Whatever their lineage, they had lost the thread of migration and now spent Wisconsin winters searching for withered grass beneath the snow.

I pondered the fate of wildness—in humans and in the more than human world—on our increasingly regimented planet. We seem intent on wiping it out, envisioning an orderly Garden of Eden without dandelions, mosquitoes, or goose poop. There are few species that do not annoy, frighten, or compete with us. Increasingly, we grant no space for the undomesticated, or for mystery, where the wild soul can explore beyond the confines of commerce. *Who will we be without it?*

⁓

The problem with styled hair, I was finding, is that you have to keep doing something with it. Mine curled like Medusa in the moist breeze off Lake Michigan. I had entered a local beauty parlor while Tom walked next door to a used book shop. A tall black man of perhaps forty greeted me with a look of surprise. I was his only customer. From his tattoos, he had obviously had an interesting youth, but time and family had harnessed him—as it generally does with those who live long enough.

"Make me look young and beautiful," I joked as I climbed into the chair.

His large hands swirled the plastic cape around my shoulders and he pumped the foot pedal to raise the chair. In the mirror I caught his look of apprehension. It occurred to me that white women probably didn't come here. Perhaps he didn't know what to do with my hair any more than I did.

I smiled. "It's just hair," I assured him. "If you cut it a bit shorter, perhaps it'll settle down. The humidity here has it all riled up."

He went about the chore seriously, clipping here and shaving there. I kept up a chatter, hoping he would relax. He told me of his three children in school. Finally he seemed to run out of places to snip and pulled off the cape. I paid and thanked him, then I walked down to the bookstore.

"What do you think?" I asked Tom. I could see he was searching for something tactful. "I look a bit like the flying nun, don't I?" My hair was shaved up the back and longer on top, giving it the aspect of an anvil. You could've stacked books on my head.

Tom remained silent, but one eyebrow drifted up.

"Okay," I declared. "I need scissors."

I was soon standing in our bathroom, hewing away as merrily as any child. I tamed my hair into a sort of pixie cut, short and wavy, and walked down the stairs feeling oddly free—shorn of something more than hair. I shook my head and ran my fingers through the short curls, trying to pinpoint the lightness. For the first time in my life, I wasn't trying to fit some vague picture of femininity. I really didn't care.

"Hi, Son," Tom's voice was gentle. "No, we're not busy. How are you?" He switched the little cell to speaker phone so that I could hear.

"I'm really enjoying my nursing classes," Lucas's deep voice entered our living room, "and Eve is dancing for joy because she's just been accepted into the Pima College nursing program for 2007! She wanted me to tell Mom that her suggestions really helped. How's her work going?"

"I'm getting my stride," I answered loudly. "I guess wherever they hire travel nurses, it'll be stressful. I've gotten the freeway driving down. A friend tells me that three days' orientation is pretty standard. That helped me adjust. People here are very supportive. You'd like Wisconsin."

"I really want to travel-nurse after I graduate," he stated.

"Your mother and I have been talking about Arizona in November," Tom said. "I think I've convinced her that Milwaukee in the winter won't be fun."

"You could live with us again." Lucas sounded excited. "Eve and Megan have really missed you. Well, me, too, of course."

I smiled and thought of living again in community. It would be so easy to let go of my quest. *What is it exactly that drives me?*

After Lucas's call, we sat watching our evening episode of *Northern Exposure,* with its surreal depiction of a quirky Alaskan town of surprising depth. Beyond the patio door, pale evening washed the sky where a harvest moon ascended through tendrils of mist above the lake. Moonlight silvered a wedge of clouds through a silhouette of trees.

I leaned back on the sofa and sighed. "That's what I'm seeking," I pointed to the diminutive screen on the coffee table, "a playful community of unique people who are at home in a beautiful world."

Tom smiled fondly at me. He didn't remind me that it was only a program. Out on the pond, Milwaukee's resident geese lifted their sleek heads in haunting song. Unlike their usual nervous barks, their voices joined in a growing twitter, rose to a hum, and finally broke into a full-throated wail. Were they calling to high-flying cousins, invisible in the night sky, or remembering their own lost journey? Perhaps the full autumn moon had awakened a memory.

We stood in the doorway and listened. *What do they know that I have forgotten?*

All that night the geese sang through our open window. Their clamor was so loud that I stuffed tissue into my ears to sleep. By morning, the windy gray water was alive with hundreds of wild ducks and geese. Thousands of gulls descended in flurries like whirlwinds of blowing paper from a charcoal sky. They settled onto the lake, all facing into the wind, and then like a great school of silver fish, flashed upward and were gone.

Winter was coming; I could feel it like a shiver through my core. The wild geese were soon drawn back to the sky, leaving our lost tribe behind on the fading grass. Like us, these birds hold their greatest strength (and weakness) in long lives and family loyalty. Bound to mates and parents, Milwaukee's geese called to the river of wonderful strangers that passed through their night like a southbound train, and their song gave voice to something within me: my tribe, too, has strayed from its natural path and forgotten the ancestral wisdom. Where are our guiding elders? I wondered. Where do I belong?

Chapter 12

WINGED MIGRATION

September 2006

Wisconsin yellowed and clouds gusted gray across the fields. Tom and I still took walks and made excursions into the countryside, but there was a somber undertone, like a minor key played softly, to our wanderings. Autumn awakened an old urge in me to hunker down—to split wood, tighten up the windows, and dig potatoes. Like Milwaukee's geese, I was homesick for a place I had never known.

In early September we drove to Manitowoc to cross Lake Michigan on the SS *Badger*. The 410-foot coal-fired ferry had been making this trip since I was two years old. Tanker trucks of milk from rural Michigan transited the lake each day to plants in Wisconsin. Local folk and tourists boarded, too—the interstate commerce of rural America.

The captain expertly dropped anchor and swung the stern around, backing the ship up a narrow slot. Trucks of coal went aboard to feed the old engine, then cars with barking dogs, motorcycles, bicycles, and foot traffic came aboard. Lines were cast off and the gray lake welcomed us with gentle rolls. We stood at the rail and watched land fall away. A week earlier, the deck would have been crowded with people sunbathing and taking pictures, but now the passengers were a pragmatic lot. Strangers spoke openly on the chilly afterdeck or hunched into the wind at the rail. There were a few older couples touring the land, European youth, and bikers in leather jackets, but most were locals commuting: hardy folk in rough warm clothing. Although the average age was over fifty, had we run into trouble, they would have pitched in without drama.

As I gazed over the swells, I remembered my autumn crossing of Great Slave Lake aboard a Canadian Northern Territories tug. I was fourteen at summer's end, 1964. My mother and I had arrived by canoe to where the Slave River pours into one of the world's great bodies of fresh water. Annie had been shipped ahead, victim of an unskilled appendectomy that almost took her twelve-year-old life in a village along the Peace River. Connie and I had continued downriver, while Annie (equipped with credit) fended for herself above a bar in the rough gold camp of Yellowknife.

Government tugboats were not supposed to take on passengers, but Great Slave Lake was a monstrous peril for us and the captain acquiesced. I was keen with excitement, wanting to see everything as land vanished to stern. Icy waves pounded over the tug's deck as I ducked in and out of the heated galley. My seasick mother finally ordered me into the first mate's cabin, which had been allocated to us during the eighteen-hour crossing. It was one of the few times I recall her pulling in my reins. Sulkily, I had retreated into the safety of a bunk, where I was hurled from side to side until land appeared out of the sunset wilderness ahead. Auroras were dancing above Yellowknife when we docked, the first that I recall seeing.

The following summer, Connie, Annie, and I returned to complete our journey down the Mackenzie River to the Arctic Ocean. The days were bright as we scuttled along the northern shoreline of Great Slave Lake. Small rocky islands were flung like jade in the blue sky-water on which we floated. We caught pike so large we had to shoot them with the .22 rifle to get them into the canoe and sometimes storms reared like dragons into an innocent day. The lake almost claimed us when we crossed the North Arm—fourteen miles of open water with a high following sea. Then one long afternoon we traversed a mirror, where bits of land seemed to float suspended and gradually a current began, funneling us out of the lake and into the broad Mackenzie River.

Now standing in rain on the rolling deck of the *Badger*, I reminded myself that security is an illusion. We never know how the story will end. Maybe there is no arrival—just life's mysterious unfolding. It is the process that matters. I had recently watched a coworker die of cancer. Holly was a decade younger than me, a gentle soul and an excellent nurse. The hospital she invested years in had named an award in her honor—the one given to me. I watched her weaken in the traces, tending labor patients as she leaned on a cane. When she could no longer work, her friends donated vacation pay so that she could keep her insurance. In the end, it was the kindness of individuals that came through.

I was there for her last steps, so mundane and priceless. Maybe that's how life is—just the ordinary miracle of each moment. I was helping her to the bathroom when she sagged into my arms.

"Oh," she said. Her voice was curious, surprised. "I guess I can't do that anymore." Such grace and dignity. That impressed me. It reminded me, too, that no matter how well one plans, there is no certainty.

If you knew that forty-two years was all you had, would you play your hand differently? I watched the majestic waves. I, too, had sacrificed for the team—wanting to belong beyond a paycheck. It was partly disillusionment with factory medicine that had set me on the road. At least as a travel nurse, the agreements were up front: I was a valuable horse. The company stabled and fed me as long as I performed, but if I broke a leg, they'd sell me for dog food.

THE FIVE ACRE PARCEL THAT my parents homesteaded on Takahula Lake in 1949 was now one of a few private holdings within the Gates of the Arctic National Park. My father held others, yet he seemed obsessed with controlling that one bit of land whose title lay divided. He had emerged the clear victor in his dealings with Connie—the Alaskan icon with wife, sons, wealth and fame—but he could not let it rest. In 1984, he leased the Takahula property without Connie's knowledge. Even when she found out, she had no resources to contest him. Two years later, she was diagnosed with advanced breast cancer. I had hoped Bud's heart would soften at this news, but he saw it as an opportunity. He told Annie and me that he would pay us twenty thousand dollars over ten years—Connie's rightful share of the lease—if we would get our mother to sign "a little piece of paper." Thinking she could use the money, I had passed the offer on to her.

"I have very little to leave you girls," she said. "I held on to Takahula for you. Don't let your father take it away. He got everything else."

After she died, I called my father to talk about joint ownership and the lease.

"I own that land, fee-simple," he stated. "I always have. The poor woman was deluded."

So I had turned it over to Uncle Bert, who ran a title search and hired a lawyer to contact my father. I recalled how our mother needed to force the fifty dollars each in child support from him (our only dependable income) by having his airplane impounded. Bud did not give ground easily. He finally agreed to share future income with his daughters, but it was one more obstacle in his relationship with me. Then in Milwaukee I received his letter telling of his planned sale of Takahula to the National Park Service. He had arranged sales before, but always walked out. I don't believe he really wanted to let go. He was now deep in negotiations, yet had failed to mention the split title to the buyer. Annie was willing to let it go and sign the papers. I was the holdout.

"Hi, Dad, it's Jeanie," I said into Lucas's cell phone. I had been dreading this call. "Did you get my letter?"

"Why, hello, Jeanie," my father's high voice was reedy. "Let me get Mother on the other line." I imagined his shrunken form shuffling into another room, his blue eyes still canny.

I heard a click on the phone. "Hi, Honey," came my stepmother's bright voice. Though high-strung and unpredictable, Martha had been generous to me.

"Hi, Mom. We're in Milwaukee. I'm working as a travel nurse, and we'll be here until mid-November. Lucas forwarded Dad's letter about selling Takahula. Did you get my reply?"

"It's all set up." Bud's tone was patient, final. "I think it's for the best. You and your sister will get a nice chunk of money, maybe sixty thousand dollars each. That'll come in handy."

I steadied myself, reaching for courage. It was still hard for me to confront him. "It's only money, Dad," I said gently. "It can't replace Takahula. I'm asking you to give your half to me and I'll pay Annie for her share. Leave everything else to the boys. Tom and I would live there and care for the place. I'm the only one who would. You speak of a family legacy, and I want that, too… you and I can heal our family."

My father's voice was cold as steel. "You never contacted me when you and Phil came to Alaska. I had to find out from strangers."

It took a moment to understand. I had been twenty-two when I returned to Alaska. Believing that the state belonged to my critical father, I hadn't called him because I was afraid of his judgment. *Point, set, and match.* It had taken thirty-four years, but I heard the triumph in his voice. His purpose in selling Takahula was to keep it from Annie and me, and to win at long last against Connie.

I took a deep breath and let go of the rope. I could end the insanity. "Okay, Dad. Do what you think best. I'll sign the papers," I said quietly. *Fifty years is long enough.* I would not leave this poisonous legacy for my son and his generation. *Maybe there are too many broken dreams for me to ever feel at home on Takahula Lake.* I was surprised that my pain was less about the land than about my father. I had hoped the proximity of death might gentle him. I was old and he was ancient. *What a stupid waste of a lifetime.*

I still needed to put my mother's dreams to rest—those five small acres of wilderness salvaged for her girls. I hung up the phone and sat in long meditation, listening to Milwaukee's wild geese through the open upstairs window and feeling the planet shift into autumn. *Freedom,* I thought, *is an opening of the heart. All things pass away; only the journey remains.* I pictured my mother's face and visualized sitting across a table from her as I told her why I had to move on. I believe she understood.

I pondered the enigma of my mother. Connie, an environmentalist before the term became popular, had fittingly died on Earth Day, April 22, 1987. Luke was just fourteen months old. Two months later, our family flew north to spend six weeks with Bud and Martha on Walker Lake. They had invited us, and Tom encouraged me to go.

"You've always seen your dad through your mother's eyes," Tom had told me. "Now that she's gone, maybe you can start over." Tom had seen the other side of divorce, and a distant daughter whose suspicion he could never bridge. His pain ran so deep that he had been reluctant to father another child.

When Bud had picked us up at the Fairbanks airport in his gold Lincoln, his first words were, "I'm sorry about your mother, but you know, she was the laziest person I ever met."

It was foretelling. We were soon isolated in my father's territory, on beautiful Walker Lake—just as I had been as a teenager. His home had grown to three stories and he now owned a lodge across the lake as well as a cabin at the inlet. Bud set us to work and lost no opportunity to make Tom look foolish. Tom would gladly have served and learned from his father-in-law, but instead came away from the summer feeling diminished and angry. He kept quiet, however, except for one point: when my father started directing me, Tom informed him that caring for our son was my role. Curiously, my father had backed down. The fact that I was claimed by another man seemed to hold more weight than my own voice.

Gazing out my Milwaukee window, I considered Bud's words about Connie. Lazy? No, she wasn't lazy, but neither was she easily channeled into work for its own sake. My mother was a wild creature, and her dreams were of open space and unfettered flight. Bud was determined to own and control that creative spirit, to harness her to his goals, but Connie could not submit to domestication—even to save herself. She was affectionate toward her children yet viewed motherhood as drudgery and often left us with weird strangers. Penniless in her forties, she traveled throughout Mexico making another film. In her fifties, she floated jungle rivers in a dugout canoe manned by Indians and was taken hostage by bandits—an experience she dismissed. At sixty, Connie was hiking the Pacific Crest Trail from Mexico to Canada, as far as she could walk each summer on her delicate feet. Wilderness remained her true love. The rest of us—husband, children, lovers, friends, fans—were all secondary. This passion for the untamed natural world was the biggest gift she left me, though it took me years to forgive her. My father never did.

A POLAR FRONT WAS EVOLVING over Canada. Tom and I stood outside our sliding glass door, staring up at the painted evening where a torrent of geese flooded the sky. Day and night their clamor had permeated our lives, but now, close on the heels of the autumnal equinox, the migration became unstoppable—birds pouring from the North in primordial millions. Never had I witnessed such abundance, such fecund wildness. Their voices rang in my heart like an affirmation from the vast and unknowable universe. Human domestication seemed but a brief aberration. This was life singing: *fly free and be joyful!* How my mother would have loved it!

"They be lots mo' soon," our neighbor's soft voice came from just beyond the patio wall. Two small children, one white, one black, stood silent behind her, big eyes open to the living sky.

"We sleep with our windows open and listen to them," I told her.

"We do too," she smiled back. Her luminous face was lifted, dark eyes shining at the heavens.

The hemisphere above was in motion—a living tapestry as far as I could see. Shifting multitudes gleamed in low sunlight, blowing like autumn leaves in great vortices that layered up and up into salmon-colored clouds. In the high distance, sparks of light revolved in glittering whirlwinds of seagulls and terns. Birds cascaded from the pastel evening until the lake was packed and yet more came. I could scarcely breathe in witness to this miracle. Canada geese are big—two feet long with a five and a half-foot wingspan—and they swung high around the lake, flying close and fast or spiraling down through the surge. Wind spilled from beneath cupped wings and tails flared as they splashed onto the crowded water or rose up in waves into the teeming sky.

There are no national boundaries when migratory birds take to the sky—only the ancient imperative and the revolving seasons. All who undertake this epic journey need havens along the way. *Let there be Life! Even in the midst of cities,* I breathed.

I recalled the passenger pigeon and the buffalo, and how easily beauty and mystery are lost to convenience. *Wild nature speaks from the soul of the world,* I thought, *calling us to remember a story larger and older than our own.*

Tom and Luke paddle across the freezing river, 1999.

Luke enjoyed time wandering alone, Kernwood 1999-2000.

Chapter 13

HARVEST

October 2006

Breezy dawn revealed that the great caravan had departed. Weak sunlight sloped between low cloud banks onto the strangely quiet lake. Scattered Vs of geese still wavered resolutely across the gray sky—like arrows pointing south—but the flocks no longer stopped. Only our lost tribe remained, talking in subdued tones. *Why did they stay?* They had simply to lift into that living river and away from Wisconsin winter, but here they waited as the northern hemisphere revolved inexorably into cold and darkness.

Humans also remain stranded and for the same reasons: caught in a web of family and familiarity—the known unhappiness preferable to mystery. I understood. I didn't fling myself joyfully into the sky either. Only when I could no longer ignore the blast of cold air, did I tuck my fears under one arm and let go of the ground. In the end there is nothing to lose, for life itself is ultimately swept away. I knew this and yet held back. Perhaps it was the mental gymnastics of choosing that mesmerized me, for once I chose, I wouldn't waste energy backtracking roads not taken. Other options seemed to grow shut: forgotten dreams of places that no longer existed on my event horizon. What if I hadn't married Tom? Had become a doctor, stayed in art glass, never had a child? These thoughts did not trouble me. It was possible futures that obsessed me.

Choosing lightens my heart. Regardless of what my father decided, my release of Takahula had opened space in my chest akin to ice going out on the river. Now I was grappling with our next destination: should I take another assignment or return to my old employer for the final 20 percent of my 401k? These are the carrots that keep us in harness. Part of me watched with amusement as my mind chewed and sorted. It was a familiar process, and although clarity rarely arose from this milling of data, I nevertheless went through it. Far from being spontaneous, travel-nursing required much planning. There were perhaps fifty credentials to maintain, contracts, interviews, and timetables. My head felt plugged with a sort of mental constipation as I processed the merits of travel, benefits, friendships, and pay. Unlike Milwaukee's geese, however, I would take wing before the lake froze over.

"Do you think we could settle here and not be domesticated?" I asked Tom as we walked the shore of Lake Michigan. The path wound through an old forest and leaves scurried about our ankles, gold and rust in the breeze. Miles of park lay deserted as if the good folk of Milwaukee were content to simply maintain them.

"People here are so genuinely well-meaning," I continued. "They really want you to get into their heaven—which I'm sure looks a good deal like Wisconsin—white fences and fat cattle. You'd end up mowing your lawn, raking leaves, and attending 4-H picnics." I was quiet a moment. "Killing me softly with a spoon."

"With homemade pie," Tom agreed.

I grinned at him. "I have to admit I feel very much at home here, even if it is a long way from Alaska. It's a lot easier than Tucson." A bumper sticker (one of the few I had seen) summed it up: "Wag more, bark less." *Wouldn't we all be happier if we did that?*

"I'm going to accept the position in Sierra Vista," I said. "Tucson doesn't really want me back. They'd rather have a lazy nurse than a 'troublemaker,' awards and all." Morale had been in sharp decline at University Medical in the spring of 2006, so I had researched and written a paper. When I sent it to management and colleagues, I was summoned to strained meetings and ordered to form committees on "staff retention" and "paperwork overload"— meaningless Band Aids with no real intention of change. Nurses, like teachers, yearn to make a difference, but burn out in systems that don't empower them to do so: another piece that nudged me onto the road.

"Sierra Vista is seventy-five miles from Tucson." Tom's voice was excited. "We can visit friends and maybe even host our Christmas Day Gathering."

"We can spend Christmas with Lucas," I said softly. "I've wanted to try rural nursing too. It's an eighty-seven-bed hospital that serves three small towns and forty thousand people—the sort of place I hope we end up. They have a hundred and thirty deliveries a month, which is a lot for the staff numbers. No onsite docs either—that'll be different."

"I can get my truck," Tom said. His old red Toyota was parked at Sylvia House.

"You've been limited here, haven't you? Stuck in an apartment all day."

"Not really," he shrugged. "I get out and walk every day. I've gotten a good start on writing a book on my life to give to Lucas. It would have meant a lot had my father done that for me. But it'll be good to have my own transportation again."

"Nothing fazes you, does it?" I edged under his arm. "You just take each moment as it comes."

"I think I learned that from you."

My laugh was a snort. "I talk a good game, but you put it into practice." I studied his familiar face. He was quietly there all the time: shopping with his backpack, anticipating my needs, doing things my way. Connie may have taught me to live my dreams, but it was Tom who daily gave me the stability to enjoy them (and not go screaming down each set of rapids). Without his steadying hand and willing heart, I might long ago have lost my nerve and settled for a narrow horizon. *But what of his dreams?* He didn't really say.

Our trail emerged from the tunnel of trees onto a sunny lawn. Ahead, the blue expanse of Lake Michigan blended with sky. We left the path, crossed a quarter-mile of mowed grass, and climbed onto the breakwater. Seagulls were riding the updraft where surf met the rocks, their cries like a memory of freedom. I leaned against a boulder and pulled out our lunch, handing Tom a sandwich. He passed me a slice of apple and the water bottle. Pressing my spine into the warm rock, I closed my eyes and listened to the hypnotic breath of the waves.

"Our lives are close to perfect," I said dreamily. "Life in the 'now' is very dear."

My childhood in Tucson created a mental schism that crystallized for me on the back roads of Wisconsin: I hadn't realized my cultural mythology was so rooted in the Midwest. Instead of celebrating the unique seasons of the

Sonoran Desert, I had been imprinted on a world I had never seen. While my young imagination was splashed in primary colors, the subtle hues of Arizona were ignored. Mrs. Frampton, my first-grade teacher, taught us to paint red tulips and green lawns. Dick and Jane of my primer lived in a white two-story house with blue jays nesting in the apple trees, and there was a big red barn on their grandparents' farm. Temperatures still hovered in the eighties when Tucson school children crafted paper turkeys and dressed up like pilgrims—they still do. Pumpkins were sold from barren lots, and withered Christmas trees were trucked in from far away. We covered our windows with artificial snow, sang nostalgically about sleigh rides and chestnuts, and dreamed of a mythical white Christmas. *How would Santa find me*, I wondered, *when we had neither chimney nor mantle?* We were orphans among cactus, while somewhere people celebrated in cozy farmhouses.

Now I witnessed the great American Midwest at harvest time and was awed by the bounty! As with the flood of migrating geese, a profound sense of thanksgiving descended upon me like a blessing. So many of my childhood archetypes came to life that I felt I had recovered a lost continent in my soul. It reminded me of giving birth to our long-awaited child. I had been so amazed that I kept repeating, "It's a real baby!"

Wisconsin in October was a storybook come to life. Unlike the ugly vastness of agribusiness, artistic deliberation and quality of life were obviously valued here. Family farms were interspersed with woodlands where leaves showered from the overarching oaks and maples. Tractors moved slowly through the browning fields, pumping forth golden streams of corn, while sandhill cranes gleaned along hedgerows. Hay was rolled into one-ton bales for winter feed on forty-cow farms, and acres of dried beans hung plump on brittle stems. *Small America may be endangered*, I thought, *but it's not dead.* Everywhere was a quiet bustle of taking in and putting by. Like a child, I laughed and pointed as we drove.

The little towns were decked in autumn—lawns and flowerbeds no less attractive than in summer. Children sold pumpkins by the roadside and fresh produce was neatly arranged beside mailboxes—the stranger trusted to leave payment. The orderly business of raking and clearing for winter could be seen on every corner. Neighbors were out repairing roofs and painting gutters, and neat stacks of split oak towered behind many homes. There was a feeling of contentment and determination in villages—very different from the playful spirit of only a month before. Approaching winter could be seen in the faces. *Perhaps it is winter that makes people pull together*, I decided. Midwestern politeness and moderation like that of Maine and Alaska may stem from a deep knowledge that snowfall is always just around the corner. Those of us who grew up in the desert never had such an unforgiving deadline.

Seeing firsthand the abundance of our nation and the basic goodness of its people kindled a profound gratitude in my heart. *I have needed this*, I thought. With all signs pointing a bony finger into the future, I was losing hope in a beautiful tomorrow. When humanity took on death without limiting birth, it created a monster. World population has tripled in my lifetime! Despite mass starvation, war and disease, seventy-five million of us are added every year—two hundred thousand each day.

"When Lucas and I volunteered in Guatemala," I said, apropos of nothing, "I came to believe we were compounding the misery." Tom and I had stopped for a simple lunch near the young Mississippi River. "Without access to birth control, women there have ten and twelve children. Half die and the others live on the edge of starvation. Think how ghastly it would be if they all survived to have babies! Where does it end?"

I lifted my eyes to the perfection of autumn along the ridge where migrating turkey vultures climbed on an updraft. "Lucas never saw it that way and maybe he is the wiser," I said slowly. "I've been grieving for our beautiful Earth and all its diversity. I've driven friends away with my ranting. I wrote a book nobody wants to publish. Perhaps all I can do is watch the train wreck. Maybe that's why I'm here—just to witness."

Neither of us said anything for a while. "Perhaps there is no grand solution," I continued, "just daily kindness and consciousness. Wisconsin isn't an antidote for the world's problems, but it has restored my faith in possibility."

THE FIRST BREATH OF WINTER was forecast in a major storm with high winds and snow. I tried to imagine my dark drive to work in blowing sleet. Pedestrians were beginning to dig out coats—these weren't cute jackets: you could wear them in Siberia. The people of Wisconsin had finally put away their sandals. Maybe they knew something that the lost geese and I were ignoring.

We were at the Honda dealer readying our car for the cold. I smiled at an old black lady in the waiting room. Her gray hair was pulled back in a neat bun. She wore gloves and a heavy knee-length coat of soft wool the color of caramel.

"I heard on the news that it might get cooler," I said. She glanced out the window at a sky like skimmed milk and the blowing yellow leaves. "Do you think I'll need more than two long-sleeved shirts and the sweater I brought from Arizona?"

I could see she didn't want to offend me, but then she didn't want me to freeze to death either. She leaned close and said, "Honey, I think you needs to go shoppin'—soon." Her eyes were concerned and kindly. "It do get real cold here."

Tom and I continued our walks on the labyrinth of paved trails as the first snow flurries sifted from an ashen sky and leaves blew thickly about our feet. The massive hardwoods were a riot of colors, each a distinct shade. You could camp in Milwaukee except for the ominous signs warning you not to drink the water. Occasionally we even spotted deer and coyote along the creeks.

Leaves eddied about our apartment door and danced down the roads. People were out with rakes or riding great vacuums that compacted them into blocks. Piles of leaves were deep at every curb. Snow fences were going up and our driveway sprouted an outline of three-foot poles. This land had serious surprises in store for the unwary. Our apartment was not well-insulated and the heater ran frequently. I was beginning to feel as out of place as the geese. We were short-timers now, saying goodbye, closing up, and moving on. In the movie *Paint Your Wagon*, a rasty old Lee Marvin says to baby-faced Clint Eastwood, "There are two kinds of people. Them goin' somewhere and them goin' nowhere." Eastwood disagrees, but Marvin interrupts him. "You don't know what the hell I'm talking about," he states flatly. Then Marvin stares off into the distance and murmurs, "I'm an ex-citizen of nowhere… and sometimes I get mighty homesick."

I too was pulled both directions. It felt right to seek a refuge at this stage in life, and yet… how I loved the next bend of the river! Domestication offers security—the promise of a food bowl in a fenced yard. It is very seductive. All we need give up is our wildness—the freedom of that mysterious journey whispered by our souls.

"I SEE HIS TRUCK," I said as we pulled into the motel parking lot in Eau Claire. We had driven west to rendezvous with Matthew, who was joining us for a last Wisconsin adventure and a visit to a small cheese factory.

Matthew waved and unfolded from the cluttered front seat of his old pickup. His large, chapped hands felt cold as he gave me a hug; his ears were red. He was dressed much the same with a frayed flannel shirt over his ragged T-shirt. "Have a good trip?" he asked in his loud cheerful voice.

"It was beautiful," I answered. "I can't get enough of the fall colors."

A chilly breeze trickled from the west where the anemic sun leaned into the autumn haze. From the motel, we sprinted across the highway toward a diner in gathering twilight. The median was already slick with frost. I walked between the men and took both their hands. Matthew stooped to pick up a discarded jug from the highway for recycling.

Integrity, I thought, watching my old friend, *is living your values, though your action seems paltry in the face of world problems. Everything we do matters.*

It was late the following afternoon when Tom and I arrived home in a steady drizzle for my last week of work. The leaves were suddenly gone; bare limbs, stark as bones, pointed at the colorless sky. The tidy folk of Wisconsin were doing a last mowing of their unnaturally green lawns. There was much pruning, edging, and pulling up of withered flowers. Ice crinkled the edges of the lake, rafting back and forth in a biting wind.

It has been said that happiness lives in the details. Tom and I snuggled on the sofa in lamplight, my feet warm beneath a blanket against his thigh. Just beyond the closed patio door our geese grazed quietly in the fading dusk. I stopped my busy mind and savored the crunch of a single wholegrain cracker with a sliver of ten-year-old cheddar made by good people we had met. A sip of white wine followed. I let the flavors melt together on my tongue and gazed out at the muted grays of coming winter. *My life is so good,* I thought, *each moment.*

Wisconsin had been an unexpected homecoming. I had hidden out at the literal end of the Earth and yet here, sequestered in the ordinary, found renewed hope. It was as if I had stumbled onto a land of industrious hobbits living quietly in the midst of a great battlefield. I knew it was an illusion—that the tide of accelerating change was still in motion—but I'd been given a brief respite. Here in the sane Wisconsin countryside, I could almost believe in a happy ending.

When Rude arrived for the downriver trip in 2000, he and Luke became close.

Rude teaches Luke how to clean his big pike, Yukon River 2000.

Chapter 14

WINDS OF CHANGE

November 2006

Leaving Milwaukee was harder than I anticipated. My coworkers sent us off with gifts of food, cards, and loving words. Many had baked special treats; two even drove to the hospital on their day off to say goodbye. I hadn't expected to feel so at home on my first travel-nurse assignment; I never intended to fall in love with Wisconsin.

Packing took only a couple of hours. Tom mailed a box of bedding to Tucson and gave the maintenance man our dishes and food. We dropped off a bag of clothes at Goodwill on our way out of town. It was as simple as that.

Indian summer lay seductively across the fields as we pulled away, but winter was already bearing down from the north, clogging the highways behind us with a foot of snow. I was tired from three hard days at work as we sped into the afternoon sunlight, southwest toward Illinois. Tom looked happy at the wheel, taking charge so that I could rest. Treating one another with gentleness was an easy blessing of years together, our differences worn as smooth as river stones. Miles clipped by to the songs of our few CDs, while trucks hauling freight into Chicago hustled us along like a minnow in a current.

The next morning we again raced south in a press of monster trucks with the storm at our heels. Illinois stretched flat and impersonal below the interstate—a smoggy expanse of factory farms. Towns glimpsed from the highway appeared neglected and sad. *One might drive the nation and never see it*, I thought.

"Is it worth a back-road transit?" I pondered aloud.

"We'll probably never see Illinois again," Tom said. "Your call."

We slipped down the ramp onto State Route 24 to discover a different world. The Illinois River wandered through a country that was hilly and unsuitable for agribusiness. Pockets of trees were interspersed with small rocky farms, and traffic on the little road consisted mainly of old pickups and tractors pulling farm equipment. Autumn still lingered here, and harvest was underway. We stopped for lunch at a diner where aging, beefy men in bib overalls talked of hogs. This was meat-and-potatoes country. My grandparents, Old Clarence and Abbie Helmericks, had farmed in Illinois until they moved to Colorado. This was my genetic heritage: hardy northern Europe emigrants—a pragmatic and unsentimental folk—grown geriatric. As in rural Wisconsin, the absence of young people struck an unsettling note. America's small farmers may be hanging on, but their children have moved to Chicago.

It was dark before we reached the little town of Warrensburg, Missouri, where my sister and her husband lived in rural seclusion on ten wooded acres. The university where they both taught was only a few miles away. Beyond the town, we turned at last into black woods and crept up a hill between great oak trees toward a glimmer of light. Silence engulfed us like a sigh when we shut off the car. A golden beam of light spilled through their storm door, welcoming us in from the night. We shuffled to the porch, feeling our way through thickly drifting leaves, and were ushered into a room fronting the old trees. Sliding beneath quilts, we soon fell into a deep sleep.

I awakened in a coral dawn to a storm of falling leaves. An occasional patter of rain rattled off the porch—skirt of the large front now dumping snow on Wisconsin. Beyond our windows, the leaves swirled in such profusion that they obscured the field across the lane and its silhouettes of cattle. Five wild turkeys slipped like water through the thicket and dropped away down the hill.

"The leaves are falling," I whispered to Tom. "You have to see this. It's like a blizzard of leaves!"

"Go put a balloon on the car so you don't lose it," Tom's eyes retreated into their wrinkles and he rolled over to claim the center of the sofa bed. His pale scalp with its scrapes and freckles looked vulnerable. I tucked my pillow under his arm and patted the quilts around his shoulders. He smiled but did not open his eyes.

I tiptoed down the hall and poked my head into Annie and John's room. "You've got to see the falling leaves," I whispered again. "It's like a snowstorm!"

"Sh—sh… it goes on all month," Annie whispered back, and she too returned to slumber.

So I was left to enjoy this miracle alone. I made a cup of instant coffee and curled up in John's leather chair by the big front window. A tabby cat was fluffed into a ball in an old chair on the porch, watching squirrels bound along branches sixty feet overhead. Below, my teal-colored Honda really was disappearing under a dancing blanket of brown, russet, tan, and gold.

An hour later John arose, followed by my sister, and laid more oak in the stove. Leaves were still driving past the window to a sound like surf in the trees. John set a kettle of water on to boil and then poured it through coffee in a glass funnel. His curly brown hair, graying sedately at the temples, was rumpled from sleep. Behind glasses, his eyes smiled at me. He and Annie were both in pajamas, quiet as cats. While John was puttering in the kitchen, my sister settled onto the sofa, her feet in woolen socks and a big mug of coffee between her fragile hands. A gray cat stretched luxuriously across her lap. The room was cluttered with art in various stages of completion and I could see her mind was already busy with a new project.

"You cut your hair," I pointed out.

Annie's hair was almost as short as mine. She was a chameleon with a flair for dressing, and could still carry herself in a manner that opened doors. I recalled our youth, my boyfriends saying, "Man, your sister is something!" While I plodded determinedly along in sturdy shoes and Goodwill jeans, my sister playfully expressed whatever light crossed her mind. She was Woman in a way I never quite learned. I was the tomboy, rooted in soil, strong and grounded as a mountain. Annie was elusive as a cloud—you thought you knew her, but then she slipped away.

She grinned ruefully. "It was time. I had a few awkward moments when some young man would happily overtake me as I walked on campus. I could see his mouth fall as he realized his mistake and the word 'Old!' form in his mind." She shook her head and grinned. "I like the simplicity. The clean lines… nothing extra."

"What do you think of Dad selling Takahula?" I asked.

She made a face. "Again? I just want closure. I've been 'stemmed' too many times." It was a saying of our father's. He would run his hand down the trusting back of a cat only to pick it up by the tail. He did it with people too, using the same word.

"I'd be surprised if it goes through," I said. "Not if he can keep the drama alive. What would he do if it was finished?"

"You know, he had so many opportunities to make Connie's life a little easier—and ours too—but he didn't."

"I never told you that one of her royalty checks ended up in his hands," I said. "It was a pitiful amount, but he cashed it! The publisher tracked me down." I was quiet a moment. "I think what I've learned from him is that anger is poisonous. It has nothing to do with whether he deserves forgiveness. It's about the quality of my life."

"It's a legacy that perpetuates itself," Annie agreed. "My first marriage, my children growing up in shadow. I believed that I could somehow heal the past, that I could do what Connie couldn't—tame the man with enough love. At some point, you just have to step away and choose today."

"So what are your plans?" John asked as he handed me a fresh mug of coffee laced with canned milk. He didn't seem to mind that I had claimed his chair.

"I start work on Monday in Sierra Vista, Arizona," I said. "We're staying in a three-story walkup in historic downtown Bisbee. I can't believe my company put us in a different town from the hospital—again! I'll have a twenty-six-mile commute. Now I'm told that day shift starts at three thirty in the morning!"

"You're gonna love Bisbee," Annie assured me. "It'll be worth the drive. It's artistic and full of quirky people. Sierra Vista is a soulless big-box sort of place. Military and retirement housing." She made a face.

"Milwaukee was wonderful," I grinned. "I never saw so much grass! My, do they mow!"

"That's the Midwest. When you live here, you realize why: it becomes a jungle in no time. If we didn't gravel our paths, we wouldn't be able to get down to the creek. It's not like the desert at all." Then she snorted. "John and I decided to let the thickets grow for the wildlife and only mow the areas we use. Within weeks our neighbors stopped by to lend us their mowers and even offered to cut it themselves. Letting nature take back the land is just not done around here."

We spent a healing day with them. While the men puttered in the yard and Annie stitched her wordless exploration of light into art, I smiled at the great trees—a much needed respite. In communion with the Old Ones, my spirit settled like the leaves and prepared for a new flowering. When evening crept out of the forest and frost skimmed the puddles, we retreated to the warm kitchen where John cooked fresh chowder that we ate with crusty bread fresh from the oven. I thought of our grandmother Winnie. Childhood with our adventurous and creative mother had often been chaotic for two little girls. Connie hated "the shackles of routine" and was oblivious to the needs of small children. Uncle Bert once said, "I don't know how you girls survived." *Winnie, of course.* Her simple and predictable home had allowed us to root in the planet. Now Annie and John had built a haven with much the same flavor—a place one could grow old with the trees and new with each dawn. *I will have a home like this,* I decided: *a refuge where I can create art, welcome friends, and plant a garden. I will choose simplicity and daily joy.* Like Janet and Bert. Like Winnie. Like John and Annie.

THE NEXT DAY TOM AND I meandered southwest, following Matthew's directions through a sunny autumn landscape along historic Highway 54. By afternoon we crossed the panhandle of Oklahoma into the dry grasslands of northern Texas. The road here was hemmed by miles of feedlots: industrialized death on a mind-numbing scale. Cattle stood packed into the distance on either side, a sea of captive backs—those living slabs of meat we try not to think about when ordering a burger. *The price of domestication.* Ahead, black clouds towered along the horizon. Suddenly, we spotted undulating ribbons flashing dark and light, high against the storm. Often we had seen immense flocks of blackbirds wavering like smoke through Midwestern fields and it was some minutes before we realized that these were vast congregations of geese and cranes—thousands of the great birds twisting like schools of fish as they fought into the winds. Watching them, my heart caught in my throat. *Wildness,* I thought, *means uncertainty. But oh! The beauty!*

Soon we too collided with that fierce storm and the highway came alive with stampeding tumbleweeds. In the sudden darkness, we switched on our headlights, while about us the land itself seemed in motion. I thought of the endless surge of buffalo that had once covered this prairie. Now only tumbleweeds galloped up the embankment, hesitated a moment, and plunged into our path. Tom slowed to dodge the ghostly herd, but it was impossible to miss them all. Around us, big trucks and many cars smashed through the onslaught, oblivious to danger and damaged radiators. Within an hour, we had traversed the storm and entered northern New Mexico.

The following two days, a deep sky—clear as in my childhood—domed the open valleys as we slipped between purple mountain ranges. I hadn't realized how much I had missed expansive horizons. We drove almost to Mexico on back roads for a quick visit to Bisbee before our long-anticipated reunion with Lucas. There were few vehicles on the narrow ribbon of State Route 80, where the tawny grassland of scrub oak climbed into the sunny Chiricahua

Mountains. We passed through the ugly border town of Douglas, then turned northwest to ascend fifty-five hundred feet into Bisbee.

The road tiptoed along an edge of the famous Copper Queen mine—a yawning red and yellow abyss that dwarfed the surrounding landscape—before slithering into the old mining town. Bisbee had grown along canyon walls, swelling into several villages, each very different, wherever the terrain permitted. Old Bisbee, the historic center, was nestled into the mountain's ribs in a steep bowl where two canyons coiled together. No one seeking a conventional life would choose to live here. In 1975 the mine had closed after a hundred years and the town became a magnet for minimalists, Buddhists, aging hippies, and artists—who set about crafting the haphazard and often dangerous structures into creative spaces. The village was at once intimate and remote, clinging to terrain so precipitous that most homes had no vehicular access. Irregular rock walls bolstered an intricate warren that sprouted from cliffs or arched across gullies. Residents parked in the Gulch and climbed hundreds of concrete steps. The few roads were more like goat trails—just wide enough for one car, with the drop onto someone's roof.

Our new home was on the ground floor of an ancient three-story hotel—oldest boarding house (some said bordello) in Arizona. "Ground" is a relative term in the arboreal world of Bisbee, where buildings lean into thirty-foot rock walls that support the homes above. Our rooms were expensively decorated and furnished. Wooden decks surrounded each floor and there was a communal back patio which resembled a sandstone canyon, deep in shade with overhanging trees. Here a six-foot sluice funneled runoff from the entire mountainside into a great stone basin and then under the building in a square tunnel as high as my head. The owners, an eccentric engineer in cowboy boots and his energetic wife, had abandoned retirement to renovate this old building, because "retirement is boring."

Driving on to Sierra Vista for a look at the hospital, we climbed above Tombstone Canyon and through Mule Pass Tunnel and then descended fifteen hundred feet along winding Banning Creek. The highway straightened and the temperature warmed several degrees as it left the mountains, arrowed across the San Pedro River, and onto the desert floor. Here Sierra Vista budded along Highway 90 into a collection of chain restaurants, lookalike apartments, box stores, and trailer parks. The hospital was pragmatic and unimposing, but the nurses welcomed me.

Two hours later we pulled in at Sylvia House, where Lucas came out to greet us with Megan and Eve right behind him. "I've really missed you guys!"

His face beamed as he gathered us up in big arms. Gazing up at him, I sighed with happiness and relaxed.

After three fast days of catching up, Tom and I headed back to Bisbee. Emerging from Mule Pass Tunnel into waning afternoon light, we spiraled steeply down into colorful Tombstone Gulch. It only took us an hour to unload the car and move in. Already I felt like an old hand at life on the wing—the simplicity of owning little, a dawning freedom. Leaning on the deck rail, we gazed across a narrow gorge at the close bowl of mountains that already hid the sun. Eighty feet below, Brewery Gulch lay purple in shadow, while across from us, buildings climbed the opposite canyon wall and snaked up ravines. The ocher, russet, rose, and yellow earth was dotted with blue-green scrub oak, yucca, and manzanita. To the south, a fifteen hundred-foot peak brooded above the town. I noticed red holes gouged in its flanks and on further examination saw great fissures extending vertically to the skyline.

"Look at those cracks!" I pointed up. "The whole mountain looks like it's caving in." I remembered bringing Luke here when he was ten. Astraddle a small train that had once carried miners deep into the earth, we toured part of the twenty-five hundred miles of tunnels. Even in summer, it was cold under that mountain.

Tom and I studied the strange peak, which glowed in the last rays of sun. "How about dinner out tonight?" he suggested.

Holding hands, we descended uneven steps into the lavender twilight of Brewery Gulch to join a happy bustle of foot traffic. The old buildings were of brick and cement, very solid and irregular, with strange passages and narrow rock staircases. People greeted us with smiles along the hand-poured sidewalks and in the winding streets. We entered a corner restaurant, its brick walls painted cheerfully, and were greeted by a dark-haired waiter in his late forties. He had the body of a dancer and soon served up excellent Mexican food with the flourish of a man who enjoys his work.

"We live such a charmed life," I grinned at Tom.

Silently we toasted the twenty-fifth anniversary of our convoluted journey together—two old friends still excited about the next bend in the river.

AS THE FIVE THOUSAND-DOLLAR COMPLETION bonus in my contract should have warned, Sierra Vista was a challenging assignment. Along with weird hours and a fast pace, there were no "in-house" doctors and I delivered many babies. The anesthesiologists (like the obstetricians) worked fast and often wordlessly, expecting me to anticipate and manage everything. In the OR there could be three doctors demanding attention. As always, there was a great deal of charting and new computer programs to learn.

Hardest of all was a charge nurse who loaded me unfairly and then criticized. She was in her late thirties, attractive and bright but volatile, and her moods set the tone. *Why,* I wondered, *do we defer to petty tyrants?* As with my father, my only defense against bullying was to duck my head and work harder. Sometimes I managed two labor patients as well as triage—the four-bed room where outpatients were assessed—while my charge nurse played on the computer. I seldom got a lunch break and was frequently on my feet for thirteen hours. Nevertheless, I adjusted. When I hit the floor, I knew where things were and what was expected. *Safe baby, safe mom* became my mantra.

Scientists measure stress as the rate of change in a person's life. Even positive change—such as a new marriage—is stressful. Each of us, however, has a different tolerance for change. I am not a thrill-seeker. I would rather slog cross-country through deep snow than glide down a packed slope. Perhaps the reason I repeatedly placed myself on top of mountains was to learn to handle anxiety. Each time I arrived at the bottom alive, I felt stronger, more balanced and—quite frankly—surprised. Nursing was giving me more than medical skills: it daily forced me out of my comfort zone. Surviving in the wilderness was easy compared with life-and-death hospital nursing.

The stress of Sierra Vista got me thinking about how others deal with change. Janet was a worrier, I decided. Though often fearful, she learned to negotiate peace with the "what ifs" in her life. Connie, too, was courageous. Although she never found solid ground, her fears did not to stop her. I recalled her nightmares: my mother's howling in the night. I hadn't been sympathetic. "Mother, wake up!" I would yell from my own warm bed. "You're dreaming again!" *What was it that chased her?* She never said and I didn't ask.

Our return to Arizona also allowed us to work on our documentary, a frustrating project of more than a decade. On my first days off, Tom and I drove to Phoenix to consult with my cousin Bert and his students at Scottsdale Community College. After several near-misses in production funding, we had accepted Bert's offer to use his video class. However, each generation of students wanted to start over with the ninety hours of the Hi-8 footage we shot during our first year in the wilderness, and our endless project was becoming known as the "Black Hole."

I WAS UP AS USUAL, watching dawn seep into Tombstone Canyon and trying to meditate. Intimate peaks glowed softly beneath a full moon and stars were paling in the periwinkle sky. Old Bisbee was decorated for the holidays, the cracked mountain lit in the shape of a huge Christmas tree. Below our balcony window, soft lights were fading slowly into the colorful town, close and comforting. *Twilight is a moment of magic*, I thought. Carlos Castaneda called it the "crack between the worlds." *But not for me today.*

I value my private dawns. As a light sleeper who never uses an alarm clock, I prefer to rise at the same time, even on my days off. However, waking at 2:00 A.M. for the long drive and grueling new assignment had thrown me into a tailspin: hot flashes and heart palpitations. The sleeping pills I took to put me under at 6:00 P.M.—the time needed for a night's rest—left me groggy. By 9:30 in the morning I had been at work for six hours. I forgot when to be hungry. My stomach balled into a knot, and my body began to vibrate with anxiety that fed upon itself. Tom tried to soothe me with meals and massage, but nothing worked.

"Want a cup of tea?" he asked from the doorway, his hair was still tousled from sleep.

I nodded. Tom disappeared into the kitchen and returned with our mugs. As he settled beside me, I leaned into the reassuring warmth of his chest and listened to the steady beat of his heart. His arm rested lightly across the back of the suede sofa, hand gently stroking my hair. Silently we watched the awakening town. Suddenly, an unexpected wave of happiness flooded me and I grinned broadly at the cosmic joke.

"For three months we've been rationing episodes of *Northern Exposure*," I said, "while I felt nostalgic for some quaint village full of friendly and eclectic people. Now we've washed up in Bisbee—against my will—about as close to 'Cicely, Alaska' as one can get in Arizona!"

"May as well enjoy it," he said.

"Indeed."

NEXT AFTERNOON THE SHADOW OF my car raced ahead over the dun-colored valley as traffic from Sierra Vista dropped behind. My eyes lifted toward the blue Mule Mountains as I relaxed into the seat and switched on my music, enjoying the gentle arch of the highway. Momentarily, the road dipped toward the San Pedro River with its outline of ancient cottonwood trees. Here the stream snaked off in both directions through yellow grass, wending between fawn-colored hills, soft as breasts.

My spirit revived as I drew near the mountains. I filled my lungs deeply with air, as nourishing as a cold drink of water, and realized that I had been holding my breath most of the day. The land swelled and opened to the road, revealing an intimate canyon. The car climbed steadily to State Route 80 then turned south into the creases of the planet. Mesquite and creosote gave way to oak and yucca, painting the golden evening a blue-green. Within half a mile, the sun had vanished behind enclosing peaks. I felt protected here, private and safe. My body trusted the embrace of the earth as I downshifted for the climb above the dry creek bed. Shadows lay deep over tumbled rocks, accentuating the pink mountain shoulders. Bare granite cliffs edged the road.

Nearing the skyline, the road twisted suddenly and dove into a rock wall, plunging beneath Mule Pass to emerge a hundred yards down the other side above a different canyon. Ahead, the cliffs blazed ochre and bronze in the glow of hidden sun. Gripping tenaciously to the gully below me was the improbable town of Old Bisbee. I was home for the night.

Chapter 15

BACKPACKING TO THE STARS

December 2006

First snow, soft as goose down, feathered Old Bisbee in Christmas white. I nursed my cocoa from the comfort of the sofa and gazed down on the picturesque town. A short distance away, the highway climbed steeply from the canyon and through the falling snow, I could see police cars blinking prettily blue and red as traffic slid off the road. Mule Pass Tunnel was closed. I considered my 3:00 A.M. commute the next morning. My car was in one of the few parking places outside our apartment, positioned for a straight slide into Tombstone Canyon. Tom's red truck stayed in the Gulch.

We were entering the contemplative quiet of yet another turning of the planet, the moment when nature pauses for breath—listening between seasons. Humans would do well to do the same. Winter solstice is buried deep in our collective unconscious as a sacred time of renewal. In the darkening days, we feel the urge to gather around a communal fire, to share the fruits of summer, and give thanks for the generosity of life. Long before there was Christmas, our ancestors celebrated this closure of a cycle and their hopes for spring.

I used to dread Christmas; I suspect many people do. My card list topped two hundred and neglected friends formed widening rings into the shadows. The "holiday season" is a time of frenetic activity and anxiety, a marathon of deadlines, shopping, wrapping, and spending money. It was Janet and Bert who brought sanity to my world when they chose to withdraw from the commercial spirit.

"Please don't buy me anything," I began telling friends. "Let's give one another our time instead."

At first I felt guilty and defensive, especially when presents continued to arrive. I schooled myself to appreciate the generosity and feel worthy while having nothing to trade. Gradually, I began to find a childlike pleasure in the season. Tom, Luke, and I created our own traditions. We decorated a living pine tree, which blessed us a second time when we planted it in January as a symbol of our commitment to the Earth. A small forest now stands witness to those celebrations. When Luke was a child, we gave him one major gift each Christmas. He in turn donated outgrown toys to a local charity. We invited friends over to prepare meals for the homeless then drove around giving boxed lunches away. We walked together through an older Tucson neighborhood that blazed with lights and song. Our big event, however, was our Christmas Day Gathering: an all-day banquet for anyone who wanted to come.

TOM AND I WERE AGAIN at Sylvia House that Christmas, sleeping in our old bedroom on the floor. Our bed had been hauled into the storage shed by the most recent renter (now gone) who preferred a more Bohemian decor. A scattering of dirty socks, hairpins, a guitar, and other oddities were still strewn about the floor. Life with young people wasn't neat or simple, but it was lively. *This year*, I decided, *I will enjoy things as they come.*

It was dark and the rest of the family was asleep as I finished making Connie's traditional stuffing and fitting both turkeys into the oven. Lucas had proudly contributed one this year, a gift from the resort where he still worked. Megan had asked me to wake her for our "special time," so I turned off the kitchen light and tiptoed to her room. The living room was softly lit by a little potted tree decorated with familiar ornaments and Christmas lights.

Megan joined me on the sofa and sleepily burrowed into my lap under an afghan. She was nine now and lanky. Her body felt solid as she compressed it into my arms. We both had coffee—hers mostly milk, the way Winnie had made it for me. The air was beginning to smell warmly of sage and onions. I stroked her hair and petted one of her hands, running my finger along the chipped, pink nail polish. Connie used to push back my cuticle with her thumbnail and tell me I had "perfect moons." *Lucas has them, too*, I thought.

"Tell me about when you were a little girl," Megan requested.

It was strangely familiar. Winnie had once been the wisdom-holder in my life. Humans have passed their values down this way for eons, sewing generations together with song and story. *What have I to offer?* I remembered Christmas Eve spent alone when I was nine. Connie had rushed my sister to the emergency room with a nosebleed. I had walked out to the street to sit on a low wall and sing *Silent Night* (all three verses) in a small voice. *How many Christmases had I allowed melancholy to tinge my experience?* Wasted years trying to mimic a cultural image and coming up empty.

"When I was sixteen," I began, "I put off shopping until the last minute. It was Christmas Eve and already dark when I set out to buy a present for my mother. Annie and I drove our mother's car around Tucson, but all the stores were closed. In those days they let employees go home to their families. The parking lot at El Con, which was Tucson's only mall in 1966, was empty except for a lone shopping cart, lying on its side. We stopped to set it back on its wheels."

I was quiet so long that Megan prompted me, "Well, did you ever find a gift?"

I shook my head. "No, we finally just went home. The sad thing isn't that I neglected shopping, but that I missed the point: my mother didn't want a present—she wanted to spend Christmas Eve with me. I didn't understand. You see, we are the Christmas gifts. You and me."

She kissed me on the cheek. "I'm so glad you're here this year."

"So am I."

The sky was paling when Tom, Lucas, and Eve joined us in the living room. I pulled up my feet so that Lucas could sit on the sofa with his coffee mug, laced with egg nog. His upper lip was white from whipped cream.

"Jeanie and I have been having special time," Megan said proudly.

"I was telling her that people in our lives are the real Christmas gifts."

"Oh, that old story," Lucas rolled his eyes at Megan. "Don't worry, you're gonna get presents. Mom's just like that." He patted my feet affectionately.

I thought of his gift to us the previous spring. He had traded a brutal work assignment for family tickets to the resort's Easter buffet. The day had been warm. Happy diners roamed between several rooms along an open stone deck. Through large windows, the Catalina Mountains towered over us on one side, while the desert fell away to a panorama of the city on the other. Eve, Megan, Tom, and I were decked in our best. Our dusty Honda had been valet parked among the Mercedes and Porches. Megan wore a flowery spring frock with white shoes and Eve was dressed to match. Even Tom boasted a button-down shirt and slacks.

While we piled our plates with "mockingbirds' eyebrows" (Connie's phrase for expensive delicacies) from the decadent spread, Lucas stood in the sun, dressed as an enormous yellow rabbit, and greeted children. His costume had elevated spring shoes and a huge head with mesh screen over the eyes. He towered above the gay mob of youngsters with his fixed bunny grin and waving paw. Often I saw him squat to hold a child on his lap as a photographer took pictures for the parents.

The crowd was dissipating when Lucas finally joined us at the table. His face was red and splotchy, his shirt soaked. I could hear him wheeze with asthma. "Did you enjoy it?" he asked, gulping down a glass of ice water. He looked beat but exhilarated.

"Are you okay? Do you have your inhaler?" I quizzed.

"Mom, I'm fine." Irritation tinged his voice. "Dad?" he turned to Tom. "Isn't the food spectacular? Did you see the ice sculptures? My friend made those." His friends ranged from management to the basement, where a host of invisible workers spoke little English and took leftovers home. People smiled and called him by name.

"It was wonderful, Son. Thank you." Tom had said.

AFTER CHRISTMAS BREAKFAST, WE ALL pitched in to make Sylvia House welcoming. We cooked ham, clam chowder, potatoes, stuffing, turkey, gravy, homemade cranberry sauce, salad, yams, hot apple cider, coffee, and pies. By the time guests began arriving, two tables were loaded and treats spilled onto the back patio.

People came in waves all afternoon, eating and talking. The day was balmy and groups overflowed into the backyard where Tom was grilling a whole salmon. I paused to savor the happy throng. Megan was playing hopscotch on the walk with a friend; Eve was deep in conversation with Terrell (a physicist who lived alone in the desert and wrote novels). Lucas was mashing potatoes, sleeves rolled up and big hands working as he talked with Charlotte Cardon, my mother's eighty-nine-year-old friend. Charlotte was wearing a white Mexican blouse with embroidered flowers. She had a plate in one hand and was gesturing with the other. I caught the words, "…Oh yes! And did you see the ruins in Guatemala?" Watching them, I suddenly realized: *This is my mother's party!*

The stigma of divorce in the 1950s had separated us from "real" families. I first recognized this when my third-grade teacher had the class draw pictures of our fathers at work. I raised my hand to say that my parents were divorced and I couldn't remember my father. Kids turned curiously in their seats and the teacher looked annoyed. "Well, draw what you think he does," she said. There was a message here, something I was not supposed to talk about. I used black and orange crayons to depict a small plane flying low over forested mountains. The teacher didn't ask to see it.

My mother's response to ostracism was to open our home on Bean Alley to other outcasts. "What kind of Christmas could I make with two little girls and a turkey?" she had once said. Some of those people were at Sylvia House this day, having shown up in my life for half a century. Winnie's home had also been a refuge for Connie and Janet's young friends during the Depression. I had merely continued the tradition.

Annie and I grew up in a "cottage" that our mother rented for fifty dollars a month. The bathroom was so tiny that your knees touched the miniature tub when you sat on the toilet. Connie slept in a doll-sized bedroom (which had no door), while we had bunk beds in the living-and-dining room. A Plymouth Rock hen, three guinea pigs, and our big dog Sylvia ran freely in the house and unfenced yard. Connie could never bear to see anything caged and we brought the hen inside each night for safety. With the first paling of dawn, Henrietta's scaly feet would thump onto the hardwood floor. If you weren't fast enough, the next sound would be the squirt of a chicken constitutional. The guinea pigs, too, ran wild inside when the weather turned cool.

Folk of every walk came to Connie's parties. Conversations were stimulating and thoughtful. Our shabby little home bulged with happy people talking and eating. Groups wiggled into the small space and onto the front porch or stood on the yellowed Bermuda grass that merged with the neighbor's backyard. My mother made mince pies with hard sauce, pumpkin pies with whipped cream, turkey, stuffing, and mashed potatoes. Guests brought food as well. A trio of aging artists always came with a gallon of Mexican rum. Connie said they were longtime lovers: a woman and two men. I realized early in my life that love takes many forms. As night arrived, I would carry Henrietta inside where she perched on her nest crate like a sleepy hood ornament, unfazed by lively discourse between artist, scientist, beautician, and mailman. From my mother, I learned to value diversity and to invite people into my life.

As time carries me over most of my mother's lifespan, I find myself stumbling across her at different ages and seeing her in a softer light. Life, it seems, climbs in a spiral so that we may revisit earlier decisions from a higher perspective. In recalling Connie, I penetrate layers of my hidden self. When some lost memory of youthful behavior surfaces, I forgive that younger me—and my mother. *How could I have known until I lived this other side? How can anyone?* Self-forgiveness is the real meaning of absolution.

So I relaxed among my improbable family at Sylvia House that Christmas Day. Our home was crowded and messy, but no one seemed to notice and I didn't apologize. Moments of grace arise when we let go of how things ought to look and simply notice that life is always perfect. *Thank you for being a part of my journey*, I thought as I studied—and perhaps said goodbye to—each beloved face. *I treasure this moment.*

THE WEEK LUKE WAS BORN, Connie discovered cancer emerging like a mushroom above her left clavicle. In a recent physical, her doctor had missed a primary tumor "the size of an orange" (as she put it) in her left breast. I never palpated her large breasts. She was heavy and shy, and did not ask. Though not yet a nurse, I was knowledgeable, nevertheless, I could not reach into my mother's pain and so I hid from it.

Connie resisted cancer with the same fierceness she displayed in her fight against old age, pollution, poverty, and the Central Arizona Project. True to character, she read every book she could find on the horrors of death-by-cancer and how-to-kill-yourself. She joined the Hemlock Society and made her plan. I was to help, maybe even inject some lethal drug. Her colorful imagination flooded with stories of bulging eyes and gasping breath. She was not going to die that way!

"Mother, I will not kill you," I had declared. "I'll read the books, support your choice, and I will be there with you—but you must do it yourself."

It was not easy for any of us. Connie was sixty-eight then and living in public housing. She drove an ancient borrowed car of a sickly yellow color with a cracked vinyl roof. The trunk filled with water each time it rained and sloshed with rust and oil. Tom and I were financially and emotionally underwater with our glass studio and newborn son. Annie had finally gathered the courage to pull free of her marriage and was supporting her two small children as a barmaid. She and I took turns accompanying our mother to doctor appointments—her allies against a calloused Medicaid system that shuffled her from line to line.

"Promise you won't leave me," Connie had pleaded the day of her biopsy.

I took her graceful hand. We were seated in the waiting room of the eighth floor obstetrical clinic at University Medical Center. The room was full of contented pregnant women and crawling toddlers. I would later come to know this clinic from the privileged side of those doors when I wheeled in women who carried tenuous pregnancies or fetal anomalies.

"Mrs. Helmericks?" A nursing assistant stood in the doorway with a clipboard. "Come with me please." I rose with my mother, but the woman barred my way. "Just Mrs. Helmericks."

"I promised to stay with her," I said.

"We'll get you in a few minutes. We're just going to get her ready."

I hesitated, cowed by the official word. My frightened mother, heavy-footed and limping, vanished through the forbidden doors and started down a long hallway.

I sat obediently, at war with courage. *NO!* I thought. *I will not leave her.* Abruptly, I stood and pushed by the protesting unit assistant in time to see my mother disappear into one of the anonymous rooms. She was wearing her red wool coat with a purple scarf. Beneath her bulk, her bare legs narrowed into insubstantial ankles draped in limp socks and orthopedic shoes.

"I told her I would be here," I stated defiantly as I barged into the room.

The aide glared at me. She had lied about returning for me; I could see it in her face. She shoved a folded gown into my mother's hands. "Take off all your clothes," she snapped. "You can leave your socks on."

Then we were alone in the cold room. I helped my mother undress and tied the skimpy gown behind her. She sat on the examining table, tugging at the short gown while her little feet dangled. Minutes later, a resident doctor tapped lightly then opened the door carrying a surgical tray. He glanced at me with irritation.

"Lie back please," he ordered Connie. His voice was colorless, flat.

I helped her change positions as he opened the tray onto a stand and spread a blue drape across her chest. I remained standing on the other side, holding my mother's hand. She squeezed so hard that my fingers hurt. Her face was a grimace, eyes darting like frightened fish as the doctor turned on the spotlight and laid out his instruments.

"Don't move," he commanded. "This is a sterile field."

"Don't forget, you promised I could have Valium," Connie whimpered in the small voice of a frightened child. I glanced at the surgeon, but he did not look up.

"Oh, this is nothing," he dismissed. "We'll be done here in just a moment."

My mother started to cry. Her eyes squeezed shut and tears leaked out the corners. Red lips pulled back from clenched teeth, and I could see her jaw muscles working.

"You promised!" Connie sobbed in a small voice. She was never a fighter. Her first inclination was to flee or plead, to live outside the rules by omission. From her, I had learned the backdoor approach: it's easier to get forgiveness than permission. Yet she needed an advocate. *What good was I, if I couldn't speak up?*

"Give her the Valium," I said.

The doctor made an exasperated noise and slid the wheeled stool backward. He pulled off his sterile gloves with a snap and reached into a drawer for a syringe.

That last year of Connie's life was terribly hard, but it was also a time of completion. Most people say that they want to die suddenly in their sleep, but there can be value in the longer path. Life's closing bell signals a time to put away the inessential. My mother prepared for death as if planning an expedition: she took her best clothes to the dry cleaners, wrote a memorial service, penciled a simple will, bought the cheapest cremation package, and had her teeth cleaned. She read voraciously about cancer and the process of dying, but whatever she did on a spiritual level, she did not share. Despite her garrulous presence, Connie was a very private person. I, who knew her rants and opinions to the point of boredom, knew little of her inner life. Perhaps this is always the case, for we see our parents through their roles. I was a cherished tributary to her life's river, but certainly not the main channel.

Luke was a few weeks old when we joined Annie and her children in taking Connie up Madera Canyon in the Santa Rita Mountains, south of Tucson. Years before, Annie and I had discovered a small tributary off the main creek—a steep ravine where people seldom ventured.

We parked in the scrub oak at the end of a dirt track and climbed a short distance into pines. Connie walked slowly, but we were in no hurry. Ben and Faith played along the creek as we ascended. The brook slid between big sycamore trunks and plunged over little waterfalls. Lichen-colored boulders sunned in the April afternoon. To either side, cliffs jutted into a blue sky and beyond them we caught glimpses of snow along distant ridges. A bed of pine needles and fallen oak leaves softened our steps. The breeze tasted of withered leaves and damp, awakening earth. For years, Annie and I had invited our mother on local hikes, but she dismissed these tamer excursions: it had to be wilderness or nothing. Now as we ambled into the mountain cleft, I saw her awaken to country she had loved in her youth and shared with us as children. She seemed to momentarily shed opinions about development, water shortage, population, and corporate greed—a snake pulling free of an old skin.

We made a simple camp, spreading blankets and sleeping bags beneath great ponderosa, whose rusty puzzle-piece bark smelled of vanilla. Dusk arrived, muting the colors, and stars began to appear in the darkening sky. Frost sparkled between the bare sycamores. A cold breeze wandered down the canyon and gusted our small fire while we reminisced of the Mackenzie River and outback Australia. It wasn't completely idyllic—life never is. Connie held forth on her strong views. Faith and Ben were restless with the uncertainty of their young lives. Luke howled his infant protests, and my body ached from sitting on the cold ground, holding and nursing him. Still it was a precious time, as we all knew—a time of closure.

The next morning we hunkered on icy boulders near the brook, roasting hunks of round steak on sticks. Camping with our mother was always primitive. We wrapped the burned, half-raw meat with cheese and tortillas and ate it from cold fingers. It was the kind of fare Connie called "real food." The canyon still hung in shadow, but the cliffs above were bathed in golden dawn. Birds whistled as they flitted through the branches. The creek gurgled under a crust of new ice.

Connie leaned against the mottled trunk of an ancient sycamore—serene in the early light, at home against her tree. She fingered the colorful scarf that draped her thick, red hair. "I really think I'll keep my hair," she said. "It's been two weeks since I started chemotherapy. Some people do, you know. I believe that dyeing it all these years has kept it healthy. I haven't brushed it much, but I'm hoping." She smiled shyly, the vanity of hair putting death into perspective, then slowly pulled off the scarf. Her hair fell away in clumps, drifting into the dead sycamore leaves like the fur of a caribou killed by wolves. "Oh well," she sighed, "it's only hair. If it were my head, I would be more concerned."

Despite her vow to kill herself, Connie submitted to a double mastectomy, chemotherapy, and radiation. The treatments were far worse than the disease. She clung to each implied hope and accepted every option. There was no particular doctor responsible for her care: just a surgeon, a radiologist, and a chemotherapist. The internist who had failed to notice her tumor would probably not even remember her. Her chest, now flat and scarred, was further scalded by radiation. At one point the doctors wanted to "place meat probes in me and microwave me." When the cancer invaded her brain, someone suggested cutting a portal in her skull to soak it with the chemicals.

"Why?" I ranted to Tom. "It's disseminated! What possible good could come from this? She's just a dot on a graph in someone's research."

"You can call a halt," he reminded me.

Tom was right. From the beginning my mother's doctors had talked to me while Connie sat on the exam table and listened with anxiety. I spoke their language, while her thoughts were fanciful and frightened. Although I had come as her ally, somehow her power had passed to me. Now her brain was affected and as the end came into view, I was the one who called the chemotherapist and said, "No more."

The doctors withdrew. Her surgeon, radiologist, and chemotherapist closed their files. She was no longer strong enough to stand in line for the disinterested internist, so I managed her care. Still she refused hospice, saying, "That's for dying people!" When Tom and I asked her to live with us, she said, "It's too far from the hospital. What if I need help?" I arranged for friends to check on her and we began taking her meals.

A year after her diagnosis, I brought Connie home for lunch on Sunset Road. It would be her final outing. Her movements were slow and careful as we walked out to see the garden and my colorful assortment of chickens. Her short hair had grown back fine and gray, curlier than before, and her skin looked somehow translucent.

My mother had never been a good listener, thinking perhaps that her opinions could save me. "You don't need any more children," she had said when I became pregnant—as if Annie's were enough. But this day was different. Connie was gentle and open in a manner I had never seen, even allowing me to give her a massage. Afterward, we sat quietly for a long time, gazing out our big windows at the fishpond and trees.

"I'm okay," I assured her. "You don't have to worry. I have a beautiful life, a husband who loves me, and a treasured son. You can let go." All of my life I had tried to reach beyond my mother's ideas about me. On this one blessed afternoon, I felt my words sink home. That one moment of clarity was sufficient to complete for me a lifetime of relationship.

IN THE FOLLOWING DAYS, CONNIE'S mouth became bloody with sores from chemotherapy and she could no longer eat the meals we brought. She started falling, her bones breaking easily as metastases invaded. She was also losing her vision. One afternoon I found her on the bathroom floor of her little apartment.

"I am going to have to call an ambulance." I sat next to her on the cramped vinyl floor and looked levelly into her gray-green eyes. Taking a breath to steady myself, I continued slowly. "Once you are in their care, you will have no choice. If you are going to kill yourself, this is the time." It was the hardest thing I had ever said.

Defiance flashed across her face and she almost bared her teeth. "You think I'm going to die!"

"Yes," I nodded. "I do."

I sat with her for a long moment and then got up to place the call.

In the emergency room, the resident took me aside and said, "She's dying. There's nothing we can do for her. You should take her home."

I thought of our glass studio and tiny bathroom, of my mother's fear. "No," I finally said. "You'll have to figure it out."

He admitted her to the hospital, where their social worker found placement in a nursing home. It was totally unsuitable for the dying: a ghastly place of dementia, crazed yelling, bad smells, and overworked staff. Although Connie could tolerate only sips of fluid, plates of institutional food congealed on her bedside tray. I bought a baby sippy cup and again hired friends to relieve Annie, Tom, and me at her side.

Connie was determined to complete her ninth book. She guarded scraps of notebook paper under her pillow, afraid someone might take them while she slept. These she filled with wandering and nonsensical prose, written in a deteriorating hand. At one point, she believed she was on the top floor of a building with wolves killing children in the street below. Her chemotherapist had mentioned that one of her medications could cause psychosis, so I badgered his office and finally got an order to have it discontinue.

Two days later, my mother was weak but clear. Perhaps stopping the drug made a difference, or maybe she pulled herself out of the fog to deliver her message. When I arrived, she looked sharply in my direction and said, "Get me out of this hell hole."

"Can I call hospice?" I asked.

"Yes. I am ready."

My mother and I had begun our separate journeys at Saint Mary's Hospital, thirty-seven years before. Now we spiraled back for another parting. Tucson's first hospital was a bit shabby from years of serving an ever greater portion of the destitute, but the hospice staff welcomed us with kindness. They gave Connie a gentle (and needed) bath before easing her into fresh gown and sheets.

I sat in the quiet room and gazed out the window at palo verde trees, yellow with blossoms. My mother was asleep, her breathing gentle. Since arriving, she had relaxed and slept most of the time. She seemed to be stepping between the worlds, wandering on the fringe of that great unknown where certainties dissolve in a land of mist. When I looked back, she had turned her face to me, eyes glistening with tears.

"Jeanie," she said, reaching for the hand she could no longer see, "there are people going backpacking to the stars. I can see them!" Her voice faltered and tears seeped from the corners of her eyes. Her skin looked pale and her mouth was dry, the lips peppered with sores. I took a pink sponge stick and dipped it in the cup of water to gently swab her mouth.

"Jeanie, I want so much to go… but I am too old and sick…" She started to cry, a dry and wheezing sound.

"You can go," I assured her, my own voice breaking. "Relax and let go. You are exactly right for such a wonderful adventure."

"Am I?" She seemed to breathe a bit easier. "I want so much to go… backpacking to the stars…"

During Connie's last few days, the larger clan gathered, taking turns at her bedside. Aunt Jane and Chickie arrived from New York and stayed with us out on the desert. Janet and Bert drove from Scottsdale and rented a motel room. We traded vigils until Connie asked us all to leave.

"It just takes too much effort for her to be with you," the kindly nurse explained. "Dying is hard work and often people want to be alone."

A day later a hospice nurse called. "Your mother is in a light coma, but very restless and anxious. Maybe your presence will help now."

The others had departed, so Annie, Tom, and I stood vigil by turns. We brought a tape deck and played gentle, evocative music. We improvised meditations, leading her down from snow line, along rippling brooks, onto a dancing river, and at last to the great sea. Connie quieted, dropping deeper into the coma, no longer fighting or afraid.

I took Annie's place late in the evening. Pulling up the chair, I settled in with a cup of coffee and reached for Connie's slender hand, the fingernails still perfect. It was cool and mottled, the color of tallow. Her peaceful breath faltered, paused, resumed. A few minutes later, she exhaled for the last time and slowly the hand turned to wax in mine, a dead thing, pallid and strange. Life does not depart from the colony we think of as "our body" in a single moment.

Cells blink out one by one. Nevertheless, a profound change washed over her and it was clear that Connie was no longer in the room. I searched my heart for her presence, but whatever makes up that essence we call "life," I found no trace. My mother had finally embarked for the stars.

We held a simple memorial at the Church of Religious Science, the same place Tom and I had been married. It was a warm day and we had a catered meal set up on tables on the grass outside. I wore my wedding dress—a beautiful flounce of cream ruffles and lace that Annie had bought. Each of Connie's family spoke. A few weeks later the clan gathered at Madera Canyon. I carried the simple cardboard box of Connie's ashes as we ascended the creek. We chose a nameless spot and buried them between the sheltering trees and close to the sound of running water. Faith braided a child's cross of twigs and wildflowers to place on the awakening earth. Holding hands in a circle, we remembered Connie and returned her to the planet she had loved so fiercely.

That night I dreamed of a great eagle, soaring along the high cornice of a snowy mountain. Below her, the land fell away—magnificent and wild. I awoke feeling happy.

Constance Helmericks: January 4, 1918 ~ April 22, 1987

Connie Helmericks paddling the Peace River in 1964.

Chapter 16
FAIRBANK, ARIZONA

January 2007

The rivers of Southern Arizona flow north out of Mexico—the San Pedro, Cienega Creek, and Santa Cruz—eventually joining the Gila and Salt on their way to the spigots of Phoenix. From there, remnants trickle west into the Colorado River to be fought over by several states. Any water that remains finds its way back to Mexico as the dead and poisonous runoff of agribusiness. However, a few miles north of Bisbee, the lovely San Pedro is still a laughing creek where it passes the ghost town of Fairbank. As the major migration corridor through the Sonoran Desert, were the San Pedro not protected as a National Conservation Area, two hundred fifty species of birds would be in trouble.

Like Bisbee, Fairbank was named after a Chicago financier who probably never visited. Founded in 1881 at a Y in the New Mexico and Arizona Railroad, Fairbank had swollen to fifteen thousand people within a year, and for a brief moment was one of the largest settlements in Arizona.

The dirt parking lot was empty when Tom and I arrived. We borrowed a map from a wooden box and started north on a three-mile loop of trail through riparian wetlands. Water chuckled between the old cottonwood trees and birds were singing in the tawny grasses. The day was sunny and I opened my shirt to let the breeze finger my ribs as I followed Tom beneath leafless trees and onto a bluff above the stream. Ahead, the path swung east toward a steep hill and the ruins of Grand Central Mill. From 1881 to 1886, the whole valley had trembled with relentless noise as iron rods in the stamp mill pounded day and night, pulverizing silver ore. Long teams of mules had hauled ore out of the Tombstone Mountains to this mill. Here it was crushed to a fine powder and mixed with water and mercury then heated to vaporize the mercury. Old pictures of the mill show a land strangely barren—mesquite trees decimated to feed the mill.

Five years after the town's founding, the mines began to flood and Fairbank dwindled away. A few dozen graves remain today, scratched haphazardly into a rocky hillside. *Where did fifteen thousand people live?* I wondered, as I gazed out at the San Pedro Valley from the lonely graveyard. I imagined tents, lean-tos, and dirty men packed into the few buildings.

Wintery sun rode down the sky as Tom and I picked our way onto the old road that traveled a few feet above a seasonally swampy bottomland. Made by human hands, this path was somehow proportional. Curve-billed thrashers flitted through the young mesquite trees, calling in evening tones. A century after the silver was spent and the people of Fairbank forgotten, the land is recovering. I thought of the damage wrought with today's machines. *What will our legacy be?*

LUCAS WAS SEVENTEEN THE SUMMER he and I volunteered in the mountains of Guatemala. He towered over the Mayan Indians like a spruce tree in a stand of alders, and I could always spot him in the crowded marketplace where people squatted in the street selling corn, fresh vegetables, lime dug from the hillsides, and dried fish. The people were poor in a way Lucas had never seen. A large family might live beneath strips of corrugated iron held aloft by four posts with boards wired between them. There would be a cook fire in one corner and old milk jugs to carry water from the lake. Children owned only two sets of hand-woven clothes—one to wear and one to wash—yet they had sunny faces. Lucas fell in love with them and started an open-air class, teaching reading and math to street urchins whose parents could not afford school. Kids would arrive with infant siblings strapped to their backs. When we walked the cobbled streets of San Lucas Tolimán, they ran up to take his hand, calling *"Libra! Libra!"* (Book!)

We had journeyed alone, but sometimes joined teams of medical students climbing single file up mountain trails through jungle to remote villages, where fields of corn and beans—no bigger than bedrooms—were scratched into clearings between giant trees. Seeing us, the cheerful little people lined up outside buildings no better than chicken coops. There are perhaps thirty dialects of Mayan and few of the Indians spoke Spanish. All afternoon our patients would flood into some stark shed; those who understood Spanish would explain their neighbor's complaint to Lucas and he would translate it into English. The medical students dispensed outdated drugs they knew little about to people whose ailments they guessed, giving instructions through this three-language barrier to folks who had no clean water, clock, or a heated home. The Indians were grateful and amazingly generous with their smiles—the only thing they had.

"I want to come back to Guatemala," Lucas told me as we settled into our damp bedding for a black night among the bedbugs.

"Then you need education," I said into the darkness. "They have plenty of warm bodies. Bring something they can use."

The town's generator was off again and we had extinguished our candle. Beneath our cots, water seeped through the tile floor where roaches and centipedes crawled. The building, we were told, had been used as a torture chamber during the Guatemalan civil war. The U.S.-backed dictatorship had killed or "disappeared" perhaps two hundred thousand people in the 1970s and '80s when the indigenous poor had asked for a portion of their lands back. The spark of Mayan independence had been soundly squashed.

Here is part of a letter Lucas wrote to his high school Spanish teacher:

> *I got back from Guatemala a couple of weeks ago, and it was such a special experience that I now have a strong desire to minor in Spanish. I always knew you were a good man, but I had no idea how much I owe you. There were volunteers who were 5th-year Spanish students and not as fluent as I was. It made me realize how easy it could have been to take Spanish and not learn anything. Because of being semi-fluent, I was able to teach three girls who could not afford to go to school. What an experience! I felt so privileged to see what it is like for kids in these countries. The girls that I taught (simple reading, writing, and math) lived in a family of 13 in a house that was so run down I was afraid to knock lest the wall fall down. There was no indoor plumbing and no floor, and it rained every day, yet these children were clean and cheerful.*
>
> *One of the most profound moments occurred one night while I was waiting for a friend to go to a dance. A young local boy came and sat down with me. I started talking with him and said that I thought Guatemala was the prettiest place I had ever seen. He looked at me and said, "This is a country where a lot of people die." I was startled and said, "True, but the people that have the hardest lives become*

the strongest." He thought for a little and then said, "This is a country where men come with pistols and kill everyone."

I feel strongly I will return to Latin America within the next few years. Perhaps there is even a career in it for me...

Your friend and student,

LUCAS

Returning home to Arizona was a culture shock for Lucas, comparing the unhappy spoiled American kids with the open faces of children he had seen.

"I'll never feel sorry for Americans again," he had declared as we emerged from a matinée movie where we had listened to kids whining about popcorn and soda.

"There are many forms of poverty," I told him. "These children are spiritually malnourished." *Without suffering*, I wondered, *how do we develop appreciation and compassion?*

THE LENGTHENING DAYS OF JANUARY brought the question of our next destination. As in Wisconsin, I was asked to remain on in Sierra Vista. The pay was excellent and being close to Lucas was a special treat, but obstetrics is a team sport. Although I was surviving, it wasn't any fun here. Then, too, you can only play the odds so long before someone gets hurt. Unfair staffing is dangerous.

"You have a triage patient," the charge nurse said over her shoulder. She and the unit assistant were on the Internet sharing pictures of someone's wedding. Triage meant a pregnant woman had arrived with a problem—anything from labor to a cold.

"Why's she here?" I asked. It was Sunday and I had only one labor patient.

"Term. Labor check. She came in earlier and night shift sent her home. She lives in Douglas and couldn't possibly have driven there and back. Check her and send her home. Don't admit her!"

Linda was a petite girl of fourteen who had been in early labor for two days. She stared at me with frightened eyes as I turned on the monitor and positioned the belts. I wedged her onto one side with a pillow supporting her back and then seated her mother in the lone chair. The mother, a slight woman in her early thirties, looked worn and tired. The girl's father stood hesitantly by the curtain.

"We live in Douglas," the father began in careful English. He was wiry and dark, his eyes intense and pleading. He was wearing a clean shirt and faded jeans, his dusty cowboy hat gripped in callused hands. "It's a long drive, Ma'am. We can't take her home. She's in, how you say? Mucho dolore."

Much pain, I nodded. *And exhausted*. Prodromal labor takes a toll. The girl's mother was silent, glancing from me to her daughter whose face was indeed contorted in pain. "Do you have friends you could stay with in Sierra Vista?" I asked.

He shook his head. "How we tell when to come?"

"First let me check her," I answered. "Relax and just breathe, Daughter," I said in my poor Spanish. "Don't fight the contractions. That's right." I held her gaze and took a deep breath with her. "Your body knows what it is doing." I continued in English—a soothing patter of sound. The girl had yet to say a word.

I continued talking as I put on a sterile glove and inserted the first two fingers of my right hand into her vagina. The baby was very low. No wonder she felt distressed. There was a paper-thin cervix and a tightly bulging bag of water. Four centimeters—that would buy her an admission. I could feel the bones of the baby's head. *All good.*

I grinned broadly. "You're going to have a baby! It's in a good position. You will stay here in the hospital."

I pulled off the glove and ran my hands along her smooth belly, feeling the child's spine. *Seven pounds, fourteen ounces*, I guessed—a big baby for her, but well descended into the pelvis. "Everything is good," I nodded encouragingly. I put my face close to hers and looked directly into her frightened eyes. "I know you are in pain," I said slowly, "but you are going to be okay. Your baby is doing fine," I pointed to the monitor strip. "Give me a few minutes. I have to call the doctor to get you admitted."

The father spoke quietly in Spanish to his wife and both parents smiled their relief and gratitude at me.

"She's active," I informed the charge nurse as I strode down the hall to ready a room. "Four centimeters, 100 percent effaced, plus one station. Please stamp up the papers and get her admitted," I told the unit assistant.

"I told you not to admit her! You were supposed to send her home," hissed the charge nurse.

"They live in Douglas," I said. "That's a two-hour drive. Her parents are very worried."

"Oh, yeah? Well, where were they when their fourteen-year-old daughter got pregnant?"

This wasn't worth a response. *Pick your battles.* At four centimeters the girl was staying. Besides, this baby was on the way.

The charge nurse dialed the doctor and I heard her say, "No real change. She's three centimeters. Night shift sent her home earlier, but they obviously didn't drive to Douglas! Maybe we can admit her for pain control… okay, we'll do that." Her face appeared in the doorway as I laid out IV tubing. "She can have Stadol for pain. She only gets one person in the room with her."

I peeked in on my other patient, who had an epidural and was asleep, and then wheeled Linda into an adjacent room—bringing both parents. The father is the backbone of the traditional Mexican family. He would stand in a corner with eyes averted, but he needed to be here. I thought of the power assumed in the name of institutions, of the dread a parent feels with a hurt child. I remembered taking Luke to the emergency room when he was little, how the kindness or mean-spiritedness of strangers can hold one's life in the balance. Living is hard and messy. We cannot keep our children safe, yet if we help them find their wings, they may yet fly beyond us. No one has walked into the world they will inherit; they need our help to find wisdom and courage. Something beyond my reticence to fight awakened. I would not let this girl be bullied! Medical knowledge does not belong to individuals, but was wrested from a thousand generations of human misery. This was a trust I would not break.

I helped Linda into a gown, inserted an IV into her wrist, and administered the drug. She dozed between contractions, buying me a few minutes to start the mass of computer, charting. Clearly, however, the baby was not going to wait.

"Six centimeters," I reported to the charge nurse. "Call the doctor and get labor orders. She wants an epidural."

Twenty minutes flew past as I worked to run in a liter of IV fluid, set up for an epidural kit, chart everything, and ready the room for delivery. This included wheeling in a baby warmer—for we only had two. Most first-time mothers progress slowly, but occasionally labor moves with violent speed. Long before the anesthesiologist or obstetrician arrived, Linda's water broke. Soon I could see the baby's dark hair.

Linda panicked and started screaming in Spanish, "I can't! I can't!"

I stuck my head out the door and called, "She's delivering! I need a nurse for the baby and a tech!"

"Daughter! Stay with me!" I commanded quietly in my poor Spanglish. "It's almost over. Pull your legs back and push! Linda, don't try to run away. Down and out—it's the only way. Push into the pain! Now… push!"

The girl was trying to escape up the bed as another contraction swept over her. I wedged her knee back with my body, keeping my gloves sterile. The other leg was kicking free. I turned to her mother, who stood paralyzed and staring, and called her over in broken Spanglish.

Keeping one hand on the baby's head I reached for a sterile towel to protect the perineum from tearing. "Get that other leg!" I told the charge nurse who rushed into the room followed by the others. Peripherally, I could see the practiced dance of readying equipment, turning on lights, and drawing up Pitocin to keep the mother from bleeding after delivery.

The baby's long brow bulged relentlessly through, followed at last by a grimacing downward-looking face. Almost at once, it began rotating clockwise. I ran my finger inside the taut vagina around the baby's neck, feeling for a possible nuchal cord, then reached for the bulb to suction mouth and nose.

"The head is out! It's almost over," I kept up a constant encouragement to the girl. "Now a big push!"

Placing my hands on each side of the baby's head, I exerted a downward pressure. It was tight, but slowly the anterior shoulder slid from beneath the pubic bone. Then I angled the head up to free the posterior shoulder. I slid my grip to the back of the neck as the rest of the body followed in a slippery gush.

"It's a boy!" I called out. "And just look at all that hair! Isn't he beautiful!" I held up the squirming infant and he peed.

The big, rubbery baby bunched up and let out a lusty squall. His eyes were squeezed shut and his little fists were clenched. Someone flipped a warm blanket onto Linda's chest. I laughed and placed him in his mother's arms as I rubbed him dry. Then I clamped and cut his thick, gelatinous cord. *Did I mention that I love my job?* The baby struggled and howled again. Then he caught his breath, opened his dark eyes, and gazed intently into his mother's face. Linda looked down in astonishment, her eyes clear and focused. Hesitantly, she cradled this new life. His tiny hand caught one of her fingers and pulled it toward his rosebud mouth.

I never tire of this miraculous flowering, that crystal moment when a girl becomes a mother. Birth is the transformation of two lives. Linda had stepped through a doorway and would never be the same. In some unfathomable way, the wandering current of her young life was suddenly both defined and expanded. Because this small human called it forth, she would be fierce and noble beyond her years—her life no longer about herself. Portals of initiation into the sacred are easily missed. Giving birth is profound. Usually, it is trivialized with chatter and hospital routine. Often the woman is only glad that the ordeal is over, her partner disappears into his cell phone, and the family begins comparing the baby with other relatives. Whenever I can, I hold the doorway open and allow the new mother to fall into—Mystery.

Babies are no more identical than old people. Although new to this dimension, they are amazingly conscious. Some arrive screaming mad, others sulky and whining; many come in wonder at the bright world—eyes quietly alive with interest. I have even seen babies whose small faces were distraught with grief when they arrive unwanted, perhaps the "wrong" sex or the result of rape. Infants are deeply connected with the web of life, boundless souls, abruptly squeezed into tight little packages in a moment as grand and terrifying as death. It is something we sense about them, what Wordsworth meant when he said we come "trailing clouds of glory."

~

"Would you like to spend next summer in Alaska with us?" Tom asked Lucas on our next trip to Tucson. We were treating him at BoBo's to eggs, toast, fried potatoes, and bacon. Lucas had ordered the biggest platter.

"We could try for the Divide," I added. "Maybe we'll finally make it."

Hiking to the Arctic Continental Divide was an elusive family dream. From our cabin it was a circuitous backpack of about one hundred thirty miles without trail or a chance to resupply. I had made the trek in my twenties, and always wanted to share it with them. The three of us had attempted it in 2000, the spring Luke was fourteen, but were turned back in the high mountains by meltwater.

"We can't afford Eve and Megan this time," Tom qualified, "and it would be helpful if they could look after the house in your absence."

"Eve couldn't come right now," Lucas said. His tone was dry. He ran a hand through dark stubble on his chin. "She's putting all her energy into nursing school and needs to make money over the summer."

"We plan to be there June through September. You could fly in with us, then charter out in time for classes," I offered.

I watched the idea taking root in his face. *Humans aren't designed to move in a straight line,* I thought. It had been a long time since Lucas had wandered free of the pavement. He had packed on forty pounds and just short of twenty-one, he was looking worn. Like many young people, his life had narrowed to a few gates in a fenced landscape.

At fourteen he had written:

> *From the time I was seven until I turned thirteen, I was someone I hated. That winter in the Arctic I started caribou hunting alone around the end of October and ended sometime in May. I would sit in*

the snow for up to ten hours with 15-minute breaks every two hours or so, whenever my toes became numb and painful. It was so quiet that I heard only my thoughts. Noise is constant in our lives. In the Arctic, often there was none. The snow dampened all sound. It was a fantasy world, a world so beautiful, peaceful, and awe-inspiring, it defies the imagination. It was like being wrapped in one of those dreams that you wake up from not remembering anything, but with an overwhelming sense of joy.

I was very sad that my friends didn't write me. I felt totally alone, and in a way I was. Maybe that is what made me who I am. The power of solitude is amazing. Gradually an enveloping calm took over my body and mind. I came to believe that the way we were living was "normal." Perhaps our society is really what is fake. Out there I had time to contemplate such questions. This was the place where I found my true self.

Now as I watched him busy with the huge plate of food, I wondered what had become of that young man.

"I've told Eve that I need some time to be single and young," Lucas said abruptly. I reached across the table to touch his arm, but he shook off my hand. "She understands. She's moving in with her brother this week. We've decided to continue as friends. Eve is the best friend I ever had. Megan took it pretty hard and that really bothers me, but I'm just not ready for parenthood."

"Just be her friend," I said, knowing that he probably didn't want my advice. "You may not have the same relationship, but you still care."

"Kids are a lot of work," he admitted. "They mess up your stuff and don't clean up. I find myself feeling resentful and that's not how I want to be."

I nodded. "Being a good parent is a full-time job. I wanted you more than anything else in the world. Had you been born earlier, I might have felt weighed down. My teenage moms think babies are 'cute' or they want someone to love them. They don't understand the commitment it takes to raise a conscious human being."

"I'll have to find other roommates that I can trust." He continued after a pause, "Let me think about it."

"We need to know in time to get you a cheap ticket to Alaska," Tom said.

Lucas raised his eyes. "Yes," he said slowly, "I'd love to come. I just need to work out the details."

We volunteer in Guatemala the summer Lucas was seventeen

Lucas works with Tom remodeling the Sylvia House for our extended family, 2006

Chapter 17

TRIBUTARIES

January 2007

I hung up the phone from an interview. "We're going to Fresno, California." Tom was reading by the window, his face lit by the fading afternoon. Beyond the balcony, Old Bisbee climbed in pastel shades through falling snow and dissolved into a milky sky. I had already scraped eight inches of snow from the car and lined it up for a straight shot into Brewery Gulch for my morning's commute.

"I don't really have a mental picture of the area," I admitted.

"I think it's flat and hot—a great agricultural valley." He set his book aside to rummage through our maps and spread one on the carpet. We got on our knees, rumps in the air, and studied it.

"Fresno could be the state's belly button," I commented, "right in the middle." The thought of California, eighth largest economy in the world, made me uneasy. *All those cars*. On the other hand, the state had passed its own version of the Kyoto Protocol—the global-warming treaty—when the United States refused.

"Look at the places we can visit." Tom ran a finger over the map. "We'll be close to the ocean and the Sierras."

"I'll be working at a community hospital that serves a diverse population, including migrant farm workers," I told him. "A thousand deliveries a month! Twenty-five labor rooms, fifty-something double postpartum rooms, and a twelve-bed triage. It pays 'crisis rates,' and I'm sure I'll earn it. There are paperwork hoops and a new nursing license to buy, but this time I'll insist that we live close to the hospital!"

"I wanna take my truck." Tom got stiffly to his feet and helped me up. "We can drive the car over and I'll fly back for the truck so we'll have it for Alaska. We can pack it with our summer gear." Excitement was growing in his eyes.

"If you get a round-trip ticket, you can return the car to Tucson in May before we head north." We grinned at one another like kids skipping school.

THERE WAS LITTLE IN THE way of goodbye in Sierra Vista, though I did make one good friend. Our last Bisbee dawn spilled into Tombstone Canyon, pushing fog up the wet cliffs. I listened to birds awakening and recalled the frenetic pace of central California. Nevertheless, I was excited at the weightless feeling of drifting free—unknown possibilities. In thirteen weeks, we would leave freeways behind on our long migration north.

We packed the old Honda to the ceiling and took to the empty road, headed first to Tucson. Every leaf was edged in light, and ribbons of snow laced the canyon walls. Gamely, our overloaded car climbed between the pink outcroppings to Mule Pass one last time. We emerged from the dark tunnel into tendrils of fog that wreathed the close peaks in shifting mystery. *Off on another adventure!*

Sylvia House was in flux. Though Lucas had yet to find new roommates, Eve was moving out and rooms were strewn with boxes. Two and a half hectic days followed: taxes, wills, financial advisor, and packing. I sorted the stifling shed, carting items to Goodwill as I repacked our next two lives—Fresno and Alaska. The former we stuffed into the Honda; the latter would remain with Tom's truck.

It was afternoon when our overloaded car struggled into the torrent of vehicles headed northwest on I-10 toward Phoenix. Beyond my window, the desecrated Sonoran Desert baked beneath shopping centers, identical housing tracts, and blowing trash. Two hours, later my cousin Bert-Son and his gentle wife Nadine welcomed us into their quiet home. Nadine was my age with long, gray hair, a lovely body pierced with jewelry, and the charm of a happy child.

Early the next morning we slipped out into a cloudy Sunday for a breakfast with my aunt and uncle. Landscaped streets opened the sleeping city for us alone—broad and tree lined with curving walls and public art. For all its flagrant misuse of water, Arizona's capital is designed for vehicles. The deserted freeway was a city block wide with bougainvillea blooming up monolithic overpasses. I pictured these vast arteries after the collapse of civilization, imagining nomads traversing them on foot. Like the Arctic, deserts heal slowly. *How long before the land takes it back?*

"Where is everyone going in such a hurry?" I mused. Tom remained comfortably silent. Years had rounded him like a river stone, smoothing away corners of argument and opinion. I wondered if his mellowing had left me with the sharper edges.

Forty minutes later, we pulled into Janet and Bert's driveway beneath orange and grapefruit trees. Uncle Bert laughed when he opened the kitchen door of their modest Scottsdale home. "They're here!" he called loudly over his shoulder. Janet's happy chirping came from a distant room.

I eased into his big arms. The flesh felt soft and the gray whiskers on his neck smelled familiar and safe. Like Tom, my uncle had gentled over time. I had some vague childhood memory of a remote man who smoked and pushed me off his lap, but Bert too had been polished in life's current. His hug buried Tom next. The two men had a special bond, cemented on their drive to Alaska a few years before. It was the relationship that my father had missed out on when he tried to dominate Tom. I wondered if he knew it.

"Well, you two are looking good." Bert's voice was still deep. Silvered hair hung in a loose braid down his rounded back. He was leaning on a walker now and there was a small oxygen tank at his waist. A thin lifeline of tubing was looped over his big ears and I could hear a faint whisper as the flow of oxygen kicked on with each breath. His skin was spotted and the hawk nose was carved with divots from cancer surgery. Dark circles hung in twin moons beneath his steady eyes, but his teeth and hearing were still excellent and he continued to volunteer doing taxes for seniors.

We sat at the table in their airy kitchen. Sliding patio doors fronted a secluded garden on one side, while an expanse of living room lay on the other. Janet and Bert had owned this home since I was a child and tailored it to age in place. Each item, from the Persian rugs to paintings by Bert's mother, held personal meaning for them. As with Winnie's house, this deliberation created a quiet feeling of sanctuary.

"Did you find someone to do your cleaning?" I asked. The kitchen was immaculate and orderly. I recalled my first nursing instructor telling us that becoming nurses would forever change us. I had become a professional busybody, always assessing.

"Oh, yes, some time ago. A mother and daughter come once a week. As you can see," he pointed at the walker, "I've got Janet's malady. Spinal stenosis.

The neurologist said he could operate. I asked what my second option was and he told me it probably wouldn't get any worse. I am delighted!" He pronounced each word triumphantly. "I can live with this—I just can't stand up very long."

Janet appeared across the living room, pushing a walker. She had shrunk six inches over the years and now inched forward in the shape of a comma. It had been some time since she had volunteered as a counselor for Planned Parenthood. The ropy folds of her neck reminded me of Winnie. Her green-gray eyes lit up when she saw me and when I rose to greet her, a smile took her whole face.

"Jeanie," she said holding my arms with her frail hands, her voice a benediction. She looked like an ancient Chinese sage. "It's so good to see you! You stayed with young Bert last night?"

"Yes," I answered, speaking loudly. She was profoundly deaf now and despite hearing aids, missed much of the conversation. "He looks more like you every day."

"Poor guy!" She laughed, showing prominent teeth as her eyes receded into wrinkles. "Are you still working as a nurse?"

I nodded. "I'm a traveling nurse now. They give us a place to stay and pay me well. We're on our way to California."

"Oh, nurses are so needed." She edged up to the table and I helped her onto her padded seat. "You saved my life, you know."

"Bert did," I corrected. "I just confirmed his suspicions." Bert had asked my opinion of a lump he discovered in Janet's breast. Her doctor and a mammogram had found nothing, but Bert was still uneasy. I had examined her and encouraged them to persist. Cancer had been found and treated in time.

"I love you so, my dear!" Janet held my hand across the table while her eyes showered me with affection. It was like sitting in the sunlight. "Did Bert tell you I have mild dementia? Not Alzheimer's," she hastened to add, "but I forget… like putting things in the icebox. Our dear Nadine is taking us to these wonderful caregiver meetings. While they're in the meeting, I attend a corresponding group. Bert is so good to me! The whole family has been going. They all take such good care of us."

"One thing I've gotten from these meetings is gratitude," Bert said. "Janet and I have it so good. Many people are dealing with terrible problems. Janet is so easy to love. She is always cheerful."

I looked over at Janet, but she seemed to be gone, drifting in her own world. Deafness, of course, curtained her off. Still she looked contented—her expression more of meditation than dementia. When the conversation turned to national politics and the Middle East, she was back, adding insightful stories about their years in the villages of Iran and Turkey. Tom and I valued the depth and complexity of these conversations. It was our heritage, I decided, from Winnie.

"What scares the hell out of me," Bert was saying, "is the growth of fundamentalism throughout the world. Islam or Christian amounts to the same thing—fanatics who are intolerant of divergent views. We can't solve our problems if we don't sit down and talk."

"What happened to discourse?" I asked. "Didn't the sixties open a time of reason? Now we're back to bigotry and superstition."

"I think people feel helpless," Tom commented. "The problems seem too huge."

"Ultimately, we're all in this together," Bert said. "We'll sink or swim in unity."

While we talked, I cooked breakfast of eggs, pancakes, blueberries, and bacon. When I placed it on the table, they were as delighted as children, celebrating each bite. Bert inhaled the scent of bacon as if it were a rare wine and Janet licked the last drop of maple syrup off her plate. I felt a wave of love for these wise mentors who walked ahead of me with such good-natured transparency on the inevitable journey into age.

"We hope to visit my father and stepmother today," I said. "We'll call when we get on the road. They spend winters in Arizona now. My youngest brother Jeff bought them a home in Salome and hauls them down from Alaska in his motor home every winter. It's in an airpark where Dad can warm his bones in the sun and listen to the drone of small planes."

"How is Bud?" Janet asked.

"Old… ninety. He has spinal compression like you. He's my height now."

"Really?" Bert said in surprise. "He used to be such a big man."

"I'm sorry to hear that," Janet said gently. I studied her face, but there was no ill will, though Bud had not been kind to her, comparing my "perfect" feet to those of her son's. It gave me pause.

"The last time we saw him, I felt my heart soften," I said. "He seemed so frail and vulnerable. As Tom and I were leaving, he suggested we move in and take care of them. I would be the nurse while Tom maintained their properties. I told him we needed to earn money for our old age and he countered with vague promises of 'being part of the operation.' I caught that glint in his eyes and realized it was the same old shell game."

"Well, it was always about him," Bert said mildly, "even as a young man.

He'd been everywhere—had even swum from Florida to Cuba! After Connie's books made them famous, they'd fly into town and he'd flash wads of cash, but let me pay the bill. He wanted us to join them in Alaska, but I knew how that would turn out."

"Yeah, it always seems like such an opportunity," I said, recalling hopeful young couples who had fallen for Bud's promises. "What I've never understood is why he lies. He is a remarkable man, a Wright Brothers' Award honoree—I think for fifty years of Bush flying without an accident—a master hunting guide. He created a life that many people would envy. I never understood why he needed to be more."

"Well, Connie built him up," Bert said thoughtfully. "She created the mythology and he stepped right into it."

I was silent, feeling this piece settle into place. Connie had written Bud into heroic proportions, but the price was a life wrapped in secrecy and the fear of being ordinary. In the Buddhist tradition, one can be trapped by attachment to the positive as easily as fear of the negative.

"He claimed to have written one of Connie's books to get into the Explorers Club," I said. "She told me she saw the letter. They didn't admit women in those days, so she couldn't get in."

"Connie wished everyone well," Janet said. "She trusted people. You know, Alaska was her idea. She was always so wild."

"Bud can't write," I said quietly. "I never told anyone. A few years ago his editor Angus Cameron started a correspondence with me. He was retired then."

"Wasn't he Connie's editor?" Janet asked, leaning forward to hear better.

I nodded. "He was her agent with Little, Brown. When Connie and Bud got divorced, Angus jumped ship. I'm sure Bud wouldn't let him have it both ways. Angus got fall hunting trips, but he lost Connie's talent. He was frustrated beyond words. 'Bud had such wonderful stories,' he told me, 'but he couldn't get them onto the page.' Finally, Angus had *Last of the Bush Pilots* ghostwritten."

I thought of my father: the pain of always having to be the best. He had written to me after I was grown, scores of letters all saying the same thing: "Life is fine. The birds are flying south (or north)." Maybe there wasn't anything else to say. *He did reach out to me in his own way,* I suddenly realized. *Maybe he couldn't break through my opinions about him.*

Janet got up and headed for the bathroom, moving the walker like an ancient snail across the carpet. Bert turned to me, "How does she seem to you?"

"Very lucid. She's better informed on Arizona politics than I am. How is she usually?"

"It varies a good deal. Sometimes she'll go into the bathroom and forget why she's there. I'll find her just sitting. She was on very expensive medication for dementia, but people in the caregiver group said it didn't make much difference, so we took her off it. I don't think it helped at all."

I nodded. "Less medication is usually better. I still think her problems could stem from pain pills. She appears more sedated than anything—the way she spaces out. Old people don't metabolize drugs well."

"Thank you for your research," Bert said. "Nadine has been reading up as well. We took your information to her neurologist and he reduced her medication, but she's in so much pain that she simply can't do without it."

"You are so loving and patient. It's a hard line to walk—honoring her independence while keeping her safe." I thought of Connie's decline and wished that I had had this model back then. I took Bert's big hand in both of mine. The palms were smooth and warm, the little finger contracted. "How are you holding up?"

He placed his other hand over mine and held my eyes. "I miss her," he said sadly. "She's the only woman I've ever loved and we have been such good friends."

As we prepared to leave, Bert took me gently by the shoulders and looked into my eyes. "Jeanie, I want you to consider how much of the negative you invite into your mind. I know the world's problems are very real, but don't lose yourself in them. Remember your mother: she was right and way ahead of her time, but no one could stand to be around her."

I thought of Connie, how she fought to preserve our natural world yet failed to enjoy the moment. She had died disappointed and angry. Her constant ranting alienated even those who loved her.

Bert's eyes softened. "The older I get, the more I appreciate Janet's sunny nature. Her joy is always a blessing." He said the words slowly, directly.

They stood waving in the doorway until we had driven from sight. Janet's little hunched figure leaned comfortably into Bert's protective bulk. With arms raised and faces smiling, they watched us turn the corner. I knew they were thinking they might never see us again. I was too.

The streets had awakened with morning traffic. We turned west on I-10, our little car struggling along in a stampede of larger vehicles. Loaded as we were, there was scant power to maneuver. Tom was muttering.

I pondered Bert's words, turning them in my mind to explore their facets. For every argument there was a counter. It was good to enjoy the end of life, but what of those who come after? Was he asking me not to stir up issues that made him uncomfortable? Was he right?

"What do you think about Bert's parting statements?" I asked. Traffic was thinning as it strung out into the steady lope of long-distance runners. The desert stretched flat, the color of buckskin, with small mountains budding purple in the distance.

Tom rolled his eye at me like a shy horse. "Is this a trick question?"

I laughed. "You know me so well." I rested my hand lightly on his thigh. "If we don't at least try to change direction, the end is inevitable. What boggles me is that so few people see it. Exponential growth is unsupportable, be it population or the economy."

Again the eye rolled my way. He didn't have to say it. I was obsessed. Finally he said, "Bert has a point. Your struggles have not changed the world. Your love and joy contribute every day."

AN HOUR BEYOND PHOENIX I called my father. My stepmother's voice rang lightly. "Yes, Honey, we'd love to see you!"

"We'll bring lunch," I told her.

We stopped for sandwiches and then hopped off the interstate, angling northwest. The historic town of Salome was an hour off the interstate on an unfenced road littered with desiccated cow carcasses and shredded tires. Salome was singularly unimpressive, like a stubborn tree you hope will die once you stop watering it. We approached through a collection of rusting machinery, boarded-up buildings, and the haze of fallow cotton fields. A low range of brown rocky hills broke the monotony. Town center was a bloom of new growth, mostly retirement homes—prefab buildings that sprouted like weeds between tufts of landscaping.

Bud and Martha were waiting in the cool sunlight on the raised cement porch of a new prefab. Jeff's airplane hangar dwarfed the house, and both were painted the color of the dirt. In stark contrast, Martha's bright flowers nodded on the deck. I remembered her flowers—the Walker Lake greenhouse filled with blossoms instead of lettuce—and suddenly understood why she had chosen beauty over vegetables.

"Well, gosh, Sweetie, it's so good to see you!"

As Tom and I mounted the two steps, my stepmother rose to give me a hug of genuine affection. Her body felt too thin. She was expensively dressed in a sea-foam green pantsuit, pumps of the same color, and diamond jewelry. She was hobbling on a bad knee and feet damaged from years in fashionable shoes, but—like my father—she would not complain. For half a century, Martha had followed his lead: loading airplanes, cooking, entertaining, and endlessly repeating family mythology for guests. The house, I knew, would be tidy and expensively decorated. I had once suggested she find someone to clean, but she dismissed the idea. "Oh, your Dad wouldn't have it. You know how he is."

I did. Years before when I had told them of Janet and Bert's decision to share skills, Martha had said, "That's a good idea, don't you think, Bud?" My father had patted her on the shoulder and smiled patiently. "Don't worry your little head, Martha. I have it all set up in the will. The boys will take care of you." Now his debility had created an unpleasant role reversal. In her eighties, Martha was learning new skills. She was spunky and bright, but also angry—unless I missed my guess.

"Hello, Jeanie, Tom." My father made a painful attempt to rise. His spine was curved like a banana and he leaned heavily on a cane. He was dressed neatly in plaid shirt and dark trousers with suspenders to keep them up. On his feet were lambskin slippers. A new gentleness rested in his face.

"Don't get up, Dad." I bent to kiss the smoothly shaven cheek. It was like hugging a dried flower—as if the smallest squeeze might cause him to crumble. Even in the sunlight, his fingers were icy. His face was still ruddy and surprisingly unlined; his thinning hair was neatly trimmed and combed. He had his own teeth, over which he wore the tight little smile I remembered, but his eyes had softened.

Martha and I did most of the talking, filling the space between us with pleasant words. Bud said little, though he followed our conversation with keen attention. His hearing and eyesight were remarkable for a man who had spent so many years around aircraft and guns. Our conversation was a guarded exchange of surfaces, floating adroitly over the thin scars of old wounds. A few times my father addressed Tom on some issue of manly interest, but mostly he watched me. Above the fixed smile, pain passed like shadows over the blue pools of his eyes.

"Travel-nursing is a way to see the country and decide where we want to settle," I told them. "They pay me well and give us a furnished apartment and insurance for me—though not very good insurance. We're both healthy and we eat well and exercise. It's better than pills."

Dad cleared his throat, his voice rusty. "You know, I always kept you girls insured. You had Blue Cross all the time you were growing up."

I tightened my lips. It was a story he had often repeated, as if to make it true. I remembered the county hospital when I had pneumonia, the Shiner's Crippled Children's Clinic that corrected my foot deformities, and how Connie worried over doctor's bills. No, either he didn't keep us insured or he never told her.

"What's happening with Takahula?" I asked, changing the subject.

"The Park Service came back with a pathetic offer. They must think we need the money. Well, we don't. I sent 'em packing."

So, back where we started. I wasn't surprised.

"You know, I once walked a mile across the tundra to get your blanket from the airplane because you couldn't sleep without it," he said, rebuilding a bridge to Jeanie the toddler. "You were such a cute little thing. I used to carry you for miles on my shoulders."

I thought of the old *LIFE Magazine* pictures, the shrouded memories. Yes, I knew it was true. I remembered how he had been with his young boys—not Jim, who had tried harder than any of us to be worthy—but the golden sons. I was sure he had been good to me too. It was the growing daughter with a mind of her own that he couldn't reconcile. Suddenly, I recalled a friend suggesting I had lived my life as a literary character, written into existence half a century before. *Who is the real Jeanie?* I wondered.

After an hour, Tom and I stood to leave and Bud painfully got to his feet. He took my hands in his cold and papery palms. "Jeanie, it's better to let the past go." He looked me keenly in the eye. There was a message, perhaps a silent plea for understanding. "It just brings you unhappiness. God has a plan for all of us."

It rang strangely like Bert's advice, but I trusted Bert to wish me well.

As we pulled away, they stood on the porch, looking isolated and vulnerable. Maybe they too were wondering if it would be our last visit.

We continued west into the falling sun and I thought of the years spent seeking my father's approval. When my first book was published, I had naïvely hoped he would be proud. Tom, Luke, and I were in Fairbanks, headed for Arizona after building our Kernwood cabin, when we learned *Reader's Digest* had bought my first book. I was dutifully washing dishes in my father's home after a lunch of pleasantries when he cornered me alone in the kitchen.

"You have no business writing a book you know nothing about." His tone had been silky, yet edged with malice. The pinched mouth was smiling, but his eyes were as cold as glass as he leaned close to skewer me with his gaze. I remember his rosy cheeks laced with little spider veins.

"But it's my life..." I had squirmed, feeling small and defenseless.

"Jeanie, you don't know anything." His tone was patient. "There's no point in making a fool of yourself and embarrassing the whole family."

"I'm not part of your family!" My eyes had suddenly welled with tears. *Why did I always have to cry?*

"Honey, this is your home. You are the one that stays away." His words were soft and reasonable as if talking to a crazy person or a small child. I could return home, repentant and docile. Daddy would finally love me.

"There isn't a single piece of me here," I had flared. "Look around! Not one picture of me in a three-story house. No one even knows you have a daughter!" Still I could not stop the tears, the feeling of being unworthy. Snot dripped from my nose.

It has taken me six decades to thank the hard teachers in my life. If my father had given me any hope of gentle affection, of being "part of the family," I would have sold my dreams to buy that ticket. As it turned out, I mapped my own course and in the end have come to see that the great Wizard of Oz was, after all, only a man.

Laurie and Lucas remain close. She visits Tucson, 2006.

Janet and Bert stood in their driveway as we left.

Chapter 18

CALIFORNIA GOLD

February 2007

We spent that night in Blythe, just over the California border. Judging from billboards, the main industry here was smog testing. I had finally shifted my sleep cycle to awaken at 4:00 A.M., but California reset our clock an hour, so my eyes popped opened at three. Rather than lie awake and wiggle, I got up to write by a narrow beam from the bathroom doorway, while Tom dozed until dawn.

The day was clear as creek water, cold and breezy, as we snaked west between towering mountains along a desert floor washed in cycles of rain and sunlight. To either side, peaks gleamed with snow, while great holes appeared in the clouds ahead, beckoning like the gates of heaven complete with spokes of light. I tried to imagine what pioneers had felt beneath these ranges. At Banning Pass, rows of windmills were harvesting the air like so many giant ants. We turned north away from Los Angeles at Redlands and up slender State Route 138 to Cajon Pass, where Joshua trees and weird sandstone formations drifted through curtains of fog.

Next day we slogged up the Central Valley, hemmed by endless vineyards of such factory precision that it felt like traversing a vast machine. The air here was as greasy as old dishwater and sad towns drifted by in a haze. In Sacramento, the tiny office of the California Board of Registered Nursing was packed with anxious faces, but I had my complex packet in order—fingerprints, transcripts, letters, photographs, resume—and soon walked free. There are advantages to being obsessive.

We found a room for the night and I phoned "Uncle Frank." He was not a relative, but had shown up like a stray dog on the Empire Ranch in the 1970s searching for "gold"—a word he spoke with a deep quaver and melodic laugh—and had been adopted by Annie and Steve. His mother had been in the French Underground during World War II, and Frank spent part of his childhood in a German concentration camp. Nevertheless, there remained something wonderfully childlike about him. Now in his eighties, he delivered flowers to help support ungrateful grandchildren and championed his lost son, imprisoned these many years. I recall the son as an obese teenager who hid in his room. Uncle Frank had tried everything to carry this son across the chasm into maturity—and failed.

We arrived at the restaurant in time to see Uncle Frank emerge from a tiny, ancient car. He grabbed me in a hearty embrace then pumped Tom's hand. He was over six feet tall and barrel-chested, but still quick and strong. His thinning silver hair was combed straight back in neat furrows showing pink scalp. Rosy cheeks were shaved to a gloss and his sky-blue eyes were those of a mischievous boy. I recalled him riding the freeway to Arizona on a small motorbike with cow horns glued to his helmet like a Viking; how he "hated children" and delighted in protruding his dentures in grotesque faces at them when adults weren't looking.

"So how are you, old friend?" I stood back to examine at him.

"Oh, not worth a crap," his laugh, the sound of a cello, deep and musically French. "I've given up everything but chasing loose women. Smoking, booze..." he shrugged. "I had to after I got the cancer. But I cured it. They can't find it anymore." Years before, he had been diagnosed with inoperable lung cancer. "I didn't need cancer, so it went away," had been his explanation.

"You are remarkable." I shook my head and Tom grinned. It was hard not to love Frank.

He led us into the restaurant, cheerfully waving his big hands as he talked. He was wearing an old fleece-lined jacket and his fingernails were grimy from work on some decrepit auto. "I'd ask you to stay with me," he said as we scrunched into a booth, "but you know how it is..." he grimaced and held up his hands in exasperation.

I nodded. "How is your house?"

"Worse than ever! They'll probably have to burn it down." That wonderful laugh again, rich as espresso.

What had been clutter before his wife went blind had become a slum after her death. We had visited on our way south from Alaska the previous year and could hardly walk between the piles. Frank had retreated to one room of the large, dilapidated structure; his Asian daughter-in-law and her three children claimed the rest. Among the chaos, I had spotted a photo of Frank's mother with a young Charles de Gaulle signed with a few sentences in French. *Treasure and trash*, as I had once said to Lucas (who sentimentally held on to everything). *You have to learn to discriminate.*

"And your heater?" I pressed.

He shrugged. "I just wear my coat. I can't turn it on. It would set the place on fire."

I looked at him sternly. "Frank, one of these days you're going to get old. You should think ahead. Your land is probably worth quite a bit. If you sold it, you could move into a little place with heat. You might even look at retirement housing."

"What! With a bunch of old people?" He rolled his eyes. I could hear the wheeze of emphysema in his laugh. "No, I'm gonna stay put. But I had a good offer on my extra lot—you know that area on the side?—I'll be able to continue my legal fight." Frank had already spent his German reparation money on lawyers for his son.

We were quiet and I smiled across the table at my old friend.

His eyes had misted over. "You know he never had a fair trial," he said sadly.

I nodded, thinking of Frank's son—no longer young—who had killed his only friend in what Frank believed was an accident and others said was in anger. Prisons have become an industry, and his son was incarcerated far away, where Uncle Frank could not even visit. It had been easier for me to offer advice before I had a son of my own.

FRESNO TURNED OUT TO BE a practical city, unabashedly devoted to commerce. It was more consolidated than Tucson and had an efficient freeway system. There were wealthy neighborhoods shaded by trees, but also warrens of Asian and Hispanic families, replete with exotic smells, and little markets selling foods I could not name. The Central Valley lay submerged under smog much of the time—like a shallow sea, flat and two dimensional—but occasionally the sky would lift to grant a distant view of the snowcapped Sierras.

Our apartment was in an older complex, nine miles from the hospital and within walking distance of stores, banks, library, and one of Fresno's few large parks. Tom and I were now skilled at power shopping and it took us only a morning to set up housekeeping. Cardboard boxes served as end tables and trash cans—for we would only be here thirteen weeks. It was pleasant, but it wasn't home. *Where is home?* I wondered as I unpacked sheets and made up the flimsy bed. At some point we would simply have to choose. It reminded me of canoeing downriver, searching the shoreline for a campsite as shadows lengthen into evening. *Not here, not yet... oh, that was lovely but it's gone now. Choose... soon. It's time to get off the river.*

"Build a home for me, where I will feel safe if you die," I asked Tom. We were eating our first dinner in the new place. Beyond the window, an artificial creek gurgled in fading light and a motley pair of ducks gabbled between the big roots of mature eucalyptus trees. Candy wrappers and bits of glass decorated the muddy shore and the water was dyed a poisonous turquoise.

Tom's eyes were kindly as he reached across to take my hand. "You miss him."

I nodded and bit my lip. A song I used to sing when I rocked Luke to sleep as a baby had been running through my mind all afternoon. *You are my sunshine*—only to me it was *son*-shine. "I know he needs to find his own strength, but eventually..." I let my hope linger, unspoken. "It's hard," I admitted.

"It's important," he reassured me. "When I was his age, I was in the navy."

Yes, I knew. Viet Nam. "But other cultures don't separate. Humans have lived in tribes for millennia before the nuclear family. I'm not so sure this isolation is always best." It was an old question between us.

"I don't care what he does or where he goes." Tom smiled tenderly. "I just want him to be happy."

It was Lucas's twenty-first birthday.

FRESNO COMMUNITY REGIONAL HOSPITAL WAS ten stories high: spacious, clean, and well-organized. They did twenty to thirty deliveries a day with three busy obstetrical operating rooms and an entire floor for antepartum patients. The hospital had a smooth process for orienting dozens of new staff each week. Nurses, many of whom were "travelers," worked cooperatively with little whining.

I was expected to manage two labor patients and care for the mom and her infant for the first two hours after birth. The pace was fast, but there was backup, including a full-time monitor nurse who watched a bank of fetal heart rates—a real safety net. There was a separate operating room for scheduled cesareans. Because cesarean delivery often arrives at an emergent point in labor, my anxiety ran high around this procedure. Usually the labor nurse must shift gears abruptly: preparing the patient and choreographing teams while charting in multiple places. The morning that I spent orienting in OR3, however, was surprisingly calm.

The usual players were present: two surgeons, anesthesiologist, scrub tech, circulating nurse, baby nurse, and a respiratory therapist. I eyed the equipment and stepped into the dance, holding the patient in a scrunched position while the anesthesiologist inserted the spinal. Then I laid her back and attached the arm support boards while the anesthesiologist placed EKG pads. I inserted a Foley catheter into her bladder and straightened her numbing legs, fastening a strap around them. I checked fetal heart tones before "prepping" her abdomen with an antimicrobial solution. I was used to doing this at full speed, but people were chatting amiably, and I began to relax.

"Are you nervous?" I asked the patient, wanting to distract her while the surgeons scrubbed in. "Don't touch your tummy—it's sterile. I know it's strange in here." She was the only one without a mask. I placed my hand on her shoulder and noticed the gang tattoo in the web between her thumb and first finger.

"A little. This is my fourth one. Another girl." Cynthia's face was round and plain. The pigment was patchy across her cheeks and chest. She had applied eye makeup and penciled in her plucked brows. At twenty-three, she was over three hundred pounds with insulin-dependent diabetes. Perhaps a quarter of our patients had diabetes. I judged this baby to be close to ten pounds.

"Are you getting your tubes tied?" I enquired.

"No… not yet. I would like to have a boy."

"You could get another girl. Raising four will keep you busy."

She nodded and looked doubtful. "I've been thinking that too. But my boyfriend, he wants a boy."

"What do you want?"

She sighed and then brightened. "How many children do you have?"

"I have one beautiful son. He's in Arizona studying to be a nurse."

"Only one?" Her voice took on the conciliatory tones generally reserved for victims of pancreatic cancer.

I grinned. "Yes. It was by choice. I didn't think I could support more."

Cynthia sighed again. "I have two in diapers still and now there's this one."

I tucked strands of dark hair into her surgical cap as the blue drapes were clamped to create a sterile field and obscure her vision. "She'll be special too,"

I assured her. "You need to take care of yourself. Diabetes is no joke. You can learn to control it with diet and exercise. Use good birth control until you are sure you want another."

"I was on the pill," she said.

I nodded. It was a common story. The reproductive system is hard to outwit.

The team pulled together with practiced ease. As the incision was made, I stepped from the room to get the baby's father. Small and skinny, he was slumped forlornly on a stool in the hall, paper scrubs pulled over his street clothes. The crotch of his jeans hung so low that it hobbled him, and his trousers cuffs were walked to threads. I beckoned and he rose with a cocky swagger, but his mask was upside down and his eyes looked scared.

"Is this your first time?" I put my hand on his thin shoulder and adjusted the mask. Tattoos extended up his neck.

"Yeah, but I'm cool."

"You'll be fine. You're going to sit next to Cynthia's head. There's a curtain so you won't see anything gooey. Your baby will be here in just a minute. We'll dry her off and then I'll bring her for you to hold." I pushed open the OR door. "Don't touch anything blue," I guided him around the maze of equipment to a stool.

The baby nurse stood at the radiant warmer where the respiratory therapist was checking equipment. Mona was stout and slow. She had hearing aids in both ears and iron-gray hair was tucked under the surgical cap.

"I just can't stay home," she told me, eyes glinting behind bifocals. "I retired three times. I don't have a husband, so this is my family and social life. I don't need the money. I took seventeen members of my family on a cruise to Alaska last summer to celebrate fifty years in nursing. Next year I'm taking my daughter and granddaughter to Europe."

"I thought they made you quit," I said doubtfully.

"You can stay as long as you can do your job. I work full time, though they pretty much let me set my own pace. The scheduled 'sections' are usually done by three o'clock. I come in five days a week and—unlike the young ones—I never miss a shift."

So, I thought, *if a big, impersonal hospital can find a place for Mona to contribute seventy-one years of wisdom and experience, I don't need to accept anyone else's script either.*

LIFE CONTINUED TO SURPRISE ME—AND usually for the better. So it was with Fresno. I was prepared for a colorless city, but people were kind, fruit trees were thick with blossoms, and red-tailed hawks were defending nest sites along the San Joaquin River. I was still mulling over Uncle Bert's parting advice. My life was good. Today. *Am I not a greater blessing when I celebrate spring with the hawks than when I gnaw on global problems?*

Each of us, I realized, inhabits a different reality. Where I saw the unraveling of ecosystems, others followed celebrities through a glittering maze of products or walked in the shadowy land of violence. My love of open sky and wild lands meant nothing to most of my coworkers. When I spoke of choosing simplicity, I might as well have been yapping like a coyote. There was no resonance in their eyes, no recognition.

"Do you know that economists assign a dollar value to human life?" I asked Tom. "If dumping toxic waste in a river outweighs the value of lost life, it's economically positive. The World Bank even justifies moving 'dirty' industries to less developed countries because human life has less value there."

"And we wonder why they don't like us," Tom said mildly.

We were eating lunch by a small lake in the Japanese garden of Woodward Park, a square mile of open space that ran above the San Joaquin River. Tom had bought a couple of used bikes and we often spent a day exploring the trails. This garden was an intimate meditation in conscious space with blooming fruit trees, mossy rocks, and banks of flowers. Petals fell like snow and drifted in such profusion that the ground was stained rose, lavender, and white. Below us, a little bridge crossed an artificial stream which was crafted with exquisite attention to detail.

I gazed about the Japanese garden. Though few people came here, someone put a great deal of attention into conscious acts of beauty. I remembered Darlene, Laurie's mother, saying, "If you can't create strength in your own community, where should you start?" Maybe it wasn't about big gestures but the compilation of little acts of courage and vision. I recalled gentle souls that I had discounted, thinking them naïve, people who didn't crow or spread their tail feathers. Maybe they were sages, choosing joy and a light step as their quiet gift. Perhaps I had never seen them at all.

I DROPPED INTO A CHAIR at the nurses' station. I had just taken my patient and her baby to the postpartum wing and "the floor" was quieting. Activity tends to come and go in waves, a pulse you can feel. The bank of computer screens showed fetal heart tracings from six active labor patients and five "antepartums," women at risk for losing their babies. In Fresno, these patients were stabilized here on continuous monitoring and then sent to their own unit where some remained until delivery.

"That doesn't look good." I leaned forward and pointed to one of the tracings. The monitor nurse clicked to enlarge it. I frowned. "Looks like an abruption pattern." This is when the placenta pulls loose from the uterine wall. The fetus (and possibly mother) can bleed to death. Frequent causes are abdominal trauma, high blood pressure, and cocaine.

"That's the patient the ambulance just brought into triage," Gail said.

"I think I'll just wander over and see if they need a hand." I pushed up from the chair, my tired feet complaining as I started down the hall.

The ambulance crew and two nurses had just transferred a woman into the cramped space of a triage "room," which was cordoned off by curtains from eleven other such areas. She was about thirty-five, a thin black woman dressed in flashy clothes with much dangling jewelry. She was writhing and moaning softly.

"Letitia, what did you take?" Kathy asked, speaking loudly. "I need to know for your baby." She shook her shoulder. "What did you take?"

"Nothin'. I dint take nothin'," the woman mumbled. Her eyes were squeezed shut and she was rhythmically turning her head from side to side.

"Are you allergic to any drugs?" someone asked. Another person was starting a second IV in her right wrist.

No answer. I glanced at her belly: about twenty-eight weeks. Bright blood was seeping down the inner thighs of shiny gold pants that were tucked into high boots.

"God, look at those pressures," Pat said. The cuff, set to go off every three minutes, was recording blood pressures around 220/110. "Help me cut her clothes off." Pat was slicing away with a pair of scissors and trying to thread the IV tubing through bra and jewelry. The jangling mass of bracelets hampered progress. Hands were taking out earrings and dropping them into a specimen bag. Someone was pulling off the black boots and tight pants. The space was suddenly packed with people in blue hospital scrubs. Unless you knew the players, it was difficult to tell a tech from a doctor.

The resident, a young black woman herself, thumbed up Letitia's eyelid. The eyeball rolled away from the penlight. "Do we have any record of her?"

"No, we're not even sure of her name. No prenatal care as far as we know."

"Get me prenatal labs, rapid HIV, preeclampsia labs, a liver panel, UA, and a drug screen," the resident said without looking up. An ultrasound machine appeared and she pushed the wand over the tight abdomen. "About twenty-eight weeks and breech. Very low. Posterior placenta… looks like a clot behind it. Give me a glove."

Speaking quietly to the patient, I pulled her quivering legs apart. "Letitia, we're gonna help you. Just relax your legs, Honey."

On the other side, a tech had pushed a pen into the patient's bejeweled hand and was trying to get her attention. "I need you to sign a consent for an HIV test and a drug screen." The patient kept up her rhythmic writhing and refused to open her eyes. Pat was still tugging at the network of clothing and jewelry. I covered the upper half of the patient's body with a gown and held the fetal monitor over the baby's heart.

"The baby's heart rate is down," I said just loud enough for the others to hear. A half-dozen sets of eyes flicked to the computer screen where the infant's heart rate had dived into the sixties. The fetus was definitely in trouble.

"She's complete! Bulging bag," the resident intoned (meaning the cervix was gone, but the amniotic membrane was intact). She snapped off the bloody glove. "Open the OR. Get me the attending and anesthesia. We're going now!"

An infant's head is its largest part. A breech baby emerges feet or bottom first, and the head can remain trapped in the pelvis. When the water broke—as it would any moment—the baby's cord could flush out, also a medical emergency. This was complicated by the bleeding and maternal blood pressures.

"Letitia," I said softly, holding her head still between my palms and bringing my face close to hers. "Your baby is in trouble and in the wrong position to be born. We're taking you to the operating room for a cesarean section. Do you understand?"

She still didn't open her eyes, but I felt her head shake yes. "Ma'am, it hurts… it hurts… ," she mumbled. A tear slid down a cheek the color of milk chocolate.

"I know, Honey. It'll be over soon. You'll be going to sleep for the operation. You just hang in there a few minutes."

A dozen people were in motion. Someone was stamping up paperwork, doing the admission, getting patient numbers; someone else was on the phone with the special-care nursery and arranging a helicopter transport to Children's Hospital across town. In the operating room, a tech was pulling open packages and laying out a sterile field of instruments. Each player was skilled and quick. I ripped open a Foley kit and inserted the catheter into her bladder, then pulled off a sample of urine for the lab and handed it to the phlebotomist who was drawing tube after tube of blood from the patient's arm. The stretcher started for the OR as I hung a second bag of IV fluid, running it wide open.

"What's up?" The anesthesiologist asked as he fell in with the procession.

"Came in by ambulance. Says her name is Letitia," I answered. "Pressures in the 220s over 1-teens. No fever. Abruption, cervix complete, about twenty-eight weeks, breech, decelerations to the sixties. Possibly cocaine. No prenatal care. Labs pending." I grabbed a mask and two surgical caps outside the OR and pulled a cap over the patient's hair as the automatic doors swung open. "Second bag of LR is running. Urine is scant and very concentrated. I'm guessing severe preeclampsia. She's sick, that's for sure, and the baby's in trouble."

The OR was bustling. I tied the sterile gown for the scrub tech as the patient was lifted onto the table, arm boards attached, legs restrained, and antiseptic poured over her exposed abdomen. Pat was on the computer charting. In an adjacent room, another crew of doctors, respiratory therapists, and nurses were checking equipment for resuscitating the infant. With no time for a spinal (and no labs to assess the risk) a general anesthesia would be used. Moments after arriving in the OR, the anesthesiologist had his tray organized. He made eye contact with each of the surgeons. Their gowns were still open in back, but their masks and gloves were on. "Ready? Go!"

A stat cesarean is an amazing team performance. The anesthesiologist pushed the plunger on a syringe already attached to the IV tubing and within seconds the patient crumpled. This is always a scary moment: the patient is paralyzed and the anesthesiologist needs to insert an endotracheal tube (not easy on a pregnant woman) to breathe for her. Meanwhile, the surgical crew cut for the baby, working to free it before the drugs reached the placenta. In less than a minute a tiny limp infant was handed off into a warm sterile drape and hustled to its waiting team. Two separate events were then underway: one to save the mother, who was sick enough to bleed to death, have a seizure, or even a stroke; the other to resuscitate the little bit of life she'd been carrying.

There was plenty of help in the OR, so I followed the baby. About one infant in ten needs assistance at birth. I watched the experts whenever I could, so that when I found myself holding a newborn with the muscle tone like a dead octopus, resuscitation steps were wired into my brain. It's that limp feeling that scares me. Babies are often born quite blue or white, but if they're rubbery, most will pink up with stimulation. They're amazingly resilient and designed in complex ways to make the transition from parasite to independence. Unlike an adult, their problems are nearly always respiratory and unless they're too far gone, they respond rapidly to ventilation.

In the stabilizing nursery, the crew was at work on a tiny boy. The pediatric nurse practitioner pinched his small cord stump between her gloved right thumb and finger, silently tapping out his pulse on the mattress. The respiratory therapist was suctioning mucus, positioning the head, and pushing oxygen into his lungs. Two people worked in concert to dry, position, and remove damp blankets from beneath him. It was a ballet in miniature.

The baby looked to be about two and a half pounds, limp and pale, but as oxygen perfused his organs, he grimaced and raised one small hand as if in protest. He had the wizened appearance of an old man, not the gelatinous skin of a preemie. He was tiny, I decided, but not really that premature. His ears were well formed and there were wrinkles on his scrotum. IUGR, I guessed: intrauterine growth restriction. He was asymmetrically stunted, with a shriveled body and the large head of a pollywog, having prioritized his brain at the expense of his body. All of this was excellent news, for size is not as important as maturity. A full-term baby can be very small if it has grown in an impoverished uterine environment—such as happens with extreme maternal blood pressures. Given the chance, these babies are ready to make up for lost time.

I felt the room relax as others came to the same conclusion.

"Come, on. Give us a little cry," the nurse practitioner said. The baby was breathing on his own, those irregular little gulps of the newborn. His eyes were open and he studied the faces with a worried frown.

"I don't think he wants to," someone said. "You're just a quiet one, aren't you?"

"What would you say? Thirty-five, thirty-six weeks?" They were curious and relaxed now, turning him gently in a head-to-toe assessment, checking reflexes, and making sure all the parts were present, well-articulated, and working.

I let out my breath and headed back to the OR to relay the news. The crew in there had relaxed as well and were talking easily as they closed. When someone tells me that I'm lucky to work with birth, I remember grief and spit-second interventions that affect a whole lifetime. Make no mistake, I am deeply grateful when I hear a baby cry.

Lucas with Megan, age ten, at the Monterey Bay Aquarium, Christmas 2006.

Jeanie on the road as a travel nurse, 2007.

Chapter 19

A Pretty Face

April 2007

The northern hemisphere revolved grandly into yet another spring, and dawn arrived earlier each morning until California "sprang forward" into darkness. One day the sun was rising as I pulled onto the freeway; the next it was still dark. It was dark when I returned home too. My biological clock was not so easily altered.

Christy was eating lunch in the report room when I joined her. "Thanks for your help," I said. "That was some trick you did. Shoulder dystocias scare the pants off me." A baby that becomes stuck as it emerges will quickly die. A few minutes earlier, Christy had straddled my patient's chest, facing her feet, and used thrusts with the heel of her hand to pop the infant's top shoulder under the pelvic bone.

"I learned it in the ER," she said. "If you ever code an adult, climb onto 'em. You really can't do much from the side."

"I see you almost every day. You must put in a lotta hours."

She was turning her neck from side to side, a pained expression on her face. "Ten days this paycheck. Ka-ching!" Christy was perhaps forty, attractive, bright, and experienced. She also smoked and drank too much.

I moved behind her and began to massage her tight shoulders. Sixty hours a week, I calculated, and she often stayed over to help night shift for double-time, making more than many doctors—maybe one hundred fifty thousand a year. My company had wanted to contract me for the forty-eight-hour week that most Californian travelers worked, but I'd held out for three twelve-hour shifts. I didn't believe I could safely do any more.

"You don't have a life," I stated. "Why so much? You're not even supporting kids." Many travelers were indentured servants who kept families in another state.

"I have two condos and a Lexus to support. I'm high maintenance." Her laugh sounded nervous. She was picking at her fingernails as I massaged, her hands raw from so much washing. "Oh, that's good… right there."

I worked my thumbs to either side of her spine between the scapulas. The muscles were as tight as guitar strings. "I'm low maintenance and take summers off," I countered. "Relax your arms and take a deep breath." I gently rotated her head. "My husband and I never made much money, but we enjoy life. You may as well have a cot in the basement as a condo—since you really live here."

"Well, real estate is a good investment." She sounded tired.

I nodded. "Yeah, but you might not live to retire at this rate. Wouldn't it make sense to enjoy part of your life now? You could work half the year and take the other half off. At your tax rate, it might come out even." I smoothed my hands across her shoulders and down her arms. "What's your life worth? Think about it."

I had to smile at my lecture. Most of my money went to Arizona, where Lucas, Eve, and Megan were all making strides toward growing up. Although they still lived apart, they remained close and supportive, and Tom and I were still part of that picture.

ON MY DAYS OFF, WE explored California. For weeks the snowcapped Sierras had beckoned me, and today we drove east toward the mountains. Blooming fruit trees—snowy white, candy pink, and violet—blurred the flat valley into a distant haze. Ahead, the earth's skin was bunched like a great carpet from north to south as far as the eye could see. This imposing barrier was visible for a hundred miles, ranges stacked one behind the other to over fourteen thousand feet.

"Hi," Eve's voice came tinny over the cell phone. "Megan wants to leave The Forum. I want it to be her decision, but I also think she should stay. What should I do?"

Early in our relationship, Tom and I had taken a human potential workshop which taught us to communicate cleanly and opened our choices beyond habit and fear. Until you examine your patterns, you have little control. We had recently paid for Lucas and Eve to take the Landmark Forum, another intense opportunity to confront one's decisions and roles. Now Megan was spending three days in the kid's Forum.

"Running away is what she does," I nodded as if Eve could see me.

"I knew she had homework last night, but she denied it. When she asked to watch TV, I asked again, 'Are you sure you don't have homework?' and she said, 'No.' Then this morning she suddenly panicked because she 'remembered' she had homework."

"She's in the right place and so are you. Some parents never stop rescuing their grown kids—but it isn't a gift."

"I feel so bad for her," Eve said.

"You think she doesn't know that? Landmark gave them homework because it's probably the biggest issue parents and kids fight about. Believe me, she won't be alone. I'm betting the day will be about taking responsibility for your own life."

"Okay," Eve sounded relieved, "this time she stays."

"You want to empower her," I agreed. "She's a full human being." I hung up thinking of science fairs and late homework. *If I could do it over, would I be less anxious?* Parents feel so pressured to mold their beautiful children into a cultural norm. *We are so fearful they will stumble and be lost.*

The San Joaquin Valley with its geometric orchards dropped behind as we climbed into sunlight. Foothills emerged, velvet green, and traffic thinned on the two-lane road as we wound steeply upward. Cattle stood in the folds of creeks, knee-high in grass and wildflowers beneath budding oak and sycamore trees. Rock outcrops that looked like dozing elephants emerged randomly from softened hillsides; the air was fragrant with spring.

By noon I could see the fallacy in my plan: one cannot drive a little way into the Sierras any more than one can drive partway across the Grand Canyon. Here geography rules. Except for a few natural routes, these mountains are as impenetrable to the auto as they had been to wagons. What an obstacle they must have been for early peoples! Roads climbed only the outer ramparts then wiggled north and south in natural creases. Sequestered in these wrinkles, we could no longer view the peaks beyond. We pulled off the road and hiked up a steep hill only to see a layered vista of mountains that hid the snowy heights.

∼

A WEEK LATER TOM AND I were headed west toward the Pacific, taking the back roads through leafing orchards and identical vineyards that twinkled past like spokes of a wheel to the flat horizon. Relaxing into my seat, I phoned Megan. "Hi, kiddo. Wanna talk?"

"Hi, Jeanie," her voice sounded excited.

"How'd you like The Forum?"

"It was really worthwhile! I learned some neat things about myself."

"I'm glad you stuck with it," I told her. "I love you, Honey." Megan wasn't much of a talker. I smiled and flipped the phone shut. You plant seeds, but you don't get to determine the outcome.

Traffic never slowed as it arrowed through drab towns that lay rusted and weathered between the fields. Beyond the car window, ribbons of geese and cranes wavered north overhead following age-old migratory routes up the long valley. *Life*, I thought, *is committed to the future.* I pictured the birds winging thousands of miles to insure that continuity. Below them, crop dusters were spraying poison on the greening land and the migrant workers. *How can we who pride ourselves on intellect be so dumb?*

As we neared the coast, the earth again wrinkled into a scenic landscape unsuitable for mechanized agriculture. Here, expensive homes lay hidden in foliage and exotic flowers bloomed. We stopped to lunch along a beach where the wind blew cold across the white dunes and kicked up a swell. Green-gray water stretched to the boundless horizon. I stood on a dune and filled my lungs with salty air, letting the surf wash into my soul. *Yes, great Mother Ocean, I've been a long time gone.* I tried to imagine living near the sea. It seemed too big a dream.

"I wish Lucas was here," I said. The wind was chilly, yet I lingered. "I always think of him when we go somewhere new."

"We gave him so many good experiences." Tom put his arm around my shoulders, drawing me into his warmth. "Remember all the trips? We did it right."

Monterey was artfully understated: little shops, flowers and trees. At the famous aquarium we stood mesmerized before the great kelp tank, swaying with fish to artificial waves and quiet music. Despite the public, it seemed holy and otherworldly—like flying. The shark is a miracle; the intelligent octopus, more than a side dish. *These beings, very unlike myself, are nevertheless worthy of respect.* I was flooded with gratitude for this glimpse into their world.

"Let's not eat farmed salmon," I said as we drove south above cliffs on Route 1 the next morning. "Wild salmon is a better choice. Did you know that rockfish can be older than you are? I don't want to eat anything that takes half a century to mature."

The day was cool and rain dampened the twisting road. We had Route 1 to ourselves, and stopped frequently to watch the painted sea where otters floated in the kelp. Waves foamed against the dark rocks below and creeks plunged hundreds of feet into hidden coves. The scent of wildflowers and salt air misted us while calls of nesting birds sounded above the surf. As we drove, the sky gradually cleared and cliffs gave way to green hills with beaches broken by headlands. It was afternoon when we came upon a score of parked cars. The beach below was littered with great fleshy logs—elephant seals! We pulled into the parking lot and walked out to a rock ledge where a breeze blew cool from the spreading sky. Beyond the beach, dark heads dotted the gray surf.

"These are mostly 'weaners,' born this spring," a docent informed the visitors. "Bulls arrived from Alaska in December, followed by the pregnant cows." She was perhaps sixty-five, a volunteer here to educate the public and protect the animals. A rope along the ledge kept the two species separated. "See that one just coming out of the surf?" she pointed. "He's a five-year-old. Bulls start growing their distinctive proboscis around six and fight for the right to mate when they turn eight. Only about one percent of them wins the privilege."

"Where are the mothers?" I asked.

"Back at sea, feeding. Both sexes fast during calving and breeding. Once a year, all elephant seals must return to land for a prolonged rest and 'catastrophic molt,' shedding their skin and fur." She showed us a small patch. "The young gain almost ten pounds a day on mothers' milk, and a month after birth, the cows mate and abandon them. Once their coats mature, these weaners will begin a solitary life, teaching themselves to swim and hunt. Already sharks are gathering offshore."

"The sharks know?" I asked, incredulous.

She nodded, gray hair streaming in the wind. "Elephant seals were hunted almost to extinction, but since the Marine Mammals Act, they've rebounded. They've only returned to this beach since 1992, but already great white sharks come from around the world when the young take to the water."

"It's a wonder any survive alone."

"Especially when you realize that elephant seals are bottom-feeders," she agreed. "They can dive a mile below the surface and stay under for well over an hour."

There's more going on than can be measured, dissected, or tracked with radio collars, I thought. *The earth is a living organism, much as our bodies are composed of apparently different organs and cells. We are one event.*

My fifty-seventh birthday set me thinking about my maternal grandmother, Winifred Browning Chittenden. Like Connie, she had two daughters late in life, so she was sixty-seven when I was born. While my free-spirited mother gave me a sense of adventure and a deep love for nature, Winnie introduced me to wisdom and self-discipline. Annie and I were the sometimes-forgotten tail of our mother's colorful kite, pulled on a chaotic journey by her dreams and fears. It was Winnie who rooted us to the planet. Her life was as simple and predictable as our mother's was impulsive and flamboyant. Winnie was a mistress of ritual and conscious space, one who walked the solitary spiritual path. Her library was rich in metaphysical books and she meditated daily—at peace with her aloneness.

Winnie was nobody's "little granny." She was tall and regal with silver hair and erect posture. She wore silk dresses with stockings held up by white garters. She had modest breasts and never owned a bra. On her feet were sturdy shoes of black or beige leather with low stacked heels and laces across the instep. As toddlers, Annie and I took turns riding those feet while Winnie pumped her treadle sewing machine mending our clothes. She dressed carefully, using a touch of makeup and the few pieces of expensive jewelry from her former life. She kept her person and home immaculate and orderly.

Winnie was not pleased to have her quiet sanctuary invaded and her daughter back. With characteristic naïveté, our mother assured Winnie that her babies would stay quietly in the front bedroom during the year it took to finish her degree in sociology. Connie graduated in the spring of 1954, but could never buckle down to being "a wage slave" (as she called it) in the "grim and regimented job" of social worker. She later got a teaching certificate, but rebelled against that, too—preferring the precarious life of an author "tied to small children" over the "drudgery" of a regular job.

I remember Winnie's house from knee-level. My memory starts abruptly with the long train journey from Colorado, as if my life began the day my parents separated. I was almost three. Spring was in the air and Winnie's yard smelled of orange blossoms when the taxi left us on the front cement steps of that solid little home across from Tucson High. I recall vivid details: the smell of crayons in the blue metal can, the corner where I played between the rocking chair and wall heater, rose-colored mantel and bookshelf with the gas fireplace that was never used, the doily on Winnie's dresser, and the linoleum kitchen floor. There was a tall dresser in the bathroom with a starched white cloth and a chair I could climb on to see. She had a claw-footed bathtub with a hooked rug over the lip. Nothing ever changed in Winnie's house. It was exactly what Annie and I needed.

I slept in the double bed with my mother in the blue front bedroom—the same room Connie and Janet had shared as girls. It was shaded by the heavy porch and orange trees, designed for Tucson heat before air conditioning. As summer came on, the quiet hum of the evaporative cooler lulled me to sleep in Winnie's starched and spotless sheets. When fall arrived, Friday evening football games lit the room and the raucous blare of the school band poured through the screen with the scent of oleander blossoms.

Connie barely knew her youngest daughter. I was accustomed to having my mother to myself, and remained her acknowledged favorite. For me, life held some continuity, but to my eighteen-month old sister, our move to Arizona must have felt like an adoption. It was natural that Winnie would open her heart to the baby's pinched face and piercing wails. Wistful little Annie soon became Winnie's baby, sleeping in a crib in her sunny western room and sucking canned milk from a glass bottle on her lap.

On weekdays, Annie and I were picked up for "nursery school" (the precursor to daycare) in a station wagon full of kids. At night, Winnie potty-trained me while my mother slept. Our bed was high, and my nightshirt (an old pajama top of my grandmother's) was safety-pinned to the bottom sheet to keep me from falling on the hardwood floor. Winnie would unpin me and take my hand "down the long road to visit Mrs. Jones." In the bright bathroom, she set me blinking and squalling on the high toilet seat to balance on skinny legs over the immense hole, eyes squeezed shut. Then she walked me back and pinned me into bed next to my slumbering mother. It was Winnie who held my sister on the taxi ride to Dr. Thompson's office, foot wrapped in a dish towel, when Annie severed the tendon of her big toe on the lid of a coffee can. I sat quietly on the seat beside them, watching blood seep through the towel onto Winnie's silk dress.

The spring that I turned four, we moved with our mother into a duplex in South Tucson on Fremont Avenue. It was a slum, infested with mice, with an unfenced dirt yard. I recall playing alone on the railroad tracks and running freely through the dusty streets with children who spoke mostly Spanish.

Someone gave me a little gray kitten that had fleas, but the neighbor ran over it. Annie was given a yellow cat and got ringworm. Summer 1954 came and torrential rains nearly swept me down a storm drain, clad only in pink panties, as I played in the gutter with shrieking children. Years later, I wondered, "Where was my mother?" *Typing*, is the most likely answer. *Writing one of hundreds of letters: a caged bird seeking freedom.*

Connie was desperate to revive her career and earn money. Perhaps she also needed to prove that she was still Constance Helmericks—educated and creative. Throughout the coming years she would board us with one family or another while she attempted to jumpstart her adventurous life again. I can count ten or more foster placements, some worse than others, and even recall waiting alone on the Tucson courthouse steps while my mother petitioned to put us temporarily into the orphanage. The families we stayed with were often rural and I think she believed that we would be happier away from the "sweltering city." I have never doubted her love for me or her raw honesty, only her judgment.

The winter after we moved to Fremont Avenue, Connie left us with a woman named Mrs. Rice and set out alone in our old black-and-white Ford on a disastrous national lecture tour. Mrs. Rice was a doughy and disapproving figure who punished three-year-old Annie for wetting the crib by making her stay in it all day until she pooped there, too, little pellets rolling into the darkened bedroom.

Connie returned to Tucson to discover that our neighbors, whom she had paid to paint the ratty duplex, had stolen her few belongings, down to the mattress and our tin-can piggy banks. As a final assault, the Savings and Loan where she had invested her meager savings, failed. We returned to that empty duplex to sleep on the wooden floor. I recall my mother's sobs and the snap of a mousetrap followed by the squeak of a soft life caught in steel.

It was Winnie who grubstaked us for another start. We moved to the cottage on Bean Alley, a few blocks from our grandmother's home, where we would remain until we set off to canoe the Peace River the spring I turned fourteen. Through the coming decade, my remarkable grandmother remained the rudder for our vulnerable little family.

She hadn't always been a city hermit. Winnie had been by turns a farm girl determined to escape from butchering hogs, a young widow left alone in Cuba by the sudden death of her beloved first husband, a working nurse at a time when women had no voice, and the elegant trophy bride of a rich and sometimes abusive doctor. At fifty, she set off with her two girls for a new life in

Arizona. She was ill, carried aboard the train on a stretcher with a nurse at her side, when she chose an uncertain future over wealth and oppression. Arthur gave her a small settlement and although they remained married, they lived apart the rest of their lives.

I treasured my evenings with Winnie. We would snuggle in her bed playing "Honeymoon Bridge" for pennies while she told me marvelous stories of her life, illuminating my own place in the great chain. Her composure was serene, but her long, cool feet twitched like the tip of a cat's tail and I sometimes grabbed the toes and tried to hold them still. Winnie thought of herself as an aristocrat in exile, a person of culture without money, but she could employ an unexpectedly earthy vocabulary—the farm girl behind the Grande Dame. Because of her, I have never been cowed by social status; because of me, Lucas enjoyed a rainbow of friendships. It was Winnie's gift. She valued ideas and discussing them. She didn't bake cookies or fuss over me, but Winnie gave me a foundation of integrity and the belief that I had a right to my own vision.

There came a point when our roles began to reverse. I was fourteen, returned from canoeing the Peace River with new strength and confidence, to find Winnie in decline. The work and chaos of our family had kept her engaged, but during the summer alone she had aged. I again went to live with my grandmother, this time to ensure that she was safe and ate regular meals. She was eighty-one then and becoming forgetful. I walked across the street to attend Tucson High School and slept in the front bedroom to the familiar Friday night football games and school band. Although her cloistered life was out of step with the outward flow of mine, it was a good period for me, a hiatus from adolescence that allowed me a larger role.

Eventually, Winnie was hospitalized with an "intestinal blockage" and from there was sent to a nursing home. She grieved deeply the loss of her privacy and autonomy. I visited, though not as often as I should have, avoiding my own pain at seeing her unhappy. Winnie, who had steadfastly taught me to be mistress of my own life—that one's thoughts and attitude create personal reality—seemed to have run aground. I didn't want to open those possibilities. *What good is learning to be centered if you lose the path when you most need it?*

After I got my driver's license, Annie and I would sometimes help Winnie dress and take her to lunch at a favorite restaurant.

"Connie," she would say to me, perhaps forgetting that another generation had come, "I am so tired." Then again she would plead, "I want to go home!" It did not seem right to warehouse her, but I had no other answer. Connie, who never was good at leadership, did her best, but was having challenges of her own.

I was seventeen when Winnie died. I saw her abdomen swelling and understood that she was pregnant with death. She didn't seem to notice or perhaps she welcomed it. She had taught me that death was a natural transition and not to be feared. That is another gift from Winnie: comfort with my own mortality. When she was taken to the hospital, old Dr. Thompson, who used to come to her home with his little black bag, said she wouldn't last a day. She couldn't eat or drink and not wanting to prolong her dying, he ordered no IV.

Annie and I tended her for a week, skipping school and practically living at the hospital. Thoughtlessly, we took our mother's car and left Connie stranded in Winnie's home, where the three of us now lived. It seemed impossible and macabre that Winnie remained alive. There was an awful tube down her nose sucking up dark grainy liquid, and she tried to pull it out until they restrained her frail wrists.

"You're going to be fine," I lied through my tears. Annie was stroking the silver hair. Winnie looked at us silently, gray-green eyes liquid and wise as a baby seal's. *Who was I lying for?* Certainly, Winnie knew.

Finally, an old nurse took us aside. She was stout and looked tired in her traditional white dress, stockings, and solid shoes. A white nurse's cap was pinned to short, iron-gray hair. "Your grandmother is only staying alive for you girls," she told us gently. "You need to let her go. You should say, 'Goodbye,' and go home."

We kissed Winnie one last time and left. She died within the hour.

Winfred Browning Chittenden: 1883 ~ 1967

I HADN'T THOUGHT MUCH ABOUT Winnie in years, until, when my picture was taken for an employee badge, there she was! Not the silver hair yet, but the same angular features, the beginning soft neck ropes, the shadows seeping from nose to the corner of my mouth. There, too, were those green-gray eyes, that straightforward honesty and determination. It startled me. I had glimpsed my mother in me at times, but my grandmother? *Do I really look that old?* Why should that beloved and powerful face cause me discomfort?

I must confess a certain vanity at looking less than my age. After seeing Winnie in my picture, I began thinking about getting a facelift. For less than the price of a used car, I could have that younger, tighter look. With a bit of help around the neck, I might pass for my early forties. I pulled back the skin like a cat picking up a kitten by the nape and studied my reflection in the mirror.

It looked good… but where did it stop? What about the tummy tuck and then those flying-squirrel things that happen under the arms?

Tom accompanied me for an appraisal. A facelift is more involved than I had thought—not just a little tuck along the neckline.

"It's your decision," Tom said, but his eyes looked strained.

"What?" I probed, watching his expression.

Lightly he ran the back of his finger along my cheekbone, over one ear, and onto my neck. "It's not the money…" he hesitated. "I love you the way you are. I don't want you all shiny and new."

Tom valued my aging face and soft body. Why didn't I? I thought of Winnie and all the elders of our tribe: what would I gain in denying age at the point of a knife? What did it say about self-acceptance and the human journey? It was one thing to care for my body out of love, but quite another to stitch it back into artificial blossom. A time to bud, a time for flowering, and a time to embrace autumn. The rest of life understood this, why did I hesitate? Then I knew: despite all my words, I've bought into the cultural belief in female obsolescence. *I am ashamed to grow old.*

Each stage in life requires a death. We celebrate our child's first steps while mourning the loss of our baby. Already he is on his way to manhood and out of our arms. I still missed my four-year-old Luke. He was gone and would never return, yet in his place stood a grown man. That is the unfolding journey. I, too, must evolve beyond a pretty face.

My generation—children of the 1960s—dreamed of changing the world. *What became of us? How did we get lost in a world of our own making?* We, who hold the power, money, and experience could still make a difference. Letting go of youth in a culture that devalues age is not easy, but the shift begins with me. Throughout our travels, Tom and I had seen our peers "retired," while a struggling generation of young people is saddled with debts before they even finish school. Winnie chose me. I think it was a good investment.

I was pondering this in a Fresno market when I noticed a little black girl of about six years old dancing in the aisle while her heavy-footed mother was pricing sandwich meats. The child saw me grinning at her and surprised me (and apparently her mother) by impulsively throwing her arms around my waist.

"You are really pretty!" she smiled up, dark eyes dancing with joy.

"And so are you," I said, as I knelt to hug her. *The role of aging mentor is a powerful one and worth exploring*, I thought. Following in the steps of my strong grandmother and gentle Aunt Janet could be one of the most important journeys of my life.

Tom and I visit Laurie in Washington, 2007.

Lucas teaches Kernwood jays to eat from his hand in 2007.

Chapter 20

SACRED GROUND

May 2007

Thirsty summer was only a vague threat in the hills east of Fresno when our old friend Matthew flew in from Wisconsin. He arrived at our apartment in motley Salvation Army clothes, the trunk of his rental compact stocked with small hard apples, day-old white bread, and generic grape jelly.

"How do you survive on that stuff?" I asked as I helped him unload.

He shrugged. "I don't think about it."

Matthew set up camp in our spare bedroom, sleeping on a foam pad he had salvaged at a rest stop along with two "pretty good" towels (which I still have). He spent his days exploring Fresno and joined us each night to share his discoveries.

Late afternoon sun filtered through eucalyptus in shifting patterns onto the glass table where Tom was serving plates of salad, grilled vegetables, and wild-caught salmon. I was tired from my third hard day of work and smiled my appreciation. Matthew was hunched over a map, his honest face intent as he fueled his body with unconscious efficiency.

"Jeanie, you have tomorrow off?" Matthew asked. "Why don't I take the two of you to Yosemite?"

"That could be fun," I said. "We haven't been there."

Tom shot me a look. "You go," he said. "I want to spend the day at the library."

"Are you sure?" I asked when we were alone in our room.

"Three is an awkward number. Enjoy your friend."

I nodded. A day in the woods with two environmentalists. *Too much information*, as the kids would say. Literally.

Early next morning I sat back and watched the country as Matthew's white rental car climbed out of the Central Valley. Green hills were dotted with great slabs of granite—dropped by retreating glaciers, he told me. The sentinel blue oak trees, he said, were ancient and because of grazing, no saplings survive to replace them. Matthew had learned more about the area in three days than I had in weeks. I smiled fondly at my old friend who had come all this way to see us. Again. What is it about lifetime friends? I thought. *They stand witness to our journey and anchor us.* I wondered how today's pelagic children—with their myriad "friends," jobs, and cities—would find their sense of belonging.

The road narrowed as it snaked into pines and entered the park. Matthew drove slowly and courteously, folded in the small car like a lean bird of prey. I looked out the window, my hand resting on his shoulder, while he told me about the land. We turned up a side road to visit a remaining stand of giant sequoias—trees of unimaginable grandeur. The parking lot was nearly empty when we stopped beneath the venerable trees.

"Shhh," I said as we stepped from the car. "I want to listen to the forest."

It was cold in the mountains and I tucked my fingers around Matthew's arm, slowing his long strides on the path. Our breaths fogged the still air as we penetrated the sacred grove through streaks of sunlight where birds sounded like flutes between the giants. Standing at the feet of these ancient beings, I felt myself expand in timeless space. It was like falling into the infinite, as if all noise had abruptly ceased. Womb of creation. Some of these trees had been here thirty centuries. There was something otherworldly about them. I felt humbled, like a vole at the foot of a mastodon.

Returning to the car, we continued our climb, twisting up through dense timber to tiptoe along a mountainside. At six thousand feet the trees were just budding out and patches of old snow crouched in the hollows. Cliffs fell away to our left, where we caught glimpses of the Merced River far below. The road edged over a ridge and dove through a hand-dug rock tunnel to emerge above the magnificent canyon. Glaciers had carved these sheer walls, leaving waterfalls to plunge twenty-five hundred feet into the shadows of Yosemite Valley, while mountains beyond climbed the sky. I had avoided national parks, fearing that a Disney version of wildness would trivialize my experience, yet cathedrals like Yosemite sing beyond our noisy minds of the sacred journey home.

Yosemite Valley is too intimate for the great numbers who visit each summer, bumper-to-bumper on the narrow road, but this early spring morning, Matthew and I had the park almost to ourselves. We drove slowly, gazing impossibly up to either side at the pearling cliffs where waterfalls arced rainbows into the sunlight and dropped in curtains of white mist into the shadowed valley. Matthew ducked his head to catch glimpses while I was free to take it all in. It was hard to believe we were not seeing the top—that beyond our vision the water was pouring from still higher.

We stopped to walk the short distance to Bridal Veil Falls, ascending a path until the water thundered overhead, showering us with spray from two thousand feet above. Signs warned of grave danger, but no fences blocked those who would climb to the very foot of the throne, and even a tourist was permitted grandeur. Wind funneled down with the icy torrent, trailing veils of mist. Matthew and I perched on the slippery path, shivering beneath that awesome blast. I reached for his big, cold hand and tucked it under my arm. My heart opened to that terrible and splendid thunder, swept into a majesty that was almost more than human senses could bear. I longed to remain forever, to freeze to death beneath that awful blast and be washed to clean white bones. For a moment, there was nothing else in my world. If only I could carry this awe back in my little cup of daily life! Yet the moment passed and we were becoming drenched. Reluctantly, I tugged Matthew's arm and we started carefully back down the steep trail.

A few days later I returned to Yosemite with Tom. It had rained in Fresno and snow had again fallen in the high country. The early morning air was frosty as we entered the sacred valley. On our walk up to Bridal Veil Falls, we were startled by the resounding boom of ice plunging over the cliffs above. At Yosemite Falls, the river was choked with sparkling slush while freezing mist coated the canyon walls. On this cold day, we walked the quiet trails almost alone to the holy thunder of falling ice and awakening waters.

ALMOST A YEAR HAD PASSED since Tom and I had taken to the road. Hills burnished gold and wildflowers withered to seed as spring again ripened into summer. The smell of orange blossoms transitioned into star jasmine, and layers of new green shaded our apartment. In nearby Woodward Park, bumblebee-sized Canada goslings grew to the dimension of footballs, their muddy-yellow bodies little resembling sleek parents. Nights resounded to bullfrog voices—like tuba players with only one note. Afternoons were hot on our bike rides above the San Joaquin River, where grass yellowed and then turned brown. Daily the Friant Reservoir dropped, exposing desiccated rings.

Fresno was far more interesting than I had imagined. California's Central Valley was a cornucopia of food. Decent wine cost less than bottled water. There were Asian markets and roadside stands beside one-acre fields where farmers spoke Mandarin, Hmong, and Spanish. For someone accustomed to strawberries with hard, yellow tops and mushy, moldy bottoms, it was a revelation in flavor. Yet there was a dark side to California's abundance. Cheap food, like cheap manufactured goods, carries a hidden price. I was perpetually hoarse from the thick smog of dust, pesticides, and herbicides, and I witnessed strange birth defects in the babies of migrant workers. Beyond roads that arrowed through dying towns, the identical rows of grape vines or apple trees marched in disquieting monotony, more like a factory than a farm, and vast feedlots harvested the misery of animals.

While I didn't become a vegetarian, our diet gradually shifted. It was sobering to witness immense stockyards of captive creatures packed hock deep in muck. I wondered at the implications of eating bodies and milk of these slave animals. It seemed a short ethical slide from treating our fellow mammals as commodity to viewing one another in the same light. *Eating is a communion,* I decided. *It matters how we consume the world.* Something in me drew back from supporting a callused system, even if it was cheap and convenient.

Recycling wasn't big in Fresno either. Tom and I generated very little trash, yet wanted to return it to the resource pool. There were dumpsters behind our apartment, but no way to recycle. One Sunday a young man came by on a bicycle and climbed into a dumpster looking for cans and bottles. He was lean and dark, his clothes faded but clean. Tom noticed him and went out.

"We don't use aluminum cans," Tom said, "but I can place a container and mark it for recycling so you won't have to climb into the dumpster."

The fellow looked alarmed. "Oh, no," he hastened, shaking his head. "If they catch me, they throw me off the property. That's why I only come on Sundays."

So, I thought. *We guard our garbage here to ensure that it all makes it to the landfill.*

Life shifts in a heartbeat—a reminder to cherish each day.

"Frances writes that Mother was admitted to hospice," Tom said. He had headed for the computer to check messages while I unpacked from a three-day trip with old friends to Kings Canyon, up a tortuous road that snaked into the impossibly high Sierras.

"You have to go," I said quietly.

It was certainly not untimely or unexpected. My first impulse was to wish her Godspeed. *There's a time to leave the stage*, I thought. Yet, seeing the pain in Tom's eyes, I knew that losing a beloved parent is never easy, even one in her nineties.

He nodded. "I want to say goodbye and be there for my siblings."

"I know."

He spent much of the evening buying an expensive ticket. In the end, full price cost less than the "bereavement" option. With our time in Fresno growing short, it felt like a sudden plunge into rapids. We had much to accomplish before heading north. Little Red Truck was already in Fresno and Tom was scheduled to drive my car to Tucson in two weeks and fly back. Nevertheless, his trip to Ohio was a crucial milestone.

It was still dark the following morning when I read Frances's email—their mother was gone. Gently I awakened Tom with the news, my eyes unexpectedly filling with tears. I thought of Mary Eva, small and determined; of her sharp tongue and quick wit. The gift of her beautiful handmade quilts. Her impish grin and rascal tricks, the mischief in those intelligent blue eyes. How good she was at cards. I recalled when she had flown to Tucson twenty-one years before to see her new grandson. Tom had shaved his beard as a joke and stood at the boarding ramp with three-month-old Luke in his arms.

As she filed past him, Tom had leaned down and tapped her on the shoulder. "Howdy, ma'am," he said in his deepest voice, "You wanna ride?" How alike they were.

We have a picture of Mary Eva holding Luke—he a huge baby and she so tiny. She had folded diapers like they were a work of art, perfect and flat, and cleaned my old toaster oven to a shine. Near our desert home, she found a stone that looked "just like a baked potato!" and took it back to Ohio to put on someone's plate.

Gone. All the words said, all the kindness and completion—done or not. It was over. The book was closed. Godspeed.

Mary Eva Irons: November 28, 1912 ~ April 30, 2007

"So what does your husband do?" coworkers would ask me.

"Well… he's… my husband. It's a big job. He keeps me fed, the bills paid, the computer running, and the car full of gas…" *He bicycles to the store for fresh food. He quietly fills his time until we head north. He writes a book about his life for his son.*

In truth, it was not full-time work. Tom was "too much dog for the job," to paraphrase my words when Lucas adopted a Queensland puppy. "If you want something to lie in the doorway and sleep," I told him, "get a hound."

Tom was no hound. He had been cheerfully running in place for almost a year, but we both looked forward to the time he would have something to build. Daily he threw his creative spirit into making dinner for me. I would arrive home from work exhausted to find exotic entrées, lovingly prepared. Tom gathered up my scattered embers and blew life back into them. I may have been driving the bus, but it was Tom who kept the wheels on.

I had never imagined growing old could be such a tender celebration. The poignant gift of mortality shining in Tom's eyes, reminded me keenly of our finite time together. Loss hovered somewhere down the path. How could I engage in pettiness with such a deadline? Always it is so, but falling leaves are a harbinger of change. We sat lightly touching as we drove or watched movies on our laptop. We shared rituals—a snack of berries with a splash of amaretto. Our bodies were comfortable with the shifting years, molded and softened into familiar contours. We laughed a lot. We breathed together at night. The familiar beat of Tom's great heart rocked me to sleep while I gave thanks for yet another day with him.

Like Tom, I'm an artist, a need I fulfilled by getting up early to write while he was asleep. I treasured the occasional day of solitude, but when he departed for his mother's funeral in Ohio, I had to admit he did more than handle chores: Tom kept me balanced. His gentle presence pulled me into participating. I liked to think of myself as complete, yet in reality, I was a human-doing—perpetually driven. Without Tom to anchor me in the moment, I disappeared into my head. I hadn't cooked a meal in days. I sat in front of my computer until my back ached and my eyes filmed over answering emails, writing—always writing.

I once spent a summer writing. Well, I've spent many summers writing. This time, I was finishing my fourth book, *Waking from the American Dream*, a researched tome on how corporate theft of our living planet diminishes human experience. "Too broad," one publisher told me. "Too negative," said another.

In the end, it was never published. Did I waste years writing it? No, I don't think so. It was part of my journey, even if it never saw the light.

That summer we had no glasswork and Tom was pacing the studio like a Queensland heeler in need of sheep. I took off his collar and sent him bounding joyfully north for a job with Alaska Fish and Wildlife among ghostly polar bears along the windy Arctic coast. Lucas was sixteen, employed a second season in Alaskan wilds doing salmon research. I stayed behind at University Medical Center, and spent every spare moment typing. Alone with my computer, I pulled food from the fridge and gnawed it at my desk. My only social contact was nursing. At the hospital I was a different person: I put on a smile and spoke with alacrity, volunteered for challenging patients, and took excellent care of them. I helped my colleagues and taught students. But on my days off, I withdrew into solitude: the Yin and Yang, ebb and flow of my personal tides.

In Fresno, I again withdrew. *Surely, this week*, I thought, *I will go for a bike ride or at least walk to the store*. I should learn to use our new digital SLR camera. I was proficient at accomplishing tasks; I just wasn't very good at fun. I didn't want to bike by myself, and would rather starve than shop alone. Eating out was a torment. I was timid and unsure of myself—a cosmopolitan hermit.

If Tom dies before I do, I thought, *I will end up a weird recluse in a nightgown hunched over a computer, subsisting on apples and cheese.* Maybe it's hereditary. My earliest dreams were peppered with my mother's banging away on her old typewriter while I napped in the hot Tucson afternoon. Connie at least made friends and went out when she could. I liked to think of myself as making friends, tending a garden, and volunteering in my older years. I will… if Tom is around. When I'm alone, my voice cracks from not speaking. As the days progress, I slip further into my own world—consumed by creativity, pregnant with vision.

I've never read all my mother's books. I intend to someday. Lucas hadn't read my work either. He shared his life candidly with me over the phone: his wins and doubts. He collected my essays and planned to read them when he was old and wanted to write about me. His voice was droll and insightful. He said he expected to end up as an eccentric English teacher in some Oregon backwater, stirring up ideas in bewildered young heads. I smiled at the thought, hoping we would live close enough to share tea on my porch, overlooking a brook shaded by great cedars. I hoped my garden would be full of personal art and jays gorging on blackberries. I hoped Tom would be there.

What is it about self-expression that's so compelling? I doubt my words or art will make any lasting impression. Blowing seasons will cover them—as it does everything from pyramids to sequoia—scouring the landscape for a new season. Perhaps therein lay my answer: creation is the fundamental act. When we cooperate with it, life dances uniquely through us. There is really nothing else to do. It is not so much a question of whether we create, but what. Only machines can duplicate. Nothing in nature—from snowflakes to feathers—is identical. That's the fallacy in comparing ourselves. Nevertheless, few people seem driven by artistic expression. Many are wistful about it, denigrating their ability as if their personal song were a competition. Children soon learn to suppress their enthusiasm and only those named "gifted" are encouraged to sing. I was fortunate to be one. My mother saw to that.

Creativity is an act of exploration, a process. I am never half so interested when a work is completed and rarely look back at the myriad of objects—books or art—that extend behind me. My attention, curious as a weasel, is focused on the play of bright water in the river ahead. When I run across my work somewhere, I recognize it in some vague way and think, *That looks familiar.* It is seductive to think one can make a living being creative, and yet the butterfly does not easily wear a harness. Better to shovel cement than force creativity into a box. Better to breathe your gift out as freely as the scent of a flower for anyone to enjoy.

Although he never said so, Tom missed our glass work. When I pulled away from designing panels, his mastery was left with no outlet. My vision and his skill had been a powerful focus in our relationship for twenty years and he longed for that too. My solitary typing did not fulfill his needs. I hoped to feel drawn to making glass again someday—if only for Tom. At the cabin he spent hours cutting and polishing unique pieces of driftwood and antlers for me to pen into figures of wolf and caribou: preparing a nest for my creative eggs. I wanted to fill that nest for him, but usually it didn't happen. I didn't really know why.

I had burned out on photography too. After decades of interest, I had been soured by our documentary—not by the filming, but the frustrating attempts at production. It was an enormous incompletion. I had hardly touched a camera since 1992. *Now that our income is no longer tied to creativity*, I thought, *perhaps I can explore like a child again.* We'd bought a good camera and I was determined to document our first summer in the Arctic with Lucas since he was fourteen, yet I had to surmount a great wall of resistance to touch the new Nikon with all its digital icons.

I recalled a picture I had taken of Luke our last winter in the wilderness—frosted and clear-eyed, hunting caribou alone at twenty below zero with my mother's old rifle. *It really doesn't matter if we make it to the Arctic Continental Divide*, I decided. I smiled thinking of the coming summer: two months of sharing the wilderness with Tom and Lucas. What else could I ask for?

Chapter 21

NORTH TO ALASKA

May 2007

"What I don't like about commuting to our cabin," I told Tom as we traveled north along the spine of California, "is the fuel needed to drive four thousand miles and charter a plane."

Our recurrent discussion about where to settle had snagged again on Kernwood. Little Red hummed along, her bed packed with summer supplies and a blue kayak lashed over the old shell. Tom looked happy, both hands on the wheel. A ball cap was pulled down to his sunglasses against the morning glare and his hair streamed in the breeze from an open window. He had chopped the sides short again, and hair stuck out along a groove worn in his temples by his glasses. His bare forearms were weathered and strong under coarse hair. A winter roll of belly fat pooched at the top of faded jeans where the holstered Leatherman that Lucas had given him was snugged against his right kidney.

"We'll use less than if we stayed in civilization," he reasoned. "No electricity, no driving or buying anything for four months. The food is already there." He shot me a sly glance. "Of course we could just live there."

"I want to be part of Lucas's life, not just a yearly visit. I don't imagine he'll spend much time in the wilderness for a while. He needs to invest in his career and find a mate." I gazed into the morning where our future, like California's yellowing rice fields, disappeared into haze. Smog flattened the sky and the sun was a low brassy glare. Occasional sunflowers dotted the freeway margin, grown unexpectedly from seeds blown off trucks.

"Here we go again," I grinned, "off on another adventure. Aren't we ever gonna grow up?"

"I hope not." We were quiet for a few minutes and then Tom continued, "When I look back on my life, I always seemed to know when it was time to move on. I remember friends saying that I ought to stay in the navy. Only eleven more years and I could retire—like those years meant nothing, were mere stepping stones. The same with aerospace: coworkers thought I was crazy leaving my cushy job with TRW to be an artist out on the desert. It was fun for a while, but it wasn't my passion. I could never see the logic in waiting to enjoy life."

I relaxed into the seat, tired from my last days at work. Fresno too had been good to me. The staff held a farewell potluck—though few had time to savor it. My mind churned over details of departing for a season: car insurance, housing deposit, credentials. There is no modern concept for genuine freedom; nothing to bridge three months out of touch. "Fax it to me, call me, just send me an email." Departing for the wilds felt like leaving the planet. *This is the barren land one must traverse to live an authentic dream.*

Let it go, I thought. *Alaska!* More than twenty years—a third of my life—I had wandered remote and wild lands. Friends questioned why. What about mosquitoes, cold, isolation, physical labor, and (let's be honest) bathing in the river and pooping in a hole? Maybe it was all right when I was young, but what could I possibly gain, they wondered, from this "hardship" in my sixth decade?

Wilderness is a homecoming for me in the deepest sense—a sanctuary to clear my head of trivia and noise. It also means freedom from the economic treadmill, a moment off the clock. While I hadn't learned to be "in the world but not of it," in wilderness I remembered. Life—simple and close to nature—was a drink of clean water after months on coffee, a place to soak up the stillness like a thirsty plant and replenish my soul. I would arrive at Kernwood trailing clouds of drama, my mind as loud and busy as an airport. Gradually the singing river would wash me clean, rinsing away the chatter until I could hear the deep rhythm of eternity. The very austerity of our days edged them with light; the deliberation of living made each movement into ritual.

I recalled Janet and Bert taking years to build their little cabin "Standwell." They dug the foundation by hand, gathered rocks for the fireplace, and cut a dead ponderosa from their acre to use as the ridgepole. Construction had been a celebration of process. I watched them negotiate: measuring simplicity against ease. What, after all, are the moments of a lifetime? What if one gains the whole world but fails to enjoy today?

"I'm excited about spending a summer with Lucas," I said breaking our silence. "I wasn't certain it would happen again. He gets so busy with his life…"

"As he should." Tom patted my knee.

"We'll see Laurie tomorrow night," I smiled. "I wish she'd come back to the cabin for a summer. I keep thinking there's something beyond the two of us—other folks who want to play and create for the fun of it." I was quiet, recalling the years spent dragging logs and laughing with Laurie. Good years. *Like Stan and Ruthie*, I decided, *we are blessed*.

IN VANCOUVER, WASHINGTON, LAURIE RAN out to greet us with hugs and her wonderful laugh—loud and raucous as a seagull. Beside her waddled an elderly Basset hound named Buddy. Laurie was plumper than of old, her bobbed hair the color of caramel. Her round, pink face was still unabashedly mobile, expressions sparkling across her blue eyes as openly as weather over a lake. She looked surprisingly at ease dressed professionally for her work with survivors of sexual abuse.

"So you're going back!" She grinned broadly, showing large, white teeth. There was no envy in Laurie, just excitement for her friends. It made me realize how often we temper our enthusiasm around those who don't really wish us joy.

"Do you think you'll ever want to come with us again?" I asked as we stowed food from our ice chest in her fridge.

Her brow furrowed and she paused to study the question. "I am very involved in my work and friendships," she said slowly. "I feel complete with that life. I don't know what the future will bring, but I don't see Alaska on my horizon right now." I watched her, sensing deep water. Always she had been my teacher, gently speaking her truth.

Tom carried our small duffle up the stairs to the guest bedroom as I helped Laurie pull food onto the counter for dinner. When he joined us in the kitchen, she brought out a bottle of bourbon with two glasses and raised a questioning eyebrow at me.

I shook my head. "Tom's still the designated drinker."

"More for us! Hey, I got to spend the day with Lucas and Eve when I was in Tucson recently visiting my mother. They go very well together."

"She doesn't let him overawe her," I said.

"They have the same droll sense of humor," Tom put in.

"He got that from you," I told Laurie. "Teaching him to read with *Calvin and Hobbes.* I could never get him back to first-grade material." We had fondly referred to Laurie as our "nanny from hell."

She barked a laughed and handed Tom a glass. "Oh, he's much subtler than I am!"

Tom and Laurie raised their glasses in a toast and I clinked my water glass. "To lifelong friendship," I said.

"So I gather Lucas and Eve are not living together?" Laurie asked. "They certainly enjoy one another."

"They're experimenting with being friends," I told her. "Eve is the only person he ever dated. She agreed that it would be good for him to explore. I'm not sure he's seeing anyone else, but he wanted the freedom."

"I like her more all the time," Laurie commented.

"I just wish she'd stayed on for the summer," I said. "Right now Lucas has mismatched roommates: a shy college girl and a strange man named Scott, who's in his fifties and has a restraining order from his wife. Lucas found him on the Internet. It sounds like a scary match to me, not to mention that everything we own is stored at Sylvia House."

"Which isn't much," Tom added, "but some things—like my tools, my mother's quilts, and our slides—are irreplaceable. Eve promised to keep an eye on things, but a lot can happen."

The following day, Tom and I crossed Washington and drove into Canada, entering the Frasier River gorge in late afternoon. Like Yosemite, Frasier Canyon is geography on a grand scale. The forest lay deep and wet, with waterfalls cascading from far above us. Spring still lingered here and patches of snow gleamed in the lowering sun as we climbed. This highway is a major artery and often crowded with big trucks, but we were blessedly alone that evening, twisting along the canyon walls and through rock tunnels above that fierce river. The air became chilly as twilight blued the gorge.

It was Little Red Truck's eleventh trip over this road. I thought of Tom driving alone to Alaska so many seasons, his old vehicle hauling truly massive loads. This five-speed, four-cylinder, one-ton pickup could tow five thousand pounds while loaded with another fifteen hundred, uphill and down at twenty miles per gallon. After more than two decades, though, it was time to retire Little Red, but we had found nothing to match her. It was a long and dubious journey for a vehicle that had logged a quarter-million rough miles. Staring out the window, I tried to remember all the times that I had made this drive.

It was May 1977 when Annie and I drove the Alcan with twenty-month-old Faith and my three huskies in a Volkswagen Fastback bought for two hundred fifty dollars. Phil and I had wintered in Arizona and planned to drive north for a summer hike from our cabin to the Arctic Continental Divide—the only time I succeeded. My father phoned in April to say that the Arctic Ocean was breaking up early and he needed help moving equipment off the ice. He offered Phil wages and a ticket north. I could drive up with the dogs, he said, and join Phil for our hike. Annie decided to accompany me.

In those days the Alcan—the Alaska–Canada Highway—was a dirt ribbon that wound above muskeg through vast boreal forests and was often deep in viscous mud. Created during World War II as defense against the Japanese, it was a remarkable monument to human effort. Annie and I were old hands from our Australian travels and thousands of river-miles, but the VW was precarious at best. We needed to push-start it the last three thousand miles. The transaxle leaked, and I regularly crawled through mud beneath the car to fill it. Reverse went out, the parking brake broke, the windshield wipers quit, and driver's side window slid down into the doorframe. We were restricted to camping on hills where we could circle around. Once the car was in position for the morning push, one of us would jump out and block the tires. Most days it rained. Every hour or so a large truck would pass, splattering us with mud the consistency of gravy. I'd pull over to wipe a circle in the windshield then peer through the streaming drops, occasionally sticking my head out the window for a better view of the road and endless soaking forest.

"You know," I said to Annie as we bounced over frost heaves on the bit of pavement near Fairbanks, "we've never asked Dad for anything. Maybe we should be humble instead of trying to prove how strong we are." We'd been on the road for ten days and had weathered numerous problems with the deteriorating car.

In back, Faith was strapped into her car seat. She had just thrown up her hot dog-cheese-and-tortilla breakfast. Her little pink face looked sad and resigned, golden hair plastered with dog slobber. Our wet tent and sleeping bags were spread out around her where my three huskies panted, steaming up the remaining windows. Rain blew onto my shoulder as I drove.

"Well, I don't feel like proving anything right now," Annie said. Then she grinned. "It's been a helluva trip, but we made it!"

I grinned back. "You and me, kid… Oops! I think the baby's gonna barf again."

The sky was clearing when our father greeted us on the steps to his Fairbanks home, which was still one floor, though he was already adding on odd rooms. We were muddy and bug-bitten; we hadn't had a bath in days. My huskies remained in the parked car along the street beyond his hedge. They had been born in the wilderness and were nervous in the city.

Faith squirmed in Annie's arms. "Down!" she said, gesturing in case we didn't understand. "Down!"

"Oh, Martha! Come see who's here!" Bud called over his shoulder. "You girls are just in time. I'm building a lanai and was just going to start the insulation. You know, I'm allergic to that stuff. Mother can watch the baby and make us all a nice dinner later." He led us through the living room and down a couple of steps to a framed addition. Handing us each a hammer and paper sack of nails, he returned to the kitchen.

"The old dog!" I whispered as we balanced on joists unrolling the pink strips and tacking them down. "Everybody is 'allergic' to fiberglass."

"So much for asking Daddy for a hand with our little problems. Where are we spending the night?"

"It's hard to push-start the car without a hill," I answered. "We'll just have to camp in their yard. At least we can use the basement shower."

"You girls can camp down at the park," Dad told us cheerfully when we had finished the job and were sitting at the kitchen table with its with matching china. "There are toilets and you'll be real comfortable with your dogs. Mother can keep the baby here. She looks happy playing, now doesn't she?"

Faith did indeed seem ready to jump ship. She cheerfully waved 'Bye-bye' from Martha's arms as she and Bud stood in the doorway watching us trudge down the street with our huskies, soggy tent, and damp sleeping bags.

"They took my baby and tossed me out!" Annie looked ready to cry.

I put my arm around her shoulder. "You'll be back at home tomorrow night. Thanks for coming."

"I wouldn't have missed it." She flashed an open smile, her face smudged and speckled with bug welts. "We're still a good team!"

The next morning was sunny and hot. We rolled the tent and Annie stuffed her redolent belongings into a suitcase. Then we walked the few blocks to our father's house for Faith and loaded my dogs into the forlorn little car. After we pushed it back to life, I drove Annie and Faith to the airport and watched them disappear into the small terminal—headed back to Tucson. I didn't want to shut off the engine; instead I drove back into town and stopped at a phone booth to look up automotive stores. My unhappy dogs waited in the running VW while I sought advice and finally bought a rebuilt starter. It wasn't clear if I needed a starter or a generator (and I lacked the tools and knowledge to install either), but it seemed a first step.

If only Phil were here! Phil was an excellent mechanic and a good worker. There was no telling how long my father would keep him, and meanwhile I had little money and no place to go. Although obedient, my huskies were as nervous as wolves around strangers. I couldn't live in the park. I bought a bag of groceries and drove back out of town. Turning onto a dirt track, I set up camp in a thicket of poplar where enough water had collected to drink. Alone now, it was harder than ever for me to push-start the car. Mosquitoes were thick as June advanced, and I felt trapped in my stifling tent. Angry and frustrated, I watched days crawl slowly by.

One morning I remembered Mark and Denise Wartes. I'd met Denise the autumn of 1975 when Phil and I paddled a homemade canoe with our dogs out of the Brooks Range just before freeze-up after eighteen months alone in the wilds. Denise was in Fairbanks for the birth of her second baby. She was staying with her toddler son and infant daughter in my father's basement until he flew them back to the Colville, where she and her husband were building a home. Denise was twenty-two then, a gentle and shy girl with blue eyes and long dark hair. Eldest of eight children, she was accustomed to doing without. In later years, I would realize that her sweet compliance was powerful—like running water that carves bedrock. She was my first example of the Taoist principle of strength-through-yielding.

I hadn't met Mark, though I knew of him. The son of Barrow missionaries, he had grown up on the Arctic coast speaking Iñupiaq. At times, he had lived with Bud and Martha on the Colville delta, best friends with my stepbrother Jim, who later married Mark's sister. So our family roots were interwoven. My half-brother was even named for him. After Vietnam, Mark Wartes returned with his young bride to build on Bud's land at the Colville under a vague assurance that he would earn "a piece of the operation." When the promise soured, the young family moved to Fairbanks and started over.

I packed my tent, loaded the dogs, and pushed the old VW down the rutted track until the engine coughed to life. Jumping in, I gunned it. The car sputtered and was making a new noise, but I was driving. Pulling onto the highway, I headed for town with the windows down and dogs' tongues out. I left the engine idling in front of a gas station and searched for Mark and Denise's number in a phone booth.

Mark was in the yard of their little two-bedroom home when I pulled up. He was six years my senior, a small man, compact and tough. He greeted me with a warm and powerful hand. His round head was already balding, and his face was more-or-less clean-shaven. He had lost an eye as a youth when a gun my father lent him blew up, and the glass one lagged occasionally so that it was sometimes hard to tell where he was looking.

"Turn your dogs loose in the front yard and pull your car around back," he said when I explained that I couldn't turn it off. "Your engine sounds pretty rough."

"I'm sorry to bother you… I don't know where else to go."

"You're family," he brushed aside my concerns. "This is your home. Let's have a look."

I could have cried with relief. I was welcome: dogs, dirt, problems, and all!

Mark picked up a toolbox and led the way. I set out my metal ramps (carried since Oregon) and drove onto them before shutting off the engine. We sprawled on our backs in the grass and inched under. For the next hour, I handed him tools while he showed me how to change the starter. Soon the little VW turned over and caught on its own for the first time since the Fraser River. My skittish huskies and I finally had a place out of the bugs, heat, and rain, with people who cared about us. They offered me whatever they had, which in those days wasn't much: a shower, a tiny washing machine, meals, and a phone. It was the beginning of a lifelong friendship.

TOM AND I CONTINUED NORTH, crossing the great Peace River a few days after entering Canada. As we climbed onto the bluff, I asked him to pull off at the overlook. I remembered this river in the spring of 1964—the torrent of mud and uprooted trees upon which my mother, sister, and I had bravely set forth—and recalled Connie's sorrow about the proposed dam. Downstream, I knew the boreal forest had been churned into a vast and stinking wasteland by tar sand extraction. I studied the fettered dragon coiling below us, green and pacific. Sun glinted from beneath a bank of clouds, illuminating its broad back in silver mail. *It's dozing*, I thought, examining the deep cut of the valley. *Time is on its side.*

As we stood in the drizzle, a Harley rumbled up and a man and woman dismounted. They looked to be in their forties, pink-cheeked from the wind, both dressed in black leather. After gazing down at the water, smooth and serpentine, the man turned to us in a friendly Canadian voice and asked, "Been up here before?"

I swelled up like a puffer fish. "I canoed the Peace with my mother and little sister from Taylor Flats clear to the Arctic Ocean when I was a girl," I said proudly. "Before the dam."

"Really? No kidding?" The woman shook long, blonde hair out of her helmet. Neither of them seemed to notice the rain.

I reminded myself suddenly of Janet. Years before, Tom and I had taken her and Annie on a four-day backpack up the north side of 9,159-foot Mount Lemmon, walking up from near Oracle following Canada del Oro. When she got to the top, Janet had spoken to people in the parking lot, telling them with childlike enthusiasm, "I just climbed all the way up from the bottom and I'm sixty-four years old!"

Days melted together and darkness faded for another summer as we journeyed north. It was early in the season and many of the small towns (often little more than a gas pump and restaurant) were locked up. We paced our trip to arrive at one of the few motels each night and planned fuel stops with care. Even today, the Alcan is no place to break down. We breakfasted on raw oatmeal, nuts, powdered milk, and fruit, and were on the road by first light, keeping a moderate speed but putting in long hours. I packed simple lunches, which we ate at some beautiful spot off the road. The Alcan is now broad and paved, arcing precisely through a hundred-yard swath of cleared trees. The curves have been shaved for speed, valleys filled in with hilltops, the bed contoured and raised. It becomes shorter and tamer each year as topography is whittled away. *When is life comfortable enough?* I wondered. *Do we really kill the things we love as Aldo Leopold wrote?*

Daily we spotted black bears foraging the new grass of the verge and the occasional moose, bison, or caribou. Judging from the highway, Canadian wildlife was more abundant than Alaskan. Looking out the window at the dark trees dampened by gray sky, I imagined migrating songbirds traveling these thousands of miles with only their skimpy fat to sustain them. How fragile yet tenacious they seem! Once we saw a ripple of cranes following the highway north; we pulled over to hear their loud musical rattles. The sight of them moved me to sudden tears.

At Liard Hot Springs we set up our two-man tent for the first time, and then followed the boardwalk over swamps through the lush woods to steaming mineral pools. A few early campers were swimming in the lower pool—a place of hanging gardens where emerald water flowed over golden sand. The hot spring had been carefully augmented with decking, a changing room, and a composting toilet.

"The upper pool is for nude swimming," a young man told us.

Tom and I climbed the hundred yards further, took off our clothes, and had the lovely higher pool to ourselves. He photographed me in the turquoise water, learning to use our new digital camera. I remembered Janet saying, "Take pictures of yourselves naked while you're young." Well, we were no longer young, but every year carried us further. I was becoming excited about photography again. *Perhaps we'll create another documentary. Maybe we'll complete the one we filmed.* Possibilities seem to open before us. I smiled, thinking of the summer with Lucas.

"Sorry I took so long," Tom said. I had stayed in the truck while he checked us into a small motel. "The owner is an old guy who wanted to talk. He just got back from taking his wife to the hospital in Vancouver. She's had blood clots in her legs before, and they thought she might have another. He closed up here and stayed in an expensive hotel only to be told it was leg cramps."

We gathered up a few items and climbed onto the wooden deck. The room was spacious and clean. Evening sun came through birch trees beyond the window.

"I don't want to be stuck out here when I'm old," I said.

"Sun City for you?"

"No, there has to be something in between. I want real life, but not isolation."

I kept thinking about the old man's question: "How do I know when to take her for help?" The following morning I wrote a page of instructions for diagnosing and treating deep vein thrombosis.

"Are you sure you should do that?" Tom was waiting patiently, the truck packed.

I stopped a moment to consider. "He asked," I finally said. "Why else did I become a nurse, if not to share?" I left the page on the table.

We were filling up at the gas station, when I noticed a man slowly exiting the sliding door of an ancient van with Minnesota tags. He was perhaps fifty, frail with wispy gray hair that fluttered in the cold wind. He had obviously been paraplegic for many years, for his legs were tiny and shriveled. Behind him, I could see a neat bed and cupboards—his tidy life tucked into the small space.

He caught my unspoken offer of help, smiled, and shook his head. With a practiced routine, he scooted over the platform, leaned out the open doors, and set a wheelchair into the mud. *Courage*, I thought. *You get to play the cards you're dealt.*

FOUR DAYS LATER WE ARRIVED in Fairbanks, just in time to pick up Lucas at the airport. At twenty-one, he had grown into a man, yet maturity seemed to weigh upon him. He wore glasses now and his face had rounded with a soft double chin filling in the angles of his jaw. His hair—glossy as an otter's and about the same color—was freshly cut, but the front cowlick (echo of mine) was still unruly. He enveloped his father in a hug while beaming at me over Tom's head.

The two stood together for long moments, breathing. "God, it's good to be here!"

"You have a goatee," I said as he turned to wrap me in gentle arms. The dark whiskers were neatly trimmed, wiry, and a bit patchy. His cheeks were rosy.

"I still can't grow a beard. I'm envious of Dad."

Lucas and Tom talked happily as we ambled toward the truck. I was silent for once, holding his free hand and this moment. He tossed his duffel in the back. I climbed into the middle of the seat, straddling the gearshift, and wedged myself onto his knee as he squeezed in and slammed the door. His head touched the ceiling.

"What do you think of the kayak?" I asked as Tom started the engine. "Our little canoe won't handle the three of us with gear, so we figured to float the kayak along behind on our hike upstream. You can have your own craft for crossing back and forth."

"Cool! I was hoping it was for me."

A few minutes later we parked under the spruce trees in front of the Wartses' large home. Mark had renovated it, removing half the original structure at a time. "Bud can't say 'Denise in her little house' anymore," Mark had declared—both of us still controlled by my father's opinions.

Mark was in the kitchen when we entered—a little balder, deafer, and rounder—and greeted us with the same generosity. He was dressed in shorts and sandals; a beer was in his hand. His skin was sunburned from playing in the deck pool with his grandchildren. A ballgame blared loudly on the TV in the family room. His eyes traveled up Lucas's six-foot-one inches as his hand was buried in the warm grip. "My God, I'm glad I don't have to feed you!"

Denise smiled up from the sofa where she was writing a grant on her laptop. The only member of her family to complete college, she had risen in the academic world to head a major program at the university. She worked with young Native people, and looked more like an Inuit elder with each season. Her hair was short and snowy now, her body rounded by the years. Her quiet energy and warm disposition had deepened with time—a steady ship in any storm.

AFTER A BRIEF DAY OF shopping, Tom, Lucas, and I crammed into Little Red for the final two-hundred-fifty-mile drive. The Dalton Highway had admittedly simplified our lives. Bladed north to the Arctic Ocean with the oil pipeline in the 1970s, it carried us easily over land that had once taken me all summer to traverse. Nevertheless, the "Haul Road" had sliced open the heart of northern wilderness, irreversibly altering its character into playground and resource pool. *In truth*, I thought, *the Brooks Range is less "a frontier" than a last remnant of the intact planet.*

"We'll get gas at the bridge," Tom was saying. The road ahead curved down in a grand view of the Yukon River. Here the muscular current gathered into a single strand—almost a mile wide—herded between hills. It was one of the few places a canoeist could be certain that the shoreline was not just another island. A bridge sloped between the hills, the only crossing in Alaska.

On the north bank sprawled a muddy parking lot and a cluster of commercial modules where we stopped for coffee and gas. The few licensed franchises along the Dalton are controlled by one company. Inside the restaurant, a busload of aging tourists were eating packaged lunches and listening to a pitch for a booklet about an old bear that had broken in during the winter of 2004 to sleep in a nest of sweaters. The trooper was called to shoot him. The broken window had been boarded up with plywood and crudely painted like an entering bear.

We squeezed back into the pickup and were soon headed north again. I was wedged in the middle and hugged myself to keep my arms out of the way. Much of the road had been paved in the past few years. The land had changed too even since the last time we'd been here. Miles of blackened snags leaned drunkenly in a pink sea of blooming fireweed. Birch erupted from hills where black spruce had ruled, flowers were replacing moss, and shallow lakes were disappearing as the permafrost thawed. We passed Grayling Lake where we had camped so many times waiting for a floatplane. There were toilets there now.

It was late afternoon when we pulled into Coldfoot along the upper Middle Fork of the Koyukuk River. This had been the easiest trip yet. Maybe I was learning to "go with the flow" or perhaps it was because we were only going for the summer. Whatever the reason, I wasn't worried about a chancy landing or the weather. Tomorrow we would find out if the cabin was standing and how the bears had treated things.

Life was good, and I had a summer adventure to share with the two people I loved most in the world.

Lucas gives me a hug on our hike up Flattop.

Tom, Lucas and me on Flattop peak, 2007.

Chapter 22

ARCTIC REFUGE

June 2007

Like the Yukon River Camp, Coldfoot was constructed to serve the Haul Road. We stopped to talk with Dirk at his log cabin on the airstrip and then crossed the dirt road for dinner at the restaurant. It was modular and had a special table and menu for truckers; everyone else ate a pricy buffet. The walls were papered with pictures of heroic machines battling river and ice. The rough-looking folk at the trucker's table were already a generation too late for their grand adventure. On one photo was written, "When we first built this camp there was nothing here."

Nothing? I glazed out at the silent mountain beyond the muddy parking lot. *How different our visions.* "Progress is relentless," I said.

Tom and Lucas glanced at one another and smiled. My son reached across the table and patted me fondly. I was reminded of my youthful relationship with Connie. The years were lapping one another—a spiral of dreams.

After dinner we drove around the end of the airstrip and into the forest a few feet above a young Koyukuk River. Lucas swung open the truck door, engulfing us in the smell of Labrador tea and spruce trees. I could hear the familiar songs of nesting birds and the sound of dancing water. Early mosquitoes welcomed us back—not in horrific numbers yet, but enough to remind us of our place in the food chain.

"Hey! I just got my first mosquito bite!" Lucas sounded elated. He and Tom were erecting our new tent while I rummaged in the pickup. Tired of toting heavier models, we'd bought backpacking tents: a two-man and a four-man. As the larger tent emerged from nylon and rods, I could see it (like its cousin) had no windows.

"I feel like a soft taco," I muttered as I crawled into our new summer home. "Chewy on the outside, meaty on the inside." I tucked my boots under the rainfly and quickly zipped the door. Lucas lay tight against the nylon wall, reading. He had spread out the pads and arranged a blanket over them, and was already dressed in sweatpants and T-shirt, using his clothes as a pillow.

"It's not a great design for bear country," Tom agreed from outside. "Do we have a water bottle?"

"Yes. Right outside the door," I answered. "The rifle is on your side—not that you can see anything. There's not much ventilation either. At least it won't get dark again until August." We had crossed the Arctic Circle, that imaginary line around the planet where the sun doesn't set at the summer solstice and fails to rise one day in midwinter. The further north you go, the more extreme the seasonal shifts.

"This is a four-person tent? Really?" Tom wiggled in, swatting small intruders. He hunched out of his jeans and pulled on his night clothes.

"I like the rectangular floor plan," Lucas commented. "I get tired of contouring myself to a tent wall." He looked happy.

I AWOKE EARLY TO A light patter of rain on the tent fly and crawled into a gray day, zipping the door behind me. Sand drifted in sheets down the exposed bar across the river. *Wind this early in the day*, I thought, *will likely worsen*. "May as well break camp," I spoke softly to my companions and heard them stir. "It'll be harder to pack up if it gets wet."

Without a murmur they began to stuff our sleeping bags and emerge. I didn't push my luck with conversation, for neither were early risers. I wore the only watch and they would allow me to define time. When canoe journeys had required us to travel before the wind freshened, I would sometimes set my watch ahead because Tom preferred to get up at "seven" instead of "four." Yet a watch was useful. I recalled a night in late August when we'd broken camp after I mistook the rising moon for dawn.

By the time we pulled up in front of Coyote Air, my companions were showing signs of life. "Hey, here's the boy from the book!" Dirk's wife, still rumpled from sleep, greeted us at the cabin door. She paused to stare up at

Lucas. "Well, I guess you've grown a bit… Hi, I'm Danielle," she said, extending a firm hand.

She was about my height with an open face, generous mouth, quick blue eyes, and a blonde ponytail. Her body, slender and strong, looked like it could handle an ax. It turned out that she did much of the mechanical work on their planes. She was wearing a "Coyote Air" T-shirt, jeans, and sandals—where a freckling of mosquitoes enjoyed her bare toes. I caught a glimpse of a girl of about eight with tangled blond hair in a nightshirt behind her. The child gave us a shy glance before darting back into the cabin.

Dirk was fueling a second Beaver—this one orange and white—before the cabin. The planes were my age: single-engine tail-dragging workhorses on tundra tires. He was wearing a T-shirt that matched his wife's, a ball cap, khaki pants, and leather boots. In one hand was a stained mug of tea. The reserved smile hidden beneath his rusty mustache seemed on the verge of a secret joke. Tom began pulling items from our pickup and stacking them in the shelter of the wing; I sorted piles and tallied weights as rain again gusted over the runway. Lucas was quiet, watching.

"Only one load today," I told Dirk. "We'll leave the rest in the truck for you to bring when you pick Lucas up at the end of July. How much weight do you want?"

He ran quick eyes over the piles. "I'd like to stick to about twelve-hundred-fifty pounds, because we don't know the condition of the river bars. The kayak should fit."

"We'll keep in touch with the satellite phone," I said. "Tom and I plan to stay until the end of moose season. How's your schedule?"

"We'll be here until October. With the climate warming, many people are hunting later." Dirk was already heaving buckets and gear behind the cargo netting, placing lighter items toward the tail. He was wiry and strong, a man of compact motions.

"Do you really eat that many pickles?" Danielle asked, pointing to the stack of white five-gallon buckets.

I laughed. "No. Those are staples—powdered milk, dried apples, dried onions. The buckets are recycled from a cafeteria."

"Do you have enough food?" Dirk asked. It was a good question. Despite the satellite phone, a lot can go wrong.

"A year's worth is stored in the cache—if the bears haven't figure out how to raid it," I said. "I always have enough food. It might be boring, but it'll keep you alive."

Danielle grinned. "Last winter traveling through South America, the kids learned to eat many things. Life is uncertain. Dirk's survival food is lard. Mine is dog biscuits. You won't eat it unless you need to. Then it'll be there."

I smiled, feeling kinship. "As an old trapper friend once said, 'The difference between what you will and won't eat is twenty-four hours.' Most people don't know that."

Dirk was all business as he belted us in and gave emergency instructions. When the plane lifted and banked, I felt my stomach lurch with the crosswinds. Lucas sat in front, chatting easily over the intercom and photographing the greening land. He had mastered the camera without reading the manual. Dirk swung his head to check on us and silently handed me an airsick bag. *Some things never change.*

I stared out my side window for an hour as we slid around barren peaks crusted with late snow and bounced through clouds streaked in sunlight. Candling ice still imprisoned the high lakes and I could see tracks of migrating caribou along ridge tops. Shifting landmarks beneath the wing began to coalesce into patterns as familiar as my palm, a terrain I had covered on foot. There were changes too: new roads pushed across muskeg and forest. Big Creek, where I had often camped in my youth, was a raw gash of gold mine and runway. A ribbon of old spruce once snaked up this otherwise barren valley, sheltering a lively creek with hidden pools. It would take centuries, possibly another ice age, to restore. Arctic willow no higher than my hand may live hundreds of years.

When our familiar riverbends came into view, my chest tightened with emotion. The water was high, but gravel and rock bars protruded from the roiling current. I tried to see if breakup had left gouges or trees stranded on the one above our cabin. Dirk swung around for another look, skimming low over the spruce forest. I soon lost track of where we were, my stomach in turmoil.

"Don't risk your plane," I mumbled over the intercom. "Set down wherever you think best. We have all summer to get home." I took off my headset and closed my eyes. It wasn't up to me. Dying seemed preferable to airsickness. Suddenly the plane banked and flared. I opened my eyes and pulled on the headset. We were coming down somewhere. Trees rushed past and then we hit, hard.

"Oh, shit!" Dirk muttered and stood on the brakes. I had no idea a plane could stop so quickly! One moment we were flying, the next the world heaved and settled.

In the abrupt silence, I released my seatbelt, swung open the door, clambered onto the thirty-six-inch tire, and dropped to the ground. Dirk had landed on our familiar bar, just upstream from the cabin. A hundred yards away, Luke's Creek gushed into the brown river. After the men unloaded the plane, Dirk paced the bar, removing debris and kicking rocks into particularly nasty holes. The ice had indeed gouged deep furrows and we had stopped just short of one.

The engine growls that distinctive Beaver tone and the sturdy old plane lifts from the bar, blowing dust over our piled belongings as it chews into the air. Dirk banks around and waggles his wings "Goodbye," and then arrows off into the patchy southern sky. We three stand listening until the drone melts into the chuckle of the river and the soft breath of wind.

"Lucas and I will check out the cabin while you sit a moment," Tom says. He loads his .357 magnum with bear slugs and straps it on. It's dubious protection from grizzlies, but easier to carry than a rifle. He leaves me with his old .30-30 carbine.

No sign indicates the fifteen years that our family has called this particular riverbend home and yet every tree speaks to me. For thirty-five years, I have belonged to this valley. I imagine my body returning to the soil, borrowed molecules sucked up by roots and transpired back into the air without a trace. *It's the least I owe.* My gaze slides north along the familiar horizon to the buttress cliffs of Flattop, climbs four thousand feet to its dome, rides down its sinuous spine eastward and up the soaring cone of Mount Laurie. Here the skyline drifts downriver into the feminine curves of South Mountain and then up the crenelated parapets of King Mountain—jagged and bare as a crown. I turn west to the breaking wave of Annie's Peak with its pink tide of fireweed and full circle north to the distant peaks of the Divide. *This is the perimeter of my life. Now I live in the present.*

My two men dwindle down the bar, ford the rushing creek in hip waders, and climb into the woods. Tom looks nimble and small beside his son; Lucas is steady and strong. His memory is photographic. At seven he recognized each campsite along a river he had traveled at the age of four. In half an hour they reappear, carrying our seventeen-foot canoe between them. They set it in the current and Lucas starts toward me across the open gravel while Tom lines it upriver. It takes them both to work the canoe around the flooded mouth of the creek. By the time they reach me, I have recovered enough to start a fire, pry open buckets, and haggle off pieces of summer sausage, cheese, and dried fruit for lunch.

"The cabin is in great shape," Lucas reports happily. He sits on a white bucket and accepts a handful of apricots. "The bear did very little damage."

I feel uneasy when Lucas chooses to paddle the kayak home in the swift current. He has never been in one and I would prefer he play around in the shallows first, but that was never his style. I think of him swimming the river at age thirteen. It takes only two trips for Tom to freight the supplies down with our canoe. We cheerfully lug totes up the familiar trail, then Tom brings up a bucket of clear water from the spring where Goldilocks's big tracks are overwritten with wolf.

The cabin looks dry and solid: the moss chinking yellow and brittle with age, sod roof already in bloom. Goldie has pushed out the window covers and bitten into the counter, but our bedding in the loft is inviolate. It's already been a long day, so we decide to spend our first night in the yard while we clean up. Lucas pitches the tent while Tom installs the storehouse door, opens the trapdoor to the cache attic, and places the ladders. They begin tacking netting over the window holes, excluding mosquitoes that are out in droves. I set up the kitchen and sweep.

"I'm glad we're sleeping in the tent tonight," Tom says when we break for coffee. Lucas has folding chairs around the fire and a pot on the grill. Tom hands me Laurie's old mug with its impressionist painting of a person fishing from a canoe.

"I'd rather sleep in the loft until Goldie knows we're home," I say.

"Old Mom is always such a worrier." Lucas smiles fondly.

Later I find him standing on the bluff, gazing across the river. I climb the few steps carved into the hill to join him. He lifts his arm to welcome me, my head as high as his shoulder. We stand in silence. Swallows stream like smoke from nest holes in the bank, their cries shrill as they weave for the bugs and snap past us like small fighters. Across the river, snow lingers in the upper cliffs of Mount Laurie.

"It's so beautiful," I say. I think of Janet. *What else is there to say?*

My son beams down at me. "I always picture you at the end of civilization, a bent old woman among the smoldering ruins, smiling. You'll look down through the ashes and say, 'Look at the beautiful flowers!' " He runs a gentle finger over my head. "Mama," he says in surprise, "your hair is turning gray."

I nod. "Yes. I may be counting more on you this trip."

"As you should. I want to be there for you and Dad, like you've been for me." He gazes north again. "I've always wanted to climb Flattop. Maybe we can do a shakedown hike up there." He glances at me questioningly.

"We can do anything we want this summer. I have no plans except to enjoy you and Dad."

While I organize the cabin and pack for a week's hike, the two men hoist Tom's handmade windsock and clear the gravel bar, marking a thousand-foot runway. Tom and I take turns showing Lucas the old haunts. He is rapidly morphing into a familiar shape, his pants becoming loose and his legs muscular. Clearly, he will soon be the strongest member of our group.

Five days after our arrival, Tom loads the canoe and ferries me across the river, then returns for Lucas. I start a small lunch fire while they carry the canoe into the trees and tie it down. We rest with our backpacks at the edge of the forest, roasting summer sausage on sticks and contemplating our route. The gravel bar below is dotted with candy pink blossoms of wild sweet pea and the delicate rose of Eskimo potato; the air is heavy with fragrance. Smoke and a light breeze keep the mosquitoes at bay. The dropping river is milky brown. Across from us, the creek has turned the color of jade.

We bury traces of the fire and shoulder our loads. Tom wears the heavy pistol on a belt, awkward beneath his pack. Lucas leads eastward beneath young poplar trees on a network of old river channels that wander between islands of mature spruce. I follow his long strides past Daddy's Magic Forest, across the rivulet of Pike Slough and onto Overlook Bluff. My thoughts, busy with details of our journey, begin to quiet as my body remembers the rhythm of movement and awakens to the familiar ache of calf and shoulder beneath the backpack. My eyes caress the awakening land. Feather moss and lichen lay deep and springy underfoot. A riot of wildflowers rockets up from roots: blue lupine, carpets of mountain avens with large white-and-gold stars, and yellow arnica. Miniature pink bells of low-bush cranberry recoil from our steps; tiny red blooms among the fresh leaves of blueberry bushes hint of coming harvest.

"There it is," Lucas intones. Ahead, black spruce trees dwindle into the Infinite Swamps of Hell, a two-mile swath of muskeg that guards the feet of Mount Laurie.

I'm too old for this, I whine to myself.

The men take turns leading; I have only to watch my footing. Cottongrass tussocks sprout like giant mushrooms over a mosaic of mud and ice. One must either lurch atop the quivering mounds or stumble over them into deep cracks.

This terrain is interspersed with bog where tough willow, sedges, and arctic birch stand rooted in knee-deep water. There is also the awful hope factor: a belief that footing will be better a bit to one side or just ahead. Every floundering step disturbs new hordes of mosquitoes that carpet our hats and shoulders in a probing mass. We frequently cough and spit them out. Our defenses—long sleeves, hats, repellant, and smoke—still leave us with a hundred bites a day. Bugs are a fact of early summer: a reason birds fly north. They are a major food base. Like anything one cannot change, sanity is found in acceptance.

When at length we reach the toe of Mount Laurie, we are wet to the knees and slimed in dark mud. The slope rises abruptly, clothed scantily in stunted spruce. I call a second lunch near a pothole where we can dip water with an enamel mug. Although waterborne illness is common on the lower river, we have never gotten ill from these mountains. Lucas builds a twig fire to deter mosquitos, and we sit on damp hummocks of blooming bell heather eating cheese and tortillas. Glancing uphill, Lucas spots White Wolf watching from a few yards away. A breeze lifts his mane and he stands a long moment, ears erect, before dissolving like smoke into the trees.

Resuming our journey, we ascend the steep shoulder, a living carpet deep beneath our boots. We curve northeast into the mountain flank, crossing gullies where slide alders tangle downward, yet the ridge never seems to top out and our view ahead is limited to thin forest and the deceptive curve of skyline. Afternoon sun swings around, lighting a panorama that slowly emerges below. We find ourselves swamping through muskeg with no level ground anywhere for a camp.

"It's not fair!" Lucas declares at one of our frequent standing rests. "How can there be a swamp on a hill? It defies Newtonian physics!"

I grin at him. He has been reading *The Elegant Universe* to me, a book on quantum physics. I have only a basic grasp and string theory eludes me entirely. I want him to listen to my thoughts on metaphysics. Tom has little interest in either.

"I'd like to go straight up this ridge to better footing," Tom says. He removes the bandana from around his head and wrings out the sweat.

"I was hoping to camp at Lake Hylaya," Lucas says. He named this tarn on the rolling highlands that connect Flattop with Mount Laurie when he was thirteen. He studies the endless slope with the eagerness of a dog.

"I don't remember seeing any trees there," I say, always the pessimist. *Realist.* "Let's camp someplace dry with water nearby and something to burn."

"And flat," Tom puts in. "Remember what it's like sleeping on the mountainside with water gushing under the tent?"

"I can't go beyond about five o'clock," I tell the others. "My legs are giving out. The map shows a series of small lakes in the folds below us. I think we should cut down and locate one."

"Down?" Tom asks incredulously. "After we worked so hard?"

"It never gets dark," Lucas points out. "We don't have to live by the clock this summer. I'd like to hike at night."

"My body is set to a schedule," I apologize. "I'm just telling you how to get the most out of the old girl."

"I think I'm getting blisters from wet socks," Tom mentions.

"I think we should camp at the first good place," I state.

"There hasn't been a reasonable spot for a tent since Pike Slough," Tom says.

We continue upward. Within a mile we reach a series of rocky knolls near a trickling bog. Lucas and Tom erect the tent, while I remove a square of sod and light a small fire in the wet earth. I find two rocks on which to balance the little enamel pot over the blaze. By the time the men have laid out our bedding, I have macaroni and cheese with dried onions, peppers, and moose simmering. I roasted and dried this meat seven years ago.

"I forgot spoons," I confess as they join me on damp hummocks. I hand each a steaming blue enamel mug with a willow stick. "I'm learning to be a minimalist."

"I like the sticks," Lucas nods agreeably.

The mountain falls away westward, revealing the valley under low sunlight. To the north, Flattop leans into a limpid sky where the sun will dip about midnight. Temperatures drop into the forties, but birds sing continuously: white-crowned sparrows, robins, hermit thrush. The call of a loon carries from the hidden ponds below. Lapland longspurs drop down the slope, skimming the bushes as they fall out of sight. I decide not to worry about bears. With our blind tent and Lucas's snoring, there's little point. We sleep fitfully on the sloped, cold, and lumpy ground—happy and at home in our world of singing birds and golden light.

I WAKE EARLY, PULL ON my damp and already odiferous clothes, and crawl from the tent into a clear morning. I feel strangely rested as I scrounge for twigs to start the fire. The others soon follow.

"Here's your cup with some rather bad instant coffee," I offer Lucas as he lowers himself onto the wet moss beside me. He was never very flexible, even as a boy. "I bought it at the Dollar Store—worth every penny. Do you want a splash of cold water? I forgot you don't like yours scalding."

He nods and I add water from an old salsa bottle that smells of chilies. "Dad likes his with the electrons stripped away," he says. "Almost plasma."

After breakfast, Tom douses the fire and replants the square of sod, leaving little evidence of camp. We continue up the ridge, where bog and thick bushes give way to alpine: a fairyland of miniature plants and colorful lichen. Netleaf willows no taller than my finger are woven with tiny lingonberry, blueberry, cloudberry, and yellow spotted saxifrage. The air is clear enough to see individual trees on distant peaks. At length we top out onto an open plateau, where lakes and streams drain three directions in hidden creases. Curtains of forest creep up the southern faces of low hills on this tableland a thousand feet above the river. Walking is easy and we companionably traverse rocky spines that separate marshy fens, often stepping in one another's tracks like the caribou that preceded us, shedding their antlers during winter migration.

Lake Hylaya turns out to be as wild and beautiful as Lucas imagines and as treeless as I remember. We keep to the high ground and wend in the general direction of Flattop. The small lakes we pass are often reedy and difficult to approach. We spot grayling in ponds with no apparent outlet and I wonder when and how they arrived. Sometimes a pair of ducks or loons is diving among cat's-paws of wind.

Two days later we start our ascent, crossing the last brushy hill and angling up the steep knees of Flattop. A heart-shaped pond falls steeply away as we switchback up the ridge. Arctic birch and willow give out, and we climb on a carpet of flowers and miniature berry bushes: fragile skin over the raw skeleton of the mountain. It is cool and breezy with a thin stream of gathering clouds—high mare's tails—harbingers of change. Lucas points out sundog rainbows that announce ice crystals in the atmosphere. Mosquitoes cling tenaciously to our packs now instead of hovering. We pause frequently for breath and to marvel at the view. Birds are left behind and the heights are silent except for wind. We spot a bald eagle soaring level with us, a tiny dot in space.

"I always feel vulnerable up here," I say as we balance on the steep shoulder. We carry little water and I have seen no potholes. Lakes glitter below, but rocks here are dry. Above us, a snowdrift crouches beneath the ridge line. In the past I've depended on pockets of snowmelt or seeps, even on top of mountains, but in a changing world, old truths no longer apply.

"I've always wanted to be here," Lucas says. Wind ruffles his dark hair. His eyes shine like forest pools with gold glints in their shadowed depths. His face looks very young with its scattered whiskers and smooth contours.

"There's nothing to burn, no place to camp, and no water," I point out. "The wind can blow you right off the mountain." *And nobody to help if you make a mistake.* Although less than five thousand feet high, Flattop towers above our sheltering valley.

Lucas smiles and pushes his warm shoulder into mine so that our packs lean together. The wind is picking up, and mist spits from the clouds that boil over the ridge. "We'll be fine," he reassures me.

I grin back. "Where else should we be? Don't ever put me in a nursing home."

"Don't worry, Mama." He places a large hand protectively on my shoulder and bends down to rub his cool cheek against mine. "I'll put you on an ice floe and push you out into the river."

We grin at one another. He knows that's what I want. *If I'm not afraid to die, why do I worry? I'm living my fondest dream and still fretting.*

Resuming our slow creep onto the mountain, we come at length under the brow of a vertical rock wall perhaps a hundred feet high, crowned in old snow. A small spring gushes biblically from its base with a swath of tiny willows tracing its descent below. We rest and drink of the icy water, gratefully filling our two bottles from the sacred fountain.

Skirting the cliff, we continue up a stony avenue dotted with plate-sized cushions of pink moss campion. Creamy stars of mountain avens speckle last year's withered grass, climbing into a sky the color of skimmed milk. Arching onto the spine of Flattop, we arrive on a sinuous ridge, where canyons fall steeply away to north and south. To the west, a precipitous dome of gray shale gleams silver in the paling sun. It is shaped like an overturned canoe with bow dropping into the saddle. The ridge is littered with balanced rock formations, delicately articulated and pockmarked with communicating holes and crevices, all orange and brown with lichen. We camp on a curved bench just off the shoulder in the tenuous shelter of a small ledge, where Lucas discovers a seep. He digs a cup-sized pothole and we dip up dribbles of muddy water.

I set dried hash browns, onions, and moose to soak in the pot, and then descend a quarter-mile into a steep swale to gather dead twigs from the fringe of miniature willow and arctic birch. Rain begins and clouds settle thickly over the mountain, curtaining the valley. I take off my outer shirt and wrap it around a scrounged bundle of sticks. Returning to camp, I secure my treasure behind our covered packs. There's no point in trying to light a fire. We crawl into the tent and eat trail mix with cold hands as rain pelts down all night.

"Breakfast is warm," I call toward the tent.

Taking advantage of a lull in the rain, I shelter a tiny fire with my body, feeding the last damp twigs into the flames as I warm last night's dinner. Icy wind rushes over the ridge. I position mugs of muddy water on stones near the fire for coffee. The tent looks like the prow of a fast-moving ship, cleaving through banks of clouds. Everything animal in me wants off this mountain. We are not equipped for severe weather in our Goodwill clothes.

"Hey, no bugs," Lucas says cheerfully as he emerges. He stands like a figurehead, arms stretched into the streaming clouds of gray, white, and shifting rainbow.

We hunch together in the wind, shoveling the awful food into our mouths with carved sticks and washing it down with lukewarm, muddy coffee. Below us the world spreads drear and wet, mountains on either side to the horizon. Clouds slide rapidly past alternately obscuring and revealing the view.

"We may as well pack up the wet tent. At least our sleeping bags are dry," I say. "I'd like to get off this mountain while we have the chance."

"I'm going to climb the peak," Lucas declares. His face is lit with quiet determination. A quarter-mile away, the gray dome stands clear and ominous against boiling clouds. It looks steep and treacherous.

"I don't think my blisters will take it," Tom tells us quietly. His forest-green fleece is zipped to his neck, and his back is hunched. "I'll wait for you."

I glance anxiously from one to the other, disasters flashing through my mind like headlines. One misstep and no backup—the story of my precarious life. I recall the suffering I have endured over calamities that never occurred: Luke's asthma strangling him in the night, Tom's back dropping him into the snow. This fear in my gut adds nothing. In *The Wisdom of Insecurity*, Alan Watts writes that our very quest for security endangers us. We are freed by the truth that we cannot save ourselves. I think of Lucas's vision of me as a joyful old woman who sees beauty in chaos. *Look at the flowers*, she whispers to me. Another possible future, just as vivid, is a fretful creature still striving to control the river. Ironically, despite my beliefs, I still do not trust life.

"We can leave the tent set up so you can stay warm," I tell Tom. "You'll get really chilled without a shelter." I've decided to accompany Lucas. To my vast relief, Tom chooses to come.

We break camp and walk the last quarter-mile to the great dome, stashing our packs beneath a shallow ledge before the final ascent. It begins abruptly and we use our hands to climb the crumbling shale into the sky. I try not to think of our descent, where one could tumble two thousand feet. Even here, hanging gardens of tiny flowers grow beneath the weak sun: purple mountain saxifrage, beautiful Jacob's ladder, yellow spotted saxifrage, and the ubiquitous mountain avens. Scattered bouquets of a phlox—ranging from dark pink to almost white—shelter between slabs of rock. It's hard to believe anything so fragile could survive in this land of ice, wind, and stone. The world drops away and I let my concerns drift like clouds over the expanse, opening my heart to the dynamic sky.

"Somebody slept here last night," Lucas points to a dusty nest stamped into the scree, "and they pooped. This is fresh."

"Here are others," Tom says. Loose rocks are scuffed into a series of terraced beds. "Lots of somebodies. Could it be caribou?"

"What were they doing way up here?" I wonder. "There's little feed. Do you suppose they like the view?"

"They could see predators," Lucas suggests.

"Or be trapped," I say. "I once found a box canyon that ended in a fifty-foot icefall where wolves had driven caribou." I pluck a tuft of silk from a shallow rock overhang. "This isn't caribou fur. Do you suppose it's sheep?"

"Naw," Tom rolls his eyes at Lucas and they laugh. "You told me this mountain was too isolated for sheep."

"Sheep," I say, decisively. "Look at the tracks: little and pointy. There's not enough food up here for a vole. How can anything survive?" We scan the distance with a new sense of wonder.

Arriving on top of our world, we explore its few acres, walking along the keel of the great canoe to the stern. Land falls eight hundred feet to the narrow ridge behind us and three thousand feet on the other three sides. Even here, a few hearty plants are tucked low behind stones. At the terminus we shelter beneath sculptured boulders, which are painted orange, black, and yellow with ancient lichen. "Worlds within worlds into infinity," I say to Lucas as I peer down into their matrix. "Like superstring theory."

"The language of life is written in fractal mathematics," he says. "Once you see the pattern, it's everywhere."

"I wish you'd let me read you my metaphysics."

He shrugs. "It's the same thing."

"I was so careful to honor your process that I didn't teach you what I believe. Now I wonder if I should have given you more tools. I wanted you to learn how to think, not what to think. I hope you will listen for the voice of your soul."

His smile is like sunlight. "Mama, I know you. Don't worry about that."

We spend much of an hour communing with the honeycombed monolith, snacking as we study the dizzying panorama of lakes, canyons, and creeks below. Patches of green forest, old loops of river now overgrown with willow, and fields of wildflowers spread in a map. Pools of shadow and color spill in shifting patterns over the landscape as clouds begin to lift, sailing like fleets before the wind. Central to everything, the blue river twists, patiently carving all we see. Clouds rush over us, periodically obscuring the valley through sun and rainbow. We plan our descent in low voices and point out riverbends where we have camped. To the north, austere peaks hem the Arctic Continental Divide—our goal in coming weeks. Lucas sets the camera on an outcrop and takes a timed photo of us. Reluctantly, he agrees to start back, and we work our way down the loose and slippery shale to our backpacks.

Our return to the land of trees and running water is remarkably easy. In single file we traverse below the dome on a trail cut by generations of sheep on their descent to pasture. Fresh tracks of a ewe and lamb precede us. We arrive at the edge of cliffs where Flattop tumbles a thousand feet into the braided river. The trail angles along the top of cliffs. More flowers appear: delicate forget-me-nots, Arctic poppies nodding among the stones, cranberries, and blueberries. Looking back, Tom spots a pair of Dall rams, white against the greening mountain and ochre cliffs. Seeing us stop, they climb swiftly to a notch and drop from sight into a canyon. This glimpse of mythical white creatures that dwell between sky and rock is worth the whole hike.

"I will never see Flattop the same again," Tom says. We smiled at one another, our lives transformed in some indefinable way.

We stop at the first stunted trees by a clear pool cupped between boulders. Flattop looms bright behind us in afternoon sunlight. A few yards away, the trail disappears in a jumble of rock and brush. Setting our packs down, we build a small lunch fire on a rise carpeted in the pink bells of blooming kinnikinnick. Our voices are a gentle murmur. The air is warm and mosquitoes are back in numbers.

Lucas steps to peer over the precipice. "There are sheep just below us!"

Three small sheep come bounding over the rocks not ten yards away.

They stop a moment to study us, and then trot up the long trail we have just descended. They look as if dressed in fluffy pajamas. The larger has the slender, upright horns of a female; the smaller two have bare heads. Ten minutes later another female almost runs over us in her hurry. We watch them toil up the slope for ten minutes, diminishing and finally disappearing against the mountain.

"I'm sorry we interrupted their breakfast," Lucas says.

"I'm so pleased we saw them," Tom adds softly.

"I love this country," Lucas murmurs.

Lucas and Tom skip stones during a break from lining upriver in 2007.

Tom and Lucas discuss our route

Chapter 23

DIVIDED DREAMS

June 2007

Lucas was seventeen when he wrote:

> When I was young I wanted to be a wizard, but the more I delved into the realm of power, the more I realized the paradox. True power is anonymity: those who remain invisible wield the most influence. For a person to master power, his original goals must be destroyed. Even if a wizard could shoot flame from his fingertips, by the time he reached mastery there would no use for it. If the ultimate goal of martial arts is to preserve peace, then the ultimate warrior is willing to give his or her life defending nonviolence. In other words, if one masters combat, there will never be an excuse to fight.
>
> Nevertheless, I continued to have fantasies of combat and mystery. It isn't much different now. When I stop fighting my path, things around me seem to click into place. Recklessness, lethargy, and contempt: all are characteristics that society proclaims preventable teenage traps. I have learned, however, that there is no such thing as a blunder or a bad choice. For me at least, the transformation into a teenager was completely unavoidable.
>
> The closeness with which my life mimics "tragic flaws" in Greek mythology is frightening. I find myself driven to do things even I label foolish, yet I have absolutely no explanation. Until I accepted the

coexistence of my youthful reality with the adult world I grew up in, my life was very difficult. When I stopped trying to justify my behavior in terms an adult (myself) could understand, I suddenly felt free to express without the need to be understood. Maybe in the end, the wizard becomes greater than he ever dreamed. For each stage in life is a different reality.

Lucas Foster Irons
May 2003

~

OUR CABIN IS A LUXURY of clean space when we arrive home, weary and footsore from our long circuit. The door and windows are still in place, but like a curious child who can't resist wet cement, Goldilocks has left delicate tracings of his long claws through mosquito netting on three windows. Tom patches the precise rents with tape. We bring food in from the storehouse, put up ladders, and pull household items out of the sleeping loft before laying out our foam mattresses. Tom and Lucas haul buckets of water to heat on the grill outside for baths in the cabin. We take turns in the oval stock trough, leaving our filthy clothes in a pile, then put on nightclothes before ascending to our remarkably flat and soft beds. Cabin walls dampen all sounds.

"My skin is happy to be out of the wind and sun," I say. My face feels tight and chapped; my hands look ancient. I sing Winnie's made-up song, "Everything is all right in our house tonight." It's a comforting ritual, invoking blessing and thanks.

Lucas joins in his deep, toneless voice, naming members of our scattered tribe—Eve and Megan first on his mind. He's been distant and quiet on the two-day hike back from the skirt of Flattop, setting a pace that is almost too fast for me. I have taken it personally, feeling hurt and confused.

"My Golden Light," Lucas says. His voice is hushed. Low sun spills from the North, pooling like honey onto logs near my head. As a small child, he used to celebrate this ephemeral radiance, wanting to be in bed for his Golden Light. "Come over here," Luke once called, "and... see... God."

"I worry about your snoring," I say into the ensuing quiet.

"You worry about a lot of things." His voice is tired, resigned.

"I'd like you to have a sleep study. You've always snored and now you sometimes stop breathing. I just have to let it go or I'd never get any sleep."

"Maybe when I'm a nurse and have good insurance," he concedes. "I doubt if the college insurance will cover it."

"You can check," I say, knowing he won't. "Maybe it's something as easy as having your tonsils out," I persist. "We'll pay for it."

"Did I tell you when we did our nursing physicals on one another, Thomas discovered that my uvula is remarkably long? It fascinated the class. I had a T-shirt made: 'Have you seen Lucas's elephantine uvula?'"

Tom rouses himself for a chuckle. "You and your T-shirts."

THE SKY IS AN OCEAN of flat blue the next morning as I lean over the tub, washing clothes. Tom has clamped the hand-crank wringer to a log and we're all working together. Lucas and Tom haul and heat water while I scrub. They crank the wringer, rinse the clothes, and hang them.

"Doing laundry is the hardest job," I say, leaning into the washboard.

"Why don't you bring in a gas washing machine?" Lucas suggests.

I enumerate my reasons, ending with, "Where would we store it away from bears?"

"You could work all that out," he says airily. A gray jay lands on his shoulder. I recall the young jay he tamed to hand-feeding when he was fourteen and wonder if this is the same bird.

"I'm not sure we'll continue building," I say. "That depends partly on your plans. We won't be able to leave the place unattended anymore. It isn't just the bears now."

"I want to share Kernwood with Eve and Megan," he replies.

"How is single life?" I venture.

He gazes toward Mount Laurie, visible through the trees. "I just want to be normal… you know—hang at the bars and pick up chicks—but I don't fit in. I want to relax at parties, laugh, and get laid like my friends." He stares into the tub of wet clothes, dejected and angry.

"I'm sorry, kiddo." I put my damp hand on his shoulder, but he shrugs it off. "You can't be anything except yourself. People always know. You will discover others who are like you, but probably not at bars."

"Well," Tom says drolly, "not exactly like you." He grins. "But there are people who share a depth beyond grab-ass."

"I want the grab-ass!" Lucas states defiantly. "At least I want to know what I'm missing. Give me shallow and insipid conversations. I'm tired of being the deep one." He hunches up his shoulders and makes a goofy face. "Gornk?" It's an allusion to a cartoon we shared about a great, awkward bird trying to fit in with a flock of mean little birds.

I laugh at his joke. Then I ponder his double-edged legacy and the loneliness of stepping beyond cultural norms. Yet divine discontent, that urge to grow beyond our comfort, is central to the human journey; without it the trip is meaningless.

We are silent with our tasks. At last Tom asks, "How's Eve doing with this?"

"Eve understands. She even comes over to help me choose clothes and gives me tips on dating. She's the best friend I ever had."

"She's a wise woman," I echo Laurie.

"I feel bad that I left her in charge of the house. I didn't know what else to do. She has no control over Scott. I don't trust him and I wonder if I made the right decision to leave him there. Part of my mind is always back there."

"It's a tough job, having the responsibility without the authority," Tom says.

Lucas nods. "I'd like to keep in touch on the satellite phone, if you don't mind."

"No. That's why we have it."

SUMMER ARRIVES OVERNIGHT, LIFE ERUPTING at a furious pace under continuous daylight. The forest falls silent as migratory birds cease their territorial songs to feed their voracious nestlings. Local birds are a month ahead; many are wise—ravens can live thirty years—and like us, invest heavily in few offspring. Established pairs have been our neighbors for a decade and more. Young ravens, jays, and owls are already learning the complex social bonds and detailed knowledge needed to survive their first winter. Most will not make it. Across the river, the Blackhearts are ready to launch two chicks from their disheveled nest in a dead spruce. Their fledglings look like black holes in the great pile of sticks and the valley rings with strident voices: a gang of bullies in a sedate neighborhood. It takes a great deal of food to grow a young raven. We have seen our pair work together to kill marsh hawks and osprey chicks.

Perennial flowers are especially profuse this year. Lupine, showy oxytrope, and wild sweet pea paint the ground in scent and color—unmistakable signs of a warming and drying landscape that twenty years before was clothed in sphagnum moss and Arctic bell-heather. White clusters of milk vetch on lush green stalks are knee-high in the older forests. There are winners and losers. I cannot judge what it means. Nature is never static, but so much change within my lifetime is unsettling. *The future rides on whispered messages. You can miss them if you are not paying attention.*

I recall how snow melts: the innocent and hidden accumulation of energy. Winter sun returns to our valley mid-January, twinkling momentarily along the rim of South Mountain. Even a faint cloud on the horizon obscures it. For two months the land has been locked in bitter cold and darkness—a world of auroras lit with the daily pastel promise of the sun's return. Inside the cabin, I feel blind, my life narrowed to a circle of lamplight; when I step outside, the air crackles, and I can see forever into starry space. Moonlight silvers the deep snow. The earth is silent, waiting. Snow squeals underfoot. It seems it will never be warm again.

Rapidly the sun gains ground—up to fifteen minutes a day. In April the stars disappear for another season, and endless light floods my world. Local birds begin to sing; moose and caribou are restless. Daily our life-giving star ascends, burning ever brighter, yet the land remains frozen; it can still dip to twenty below. We lengthen our snowshoe trails, traveling miles to old haunts, eager as the moose for the first green. Willow buds burst into bloom, icicles form, and the snow turns granular under foot. The river ice floods, gurgling sea-foam green over the old crystals and refreezing. We play, sliding over the changing whorls. The creek becomes a dangerous torrent, racing loudly under the ice. And yet the snow lays deep, the consistency of mashed potatoes.

Then, in three days, it is over! The inexorable momentum of spring melt culminates in a dramatic transformation. Snow disappears, ice flushes down the river, and summer has arrived. Just like that. *Climate change can happen that way too*, I think. *You have to be conscious of the little signals or you may be caught unaware.* In part it has to do with the nature of water, for it takes a great deal of energy to change it from one state to another. All that gathering of energy occurs with little noticeable activity. Ice at thirty-two degrees and water at the same temperature have very different consequences.

As I walk the valley this summer with Tom and Lucas, I listen to the changing voice of the land and wonder what it is saying.

"Good morning, Son," Tom smiles as Lucas joins us outside at the raised fireplace under the trees.

"Don't you have any more books?" Lucas asks, opening his folding chair.

He's been reading one a day.

A week has passed since our return from Flattop and I am packing for the next journey—our hike to the Divide. June sun stands bright above Mount Laurie. Herringbone clouds stream from the southwest while lower banks travel transversely, crossing the sky like quiet ships in three dimensions. I lift the blackened coffeepot from the grill and stir with a special stick before pouring through a strainer into Lucas's mug. I shake in powdered milk mixed with sugar and hand it to him: our life a ritual.

"Try Edward O. Wilson's *Consilience*," I suggest. "I think that's up your alley."

"There are plenty of books in the cache," Tom says. "If you run through this year's, we have over three hundred in storage—everything from deep ecology to novels. Just dig through the totes."

"When do we take off for the Divide?" Lucas asks.

"When I finish packing food and preparing," I answer.

"I don't care what we eat. Let's just go."

"You will when we're out there. Give me one more day."

Our trek to the Arctic Continental Divide—those precipitous and barren mountains where rivers flow north into the Arctic Ocean or south to the Yukon River—is a quest long delayed. We tried early in the spring of 2000 when Luke was fourteen, pulling our canoe upriver until we entered a gorge. Here we cached the canoe and continued north on foot under heavy packs. "Antler Creek," which I had remembered as a lively stream when Phil and I ascended it, was a roaring monster. Every runnel was also impassable with snowmelt, and after a couple of weeks we had turned back.

We plan to again line the canoe upstream with extra supplies, trailering the blue kayak behind. The river forks before it enters the steep mountains: one channel braiding out to climb into an amphitheater, while the other enters a cataract. Last time we chose the gorge, but now we will take the wider valley. When we can no longer pull the canoe, we will cache it and put on packs, wending into the raw country above tree line. It is surprisingly easy to get lost at that knife-edge of possibility, where ridges and snowfields form a maze a thousand feet higher than Flattop. It will be a long journey back to our waiting canoe.

Summer solstice marks the start of our trip. I have prepared dried meals and packed them in five-gallon buckets: breakfast, lunch, and dinner. These will ride watertight in the canoe and be used as seats in camp. An active person eats two or three pounds of dried food each day, which adds up on a long trek. We also need a tent, bedding, cookware, clothing, camera, satellite phone, ground-to-air radio, and pistol. Our packs are flattened and strapped together. Our two sleeping bags, three pads, and tent are in waterproof bags until we leave the river. There is nothing extra. We each have a raincoat, fleece sweater, pair of long underwear, four pairs of socks, two T-shirts, a long-sleeved shirt, and a second pair of jeans. We have two caps—one for cold weather and one for every day. Tom will wear hip waders for the upriver walk, while Lucas and I wear knee-high rubber boots. We each have good hiking boots and a pair of camp moccasins to allow our feet to dry at night. It comes to about one hundred eighty-five pounds. In addition, Dirk has dropped off a twenty-gallon drum of supplies high upriver.

We store away bedding and food, remove the cabin door, and close the cache. It's a hassle to break down our home, but necessary. Tom and I divide up familiar tasks; Lucas tries to help, but becomes frustrated and retreats to the bluff.

"It's not easy to dance with us," I console, coming up behind him. "We've been doing this for so long that we each know our part."

"It's not that," he sighs. "I miss Eve. I wish I could share this with her. I keep thinking that if being free means being unhappy, I might as well be with her."

"All I can advise is to follow your heart. The head is just for working out details."

He doesn't speak. I stand beside him companionably, not touching. When he was an infant, I always knew when he was cold. I would wake from a deep sleep and go into his room to cover him. We had an almost physical connection. Now I pull back, giving him privacy.

"You are so lucky to have found Dad," he says. "He's an old man of the woods, like something out of a fairy tale. Not many people would have taken to this life. I think Eve will. She tells me she wants to come."

"I didn't just find him. We've evolved together for twenty-six years. When I first met him, he didn't want to come to Alaska. Remember how critical he used to be? He's gentler now, a different person. I think the most important quality in a mate is being willing to listen and grow."

"I don't have twenty-six years," he says. He glances at me as if I'm as dense as cordwood.

I smile at him fondly, seeing the impatience of youth. We want to hear one another, but our messages originate in different dimensions. "One day at a time," I say reassuringly. "That's how life unfolds. Like a flower. You look at a photo of a child and recognize an old man that you know, but you cannot reverse the process. The future has yet to be written. Just know it is more wonderful and complex than you can imagine. Be open to that. Choose from your heart and enjoy the ride. It's really very short."

"People told me it would get easier when I got older. Well, it hasn't."

"Life flows in a spiral. Each time you come around, you see the same question from a higher vantage. Experiences that look like unnecessary side trips may in the long run reveal patterns. Sometimes you have to find who you are not, before you can see who you are."

He is quiet a long time, gazing at the slopes of Mount Laurie. I edge into his space and he welcomes me under his arm. I relax with my head against his chest, hearing the muffled sound of his great heart.

"That winter when I was thirteen, breaking trail through the snow here and learning from the caribou, I found myself so clearly," he is speaking to himself. "I thought I could never be lost again, that I could inspire my friends to look up from their narrow lives. Instead, I strayed into a crowd of blank faces and I forgot. I use the genus name *Rangifer* as my email, just to remind myself of that winter with the caribou. It's my totem."

"I know… the human journey. Read Joseph Campbell's *The Power of Myth*. I think that book is here. Your friends can hide out, but they too will have to face it. Ultimately, we each must set out to discover the gift we alone were born to carry."

He turns and looks me in the eye. "Have you found yours?"

"I don't know," I admit. "It's an evolving creation, but the journey is everything."

THE RIVER HAS DROPPED, REVEALING rocks and shoals as it turns jade green. We eat a snack on the beach beside our piled belongings and then Tom loads the canoe, hitching the kayak behind. When he is satisfied, he shoulders the rope and starts upriver, pistol on his belt and hip waders pulled up.

Lining a canoe takes a balance of tension: one end of a long rope is clipped to the bow and the other to the rear thwart. Current against the shallow keel ferries the canoe out from shore as you walk. Lucas and Tom trade off with the load, leaving me free. When the shoreline deteriorates into a cutbank or brush, we don life preservers and paddle our two crafts across the river—dozens of times each day. Occasionally, we make headway by paddling up an eddy close to shore.

We make good time that first day, traveling quietly through familiar lands. Each of us knows the crossings, rehearsed through years, and notes the changes. The river shifts, moving as a person in sleep—fitfully with long periods of apparent stasis—and life dances with it. The land reveals itself to one afoot, season by season, in ways that can never be grasped from a car or plane. The real story is not in data, but told to nose, eye, ear, and heart. My feet know the history beneath the sod, though the old riverbed be buried a thousand years. This land is all in motion, a living symphony played in a key we do not often register. It sings of the changing relationship between organisms in synergy with a breathing planet, of time, water, earth, and sky.

This is my natal landscape, yet I am not naïve about it. Tom once shot a charging grizzly from five feet; I have nearly drowned in this beloved river, come close to starvation, been lost, and frostbitten. I have no illusions about my mortality. I am not afraid, and yet it seems unwise for an aging couple to live here alone. *If I play in this land long enough, it will claim me. Would that be so bad?* To wash away like leaves so the next generation can flourish on clean ground, returning my borrowed molecules as graciously as a tree. Death can be a magnificent giveaway—an exploding star that seeds possibility. Fly larva to fish to bear to poop, into the moss and up the silent trunks of trees: a wholesome journey.

"What a difference low water makes," I comment to Tom as we walk together on a gravel bar. Lucas has the canoe and is splashing out on the slippery stones a few yards away—the river too shallow and rapid here to line from shore.

Afternoon thunderstorms play about us, highlighting the vast sky and freshening the wind as days slide behind. Flattop becomes unrecognizable, its appearance shifting three-dimensionally with each bend: a great presence beyond name.

"It looks more like Pointytop," Lucas say as we lunch on a warm sandbar.

"I think I see our sheep," Tom remarks. "It makes me happy just to think of them." He cranes his head back, peering up at the cliffs. He is roasting summer sausage on a stick over the fire. The canoe and kayak are beached a few feet away, trailing into teal-colored water. Clouds move rapidly, dappling the valley in sun and pools of shadow. A shifting rainbow highlights the mountains behind.

"We sure haven't seen much moose sign," I say. "I wonder if hunters are taking a toll."

"We haven't seen many bear tracks either," Tom remarks. "You need to be prepared—one autumn, someone may shoot Goldilocks."

"I know. Someone who doesn't know him." I think about how we see the world through our fears and prejudices.

Lucas is lying on the warm stones gazing up at Flattop. He has his boots off, drying his wet feet. His voice, and perhaps his thoughts, are still.

We pass the main fork and enter a realm of peaks, seen only distantly from the bluff at our cabin. Tree line runs close here and the channel wiggles in tight curves between barren mountains. It's rewarding to chart our progress by the sliding contours. Our camps are often wet now, planted among blooming flowers and deep in moss. Our clothing is rarely dry. Rain comes more frequently as we burrow into the mountains, and clouds play along the high rim of our world in a kaleidoscope of weather so that we walk in and out of storms. Sunlight sparkles with raindrops as the sky vaults over us—at once expansive and intimate—framed by peaks. The air holds that peculiar Arctic clarity, every detail etched by the low angle of sunlight. *Home. I would know it anywhere.*

One evening Lucas returns to our fire after a brief conversation with Eve on the satellite phone. I still marvel that we can now reach out across these mountains. He sits on a bucket and holds his hands to the blaze. Steam wafts from his wet jeans. His face is troubled.

"Scott is behaving like a bully. He told Eve that someone stole things from the shed. She thinks it's him."

Fine rain is falling as evening settles gray about us. The sky is soft and muted. Through the trees we can see a loon holding its place in the current, fishing. It stretches its neck and calls into the cold air. Tom is patching Lucas's cheap rubber boots again, bought last minute in Fairbanks. They are disintegrating, leaving a raised honeycomb of plastic and metal. I fashioned makeshift insoles, but his feet are sore and blistered. I feel responsible. I try so hard to plan, but cannot anticipate every potential. *A few more days*, I think, *and we'll switch to hiking boots.* I want so much for this to be a perfect trip.

"Do you want to go home?" Tom asks him softly.

Lucas shakes his head. His eyes are on the fire.

He is quiet and remote the next morning while we break camp and again walk the riverbank. He has put on his hiking boots and sloshes along, wet as he had been for days, but with better support. Rain drizzles out of the sky and the mountains are veiled.

Around noon, Lucas grounds the canoe and its trailing kayak on a barren stretch of wet rocks at the head of an island. It is an unlikely place for a lunch break. Tom and I are walking together a few feet behind. Lucas approaches us, face miserable. "I have to go back," he says simply. "I'm so sorry about your trip, Mama. All your planning…" He looks ready to cry.

"It's okay, Son," Tom says. We gather him into our arms and the three of us huddle in the falling rain while the gray river rushes noisily to either side.

"Let's see if we can get a fire going and have a bit of lunch," I suggest at length. "Then we'll go home."

"I bet we can make it tonight," Tom says brightly, "and sleep in a dry bed!"

Tom and I board the canoe; Lucas looks like a duck in the blue kayak. It is not a good craft and too small for him, but he is delighted to be paddling solo. We quickly lose the ground gained in a week of toil. It's remarkably difficult to recognize the various riverbends from this perspective—land I walked only days before. We are swept out of the mountains and rain is left behind. Each bend reveals dappled vistas hung with rainbows in the low afternoon sunlight.

I hold my tongue when Lucas chooses to run the middle of rapids rather than the safer channels. I peer around anxiously, trying to see him as he explores the other side of islands.

"What if we get separated?" I ask.

"He needs to do this," Tom tells me. "Let it go."

At the head of the worst rapids, we converge and pull ashore. "I am going to run the haystacks," Lucas declares. "I'd like you to take pictures." He eyes me, waiting. I nod.

Tom and I skirt the torrent—now brown and high from the rain—and pull ashore below the rapids. Lucas waits until we are in position and then takes to the water. His hat is pulled low and he is paddling hard, almost disappearing into waves. I snap photos. In the end, my son does not belong to me. He has his own journey. At his age, I set out in a canoe for a year of living off the land. Knowing the dangers, my mother had advised and encouraged me, then let go. *God, it is hard!* I scarcely breathe until he beaches the little plastic kayak next to our canoe.

His face is radiant. "Wow! Did you see that?!"

I grin. "I got some good photos." I think of the price of domestication and the illusion of security. I recall the caribou. *Rangifer*.

"Are you okay?" Tom asks gently as we stand together watching the plane dwindle into the southern sky. He puts his arms about me and sinks his scratchy beard into the hollow of my neck. We stand together on the familiar gravel bar, listening to the song of the river. Nothing has changed. *Everything has changed.*

I blink back tears. "I'm disappointed," I say at last. "I was so looking forward to a summer with Lucas. But I am happy we got the month."

"I think it was just what he needed," Tom says. "He always grows in quantum leaps. I saw a lot of change in him during this brief time. It was the right thing, and it was worth it."

"I know." I am silent and Tom doesn't try to fill the space with reassuring noise or advice. Finally I say, "Do you think we could still make it to the Divide—if we set off now?" My voice sounds small and plaintive.

Tom watches me gently for a moment. "Maybe not this year."

"Do you think we need an unattainable dream? Just to keep us going?"

He doesn't answer.

"What are we going to do with the next three months?" *Maybe I'm still a human doing*, I think. Tom is content with whatever the day brings. My mind is searching for possibilities. "What about building a laundry room? Somewhere that we could keep a wringer washing machine."

He smiles softly. "Would you like that?"

"It'd give us something to do and a fun project."

He nods. "Yes, it would."

Chapter 24

Distant Rapids

July 2007

Lucas calls to sadly inform us that Scott has indeed been busy. It is uncertain what is left in the stifling chaos of our shed, but clearly much is missing. The young woman roommate has fled, leaving the older man to pick through our belongings at leisure. Lucas surprised Scott and threw him out, but the damage is done. The police are not interested.

"It's only stuff," I say gently to Tom

"Our stuff." He is not so easily consoled. Nevertheless, as the kids say, *it is what it is*. We both know that.

Our days settle into quiet ritual worthy of my grandmother, Winnie: the Zen of simple chores done attentively. It is (quite literally) the "drawing of water and chopping of wood" referred to as Karma Yoga—life as process. I rise early to write on my laptop, recharging batteries every few days with a tiny generator. When Tom awakens, we sit outside by the fire, drinking coffee and planning our day beneath a dynamic sky. We never hurry this part. Birds and small mammals often join us for no apparent reason: squirrels, ground squirrels, hares, voles, robins, juncos, chickadees, waxwings, flickers, woodpeckers and, of course, gray jays. Even a golden-eye duck sometimes waddles inexplicably by. Perhaps she has a nest, but we never see one. As summer advances, a family of spruce chickens peck gravel along the path. The Blackhearts keep us under surveillance, but remain aloof. Only when we leave fish guts on a rock do they send a messenger to sing in our yard—voice like a harp.

Our diet is simple. Breakfasts of raw oats, granola, raisins, and nuts with powdered milk. I bake bread in the stovepipe oven and pies as the berries ripen. We eat dried staples: beans, pasta, cornbread, powdered eggs, and rice. We keep cheese and margarine in the cool storehouse. I grow sprouts, which we enjoy with mayonnaise, pickled peppers, and sun-dried tomatoes. Many of our supplies are nearly a decade old, but are frozen most of the year. Daily Tom hauls about fifteen gallons of water from a little spring that bubbles up near the river. Sometimes he catches a grayling or two for dinner, but we're careful not to overfish. These small and beautiful jewels grow slowly and over three decades.

On calm days we sometimes fell dead trees. Warming climate has fostered an explosion of bark beetles and many of the older spruce trees are dying. We are careful of the forest floor as we carry branches to the river bar, allowing sunlight to reach seedlings. Baby trees thrive where we've logged in the past, though it is a remarkably slow process. Even willow bushes show little change over two decades. As I distribute ashes from our stove around the trees, I think of Janet pouring her dishwater on pine saplings at Standwell. *Maybe my small actions make no difference in the big scheme, but living consciously matters to me.*

Tom drops snags and cuts them into lengths we can handle; I come behind with my ax, cleaning logs. I recall my mother's story of an old trapper—a man of ninety. "He could chop wood all day, just lifting the ax and letting it fall," she told me. "He understood the grain so well that it split apart with the flip of his wrist." I'm not there yet. Tom and I work together, dragging logs down a path to the riverbank. It takes all day to accumulate enough for a raft, which we'll build and float home another day. Closer to home, we carry logs on an ingenious set of wheels Tom has designed. We laugh at our slowing rhythm—logs and workdays shorter each year—yet somehow pounds drop from our bodies without effort as muscles remember their purpose. There is no hurry.

Each action is a communion. I drink from the river—atoms ancient as the solar system. This air was over the Asian steppes only days ago: breath of the planet, now breath of me. Sunlight stored in a tree before I was born cooks my lunch. *When one looks closely, everything is sacred.* I watch the trees sway in an ocean of air like anemones, picking up what they need, letting the rest go. No grasping, no worry. I lie on the moss and feel the ground swaying as an interlocking web of roots moves with the wind in the trees. Surely trees communicate, perhaps even as our neurons do, in that darkness. Their intercourse with mycelium alone is unfathomably complex. What we call a "mushroom" is but the fruit of an entity that may span acres and hundreds of years. It is all alive, all aware. Under the broad sky, I am part in a living world where even the rocks are conscious. *The planet is breathing me.*

Tom and I often spend a day exploring the valley, overseeing the changing seasons like two old gnomes. We pack a simple lunch and walk until I tire and then we build a small fire on some knoll, perhaps overlooking a pond where loons nest and red currants ripen. There is always a surprise. No matter how cyclic in appearance, each year is unique.

As if licking its parched skin from recent fires, the land wraps itself in mist. All summer a fine rain shimmers through sunlight, rarely heavy enough for raincoats. Still the river continues to drop until we can wade it in places, every stone visible through the teal depths. There is an unusual abundance of berries and cones, but it is the mushrooms that astound us. Punctuating every foot of land are fungi, some the size of platters with backs patterned like turtles, others that look like ginger cookies. There are mushrooms that remind me of tiny bells—no bigger than sesame seeds. We find a peach-colored fairy ring that circles a lone tree, and we step over miniature parasols, clumps of creamy mushrooms, snowy ones stacked in interlocking columns, mushrooms like flung copper pennies, and nests of prickly puffballs as beautiful as eggs among the red bearberries. Tom waits patiently while I crawl through the diminutive worlds with our camera. The squirrels seem overwhelmed, decorating trees with drying mushrooms.

A multitude of tiny spiderlings hatch from the sacks their mothers have carried all summer and climb trees to parachute off on glistening threads. Evening light sparkles off their shifting strands of gossamer. Young swallows launch over the river from nest burrows in the bank, soaring high where the wind carries a river of insects on their journeys into the future. Plants, too, send their hopes aloft to colonize distant vistas: willow, mountain avens, dryas, and fireweed—fluff on the wind. The sky glitters as with myriad stars sparkling—up and up—as insects, spiders and seeds take to the air.

"I can't get over the wonder of picking berries," Tom says when he returns with his full pails. "They are such a gift from the land."

"Child's play," I say. "That's our life here. Little sticks and stones that will wash away. The next generation doesn't need our monuments. Let them build something new on this good Earth."

Days shorten and we light the stove, simmering beans while we work on art projects or read. When stars return, Goldilocks visits more frequently, leaving big tracks by the cabin. Like early humans, he migrates to seasonal foods and has learned that hunters now come in the fall to kill moose. It is a dangerous game, but worth the risk in a land where food is scarce. Occasionally he pushes over our windsock but never damages it. Perhaps he sees it as territorial behavior and is adding his comment. Maybe he is just playful. I am sure Goldie knows his territory as intimately as any urban dweller knows the streets. While covering his fifty square miles, he steps in the same places, rounding this rock here, rubbing against that tree again, always aware that death waits somewhere.

When I was young, the Athabascan elders told me they didn't hunt grizzlies, regarding them as mysterious and close to human. Phil and I passed through the village of Venetie in 1972 and Jessie Williams advised me, "If a brown bear comes into camp and you are alone, you say to him, 'Go away, Old Bear,' and he will go, but if there is a man with a gun, that bear will attack."

I think of great white sharks gathering when elephant seal pups take to the ocean. Somehow, those ancient beings know, and yet their allotment of brain tissue—our uncompromising yardstick for sentience—hasn't changed much in four hundred million years. *How do they do it?* Instinct, we say. We might as well say, Magic. We don't know. The rest of life is cohesive on a level we dismiss because, in our presumed dominion, we have stopped paying attention.

How do we rejoin the greater community of life? I wonder. We are not an accident, but children of Earth. The journey to wholeness isn't neat or safe, but it is our great task. Rumi filled books about silence—doesn't that seem ironic? "A finger pointing at the moon," the Buddhists say. "Don't look at the finger!" In this beloved wilderness, it is easy for me to walk in grace and gratitude. I just don't know how to do it among my own kind.

THE SUN IS LOSING POWER, falling daily in its arc like a cooling balloon in the morning transit above Mount Laurie. Cherry red, it now bathes the peak's flank in soft light. I warm my fingers over the fire, waiting for coffee water to boil, and watch it pale to gold as it ascends through cirrus clouds—tenuous as blowing hair. I stir coffee into the pot using the familiar stick and pour it into my mug. Leaning back in my canvas chair, I release my musings and suddenly, inexplicably, I am happy.

The cabin door opens and Tom steps lightly into the day. "Coffee ready?" he asks. He sits in the chair I have placed for him by the fire. "Isn't it a beautiful day!" It seems so easy for him.

I fill his mug from the blackened pot, straining grounds out with a little sieve. "Yes," I agree. "I heard the loons calling again from Lake Eugene."

Gradually the laundry room rises, articulating into the cabin's north wall. We skin and notch logs, twisting the augur and pounding in dowels. It is a small structure, but massive, accessed from the outside like a built-on shed. The architecture is complex, a study in process. There is a clerestory that coincides with a loft window, and a staggered roofline.

I straddle a log ten feet above the ground and wedged under the cabin ridgepole beneath the eave—a difficult place to auger. The sky is heavy with rain and wind gusts from the west rocking the spruce tops. Across from me, Tom is smoothing off a dowel with his jack plane. His shirt is filthy and stained with pitch, the elbows ripped. His white beard blows shaggy in the wind.

"You are becoming the 'old man of the woods,' " I say. "Lucas called you that."

He glances at me, askance.

"I guess we've decided to come back?" I rest. The auger has crunched through the top log and chips are beginning to jam in the one below. "Why else are we building?"

Tom nods. "Looks like it."

"Does that mean we'll spend every summer here protecting our cabin from hunters? That doesn't seem like freedom." Guides now want to use our cabin. One even told us we couldn't keep him out.

"Why not?"

I try to imagine the pattern of coming years: travel-nursing nine months, then home to our cabin. I smile at the thought of putting that on my driver's license. In Alaska, I could. *Maybe I will get an Alaskan license.* This is the only place I call "home" anymore. *But what of community?*

"We could settle in Fairbanks and not have so far to drive," I say. "Now that we have less to move."

It isn't a good joke. Tom is still mourning the theft of his tools and guns from Sylvia House, things his father left him, not even insured.

"Change," I say. "The one constant."

MOOSE SEASON OPENS. WE SEE planes daily, but our area remains serene. It seems odd that people invest so much in this frenzy of taking, while the real treasures—grace and beauty—lie uncontested these long months.

We pull the canoe two miles upstream to Wandering Slough, where pike are beginning to cluster. We plan to catch three and smoke the filets, which will now keep and will add greatly to our diet. The Blackhearts have been waiting too and we know there is probably a scout following us, unseen along the bluff. They are secret folk, but little escapes them. The day is sunny with only a hint of frost as we easily line up the shallow current. Autumn glows brilliant: gold, burgundy, rust, ocher, and red contrasting with spruce green. The river is remarkably clear, like mint jelly tumbling over rocks. Twice Tom crosses it in hip boots, toting me along as baggage in the canoe.

"Look!" I point to the fresh tracks of a modest-sized bull moose in the wet mud of a bar. A mile below we have seen tracks of our lone cow and calf, the only moose noted all summer. The calf prints are larger now and well-spaced. "Well, at least there are three moose. I hope they find each other."

September 10 and moose are beginning to rut, bulls traveling vast distances in search of cows. They do not feed in rut and may run off much of their summer fat, entering winter in poor condition. A surprising number of winter-kills are bulls. Normally shy, they are now curious and incautious. In this land of little cover, their flashing antlers and great bodies stand out to low-flying planes. It's not legal to hunt on the day one has flown, but there is no one here to notice.

We arrive at Wandering Slough and Tom spots pike lying like speckled logs where the tea-colored slough curls into the river. I build a small fire on the point and set up my board and bucket. He has soon caught three fish while I squat on the gravel filleting the big paddles of white meat. This will feed us through September. I lay the heads and guts on a rock, thanking the fish for their gift. I search the high bluff across the river for the raven I know is watching. A young osprey rides the wind over the bluff, peeping loudly. I smile. *So they have fledged one this year!*

As I squat in the shallows, raking the heavy scales off the third pike with Phil's old Buck knife, I notice the persistent whine of a plane circling somewhere downstream. It comes and goes on the light breeze, annoying as a mosquito.

"What do you say we cut the day short?" I rise stiffly and stretch. "Let's eat lunch at home."

Tom gazes south along the broad sweep of river and islands. The plane sounds like it's banking. Hastily we load the canoe and shove off. Paddling strongly for home, we skim over shallow rocks and rapids. As we round the last bend we see two Cessna 170s parked on the bar across from our cabin: a gold plane with red patches on the wings, and a white one with a band of red and blue waving along the tail like a flag.

After stashing the fish in our cool storehouse, we paddle across to introduce ourselves. Three people are unloading duffel onto the bar. A small, older woman with gray hair and a winning smile introduces herself as Jackie. A heavyset fellow, who I assume is her husband, says little except his name: Terry. The other man is Dennis.

"I'm Jeanie Aspen and this is my husband, Tom Irons," I say, putting out my hand. "We live across the river. We wanted to be sure you didn't shoot in our direction."

Dennis shakes hands vigorously and starts talking in a nervous, overloud voice. He is lanky and perhaps forty-five with graying hair and a stubble beard. "We camped here last year. We're not really hunting. It's more like a retreat. We just come up here to get away. Last year we turned down several bulls until one just walked into camp and committed suicide. Can I do anything for you? I'm flying back to Coldfoot for my wife and son and more supplies."

"No," Tom answers quietly. He has taken a step back.

"You sure now? I have friends who live out in the Bush. I always bring them salad and apples. If I really want to impress them, I bring them a gallon of ice cream."

"They'd have to eat it all at once," I say.

"That's part of the fun! Watching 'em try. You have a real nice cabin over there. We looked it over last year. Nobody touched nothin'," he adds quickly. "You'll have to come over one night for dinner. The girls will fix us up a spaghetti dinner. We caught some of those grayling last year. Have you tried 'em? They're really good eatin'."

"Come on." Terry's voice is sharp. "We gotta get goin'."

The two planes roar down the bar, trailing one another into the sunlit sky. Jackie is left to haul baggage and set up camp.

"Can I give you a hand hauling stuff?" I offer.

"No, I got it all handled."

We turn toward the canoe and I hesitate. "We have a big grizzly that spends time around here. He's used to us. You might want to keep a good eye on your meat."

"Oh, we're fine," she smiles.

As we walk back to our canoe, I say to Tom, "Dennis asked if we knew grayling were good to eat. What he didn't ask was if camping in our lap was a problem."

"I didn't like him," Tom states. I glance at him sharply. His brows are knit. "He's too…" He lets his words trail off.

I nod, keeping pace across the uneven stones. "Yes," I agree, "he is. In biology it's called 'displacement behavior,' what animals do when they are torn between running away and aggression. What about the other guy? Terry?"

Tom is silent as we walk. His pace is always faster than mine unless he slows or I hurry. "A closed room," he says at last. "I get no impression at all."

"They said they were from the Kenai Peninsula," I continued. "Sterling and Soldotna. Couldn't they find somewhere closer to home for their 'retreat'? It's nine hundred miles—not cheap." We pull on lifejackets and slide the canoe into the river. Even as we paddle for home, another plane buzzes low across the bar. It's close enough to make eye contact with the pilot. We are suddenly back in the twenty-first century.

The planes make several trips that afternoon, bringing people and setting up an extensive camp. Next day, the white Cessna with the red-and-blue band takes to the air in a pattern that will govern the week. Especially in the evening—when moose are active—it scouts every pond and bar up and down the valley. Always within earshot and only a couple hundred feet above the trees, the plane circles and circles. Often it swings unnecessarily over the cabin, thundering by just overhead and rattling the windows. From the pattern, we guess there is another camp with the third plane somewhere upriver. I begin keeping a photo record and log of activity.

Moose, greatest of the deer, are elegantly efficient. Designed to cover broken terrain while conserving energy, they are powerful swimmers that can flatten their nostrils to feed underwater. As browsers, they eat twigs and leaves all summer and slowly starve during the winter (when the stress of being chased with a machine can kill them). Bright and sociable, moose have been used as draft animals, but cannot digest hay and die easily from livestock diseases. Moose calves depend on their mothers for a year and if raised by humans will cry pitifully when locked outside. Although solitary as adults, they form close bonds. Older bulls are gentle when sparring with smaller animals, only doing battle with equals during the rut.

The "retreat" across the river explodes with gunfire. It's like living in the middle of a war. At least four moose are killed, one apparently shot from the plane. With a single state trooper north of the Yukon patrolling an area larger than Texas and the flood of hunters, there is little enforcement. The sudden violence of high-power rifles reverberates in my chest like physical blows, leaving me nauseated. All my calm and presumed at-oneness-with-the-process is shattered.

Distant Rapids

I COME SWIMMING UP FROM a nightmare—the first in a long time—yelling, "As long as I'm here, the children will have enough to eat!" when someone grabs me by the hair. Then Tom is there, gentling me in the darkness of our cabin.

It's cool and rainy next morning as we breakfast at the handcrafted table. Our stove pops cheerfully, warming the cabin. Gray jays are pecking about the sodden yard. "Remember Kipling's story, *The White Seal*?" I ask. "Kotick spends his life searching for an island inaccessible to men, a place where seals can thrive."

Tom sips his scalding coffee and waits for me to continue.

"Well, there is no place to hide. The seals were almost exterminated. It takes the Earth a very long time to recover."

"But it does."

"I'm not so sure anymore. In the three hundred years it took Clovis hunters to migrate from the Bering Sea to the tip of South America, they exterminated all megafauna from both continents. The land that the Europeans discovered was already impoverished, and we've finished off most of what was left. It's more than just beauty and diversity at stake."

"The planet has recovered from worse," he reassures me.

"In *The Ages of Gaia*, Lovelock claims that life evolved when our sun was cooler, that like our bodies, the biosphere creates favorable conditions. He says that if we damage ecosystems beyond a tipping point, Earth's temperature could spiral out of control leaving our planet as dead as Mars. I just can't go there."

Tom doesn't comment. For some reason, I recall my father saying, "I wish they'd leave my world alone." I had discounted his words, feeling a certain smugness. *His world?* Well, now I feel the same way.

"Do nice guys finish last?" I ask. "Do the most ruthless always prevail? If so, why hasn't life run down into chaos?" *There has to be something more.* Then another thought: *Does my pain change anything?* Eckhart Tolle writes that there are only three sane responses to suffering: leave the situation, change it, or surrender to it. Anything else is madness. *Well, I've certainly spent the last ten days in madness.*

"My mother taught me to run away," I continue. "Like a caribou, it was her main defense. I've run all my life, but there is no place to get off our shrinking world. I have tried to change our voracious culture and ended up ranting. Yet, I cannot accept the desecration of our planet. That leaves me back where I started—wedged between the horns of an insoluble dilemma."

Tom is as quiet as the Arctic beyond my window. I take a deep breath and smile. "They didn't invite us over for spaghetti," I say.

"That's the good news."

THE HUNTERS DEPART, FLYING TRIP after trip of boned meat to Coldfoot. It has been a well-planned coup. The valley sighs in relief—*or is that just me?* I can't be certain. The wilderness broods silent and vast, emptied and somehow impoverished. The fragile landscape of my mind, my sense of home, feels forever altered: a raped maiden pulling her gown about her.

Tom and I paddle across to Pike Slough, hesitantly examining the bar like a fresh wound. Near the big mound of ashes, stashed poles speak of intended return as do platforms built between spruce trees at critical junctures. The Blackhearts have company, and querulous raven voices reverberate down the river. There is plenty for all. Seagulls and a pair of bald eagles with their great fledgling are busy cleaning up the carnage, making the bar wholesome again. We see tracks of the wolf family and Goldilocks—still alive one more season.

The planet accelerates its familiar swing into northern winter and days rapidly shorten. Stars glimmer unimaginably bright in the freezing night where the aurora wavers over the quieting river. Tom and I move inside and put away our outdoor cooking pots. We read by lantern light and begin to speak of that other world.

In the 1970s I could walk across the frozen river by the end of September, but in 2007 it is running clear of ice when we use the satellite phone to call Dirk. Again we close the cabin, pull out the windows and door so that Goldilocks can come and go, and stash our supplies out of reach in the storehouse-cache. This time we take a minimum of things: guns, medical kit, laptop, Tom's buckets of cranberries, and pint jars of blueberries. If we are really coming back, it is pointless to keep hauling so much.

We arrive in Coldfoot on a clear afternoon. Tom's Little Red pickup seems tired, its battery dead. He reconnects the cables and Dirk gives us a jump-start after tightening a spark plug. The cracked manifold mutters and the door creaks with dust as I settle into my familiar seat. After twenty-one years of hard use, the old Toyota is running down. Tom and I both know her days of faithful work are numbered. We must surely replace her this winter.

Although we stop to stretch, Tom keeps the truck running all the way to Fairbanks. Daylight fades and a full moon rises golden, sliding along the ridge and never seeming to gain elevation as we drive south. Winter disappears behind us and the brilliant yellow of autumn stretches like a glowing quilt over soft hills as we travel toward Fairbanks. We puzzle at a green band of smoke that trails across the sky ahead.

"Of course!" We laugh suddenly as the band flames. "The northern lights!" How could we have forgotten?

Tom roofing our "laundry room" in 2008.

Tom and I use his "log wheel" to haul wood.

Chapter 25

LITTLE RED TRUCK

October 2007

I was hunched outside a Fairbanks restaurant with Lucas's cell phone. Patters of rain blew from low clouds and the wind smelled of snow. Fresno wanted me back, but because I'd been unemployed more than ninety days, I would need to go through orientation and drug testing again. I twisted the phone, trying to keep the signal.

"No, Kelly," I stated, "you can't 'overnight' anything to Alaska. It won't arrive before next Monday, and I'm not staying around for the weather to get worse."

"I don't make the rules, Jean. You have a contract." My recruiter's voice sounded exasperated and tinny through the phone. I was obviously an unsettling anomaly in her life. "Your drug test needs a chain of custody from Florida!" She said it like Moses handing down the Ten Commandments. I imagined her in a carpeted Florida office—palm trees, white sands, headset, computer.

"I don't care about rules. I'm headed south, and once we're on the road we'll be out of touch for a week. Find a way to originate it in Fairbanks."

"And you need a TB skin test! You'll have to hang around at least forty-eight hours so that can be read."

"I am dealing with real geography and the real possibility of freezing in some snowbank. It's a thirty-five-hundred-mile trip—like you driving to Los Angeles and back—only with no helpful gas stations." *Welcome back to the land of straight lines and little boxes.* What did I gain seeking enlightenment in the wilderness, if I was grinding my teeth within four days of hitting town?

I took a deep breath and tried again. "Go to Google Earth." I knew Kelly was practically wired into the wall. Even as we talked, she would be typing notes to other clients. "Okay, now find Alaska," I continued. "Notice how far away it is, and how big? It's not a little island off the coast of California—like it looks on some maps. Trace the highway out of Alaska…"

"Which one?" She sounded irritated.

"There's only one." I waited as the silence deepened.

"Oh…" she said. Then came another, "Oh…"

"Okay, follow that little line south looking for towns. Go slowly. Notice those big mountains? Can you find any towns? Those few little dots with names… they're cabins that sell gas and bad coffee during the summer. They are closed in October."

Kelly was uncharacteristically quiet. Her thoughts might zip around the globe arranging contracts in cyberspace, but somehow the physical reality of the planet had eluded her. After a spell, she said, "I see your problem." Her tone had lost its bright edge. "I'll do what I can. I'm not promising… this is highly irregular."

"Thank you," I said. "People up here are accustomed to irregular. I think you'll find them unusually helpful. It's a big, cold, remote land."

"All right, I'll get back." She had regained her business tone.

"One last thing," I said somberly. "When you arrive at your sunny office with your latte and bagel tomorrow morning, don't call me. It'll be four o'clock in the morning—cold and dark here. I will not be cheerful."

"THE TRUCK IS OVERHEATING," TOM said. It was the sound of the other shoe. We were following the twisted road along the foot of a mountain.

For days we had journeyed through a wild and beautiful land. High mountains frosted in snow hedged the road for two thousand miles with golden birch trees incandescent against the dark green of spruce. Lakes were crinkled with new ice. The road snaked in and out of snow line as it wove between the peaks. We had photographed three grizzlies in good fall condition and a pair of moose consorting. The barren crags cupping Kluane Lake were dotted white with sheep. We frequently slowed, allowing migrating caribou to cross the otherwise empty highway.

Always the truck had been on our minds. Tom had bought a new battery in Fairbanks, and despite being booked for a week, the dealer fit us in to replace our leaking rear seal when we said we were driving "Outside." Our first morning in Canada, we had stopped to photograph dawn light on snowy peaks reflected in Pickhandle Lake. When we restarted the truck, the charge light came on. There was no point in fretting: with few towns of note ahead or behind, we had no backup plan.

We had driven much of that morning, but just out of Haines Junction, the engine sputtered and died. The battery recovered just enough to nurse the truck into town, where it quit for good in front of one of the only motels in a hundred miles. A local mechanic put aside work on big diesels to diagnose a bad alternator. He whacked it to "loosen it up," then recharged our new battery. The following morning we had driven through light snow for three hours into Whitehorse, where we found a rebuilt alternator and then a mechanic to install it. By afternoon we were again headed south. That had been yesterday.

"It's never overheated before," I commented unnecessarily, "even in Arizona."

We were silent, watching the gauge. Tom turned up the heater to help cool the engine. "We're losing power," he said." I'm pulling over."

Coasting to a stop along the shoulder, we climbed out. New snow glistened in the yellowing autumn grass along the verge of the Alcan. Somewhere off to our right, the majestic Coastal Range—a wall of mountains and glaciers soaring to sixteen thousand feet—lay hidden in clouds. Eighty feet below us, the gray-green Liard River thundered against boulders the size of houses.

An icy wind carried deep tones up from the river as Tom lifted the hood. There were those mysterious greasy innards again, just like yesterday's breakdown four hundred miles to the north. We picked desiccated bugs from the radiator—there since Fresno—fiddled with a few wires, and checked the oil. The engine rapidly cooled and Tom removed the radiator cap. It took two liters of water, another ominous sign. The truck had never used water before either.

"Might as well go on," he said. "I think Liard Hot Springs is only a few miles ahead… if they're open this time of year." He tugged the cap lower on his balding head. I was beginning to shiver. It had been an hour since we'd seen another vehicle.

"It isn't just the radiator," I stated. "Not much chance we'd have two problems at once—loss of power and a low radiator." The little truck started and pulled gamely back onto the road. Towering mountains peeked through the shifting clouds, dappled in sunlight. I sighed and gazed out the window.

Tom didn't answer. He was watching the gauges. The road wound over hills, revealing scenery out of a postcard. After a few miles the heat gauge began to climb, and we stopped to top off the radiator with the last of our drinking water. By the time we limped into Liard Hot Springs, the engine had again overheated. Little Red seemed to be heaving for breath, and we both knew that something was terribly wrong. The game little workhorse, bought the year Luke was born, was simply wearing out.

"It's a blown head gasket," Tom announced with finality as he switched the engine off in front of the lodge-and-gas-pump town. He'd been working through the possibilities in his head. "Let's get a room and figure out what to do."

"Are you sure? I hate stopping at a pricey lodge." I glanced up at the attractive two-story log structure with its red roof. We'd spent most of our Canadian cash and much of our allotted time on breakdowns. *Maybe it's just colic, something that will heal.* I had a contract—our first paycheck since May—and there would be stiff fines if I was late. Our safety net seemed so flimsy. "What if we go on… try to coax the truck into Fort Nelson?" I asked. This was nearest real town, four hours away. "We might find a mechanic there." What else could we do? We had tried calling AAA—satellite phone and cell phone—and couldn't even get through.

Tom shook his head. "We'd be stranded on the road. It's not worth the chance." His kindly eyes looked worried. He was leaving it to me, but I could see he had grave misgivings. When I hesitated, he placed his hands on my shoulders and looked me in the eyes. "I don't want you out on this road tonight. I strongly feel that we need to get a room while we can."

He so rarely pushed a decision that I did not protest.

We peeled out one hundred twenty dollars for the last available room—a tiny garret with sloping ceiling—and lugged our overnight case and cooler up the wooden stairs. While Tom conferred with travelers in the café and parking lot, I borrowed a phone book and stood at the pay phone by the front door trying my American calling card and the toll-free numbers for the Toyota dealer in Whitehorse, to no avail. A generous waitress lent me her Canadian calling card, but I couldn't get that to work either. The afternoon ticked away.

"Two girls was here just las' week in the same situation," the aging waitress told me as she puffed a cigarette outside the front door. "A trucker offered to load up their car, but they couldn't find no way to get it aboard. We don't have no ramp." She hugged her thin ribs through a sweater, gray smoke drifting from colorless lips. She was from Newfoundland, she told me between coughs, her accent thick and her voice kindly.

I gazed down the empty road, first one way and then the other. Snow was sifting prettily, obscuring the mountains and smudging the edges of visibility in failing dusk. Ahead lay Summit Pass, the highest and most treacherous part of the journey. My guts were in a knot, my breath high in my throat. I tried to bring it down to my diaphragm, but there seemed a tight band around my chest.

"Don't you miss your family?" I asked, wondering at the ordinary courage of people.

She nodded. "My husband works out of Fort Nelson, but he's gone most of the time anyway. I get back every couple a' weeks. I'd love to see my grandkids back in Newfoundland." She pronounced it "New Found Land" with the emphasis on the "Found."

"I was hoping to hitch back to Whitehorse and buy another truck," I said, "but I can't even get through on the phone."

"It'd cost you about $8,000 more than stateside," she warned. "People go down to Seattle to buy vehicles if they can. I think the salesman has to buy it and then sell it to you used the next day or something to make it legal for Americans."

"I don't know what we're gonna do." I was running my fingers repetitively through my short, wavy hair. It had picked up more gray over the summer. "I have to be at my job by the fifteenth or they'll charge me twelve dollars per hour for time missed."

She stared at me wordlessly, and it occurred to me that she might be delighted to make twelve dollars an hour. I had so much to be grateful for and so little to whine about in the big scheme of things. It just didn't feel that way at the moment.

Returning to our cramped room, I found Tom sitting on the bed and paging through the phone book. There were holes in the plaster of the sloping roof, knocked by errant heads. Perching next to him, I took out a pencil and began a flowchart on the back of an envelope.

"Let's pool what we've discovered," I said. "Either direction will entail great distances and be difficult to reverse."

Tom eased onto the only chair and gave me his attention.

"We have two options," I drew headings, "tow the truck or abandon it. If we tow it, what does that look like?"

"It'll cost two thousand to tow it to Fort Nelson. Even so, we probably won't find a mechanic and the parts to repair it in time. It will be safer to leave it here."

"We could hitchhike back to the Toyota dealer in Whitehorse, buy a truck, and then return to tow Little Red to Fresno," I suggested.

Tom considered this and then shook his head. "No telling if we'd find a vehicle, what the price would be, whether we'd have trouble with customs, or even if the new truck could tow Little Red. Too many unknowns."

I nodded. "Okay. We leave the truck here and hitchhike south. I can rent a car in Seattle and drive to Fresno in time to start my job. You can buy another truck and come back for Little Red. That would add perhaps four thousand miles to this venture with winter descending."

"I'll ask the manager if we can leave our pickup here until spring when we can tow it back to Fairbanks on our way north. That would be my preference."

He departed to explore options while I started another list of what we'd need to carry with us. When he returned to the room he said, "The manager won't let us overwinter the truck. I finally persuaded him to let it stay until I get back. He's charging five dollars a day—our last hundred and fifty Canadian cash—for a month. I can't blame him for not wanting abandoned vehicles. It'll cost far more than the truck is worth to get it hauled out. There's a 2:00 A.M. bus leaving Fort Nelson that'll get us to Seattle for three hundred dollars."

"Maybe we can hitch clear to the border," I suggested. "Let's sort our belongings while it's still light. We should take anything we'll need before spring. There's no telling how this will end."

As we stood in the muddy parking lot pulling scuffed totes from the camper shell and sorting our lives into a pile that we could carry, a snowy evening settled upon the mountains, muting the light and wrapping the vast land in mystery. A raven sailed low from the north like a messenger, a shadow in the swirling snowflakes. He circled once, uttered his musical winter "*plunk-plunk*," and then disappeared silently south. I took a deep breath of the clean air and rested in the hush of the moment. The cradle of wilderness spread out for hundreds of miles in all directions. It's always hard, this crashing into the twenty-first century after months in the Bush, and these past ten days had been particularly stressful.

Tom locked the truck and we lugged the remnants of our lives into the warmth of the lodge and up the artistic stairs with their diamond willow banister. We would take our electronics (laptops, satellite phone, ground-to-air radio, and expensive camera), important papers, items necessary for my job, our medical kit, a couple of changes of clothes, and our heavy jackets. I made lunch for the next day and gave the remaining food away. Even half a loaf of bread was eagerly accepted here. Hardest of all, Tom parted with his summer pickings: five gallons of low-bush cranberries.

Darkness claimed the land early. We curled together into the small bed, my head on Tom's left shoulder where I could hear the dependable thump of his aging heart. My mind still jumped about like a small animal in a cage. Noises carried clearly through the walls: voices, footsteps, the flush of a toilet. From outside, a neon sign lit the room in orange.

"Four years ago we had a business, family, friends, five acres, a home, and a guesthouse," I murmured. Tom stroked my hair and I began to relax. "I wanted to simplify our lives and now look at us!" He was silent, continuing his gentle petting. I sighed. "Tomorrow we'll set out on foot down a snowy road in the middle of nowhere with only the items we can carry. It's simple—but not exactly what I had in mind."

"Today has been a real lesson for me." Tom's quiet voice was soothing. He rolled onto his side and pulled me close. I nestled into the familiar contours. He was thin and wiry now, down thirty pounds from that ancient past. I could feel his ribs as I nuzzled into the warm hair of his chest.

"Everyone should have to prioritize life from time to time," he said at last. "Today I got to see that you and Lucas are all that really matter. I was terrified of breaking down with you out there. I'm supposed to protect you—not that you aren't capable—but it's my role. As long as I have you, everything else will turn out okay."

I had never heard him speak this way. A wave of gratitude flooded me. *What a privilege to be alive!* "Think of all the times we could have broken down when it would have been so much worse," I said. "Like when you were hauling a trailer north with our dreams and no money or alternatives. What would we have done?"

I felt him sigh. He hadn't always been so balanced. Once I had tearfully asked for ten minutes a day of "lap time." I just needed to be held and stroked, but in our early years, he was often too busy to notice. He used to get irritated, ready to do battle, when life took an unpleasant turn.

"How did you become so mellow?" I asked.

"You taught me."

"So why haven't I learned? Things always turn out. I know that and yet I am fearful. Remember when our roof blew off in 1982 and rain poured through the ceiling? You took it so hard. You didn't do that today." I thought a moment then said, "I think we both handled it very well."

My body relaxed under Tom's caress and my thoughts drifted in a current of free association, touching memories of past trials like old friends. "Remember when you almost died of pneumonia in the wilderness, and then the squirrel bit Luke and I was so worried about rabies? Or when my mother was dying and Luke was newborn? What about all the years living on a shoestring, never knowing where our next dollar would come from?" My lips twitched in a smile. By the orange light from the sign outside our window, I pulled back to gaze fondly into his eyes.

ENLIGHTENMENT IS A JOURNEY. I break into an occasional clearing, but am soon drawn back into the thickets of unconsciousness and forget the sunlight. Life devolves into struggle and effort. There was much of that yet to come. I felt like we were tiptoeing along a knife edge. Nevertheless, events funneled us safely through with breathtaking synchronicity.

The next morning we checked out and stashed our duffel by the entrance. I stood in the empty parking lot in falling snow holding a paper bag on which I had written, "SOUTH." Only an occasional traveler stopped for gas or a bite to eat. The waitress informed guests of our plight and soon they too were appraising each new arrival. Most had no room. A man who walked heavily with a cane needed our help. He was towing a U-Haul trailer when it blew a tire a few miles north of town. Tom went with him to replace the flat, but there was no spare. The man would need to drive to Fort Nelson to get it repaired and then return.

It was late morning when a Ford F-350 towing an enormous fifth-wheel with Alaskan plates pulled in for fuel. When the lone man emerged, I approached to ask for a ride. He was about Tom's age and height, clean-shaven with short, gray hair and reserved brown eyes behind glasses.

He drew back and studied me. "Are you planning to mug me?"

It was a startling (but relevant) question. I told him our story and then ran to get Tom, who had just returned from changing the tire. Tom had trimmed his beard and looked like an aging poet in Goodwill clothes. The two shook hands and assessed one another.

"I'm sorry, but I'd like to see some identification," the driver stated.

We agreed to go into the restaurant to talk, and Tom bought a round of coffee. Twenty minutes later, we loaded our belongings into the trailer and climbed aboard the truck, trying not to track mud on the beige carpet. Don turned out to be an agreeable companion, accepting only a sandwich and dinner in payment. He was headed for Montana and offered to take us as far as Dawson Creek—five hundred miles. Summit Pass was already layered in two

Little Red Truck

feet of snow, but because of Don's kindness, we traveled over it in warmth and comfort. In unaccustomed luxury, we watched Stone sheep, migrating caribou, moose, and buffalo as we exchanged bits of our lives.

That night we stayed in a motel at Dawson Creek. Don accepted our dinner invitation and got up before dawn, insisting that he drive us to the bus station. From there, I recall a kaleidoscope of images as the bus rocked along the autumnal roads for thirty hours and a thousand miles. Sometime during the night, some drama arose between the driver and a drunken passenger. There was also something about kids who had boarded by mistake and had to be taken back. The bus stopped at various hamlets. I put my fingers in my ears and tried to sleep, curled against the cold window, hoping no one would steal our camera, briefcase, or computer from the overhead rack.

It took four hours to clear U.S. customs the next afternoon. We arrived exhausted in Seattle a little before dark. The bus station was a tawdry scene of people fallen through cracks in the American dream. Adrift among the stoned teenagers and despondent old men, the tired babies and hopeless transients, we were just one more hard-luck story that no one wanted to hear.

Tom left me guarding our baggage while he scouted for a hotel. He was sneezing with a cold and my head was spinning with fatigue. We had eaten nothing but bagels all day. I reached Lucas on the little flip phone and told him we were back in the States. Then with Tom leading, we walked the few blocks, dragging and carrying our worldly possessions. The hotel elevator wasn't working, so we walked up the four flights. Our room was expensive and squalid, with bare electrical wires hanging from walls that were painted the color of egg yolk. The stained mattress sagged and the sheets were dingy. Nevertheless, it was ours for the night.

"I think we can walk to both the Toyota dealership and our bank," Tom said when he emerged from a chilly shower the following morning. "Of course, it is Sunday."

"I've been trying to visualize what we need," I told him. "If we're going to live in Alaska, we should have four-wheel drive."

"Five-speed and four-cylinder. I don't want an automatic," Tom stated. "Like Little Red, only newer. I'm not keen on used vehicles, but it's what we can afford."

"Extended cab, so we can keep our travel gear and electronics locked up and available. With a camper shell."

"I think you have to buy the shell separately."

"Silver. It would be nice if it were silver and had a CD player."

Walking in to buy a vehicle does not put one in a good bargaining position. The Toyota dealer had only one used truck: a silver 2002 Tacoma, long-bed with extended cab, four-wheel-drive, and forty thousand miles. We had to wait until the following morning to complete the paperwork. This too was a cliffhanger worthy of fiction. After all the dickering and signing of papers, we handed over a check for twenty thousand dollars written on the Sylvia House equity line— only to have it rejected as "out-of-state." It was Columbus Day, and most banks were closed, but we walked several blocks and found ours open.

"This will take a week to clear," the well-dressed young manager said as she fingered our check. Tom and I were seated like supplicants before her spacious mahogany desk. I was clad for hitchhiking in snowstorms.

"I have a very good job, but I need to be there by next Monday!" My voice began to rise like a bearing going out. I rummaged through our battered briefcase and slapped credentials onto the polished wood. "We can't wait in Seattle," I snarled. "Here! I have four nursing licenses that let me practice in twenty states. Here!" I slammed down another document, "is my certification in obstetrical nursing. This is the clear title to our house in Arizona! Here," I yanked forth wads of paper, "are mutual funds, CDs, saving accounts… We have the money! We just need to get at it. Today!"

I was half out of my seat, shaking and sputtering like a teakettle about to emit a piercing wail. An avalanche of recent events had started its reckless descent, burying me to the eyeballs. Tom collared and gently pushed me back into the chair. "It'll be okay," he soothed. He nodded pleasantly to the manager. "What can you do for us?"

She looked as if she expected me to spring across the table. "With your history and credit rating," she said tentatively, "I think we can write you a signature loan."

Forty-five minutes later, Tom and I walked back to the dealer with a certified check. The next snag was registration. We were only passing through Washington, and didn't live in Arizona either. Alaska was the one constant in our itinerant lives. After a series of calls and a walk through downtown Seattle to the FedEx office, we mailed the title to Denise. She had come to our rescue again, offering to carry the title through DMV and smog-test exemption in Fairbanks.

By afternoon we loaded baggage behind the seat and climbed into our shiny pickup. It was raining as we pulled out of Seattle, and we stopped in a small town off I-5 to buy windshield wipers. I read the manual aloud as the new wipers and big tires sang down the highway. We were driving again! A day later we stopped at an Oregon dealer wondering why the "check engine" light was on. The mechanic said he didn't know, that perhaps the generic gas cap didn't seal well. We listened to the engine and watched the gas gauge with apprehension, trying to divine our future.

When Laurie and her aging Basset hound welcomed us home, it felt like we'd swum the ocean and finally made it to shore. We rested a day while Tom researched ways to get Little Red out of Canada. He found a grocery truck returning empty from Alaska. The company would fax our title to the driver, and if he could coax our wounded pickup aboard, they would haul her to Seattle for a thousand dollars. The following morning we again raced south for a second go at Fresno.

Lucas visits us in Homer in 2009.

Lucas holds Tom on his lap when he visits, spring 2010.

Chapter 26

LOST AND FOUND IN AMERICA

November 2007

With my iconic father and imaginative mother, being "ordinary" never seemed an option for me. I have said that my first memory was the train trip from Colorado, but another is stronger. I'm standing on the stage in a spotlight looking out into the darkened auditorium of the University of Arizona. A thousand faces dwindle into the blackness. There's even a balcony where the projector beams down like a train light.

"I am Jeanie of Alaska and I am three and a half years old," I intone solemnly into a microphone. My voice is huge. My first stage fright. "I am Jeanie of Alaska and I am three and a half years old…" I repeat. Apparently this is my only line. "I am Jeanie…" I begin once more.

"That's fine," my mother says softly. She pats me. "That's enough."

She's been up here with me all along. She is radiant in front of the audience. Young and slender, she is wearing heels and a dark, fitted dress with nylon stockings. Her white fox drape—the one she trapped herself—cascades like snow to her knees.

With relief, I step from the brightness and am handed down to an older couple, Clyde and Marion Bell, who sit in a front-row seat. Clyde has a gray mustache like a little brush. His shoulders are bony under a tweed jacket, and his arms are soft and unsteady as he receives me from the stage. Why should

I remember the Bells? They never played a central role in my life. *Why not my father?* My young memory is clear, yet I saved not a scrap of him. It took me sixty years to discover how hurt and angry I felt at that loss.

"That's me!" I pipe up, pointing to the giant toddler that flickers across the screen on snowshoes. I am sitting on Marion's skimpy lap. She has on a dark silk dress with little white dots. From the black depths behind us comes the hushed rustle of the audience.

My father isn't present, but he certainly is represented—fifteen feet high on the colorful, silent screen—while my mother's well-rehearsed lines reverberate through speakers. There he is: tall, handsome, far larger than life, hoisting a great log onto his shoulder, landing our Cessna on the arctic pack ice, shooting a polar bear, catching fish, and carrying me across the muskeg. He appears graceful and confident. His blond hair is trimmed and rosy cheeks are neatly shaved. The severe cleft in his square chin is as sharp as the cut of an ax. Even when he smiles for the camera, there is something pinched—almost priggish—about his mouth.

My lovely, flamboyant mother looks innocent—not in a prim way (for she loves to flirt), but as if she expects kindness. She is girlish on the screen, paddling her kayak over the jewel waters of Takahula Lake with me wedged safely between her knees. I see her holding my hand while we snowshoe in Native parkas on the polar ice, and tucking me into a sleeping bag in the snug wall tent. Little Jeanie seems completely happy. She is a perfect blend of her parents: a vigorous child with her father's blooming cheeks, golden skin, and that dimple in her chin, her mother's gray-green eyes and the moons of her fingernails. *Oh, yes, like it or not, I am their daughter.*

I still dream of Takahula—emerald water deepening below the kayak as the ground falls away. There are old trout and char as large as myself in the sunlit depths. In my dreams, I swim among them, breathing that beautiful water, the surface of the lake dimpled and blue far above. An impartial observer might comment that I built the rest of my life around my parents, that my own journey has been but a shadowy re-creation of theirs. I would deny it, but that doesn't mean it isn't so.

I once asked my mother if I had been born as a photo prop. She thought a moment before answering. "No," she replied candidly. "You were a surprise. But a nice one," she added as an afterthought, patting me on the knee.

"What about Annie?" I pressed. My little sister had followed closely.

"Your father wanted to spend a year hunting in Africa. We'd already bought the truck. He could never get enough of shooting things, and I couldn't face another continent full of new animals to kill. Annie was my way out."

Bud would take his new wife to Africa and to India as well. His homes became museums of exotic dead creatures—from elephant to monkeys, tiger to polar bears. Like a frozen Noah's Ark, they peered from every wall, looking sad and slightly surprised. He never posed them snarling. Perhaps this was his way of holding back the river, attempting to capture that essence of life, whose very nature is movement.

When Connie died, I discovered a score of Bud's letters saved in the small bundle of her possessions. Searching for signs of my father, I found mostly an account of what he ate or wore on lecture tour, the cost of items, and how much money they could make. There was a sense of grandeur: plans for more, bigger, and richer successes that would further elevate them above the "hares." Underlying it, there may have been a current of affection, or at least a need for her guidance and approval. It was as close as I got.

For her part, Connie saw the world as colorful and exotic. Friends became characters in her imagination, and she generously wrote us into the best parts. After being fifteen feet tall on the silver screen, how could my father ever settle for life-sized? I caught only the edge of the spotlight, yet it has taken me a lifetime to make it to solid ground. *Who am I?* This is the question each must ask, made no easier when someone else writes the script. We all come from people with answers, people who have yet to find their own way.

How much of my early life was staged? Annie was already born when our parents filmed *Jeanie of Alaska* under contract, and the happy scene was fraying below the surface. I must have sensed that discord, yearning to save my parents. As for my sister—apart from a few black-and-white photos, a birth announcement, and a pair of gold-plated diaper pins in the scrapbook—she is conspicuously absent from the family story. In the few inclusive photos, I am a robust child, smiling and self-confident. Beside me, Annie seems a fragile doll, pale and unsure of her grip on life: our mother's excuse for not going to Africa. Connie later told me candidly that when they divorced, Bud asked for one child—she could pick. That had seemed fair to her, but Winnie spoke up, saying, "You can't give your baby away like a puppy!" So Connie had kept us both.

Life in Tucson was an odd sequel. I think all three of us felt displaced. Like my mother, I wanted to say, "This isn't my real life!" When visitors came to our shabby cottage on Bean Alley, I would run to the heavy scrapbooks (kept always on our coffee table) and turn to publicity shots and newspaper clippings of me. Annie would pipe up, wanting acknowledgment for her small place in the family archives, but of what merit were gold-plated diaper pins?

Our mother continued to tell us that we were somebody. "Class," she said, "is a matter of values, not money." We were "upper class" and as such had a responsibility for our world and to the poor. It seemed an odd dictum: as far as I could see, we were "the poor." Nevertheless, such inconsistencies dwell in the minds of most humans, sharing time with equally unlikely ideas. It was a raft that kept my self-esteem afloat in the judgmental world of the 1950s, but even to a child, it didn't feel like bedrock.

The one thing a Helmericks could not be was ordinary. The mandate to be unique came from both my parents, but while Connie celebrated her children, Bud required them to reflect his image. For him, disloyalty was the biggest sin. There was never any pretense of equality among his children. As Bud's oldest biological child (and a male), my half-brother Mark got the largest helping of specialness. He would be governor of Alaska one day and—who knew?—maybe president. Mark grew up on a sharp pinnacle with no place to step but up. The other golden boy, Jeff, was groomed as Mark's second: Prince Harry to Prince William. As a stepson, I don't think Jim even placed. Curiously, of all Bud's children, Jim deserved the title of successor. He was the one who continued the legacy of life at the Colville. Annie and I didn't exist in Bud's fabled pedigree at all.

Like Connie, I chose a nebulous place in the social hierarchy. Even if I didn't have money, as an artist I wasn't a "hare." Nursing, however, pushed me into a whole new game and the humility of starting at the bottom. I knew how to be alone on stage, but nothing of collaboration. As I struggled for footing in this new environment, I began to drop my story. I was no longer "Jeanie of Alaska," but just Jeanie. It came as a surprising relief. Taking good care of patients and being an asset to my peers was satisfying in ways that I had never imagined. Far from disappearing in anonymity, I found it freeing. *What if everything I have always believed is wrong?*

IN FRESNO, THE CURRENT OF our lives again slowed to a meandering channel. I was grateful to be back in familiar surroundings and for the respite from change. My coworkers welcomed me and there was an illusion of safety. Nevertheless, I caught myself listening for the sound of rushing water. Life flourishes on the edge of an abyss—each day an ordinary miracle. The rapids, like the beating of our hearts, whisper a reminder.

In the wintry mountains of British Columbia, Little Red started her sick, old engine and climbed gamely aboard the empty grocery truck for the ride through Canada. In Washington, she transferred to an auto-hauler and was delivered like an ignoble package to Fresno, completing our agreement to remove her from Liard Hot Springs before the deep snows. Tom had wanted to repair her for light duty, but the dealer's six-thousand-dollar estimate was three times her value.

She was parked behind a chain link fence like a forlorn dog left at the kennel when we came for our weathered belongings. I felt disloyal pulling totes of clothing from the shell and loading them into the bed of the silver Tacoma. The newer vehicle looked muscular next to our squat little pickup, but it was all show. Its shiny body was fragile, the engine gutless, and the suspension built more for light touring than real work.

"Pretty Boy," I muttered as I climbed into the clean bed to arrange our load.

Tom quickly found a new owner for Little Red, someone who could do repairs in his yard. For years, men in dusty clothes had gravitated to the tough little workhorse, leaving notes on the windshield: "If you want to sell your truck, please call Manny…" Taking only a few wrinkled bills from the man's calloused hand, Tom handed the keys to an immigrant of hesitant English who was working his way up the American dream. Gently Tom closed the door on two decades and walked away without looking back. *For every birth, a death*, I thought. *It is the law.* Yet as our old life fell irretrievably behind, I could see no land on the horizon.

Eve and Megan returned to Sylvia House, where Lucas was in his second year at the University College of Nursing. Eve was attending the Pima College associate degree program—an abbreviated path to registered nurse. They again shared growth and parenting while Tom and I picked up much of the tab with two-thirds of our income. My plan that Sylvia House help pay Lucas's way through college hadn't quite worked out.

"It's a good investment," Tom reassured me.

I nodded. "Not in our future, maybe, but in life."

At Christmas the little family came to see us in Fresno, driving in a marathon day from Tucson in Lucas's old Honda. He had kept his weight down and his face looked happy. On his left hand he wore Eve's ring, and although he was not talking forever, he was considering it. The three young people settled noisily into our spare bedroom—not unlike a nest of ravens. We spent a week in celebration: playing games, laughing in the Jacuzzi, and biking in Woodward Park. In the Japanese garden, Lucas enticed a goose onto his lap where it rested, gazing over the lake with him like two old friends. We rented a van and drove to

Monterey, having the aquarium surprisingly to ourselves, then back on Route 1 to see the dozing sea elephants. Too soon the kids squeezed aboard the old car and disappeared south into their busy lives.

Just after New Year's 2008, Annie phoned to tell me that my first husband Phil Beisel had died of cancer. I recalled twelve sweet years together. I had gifted Connie's vision of Alaskan wilderness to Phil and he had taught me how to craft my dreams into reality. Even as our lives were drawn apart, we had treated one another kindly. In time, the amputation of divorce healed and I came to realize that his abrupt departure had not been personal, but a necessary divergence of two souls on different paths. For me, the numinous quest has always been a driving fire, but Phil was uneasy below that shifting surface. Sequestered in friendliness, he was as private as a spruce tree and whatever he believed about the larger human journey, he did not share. In leaving our marriage, he chose a safer mate with definitive answers to life's larger questions. He had also freed me to seek where I would.

Most of us end up far from our original heading—whether we choose our lives or allow circumstances to define them. Phil settled for domestication and success. Yet in 1990, Bush pilot Dave Ketcher recounted a salient story to me. He had flown to a remote lake to check out a downed airplane for salvage. As he circled the wreck his own plane faltered and he was forced to land on the pond. He was puzzling over his plight when a lone man with a backpack and rifle stepped from the forest. It was Phil.

"Sounds like your magneto is going out," Phil had said.

"I lost radio contact coming down in the mountains or I'd call in a mechanic."

Phil, who was a licensed aircraft mechanic, had removed the failing part and replaced it with one from the wreck. Dave had given him a ride back to Fairbanks.

I last saw Phil in Tucson at Christmastime, around 1995. His father had died and he called me from Alaska to ask if I would help move his mother into an assisted living complex. Marion Beisel had always been kind to me and I was pleased to help. Tom offered the use of Little Red. Luke, who was about nine and curious about my past, accompanied me to the airport to pick up Phil. Luke was intrigued by Phil's bright edge, but wary of the rough-and-tumble kidding.

Phil and I spent three days moving his mother's belongings and cleaning out the old apartment. He was as agile and strong as ever; still outgoing and personable, still elusive. As we worked—his every movement so familiar—I thought of our years together and toyed with the path not taken. I drove him back to the airport and waited with him. Would he hug me goodbye? What would I say? Ahead of us in the line of travelers, an older woman with white hair and an open face was greeting strangers and handing out snowflakes that she had crocheted. I still have one. They were the size of my palm and carefully crafted in fine, white thread.

Phil grinned and said, "Look, a little old lady with snowflakes."

"Phil, that's patronizing," I said, turning to study this handsome stranger whom I had once married. It was a curious completion for me, a sudden validation of our different roads. As he walked down the ramp toward the plane with that familiar pigeon-toed, confident stride, I noticed that Phil was carrying a Bible under his arm. I hope it brought him peace.

Philip Karl Beisel: July 2, 1948 ~ January 4, 2008.

TOM AND I WERE MARKING time. By returning to Fresno, I had foregone growth for the illusion of stability. We still had our gentle rituals, but the city was hard and ugly; visibility was often less than a mile. I developed a chronic cough and my focus narrowed to the next paycheck or run of work. It wasn't so bad, this little death. Most people do it. The routine was familiar and they paid me well. So what if I shuffled home hunched with fatigue? *But where is the sparkle?* I watched people in stores—disappointed faces, bodies molded with tension and thickened with unconscious eating. Even children plodded grimly through the noise of traffic. *Is this it? Life?*

I recalled another Kipling story my mother read when I was a child: *The Miracle of Purun Bhagat*. It is about a high-caste Indian Brahmin who spends his first twenty years as a youth, the second centered on family, and the third as a celebrated statesman. At the pinnacle of success, he abandons everything to walk barefooted and anonymous onto the dusty road, following the inner path of a holy man. It intrigued me to think life might be lived in chapters—each a different journey. *What template have we?* I wondered. *Do we simply spin down like battered tops and fall over?*

In health care, the bundling of human affairs continued under federal mandate—new edicts clicking into place with mechanical regularity. Meanwhile, Fresno's Community Hospital was under massive renovation, which seemed to have run aground on infrastructure. Daily I skirted men on ladders as I rushed to the operating room on the life-and-death business of birth. Vandals trashed a half-dozen cars each night in the employee parking lots. This chaos felt like ice splintering on a frozen river—an uncanny reminder of water underfoot—and it signaled a time for me to float free. I tried to remember that the river knows where it's going, but here—where the future disappeared into mist—I still paced and fretted.

We might have hunkered in Fresno until spring had the hospital been extending contracts. Instead, they offered enormous bonuses to travelers who would sign on as staff. Many did—a two-year commitment for a huge bowl of food. *Two years*, I thought, *is a sizable chunk of my life—maybe all of it*. I decided to take my chances as a coyote, lean and vulnerable, but alive every day. Suddenly, I was no longer afraid. Willie Nelson was belting out *On the Road Again* as I sped to work in the crush of vehicles and murky darkness. Only the week before, one hundred cars had collided on this stretch of freeway. I laughed and joined Willie at the top of my lungs. *Life is not about survival!* What was I doing in Fresno, remote from my roots in this beautiful planet? Somewhere invisibly ahead, our wandering days would end. Against all logic about old age in a dark and frozen land, Alaska held my heart.

Our immediate future crystallized when I signed a contract up the coast in Olympia. Prophetically, coastal Washington had been our original destination when we embarked long ago. In my phone interview, the nurse manager spoke of Olympia as "a thoughtful community with counterculture overtones." The hospital, she said, encouraged families to have a birth plan and to participate in decision-making. Perhaps we would discover a healthy relic of the sixties—a prospect as exciting to me as finding a live mammoth in the forests near Puget Sound.

"It looks like Mordor out there," I intoned.

Tom was jockeying our loaded pickup south through traffic for a brief visit to Tucson before we headed north to Olympia. The new silver shell over Pretty Boy's bed was filled to capacity. Above the smog it was late afternoon, but California's Central Valley lay smothered in dark murk—trapped by the high Sierras like pea soup in a bowl. Buildings appeared to drift, suspended and vague. Along State Route 99, ravens were scavenging the blowing trash. Like humans, their dependency appeared sordid and debased. I thought of our proud Blackhearts living close to the edge, fiercely independent. These scabrous birds seemed a caricature of wildness.

Evening pulled down as we climbed out of Bakersfield toward Tehachapi Pass. Fields and towns gave way to steep rangeland with scattered trees. As we ascended, the air thinned until we topped out above the pall. Behind us, peaks floated like islands in the miasma; ahead the view opened—vast and inviting.

"Look! Stars!" I exclaimed. Brilliant pinpricks appeared in the velvet sky. My eyes lingered on a sharp edge of mountain where purple dusk faded into salmon. A dusting of snow sparkled white in our headlights. "I had forgotten the stars," I breathed. "I think Bisbee is the last place I recall seeing them."

That had been almost a year ago. We had traveled to Fresno and then into the constant daylight of Alaskan summer. When arctic night crept back, I relinquished it to the grizzlies. Back in Fresno again, we were submerged under a noxious blanket in a colorless world. *It's so easy to lose one's vision,* I thought. A generation grows up without stars and memory fades. *How can you miss what you've never known?* Bottled water exchanged for clear streams, malls instead of a town center.

The purpose of this long drive between my assignments was to visit friends and, of course, Lucas. Although we kept in touch with email and phone calls, we missed him. With Eve and Megan at Sylvia House (as well as a new roommate), we chose to stay with friends. We took Lucas to dinner and shared as much of our scattered lives as time permitted. There seemed a quiet sadness about him, a resigned heaviness of spirit as well as body that he did not share. Two days later, we were back on I-10, headed north through Phoenix.

Uncle Bert's face lit up when he opened the door of their Scottsdale home. He was stooped now, leaning on a walker and wearing oxygen full-time.

"I am delighted that I can still make new friends at eighty-seven," he said when we were seated in their comfortable living room. "I never expected that. I'm representing people with Alzheimer's, not just caregivers." He had addressed the Scottsdale City Council, he told us. Although the exertion pushed him into a heart attack, he was still writing, speaking out, and bringing people together around this complex issue. "I'm the caregiver now," he continued. "It's a role I never anticipated. It surprises me how much joy I get from giving back to this wonderful woman who served me most of her life."

Janet beamed angelically from the sofa, tiny and fragile. "You see, I've been diagnosed with Alzheimer's," she said. "We had hoped it was some other form of dementia. Rats!" Then she grinned.

"How are you doing with that?" I moved next to her and took her hand.

"I sometimes forget things, but my memory of long ago is very clear—when your mother and I were children. Connie was so good to me, Jeanie. You remind me of her." Janet's wonderful smile lit the room. "I am very happy." Her hand lay light and dry as a leaf in mine and her eyes glistened with affection. "My Bert is so good to me. You see, I've given up competing. I simply enjoy each day. Joy!" She let the word hang in the air.

"When we see you, we always think, 'This is the last time,'" Bert said when they walked us to the door. "Then here you are again!" He hugged each of us in turn. "Never forget that life is good," he told me pointedly. "You have to focus on the blessings or you'll miss the best parts."

It was the last time we would see them—standing together by the front door, hands upraised in farewell until we turned the corner.

As we drove away, I kept thinking of Janet stepping into the darkness without fear or drama. I remembered the book, *A Three Dog Life*, by Abigail Thomas, whose husband had lost his past and future to traumatic brain injury and yet his words were often profound without context. "Alzheimer's seems like the very worst calamity," I said to Tom. "Take my mobility, even my life—but not my identity! Yet maybe enlightenment happens beyond our brains. What if we can live joyfully regardless of circumstances?"

That night we stayed with Bert-Son and his gentle wife. Nadine's life was of playful service. She saw the best in everyone, and people bloomed in her presence as easily as geraniums.

"There's something different about you," I said to Bert-Son, "a new sense of balance." We sat facing one another on the sofa, knees comfortably touching, while our mates cooked dinner. Seeing him was strangely familiar, like looking into a mirror.

"I've been exploring life as a spiritual journey," he said. *Winnie's gift, of course.* Like his father, my cousin wore his hair in a long graying ponytail. Like Janet, he now had hearing aids. "I thought for a while that I might be Buddhist or Taoist, but there is no name. Ritual keeps the mind busy so that you can discover the silence below it. Most people get stuck in ritual, yet the message of the Masters is simple: Be present."

I sank into his familiar eyes and we both took an audible breath.

"I care about my students," he continued, holding his palm up, "and I don't care." He turned his hand over as if letting sand fall, and watched me to see if I understood. "I am completely committed… and I am at peace with their choices. Perhaps failure is the experience they need. I am spending more time in that space between everything and nothing. Possibility and Void." He held my eyes.

I nodded. "I can let go of almost everything," I said at last, "except this remarkable living world! I am so saddened at what our human greed and carelessness are doing to Earth, and so helpless to change any of it."

Bert-Son held my hands between his and said, "Gaia."

I was silent, allowing him to see into my pain. "If only I knew that it would be all right," I whispered. Grief welled up in tears.

"Gaia will survive our tenure." He spoke slowly and with such certainty that I almost believed. "Earth has weathered worse. What humanity is doing cannot compare to a comet hitting the planet." He brought his kindly face close. "Earth has been through many lifetimes, evolving between devastation and rebirth. I admit there are a finite number of lives—even stars burn out—but that time is not yet. Even if it were, universal progression is unstoppable. Countless planets are awakening at this moment. Your grief serves no purpose."

I considered the Serenity Prayer: *To change the things I can, to release those I cannot change, and the wisdom to know the difference.* Then I thought of the planet that my mother had entrusted me to save. Taking a deep breath, I felt suddenly light. Perhaps it wasn't my job. Maybe I was present to witness—to learn to see beauty, even in the face of destruction. Alan Watts writes, "The meaning and purpose of dancing is the dance." *Could it really be that simple?*

Tom and I again took wing in the morning light, choosing a quiet route north. In the cab of our new pickup it felt almost like flying low through the mountains. *How different this journey would look afoot!* Out of Parker, Arizona, the green Colorado River slid by docile and harnessed, its shores tiled white with homes and boats. It appeared neutered: a Disney version of riverbank. Hugging the captive river, the highway snaked beneath silent red domes painted against a blue sky like the backdrop of a travel poster. I silenced my judgments, trying to see it as the first people had, to touch the wonder and remember the wild river whose journey had carved through a mile of rock. I smiled, doubting that a few dams would keep her captive. *The planet is patient; life mysterious and tenacious.*

"I'm not going to rant anymore," I said.

Leaning back, I allowed my gaze to ride like a blue heron along the sunlit cliffs over the river. Even the arrogant boats failed to annoy me. The planet will survive our tenure! I held my cousin's words like a warm stone close to my heart and was suddenly happy. I hadn't a clue where we were going, and it didn't matter. What a joy to live on the wing and be part of it all!

Tom lines our canoe upstream for a day trip together

"Rude" Amerud, man of wild places, wandering at Kernwood, 2009.

Chapter 27

OLYMPIA

February 2008

I was quiet as we drove north—engrossed in the changing scenery with the delight of a child. It seemed so easy to just be.

There is power in declaration, I thought. I had once stated that I was "through getting my feelings hurt." The words had surprised me, seeming to come from nowhere. "My pain is real," I had said to Tom, "but on some level, I must have learned it as a way of controlling others. I'm not saying I'll never experience that sinking feeling again, but I am committed to seeing beyond it."

I had been the "sensitive one" in my family, falling easily into a hole of low self-esteem—especially after the winter with my father. Although my mother and sister tried to coax me out, it was an endless chore. Trapped in my own beliefs, I alone held the key. Choosing not to indulge in hurt feelings had freed me in unforeseen ways. I no longer needed to defend myself and could even learn from criticism. If I sensed that someone didn't like me—and because I still carried uniqueness as a shield, many people didn't—I had options. "Have I done something to upset you?" I would ask. It was a powerful tool.

This declaration to cease ranting shifted the mosaic again. Clearly, anger and joy were incompatible; my grief for the planet healed nothing. *Perhaps, we need crisis to evolve,* I thought, *like an alcoholic reaching bottom. Maybe it's supposed to happen this way.* When one is skewered on the horns of dilemma, answers must arise from beyond our belief in opposites. Einstein said a problem cannot be solved with the consciousness that created it. Chief Joseph chose empowered surrender by declaring, "I will fight no more forever." Against all logic, struggle does not bring freedom. War begets only war.

Most people believe that a caterpillar "changes" into a butterfly (a nip here, a tuck there), but the truth is catastrophic—and miraculous. Within the crawling caterpillar are dormant "imaginal cells," which carry the dream of a new being. When the humble caterpillar spins its cocoon, these cells awaken and release enzymes that digest the wormlike form. From these raw materials, something completely novel is birthed. In a similar process, we harbor the template of a new paradigm invisibly within us. Like the caterpillar, we do not control this process. Awakening is a painful and cataclysmic ordeal. It dawns through us in its own time and is not of our making.

As Tom and I traveled north through snowy redwoods, skirting washed-out highways above the wild Pacific in the wake of a major storm, I recalled moments of awareness when I had seen threads of light—delicate as spiderwebs—connecting the living woods: leaves, moss, and stones. *Nature is an evolving collaboration*, I thought. *Earth brought forth our intelligence as its next, great unfolding. We are the Planet awakening to its own beauty.* It was a grave risk, for until we mature as a species we endanger all living things. *I will learn to walk between the worlds*, I decided. *May I be a blessing.*

Again we stayed over a day with Laurie. She and I arose to share dawn in front of her large windows, where a full moon was garlanded in fading stars above the frosted lawn. In the courtyard, a raven was drinking from the freezing fountain. Laurie cupped a steaming mug of coffee between her palms and snuggled into an overstuffed chair. I heard Tom's feet on the carpeted stairway.

"You're up early," I said as he joined us with his hot mug.

"I didn't want to miss anything."

There was something tribal about our friendship. We had trusted one another with our lives. I thought of Laurie skinning a grizzly in the snow the morning the starving bear attacked and of hauling logs together like a pair of sweating mules. I recalled how she always treated young Luke as an equal.

"Can you remember having a 'perfect day'?" Laurie asked.

"Yesterday," I said. "We woke along the beach and watched the moon sink into the ocean and then spent the day driving through forests above the surf. Today we're here with you. Really, most days are perfect. I just forget sometimes."

"For me, it's little things," Tom added. "Berries on my oatmeal, a hot shower. Our dinners together—little rituals."

"Even when things go wrong," I said, "my attitude colors everything."

Laurie listened and nodded.

Olympia

"I'm excited about exploring the Olympic Peninsula," I told Tom as we drove into Tumwater looking for our apartment.

Secluded old-growth forest loomed in the mist beyond the truck window. Less than fifteen thousand years ago this coast lay buried beneath five thousand feet of glacial ice. It is a geographically complex landscape cut with fjords, skerries, and drumlin hills. Today, one hundred thousand people live astraddle I-5, where the thumb of the Olympic Peninsula points away from the continental palm and the collision of land masses slowly rips it apart.

We found the apartment complex on a steep and winding road up Tumwater Hill. Below and to the west was an intimate harbor where sailboats were moored. The women who managed the complex were an odd pair: the dark-haired one was frosty and humorless, while the blonde with the little-girl voice minced around on high heels with the bright expression of a Barbie doll. They handed over a thick folder of rules and watched us sternly like grade-school teachers who expected the worst.

"Did we do something wrong?" Tom wondered as we crossed the parking lot to our new home. It was the first place that no one had walked us over. "Maybe it's our clothes?"

"Or our levity. They think life is serious." It was true we were openly happy.

"This must be the one." He stopped before a gray door trimmed in purple. It was identical to its neighbors—the ground floor dropped into the hill below grade, while the living room and kitchen fronted a road on the other side. The apartment was clean and tight, but lacked the spacious (if drafty) quality of our Fresno abode. There was onsite recycling with containers for each type of material.

"We're supposed to vacuum the blinds, clean behind the refrigerator, wash the screens, and run vinegar down the garbage disposal." I said, thumbing through the rulebook. Tom was opening drawers and peering into closets. "Do you suppose there will be surprise inspections?"

"I wonder how the thermostat works," he muttered. "I think it's on a timer."

"I'm not going back to ask."

Our rental furniture hadn't arrived, so we slept that first night on the clean dove-gray carpet. I wasn't sure if a dresser and queen-sized bed would fit in either diminutive bedroom, but the polite young men who delivered them squeezed it all in. If we stood to one side or sat on the bed, we could open the drawers. We soon discovered that despite the thermal efficiency, communicating walls were flimsy and we were privy to neighborly noises—peeing, drawers closing, steps overhead, and the incessant tirade of television talk shows.

Fortunately, the managers turned out to be an anomaly. Olympia had a prevalence of aging, thoughtful folk with long gray hair, sensible shoes, and old woolen sweaters. We saw them mowing lawns, pulling weeds, and walking. I imagined them sharing wine at potlucks after a day of volunteering with the Nature Conservancy. Strangers were playful and often initiated conversations or joked with us, and we found it easy to make friends. Families seemed wonderfully balanced, speaking calmly to children who behaved responsibly. Unlike Fresno—where only the poor walked—Olympia was a very pedestrian town with dependable public transit. The bus driver directed us to a natural food co-op and "the best barbecue in town." There was an excellent library where Tom (as usual) got a card.

The Olympic Peninsula is an area of microclimates, offering a smorgasbord of weather—most of it wet—on a walk. It could be snowing on our hill while rain fell two hundred yards away. My dark commute to the hospital was a five-mile drive up Route 101 blending into the troublesome I-5, then off on twisting coils. Twice I got lost in blowing sleet. Skies were in constant motion: sunlight to snow flurries, mist, and hard rain throughout a morning. Locals seemed to take pride in the rain—the way Alaskans do in cold—and we rarely saw a raincoat. They walked cheerfully in all weather and few of them were fat. Mothers were swinging toddlers at the park, everyone having a wonderful time beneath curtains of rain. Like Inuit—who have many words for snow—Olympians have a vocabulary colored in shades of rain. A clear winter sky (which could cycle through a dozen times each day) was more like a bright mist than anything one would see in Arizona. Water burbled, icy and clean, for weeks down the center of our parking lot. Moss grew deep velvet around the trees, just as grass would in the Midwest.

"If you wait for it to stop raining, you'll never do anything," one of the nurses at the hospital told me.

So Tom and I put on our raincoats and went out. We walked through drifting fog in parks reminiscent of the Pleistocene; ferns grew high in ancient trees and the air smelled alive. Moss climbed roofs and covered curbs, slick beneath the foot. On someone's advice we toured the local dump, which was immaculate and had gardens devoted to education on composting.

"Recycling is a sport in Olympia," Sara told me. She was a buxom blonde nurse who loved natural childbirth. "You're gonna fit right in. We're all very different, but we celebrate it."

"You caught us at a bad time," Dot chimed in, her expression worried. She twisted a strand of long, graying hair. "With all this construction and now the new scan-the-band computer system coming, I'm ready to quit."

Sara dismissed her with a cheerful wave. "We've been under construction for years. They never finish."

Welcome to my world, I thought. *Wherever they hire travelers, there's chaos.*

"It's like Harry Potter and the changing walls," Dot continued. "Every day we have to find a different route in."

It was true. I felt like leaving a trail of breadcrumbs. The maternal-child labyrinth could easily accommodate a thousand deliveries a month, but served a tenth that number. It ran along the exterior ground floor for more than a hundred twenty yards with large windows fronting venerable trees. Colors were warm and inviting, with inlaid vinyl floors that looked like hardwood. Patient rooms were spacious and had the newest technology. There were Jacuzzis for those in natural labor and "big girl" rooms with ceiling hoists to position the larger patient and get her out of the tub. Apart from the changing walls, the main problem was vastness. "Aerobic nursing," I called it. It was a long hike to get anything—including help in an emergency.

It was the parking lot, however, that won my heart. Saint Peter Hospital was secluded in old-growth forest, and parking spaces were insinuated between giant spruce and cedars. It was something elves might build if they drove to work. Arriving in the icy darkness, I would follow paths and twinkling lights toward the hospital. People obviously valued nature over expediency here. This "green" philosophy was echoed throughout the organization. In Tucson, when I had wanted to recycle soda cans, I'd been told it was unhygienic, but here recycling bins were everywhere. Juice was dispensed from machines and patients were given sturdy mugs instead of Styrofoam cups. The staff lounge was equipped with dishwasher, plates, and silverware. Towels and cloth underpads were used instead of disposable ones for labor patients.

Awakening is a moment of grace, but remaining aware requires discipline. In my new commitment not to rant, I attracted curious allies. There was the Korean nurse, who hummed and nodded sweetly. When I mentioned that I was trying to remain centered, she smiled and said nothing. Yet whenever I found myself pulled into the daily complaint session, she accidentally kicked me under the table, seeming not to notice.

One night I was reporting off to a nurse I knew only slightly. I had missed something about a patient and was apologizing. "I'm dumb," I said in an offhand way.

She stopped me with a look. "Never say that!" she stated with quiet intensity. "Never think it. Words are powerful."

"I HAD TO LEARN ANOTHER computer system," I told Lucas when he called. "All this charting for lawyers!"

"You might find the new technology actually speeds up your charting." His tone was mild.

"That has never been my experience," I replied sourly.

"Get over it," he advised. "Stop resisting and learn to use it."

"I have to learn new computer systems every thirteen weeks! Plus door codes, communication systems, IV and epidural pumps, glucometers, baby security systems, and medication computers. In two years I've used Watchchild, four versions of QS, and assorted lab, pharmacy, and clocking programs. Here they use ProvCare for labs and ProvClinical to integrate Care Organizer with Star. There is HOM, HED, Admin RX, and Carefusion. Linked with these are QS, IBEX, HMM and HSM. Do I sound a bit nuts?"

"Get over it," he repeated. "All your flapping is a waste of energy."

I paused. There was truth in his words. *Ranting is like praying for something you don't want.* It was one more piece that I needed. In the following weeks I would share his words with angry coworkers. "Get over it. Stop feeding the chaos with your outrage."

"Some of my instructors don't like me," Lucas confided when I paused, "and I'm not sure what to do."

I sighed. "I understand. I almost quit in my last semester because a teacher bullied me. Everyone was afraid. I remember students throwing up before class."

"It hasn't changed." He sounded sad and weary.

"They hold all the power," I agreed. "After graduation I wrote a letter to the administration, hoping for change. Later, three instructors were murdered."

"By a male student," he said pointedly.

I sighed. "They say, 'Nurses eat their young.' Of all professions, you'd think we'd know better. So the college didn't get the connection between the way students are treated and that tragedy?"

"No, they just installed security. All those bright faces in my first-year picture look anxious and haggard now. Many are taking antidepressants; some have gotten fat or started smoking. Teachers pick on individuals like a wolf pack testing for a weak caribou. You just want to escape notice—and I don't exactly blend in. My psych teacher ridicules me in class to the point that even students have protested."

"Have you thought of talking to the administration?"

"It's the same group! There's supposed to be confidentiality, but it's a sham. She 'accidentally' emailed my last paper—and her critique—to the entire class. It's vicious."

"It's dumb," I sympathized. "Students in my class figured out IV lines and dressing changes alone—hiding from teachers instead of asking for help. You're not stuck there. Dad and I support whatever direction you take. I'm sorry I encouraged you to go into nursing."

"I'm not. I love my patients and I will be an excellent nurse. Eventually, I want to teach."

"Mentor the young ones—that's how we'll grow a healthy culture. Remember the award I got from the medical students? Their education is just as ugly. They appreciated that I was someone they could trust. Have you made any friends?"

"There's one guy, Thomas." His tone was warm.

"I thought you might find a group. When I was your age, we'd sit in the student union and talk about life."

"That was the sixties. Kids are different now."

"Nursing students must be bright," I countered.

"They're smart, but shallow. The only thing they read is class material. On NPR last week, the commentator said my generation has no sense of time as a continuum. They 'friend' people on Facebook, but don't develop lasting relationships."

"Maybe they need someone to awaken them."

"When I open my mouth, they look at me like I'm from another planet. They're here to learn tricks for making money. Thomas and I keep one another sane."

"Surely, young people are still curious and full of life?"

"Not really. It's creepy how detached they are."

"I love you, Son," I said as Lucas hung up.

I stood clutching the little phone. Maternal worries did not help him, and yet that was one piece I seemed powerless to release. I recalled Gibran: "Your children are not your children… You may give them your love, but not your thoughts."

THEN IT STOPPED RAINING. It didn't cease abruptly, but faded gradually over several days, like a slow-motion dawn breaking over Puget Sound. The drizzle became fine mist, and then a heavy fog. Patches of dry pavement appeared and the artesian well in the flowerbeds began to slacken. Velvet moss on the curbs was no longer slick. Great cedar trees loomed like something primeval beyond the hospital windows where birds sang, sweet and invisible. The rich air smelled of lavender.

One morning I saw stars on my way to work. A paling sky told me that our planet was again revolving into spring. Shy peaks and glaciers appeared across the sound on the Olympic Peninsula, and Mount Rainier rose in the east—a frozen portrait of chaos and splendor. Emerging from the building one night, I stood spellbound beneath the orange ball of a lunar eclipse, perfect above the frosty trees. I had not been aware of it and yet had arrived just as it dipped to totality. I stood transfixed by the serendipity of my life.

I was still working on awareness, studying Ursula Le Guin's translation of the *Tao Te Ching*. I tried to focus on being present and calm, but fell in and out of it. It was frustrating to see how easily I resumed old habits. Apparently, one did not "become enlightened" conclusively.

"What do we do about inequity?" I asked Carola.

Tom had arranged for me to get bodywork from a Rolfer, and she was freeing space to breathe along my rib cage.

"When you hate something," she said, "you become the other part of it. To heal, you must shift your attention to the result you want. Nobody could have predicted that the Berlin Wall would come down and then one day nothing could stop it. Transformation happens like that. A few people see a possibility and then a few more. Suddenly the hillside blossoms right under your feet."

I considered her words, how it requires a new idea to create a different experience and that one person could anchor this possibility in consciousness. The Apollo photograph of Earth—heartbreakingly alone and lovely in the blackness of space—had altered human imagination forever. I recalled pivotal experiences in my own life. Luke was eighteen months old when I took him for swimming lessons. All the mothers were singing *Ring Around the Rosie* and then dunking their babies, "Whee!"

It took only one chorus for Luke to figure out the program. Nope. He'd seen enough. In that uncomfortable moment, I gathered the courage to step out of the happy circle and allow Luke his own pace. When his need to control the dunking was honored, he learned to swim without lessons. It was always his pattern.

A second awareness came after that class when the noisy crowd of mothers stood in the showers with their toddlers. Some were pregnant or rounded with extra fat; others had stretch marks and breasts heavy with milk. Not one would have been featured in a magazine. Gazing at them, I saw these beautiful healthy women for the first time beyond my judgments. They were like ripe fruit, perfect—exactly as they were—these strong feminine bodies carrying the future of our species. *This is how women's bodies are supposed to look!* I thought. That moment allowed me to accept my own body and to later assist women and their babies through the miraculous journey of labor.

Travel-nursing was now transforming my beliefs about birth. Before working in Wisconsin, I had rarely seen natural labor. I had been taught to treat birth as a procedure that separated two people in the quickest, safest, and cheapest manner. Interfering with it, I realized, often caused the problems I was trained to manage. There is a place for medical interventions, but in Olympia I learned from nurses who worked tirelessly to keep their patient focused and help her rotate the baby—avoiding cesarean deliveries with age-old wisdom. I was amazed too at the courage of ordinary women giving birth. Daily, I saw them fall in love with their newborns. Until that instant, the child is an idea, and then beyond all thought—she knows!

In Olympia, yet another awareness opened for me. Ten labor nurses had recently traveled to Kauai on retreat and Tyra shared the photos with me. The pictures were common and technically imperfect, yet somehow arresting. The women stood together on a beach, gray hair blowing in the Hawaiian breeze: colorful clothes, open smiles, wrinkles and glasses, fat and thin. Suddenly, I *saw* them! Hidden in the ordinary, stood the wise-women of my tribe, elders with their own faces. *These are the medicine women who daily lead children safely into the world and I am one of them!* In a culture that tries to control and fix us, we are still perfect.

Rude and Tom complete the smokehouse, 2009.

Our bakehouse-smokehouse.

Chapter 28

Uncommon Ground

April 2008

I grew up on a geographic grid: Tucson is laid out with the monotonous pragmatism of a city intent on filling the valley; Fresno can be learned in an afternoon. Apart from a few artsy flourishes, their streets are aligned in unimaginative squares. Olympia, however, is defined by an intricate landscape: fjords, estuaries, and hillsides. Direction here is indefinite and roads meander off in vague ways that imply that the journey is of value. Like a three-dimensional rainforest, this complex natural space also creates an exciting human habitat, fertile ground for small businesses and people on foot. It is this subtle conversation between unique geography and human imagination that make San Francisco, Bisbee, and Olympia vibrant places to live.

Late one golden afternoon Tom and I set out for a walk and found ourselves trending down to the little harbor where sailboats gleamed like lilies in a bowl. Accustomed to a gentle mist, Olympians blinked like groundhogs under the bright sky. A group of neighbors with shovels and wheelbarrows were pulling invasive plants along the path. Crocus and daffodils were coming up and trees had the blush of new buds.

"I should've brought Diana's number," I said. I wanted to introduce him. "She lives down here." Diana and her husband sailed to Olympia for a travel-nurse assignment. She had signed as staff, but they still live on their boat.

"We'll run into her if we're supposed to," Tom said.

Ten minutes later, Diana came toward us along the path. She was nearly my age, yet trim and agile. Dark collar-length hair bounced with her stride. Gray eyes took us in as she smiled in welcome. "I don't usually go for a walk this late in the day," she said, "but it's so lovely. Would you like to see our boat?"

Indeed we would.

Diana led the way along the wharf to a small wooden sailboat. It was meticulously neat and clean, rebounding gaily as we stepped aboard. In single file we wiggled down the hatch, descending like rabbits into a hole. Beneath a warm vault of wood we found a rare display of consciousness—two lives tucked neatly into a space not much larger than a car. Living here carried simplicity to a new level even for me. I thought of the icy mornings I had commuted in the dark and pictured Diana emerging onto the slippery dock.

When her husband Mike arrived from work and suggested we "go out for dinner," I thought he meant to a restaurant, but there ensued a flurry of activity as lines were cast off and we motored sedately into the quiet bay. Mike was a handsome man, robust and Nordic, with cropped sandy hair, cleanly shaven cheeks, and engaging blue eyes. He included us in the activities and soon I was feeling relaxed at the tiller while Tom helped him unfurl the sail. It was not surprising to learn that he was a teacher.

It was a perfect evening, with a whisper of breeze ruffling the water. As Tom and Mike raised the sails, Diana stood chest-deep in the hatchway handing up steaming bowls of bean soup with fresh, dark bread. We ate from their two bowls while they used the two cups. To either side, lights began to twinkle along the intimate shoreline and the sky paled to tangerine. Seabirds came winging in, alighting on buoys. It was almost dark when the harbor lights guided us back under a starry sky. After we tied up, Mike pulled out a guitar and we sang together—snug as chicks in their intimate nest.

The next day Tom discovered a group of young men who played volleyball in the gym of our apartment. He had been competing in the sport before they were born, but they agreeably invited the old fellow to join them and soon found him to be an asset. Not only was Tom still quick and skilled, but as a former referee, he helped them hone their game. He returned home flushed with excitement after two hours of hard running. "Old age and treachery," he grinned wickedly, "makes up for youth and ability." There was a fire in his eyes I had not seen in some time.

One night a little boy was watching from the sidelines as Tom covered the court in his light dance—that familiar springing crouch which allowed him to fly in any direction. He had just saved a ball by diving to the floor and bumping it up for a set-spike. The other team hit it out of bounds and the child ran to pick it up. Tom dashed across the court and landed in front of him with arms outstretched and a grin on his face.

Still grasping the ball to his chest, the boy peered up and asked, "Are you really old?"

Tom nodded solemnly. "Yes. I'm really, really old."

The little fellow looked perplexed. Slowly, as if shaping his thoughts, he shook his head from side to side. "No," he clarified. "I mean are you old, REALLY?"

How, he was asking, *could anyone who looked so ancient move that fast?*

I sometimes wondered that myself. He was almost sixty-two now and to the casual glance, a rather modest aging male: scanty hair, paling beard, wrinkles, and mild eyes behind glasses. Yet when I looked with my heart, I saw strength, integrity, and a person I could trust with my life. He shone brighter every day. *Who are we?* This radiance hidden beneath common clothes? When you really look, it takes your breath away.

Spring arrived. Tom and I walked through the Farmer's Market with plum trees arching pink over winding streets and blossoms drifting like snow. Daffodils erupted between the mossy stones—blazing suddenly yellow in the rising mist. A great horned owl sang his booming call from the deep woods that dropped away to the south of our apartment. The morning grass outside our window sparkled with a late March snow where robins were pulling torpid earthworms from the greening lawn. The parking lot was crisscrossed with soggy worms. Sometimes they crawled onto the cobbled foyer and under our doorsill. A mile away, Tumwater Falls thundered. We ambled the path along one wall of the canyon where water gushed from ferny cliffs. A father and his toddler splashed happily through the puddles, their faces turned up like flowers to the drizzle.

"Our life is magical," I said.

As the season advanced, we explored the Olympic Peninsula. There were no easy routes. Winding roads hugged the channels that fingered between mountains like the veins of Puget Sound: a lung breathing in and out with a gentle sea. We traveled to the northwest tip of the peninsula through old-growth forests, catching glimpses of the Olympic Peaks, and finally along a cliff above the ocean where a dozen bald eagles stood vigil against the snowy mountains of Canada's Vancouver Island across the water. Everywhere massive trees were decked in ferns, an arboreal ecosystem that some trees support with climbing roots. "Survival of the fittest" is but a skewed fragment of the truth.

One evening at a small motel in Port Townsend, we were supping on the deck above the sea, eating local chowder as the sky lifted momentarily vast and blue above Puget Sound. Ducks dove for mussels a few feet from our table, disturbing the reflection of sailboats in the low sunlight.

"This feels like home," I said. "Maybe this is the place. We could take the ferry to Alaska each spring. We'd buy a tiny car for here and leave our truck up north."

The next morning we boarded the state ferry for Whidbey Island, paying eleven dollars, which included the truck. Dolphins played off the bow wave and children were laughing on deck. I took pictures until my fingers were cold. An old man in overalls and frayed sweater was leaning on the rail. He told me that the senior fare was a dollar and fifty cents. "There's a free bus ride up the island," he said. "I'm going over for lunch and cards with a friend. We do it every week."

As we tunneled beneath the trees on Whidbey Island, I smiled in recognition. Humans were playfully engaged with the landscape here. This art can never be mass-produced, for it emanates from love of place and daily choice. We stopped for lunch at the farmer's market on a green hill where kids were hunting for Easter eggs. No one objected to the Canada geese sharing the grass and ponds.

Stopping, as we often did to consider employment at the little hospital, we found a central desk with two nurses who were happy to chat with us. There were only half a dozen patients. "You'd need to be flexible—everything from labor to hospice," one of them told me.

"If I find the right place," I said, "I'll clean toilets."

A kindly older man was making rounds accompanied by his grandchildren. When another fellow arrived, the doctor turned to me and said, "Have you met the chief of surgery? That's him," he pointed to his companion.

"Well, he's the chief of staff," the other accused.

"We take turns," the first admitted.

I could work here, I thought.

On the ferry back to the mainland, I suggested we drive up the coast. My contract was ending and I needed eight weeks of work before summer in Alaska. Everett, a city just north of Seattle, was seeking a traveler for thirteen weeks. Perhaps they'd deal.

The road north meandered beneath blooming plum trees through a hilly land painted rose and green. Everett seemed a practical place of old houses, military families, and shipping. There was a big hospital with a split campus. It was a Providence Hospital (sister to the one in Olympia), so I was familiar with their computer systems. I decided to apply.

Rain returned during the night and we awoke to leaden skies—hushed and dripping. A few hours and a hundred miles south, we arrived home in time to rescue lost earthworms on the gray carpet. An email awaited me from my father's lawyer. I could participate, it informed me, in a court hearing over Bud's "thousand-year trust" (as my father called it), where he had buried his half of the Takahula property along with his other holdings. It seemed unlikely that Annie and I would ever see our mother's inheritance without a legal battle. My half-brothers had already spent over a million dollars fighting one another. This was our father's real legacy: division and dissent. I recalled Mark once saying that he and Jeff were like two ends of a propeller—when one was up, the other was down.

"I will not fight my brothers," I had told him. "I'm not choosing sides."

"You'll have to," he had said. "You'll be like a bird between two cats."

I recalled them as little boys, giggling as they played with me on the freezing potholes along the Arctic coast. I pictured Fairbanks in April: bright now under a growing sun, snowbanks melting, and the sky wheeling with excited birds. *My father feeds the birds,* I thought suddenly. *We have this in common.* Then I turned the key in my heart and released the ancient pain. Rusty chains clanked down around my ankles as I surrounded my siblings and parents with affection—all of them doing their best. Maybe, like Bert-Son had said, they needed these events. As I'd told Lucas, you discover who you are by exploring who you are not.

As usual, the Saint Peter Hospital approached me about settling down. In Olympia, I could have a regular food bowl and the implied security of friends and health insurance in exchange for my wild summers. *It's tempting,* I thought, *but no.* Had they been willing to take part of each year, I would have signed. Suddenly, our future crystallized—pieces settling like geese out of the swirling sky. Everett Hospital called to say they wanted me and would take eight weeks! We could go from one tight home to another without a pause in paychecks. Tom began researching the possibility of taking the ferry to Alaska and Megan, who was ten now, wanted to join us. I couldn't stop smiling.

Nevertheless, the completion of our third year on the road found us no closer to a safe haven. *Maybe there is no perfect place,* I thought. You could move to Olympia and complain about the rain. Alaska is cold and buggy. Arizona is drying out; California is crowded; Pennsylvania, smoggy. There are hurricanes in Florida and tornados in the Midwest. And everywhere nature is under attack from our careless species. *There is no place to hide—even in the Arctic,* I realized. Somehow I had to find peace on this shifting river. For the first time, I caught inklings of life beyond struggle. The Buddhists say attachment is the root of suffering and that accepting what *Is* leads to peace. Instead of orchestrating my life, maybe I could live the day that arrived. Einstein wrote, "There are two ways of looking at the world—either you see nothing as a miracle or you see everything as a miracle."

A few days later we were at a small bookstore in Olympia. It was raining hard outside, the afternoon gray as lead. I stood at the checkout with my arms full of treatises on deep ecology and planetary crisis. Some were obscure, and Tom was pleased to have found them for my summer reading. He had his wallet out at the cash register. I stood thumbing pages and feeling bleak.

"I can't," I said.

Tom and the clerk looked at me in surprise.

"I just can't read any more of this. I know enough about what is wrong with our world."

"What are you going to read this summer?" Tom asked as I returned the books to their shelves.

"I don't know. Something that will guide me in finding personal balance. That's what I need right now."

CHERRY BLOSSOMS DRIFTED LIKE YESTERDAY'S confetti, blanketing Olympia's streets. Sunlight burnished the misty forest on my commute to the hospital and shafted between the giant cedars as I returned to the truck each evening. Birds sang high in the sacred cathedral of trees that was the hospital's "parking lot," where a chorus of frog voices resonated in the gold of evening. We were saying goodbye again. I savored that buoyant feeling, the lifting of my hull on a gently rising tide. It was always bitter sweet. People hugged me in the halls, inviting me to stay. I thought of the melting snows along the Alcan. Then I thought: *Maybe Hawaii next winter?*

A misty dawn heralded our last day in Olympia. Tom and I were now good at moving. We cleaned out the apartment, sweeping it on hands and knees and—yes—behind the refrigerator. Blonde Barbie teetered over from the office in her spiky heels, looking smug and suspicious as she peered into every corner to be sure we had vacuumed the screens and vents. We did not own a vacuum, but kept the Alaskan custom of removing our shoes at the door. Closing that door, we rode the crest of spring northward, just as we had descended the continent on the darkening wings of autumn. Orchards had been in bloom when we departed Fresno and now cherry blossoms had peaked as we left Tumwater. The trees in Everett were just bursting forth when we pulled in, frogs singing in the damp of evening.

Compared with Olympia—where trees are revered and human needs tempered with restraint—Everett's sprawl seemed mundane. A century before, forests and a natural harbor had fostered a lumber town that devoured the ancient trees and stripped away the magic. Today the cleared hills support a practical populace devoted to commerce. It's a pleasant and efficient place, but strangely sterile. One can barely sense the ghosts of departed trees. Gone are hidden dells and dripping banks of ferns. Gnomes don't live here anymore.

Our new apartment, located in Lynnwood—an area that boasted three times the national average of car thefts—was a showplace for the development. There was a relaxed air of community about the large, circular complex. In the center was a "wetland habitat" blown with litter, but nevertheless ringing in birdsong. From our front window we could see families playing and exercising their dogs on the commons or pushing lame vehicles home. The air smelled of flowers, mown grass, and ethnic cuisine. We soon found the library and places to walk by the ocean.

The hospital's Pacific Campus, a twelve-mile commute up I-5 from Lynwood, was modern and well-staffed with a view of the harbor. Patients usually had prenatal care and were low risk, for those with serious problems were transported to Tacoma. I didn't go through my usual stressed learning curve, but instead imagined myself as the eye of a storm, centered and calm.

Everett was the most balanced place I had yet worked. The charge nurse acted as captain of the ship, responsible for orchestrating the kaleidoscope of activities. There were usually two "float" nurses for backup and giving breaks. Phones and assignments were arranged in advance. I found a collegial attitude between the disciplines that made things run smoothly. Anesthesiologists were courteous and cleaned up after themselves, doctors treated me as part of the team, and a good use of techs created an efficient and safe flow. There was also a sensible balance between allowing labor to progress naturally and intervening when needed.

I recall a big girl with an epidural who was "laboring down"—sleeping while her contractions worked the baby through the pelvis after the cervix had opened. If the mother is comfortable with anesthesia, this is often better than actively pushing for both her and the baby. The midwife was in a nearby room working with a patient who had chosen to labor without medications.

I found myself increasingly uneasy, a tightness building in my diaphragm. The baby's heart rate showed decreased variability, but nothing ominous. When I put my fingers on her head, I found that she had ceased descending. My touch also conveyed something else that I couldn't articulate, but it felt as if the baby were losing hope.

Softly I entered the other room. "I'm sorry to bother you."

The midwife, Sky, was sitting on the side of the tub, pouring warm water over the other patient's abdomen and encouraging her to breathe through a contraction. Her husband looked at me with frank irritation.

"The baby in the other room needs to come out," I said quietly. "I would like to have her start pushing."

Sky studied my face and I felt a connection. She did not question my judgment or ask for reasons. She was a graceful woman of perhaps thirty, blonde hair piled under a cloth cap, long fingers strong and competent.

"I'll be right in." Turning to the young woman, she said, "I'm sorry, but I need to check on my other patient. I'll be back as soon as I can."

Sky followed me into the room where my patient was resting. I had set up the delivery table and turned on the infant warmer, which contains all the equipment to resuscitate a baby. Briefly, I spread out the fetal heart monitor strip. The midwife glanced at it, but was more interested in touching the baby. I positioned the patient while Sky inserted the first two fingers of her right hand then looked at me. She turned to the patient and said gently, "I want you take a deep breath and push."

Together we worked with the patient and gradually the baby's head descended. My stomach was still knotted. "Do you want NI?" I asked.

"If you think so, yes."

I pulled the phone from my pocket and called the charge nurse. "I want NICU and RT in room 315 for delivery now." Then I turned to the patient and her anxious husband. "We'll have extra people here, just in case the baby needs a little help. Sometimes a baby gets stuck coming out. If that happens, I'll need you to work with me. This stool," I pointed it out to the husband, "is for me to stand on. We'll pull your legs way back," I said to the woman, "and I'll use my fist here to push your baby's shoulder under your pelvic bone."

The next minutes were a blur. The baby was large and her shoulders became stuck with her pale head protruding. Her eyes were open, but she did not grimace or struggle. The room suddenly filled with people. While the team checked the equipment, the midwife and I flexed the patient's legs back and I jammed my fist above the pubis to rock the shoulder loose. When it popped free, we all gave a sigh, but it was not over. The baby's body was stuck tight as a cork and had to be twisted and tugged. Finally, she slid free and was handed off to the waiting team, to be bagged with oxygen. It was a long minute before we heard that thin wail. My eyes filled with tears. A baby's cry is the best sound in the world.

Later at the nurse's station, the midwife came up to me. "I felt the life very faint for a while," she said. "She seemed undecided about whether to live or not… like she didn't care, had just given up. Thank you for calling me."

Nurses and doctors are taught to be objective. This baby's heart rate had been an indication that there could be problems, but I have seen far worse. It was something I felt—a silent cry from someone trapped and sinking. Sky had felt it too. I have learned to honor these intimations.

"Mom, I'm so sorry," Lucas sounded ready to cry. "I failed my psychology class."

My heart sank. "Okay. What's the next step?"

"I don't know. There's no clear path. The class is broken into two segments, classwork and clinicals—you have to pass both and they're not added together. I passed the clinicals and all the exams, but my instructor failed my main paper. Seventy percent was passing and she gave me a 69 percent. I don't even know why. It's all subjective."

"Can you redo the paper? It seems terribly harsh to fail you without recourse. Can you appeal?"

"No. I can finish up my Critical Care class and then I'm out of the college. My only hope is to write a letter to the administration, admitting blame, promising to work harder, and asking for re-admittance. They might let me know by summer."

Do we have so many beautiful children that we can afford to throw them away? I wondered dismally. Nothing had changed in the ten years since I graduated from the University of Arizona College of Nursing. If a student stumbled, five years of prerequisites and nursing college went nowhere. Without the nursing degree and the RN registration, all that preparation led to a dead end. There was no other pathway. The gatekeepers determined who had a career and who would be bagging groceries to repay college loans. Meanwhile, the U.S. was importing nurses—people who often did not meet training standards or even speak reliable English—to fill the desperate need.

"I wish I could help, Son. You are up to this. Go find the hoops and jump through them. I suspect they just want to humble you. Write your letter and do your best in Critical Care. Meanwhile, look into transferring to Pima College or to Northern Arizona University, or even the University of Phoenix. There has to be a way. Check all options."

It's so easy to get tunnel vision and make choices out of fear, I thought as I snapped the phone shut. I could face my death without blinking, but fear for Lucas still drove me into a dark place. I sat, trying to make friends with fear. I didn't want to be carried down life's rapids thrashing and screaming. *There is no safe shore,* I reminded myself. *It's all in motion. Within that motion is power and great beauty.* I sought to recall what that felt like, but at the moment they were just empty words.

Chapter 29

MOMENTS OF GRACE

May 2008

I awoke in fog to a land muted and mysterious. The cold drizzle had ceased and beyond my windows, cherry blossoms descended like pink snow on the green lawn and collected in drifts against the curb. In the near distance, identical spruce trees marched obediently into the mist where birds were nevertheless singing. As the sun climbed, a breeze sprang up and the falling petals became a blizzard. By noon, the city lay revealed under a hot sky and the trees were clothed only in new leaves. Down the street, flowers blazed neatly and lawns stretched uniformly verdant. Summer had arrived in a morning.

My own life was also undergoing a similar transformation. I too slipped in and out of fog, yet beneath the details a current was gathering—as elusive and profound as melting ice. "I was blind, but now I see," wrote John Newton in his song *Amazing Grace*. In 1748, he had survived a pivotal storm at the wheel of a slave ship, yet it took him forty years to make a stand against slavery. What we sense in this hymn is an irresistible upwelling of the soul.

Events dropped into my gathering stream like stones. First, my conversation with Bert-Son had freed me—not from responsibility, but from hopelessness. Earth now seemed like a big, wet dog rising from the mud and starting to shake. Cleansed by comet, solar flares, reversal of the poles, ice ages, volcanoes—or humanity—life will run free. That is its directive. This domestic grass will tangle higher than my head and burrow through concrete. Bugs, worms, and fungus will joyfully recycle and rebuild. A second channel joined when Lucas told me, "Get over it." *Life isn't fair. So what? Embrace the day, bloom where you are planted.*

Now a third insight came through my half-brother, Jeff. Because our father had blocked communication between us as children, we were practically strangers when he phoned from Arizona.

"I'll be driving the motorhome back to Alaska in a few weeks with Mom and Dad," he said. "I'm having a place built for them near me in Palmer. They can't live in their 'Winchester House' any longer."

I laughed, Jeff's trenchant wit reminding me of our father. Bud's plan to live above the crowd was proving sadly hollow. No longer able to climb to the tower of added stories overshadowing their neighbors, he and Martha were sequestered in a few dark rooms of their strange Fairbanks home.

"Denise Wartes figured she'd end up with them," I said. "She keeps an eye on them, but they never reach out."

"No, they wouldn't," he agreed. "They were just gonna sit there."

"Well, one of them would have fallen. That's what usually happens."

"No one else was making any decisions, so I did. I just told them they were coming with me. Dad made surprisingly little fuss."

"You aren't the favored son," I remarked.

"No, but so what? A fellow only has one set of parents. I always thought I was stupid and Mark was the smart one. You know, I idolized him. I just don't understand what happened."

"Well, I think Dad set the tone." I recalled Mark's comparison about a propeller.

It wasn't long after this conversation that I awoke from a gentle dream of my father. I don't recall the details—perhaps a remnant of long ago when he had carried me on tireless shoulders across the tundra. He was ninety-one now, and I suddenly realized that if one of us were going to forgive, it would have to be me. I wasn't sure it was worth it. I thought of our abortive reunion when I was fifteen: he expecting the beautiful, compliant two-year-old, me seeking the loving father. *I must have been quite an intrusion into his carefully choreographed reality.* I thought of his tight little smile and his fierce eyes full of pain.

I hold a key for him. Stingy not to use it. I flipped open Lucas's phone and pressed the numbers. Martha answered. She handled their lives now. As with Bert and Janet, my father's decline had forced unexpected growth in her.

I spoke openly, dropping the social dance we had lived with so long.

"I don't know what to do," Martha confided. "He just sits. It's like living alone."

"He's probably depressed," I said, switching into nurse mode. "Depression often goes undiagnosed in the elderly—most young people think, 'Of course they're depressed, I would be too if I were old,' but depression isn't normal at any age."

"Maybe that's it," she agreed.

I took a breath. "Mom, I'm ready to let go of the past and just enjoy him. He doesn't have to change."

"Well,... you know Bud." She laughed.

I laughed too. Yes, we both knew.

"Oh, here he is now! Let me put him on the line." She sounded excited.

It had been some time since I had spoken with my father. There was a pause and then a hoarse whisper, "Jeanie?" I could hear him mustering energy to reach across the distance.

I don't recall much of our conversation, but the tone was warm. At one point, I said, "It's easy to look back and wish we'd done things differently. You can't fix the past, but you can forgive yourself and move on."

"Yes," he whispered, "forgive yourself and move on."

I thought of my father's cornered eyes and my mother's fanciful stories. Then I remembered how angry and frustrated I had felt when she failed to see me. She regarded her children fondly and with humor, but penciled-in lines that didn't allow for growth. Finally—just for a moment—I realized that I did the same thing. My opinions limited people, freezing their rivers. With that, I stopped cradling my old stories. The miraculous part is that—in that moment—I think my father did too. Perhaps I had always known that were I to release my hurt (even if I never told him), he might change. Forgiveness transcends time and space. There are no villains, only facets of expression, the playing out of endless variations of who we are not, so that we may at last remember who we are.

I started to recall good things about my father. Without my bitterness, I could see the careful pilot, the craftsman, the man who could butcher a moose and not be mired in blood, the woodsman who traveled beyond a fenced life. There were also pieces of myself to reclaim, bits thrown away in anger. Without my father's practical strength, Connie would never have made it to the wilderness—and neither would I.

THE TREES WERE LEAFING OUT the evening Jeff arrived in Everett with Bud and Martha. They were too fragile now for the airlines, so despite the demands of his high-pressure life, Jeff was driving north at their pace. He was an empire builder—defining his worth by expansion like our father—but unlike him, modest and introspective. My half-brother was tall, handsome, and unconsciously graceful in his restless movements. His light hair was receding at the temples and he wore reading glasses now. He had Bud's high color, but not the cleft, and Martha's pretty dimples. His face was more oval than square, reminding me of Annie. His eyes were Annie's too.

Jeff docked the leviathan motorhome at a mobile home park for the night and Tom shuttled the three of them to our apartment in our truck. My father came first: tiny, twisted, and slow as a vine. I carefully lifted his feet out of our silver pickup and hoisted him upright onto his walker. Taking hold of his frail arm, I accompanied him on the painful trip over the thick lawn and up the walk, a shuffling journey of several minutes that took all his strength.

"Jeanie," he said, in his scratchy voice as I lowered him onto the sofa. "You were my firstborn and I have always loved you." Then he smiled at me. It was a smile I had not seen in fifty-five years: golden, open, and devoid of guile or reproach. The familiar blue eyes were strangely warm.

"I know." I let his words sink in, not resisting or adding to them in my head. Beyond all the drama, it was true.

I smiled back—not the cautious smile we had always exchanged, but the Big Cosmic Joke smile. He knew, and I knew that he knew, and he knew that I knew. It was a piercing beam of light. There was a glow about his face, a quiet acceptance so different from the man of only a few months before. Age had humbled him and somehow made him whole. He had nothing more to prove. Neither, I discovered, had I.

Would he choose a different life if he could be young and strong again? Honestly, I doubt it; only he could answer that. Does it matter if enlightenment comes at the last? Maybe the hard road is necessary. Who am I to judge?

To be honest, this acute level of intimacy did not last. Does that mean it wasn't real? Love transcended our history, converging in a perfect moment that had somehow always existed. This makes no logical sense, but it was nevertheless true. For that instant, I was lifted above my life's story. My parents were exactly the ones I had needed. They in turn had done the best they could. It had always been perfect.

It was late May when Tom and I pulled out of Washington, headed for Alaska. An afternoon breeze drifted warm through the open truck windows as we waited, engine off, for the Mukilteo ferry. Megan's ten-year-old legs were scrunched behind the pickup's main seat, where she curled sleepily on the cramped bench. Tom had picked her up at the Seattle airport three days previously. She spent much of the intervening time playing with our ebullient and bossy neighbor girl. Their friendship had culminated in a sleepover that had little to do with sleep. Megan's hair was still knotted in a styling attempt and she looked relieved to be dozing.

After the short trip across the bay, we drove the now-familiar winding road up the backbone of Whidbey Island and waited for the Port Townsend ferry. Along with a dozen other parties, we left our vehicle and hopped boulders on the rocky shoreline, watching crabs scuttle with the influx of tide. Despite the unmistakable smell of sea, there were no waves in the shelter of Puget Sound, just the quiet flood of water overtaking the rocks.

Megan squatted near the tide pools. She was almost my height now, with coltish legs, dark, shoulder-length hair, and a flawless complexion. Her brown eyes were fringed with curly lashes. She kept her belongings neat and was a cooperative (if sometimes remote) companion.

We spent that night in Port Angeles and at dawn boarded a Canadian ferry across the channel to Vancouver Island. Megan and I huddled out of the wind on the aft deck, watching the Olympic Peaks diminish. Her main concern was a last call to her mother before entering Canadian waters. I put my arm about her shoulders and she snuggled into my warmth. Riffles crosshatched the gentle swells, scattering the reflection of salmon-colored clouds. In the distance, oceangoing freighters dotted the channel where water and sky blended to violet.

"What did you think of your day at Greenfields?" I asked. Lucas had worked to get a partial scholarship for her to the private school he had attended. As an alumnus, he had priority and we had offered to pay the rest. Like us, he valued education and although he was not ready to be her father, he was her champion and close friend.

"I really enjoyed it," she admitted. "They do a lot of interesting things."

"Are you planning to go next year?"

"Well," she hesitated, "I like the school I'm at. My friends and all. I could always go some other year."

"You'll need to choose before we head to the cabin so that I can send your mom the money. No one will make you go, but I encourage you to take the risk.

Being willing to try new things, like coming here, will open opportunities. I used to tell Luke that he might not have a good time, but he would have a new experience."

"My mom made me come this summer," she admitted.

"Well, thank you for being a good sport. Tom and I won't make you come to our cabin, but we'd love to have you all summer. It has to be your choice."

Soon we were driving through the quaint town of Victoria and up the inland coast of Vancouver Island. The road ran for three hundred fifty miles through forests above a gentle beach, protected from the North Pacific by snowy peaks to the west. We took our time and stopped often. The first evening we stayed in a small motel overlooking the narrow passage. As we sat in lingering twilight, three great cruise ships, lit like Christmas trees, passed the patio window. I tried not to think about all the poop they emptied into the water. Two days later, we departed the windy northern tip of the island.

The deck was familiar and alive beneath my feet. For a long day the Canadian ferry traveled up the coast to Prince Rupert, where we stayed overnight and boarded an Alaskan ferry the following afternoon. Now we meandered between forested islands, never far from land. Sometimes the channel pinched tight and cliffs rose steeply on either side, where waterfalls foamed between the trees. In the shifting mist and sunlight, bald eagles seemed as common as crows. Whales breached and orcas tipped the surface. The air grew colder and we could see glaciers in the distance. I fell asleep each night to gentle rocking as northern wilderness slid past our cabin porthole in the lengthening twilight of summer. As always, I thought of Lucas, and visualized moving curtains of light like aurora borealis surrounding him at Sylvia House. He had sounded happy about Megan coming and wistful too. I wished I could share this wonderful voyage with him. He still had no answer from the College of Nursing.

The ferry stopped at little towns as day and night we chugged northward. The passengers were adventurous or local folks talking easily together. There was a feeling of community as our little group journeyed through a vast and beautiful sea. Many people slept on the open aft deck—which was covered and heated for camping—and ate food they had brought along. We purchased a few meals onboard, but mostly we ate from our ice chest. Megan did not complain at the repetitive diet of sandwiches, cheese, crackers, and instant soups. Always one to hold her cards close, she was nevertheless taking it all in. Tom even managed to arrange for a rare trip to the bridge, where Megan had a chance to steer the ship.

"I got my start on Lake Michigan as a boy," the captain told us. "When my mother took me across on the SS *Badger* and the captain showed me the bridge, I knew that I belonged here. It's important to give young people a chance."

We woke early on our last morning aboard and packed up our things. Beyond the cabin porthole, snowy peaks loomed over the ship, plunging steeply into the dark channel to either side.

"You guys are easy to be with," Megan said over breakfast in the cafeteria where big windows framed the changing world.

"You are too," Tom smiled.

We again took to the road at Haines, reentering Canada on a narrow highway that wiggled up a canyon and then climbed steeply above tree line between lingering snowbanks. There were few vehicles and we pulled over to play in the crusted snow. At Haines Junction we picked up the Alcan and turned northwest. Although it was almost July, the bright air was still crisp with the feel of early spring. We were arriving a month later than usual and yet flowers were just budding along the road cut.

In Fairbanks the sun rode high and although it set briefly, the sky never darkened. Children played ball and rode bicycles at midnight. Locals were upbeat, striding purposefully or chatting with neighbors, their bare skin pink beneath skimpy clothes. Nevertheless, frost lingered in the back of their minds, and they counted days until snowfall the way people elsewhere worry about shopping days before Christmas. The feeling seemed more strained this year because of the late spring and escalating costs in gas and heating oil. Tom and I traded in our Arizona driver's licenses and registered to vote—making our move to Alaska official. Kernwood was now our legal home.

No seed is ever wasted, I thought as we watched Megan board the plane for Tucson. A man with six children had once given me a ride when I was twenty and hitchhiking through Iowa cornfields. Concerned for my safety, he took me home to his family and bought me a bus ticket to Idaho. When I was six, a kindly woman replaced four amber drinking glasses when she saw me crying on the steps of a store. I had tripped and shattered my mother's Christmas present. My seventh-grade music teacher helped me style my hair and my eighth-grade math teacher trusted my integrity—even though we both knew I didn't deserve it. Many gentle strangers have shaped my life. *Thank you.*

GOLDILOCKS HAS BEEN IN OUR cabin, leaving his usual muddy paw prints and coppery fur. "I wish I could see him this summer—from a sensible distance,"

Tom says as he stacks the scattered firewood. It is a quiet return, our lives simpler now, but the first day of flying and hauling supplies is always a challenge.

"Remember when Luke was six, how he used to hide firewood?" I ask.

We pause and smile at one another. "He thought it too beautiful to burn," Tom says. "I think of that every time I split wood that has a pink sheen."

A few days later we set off for Pike Slough. Tom carries his fishing pole and I have packed a lunch. The water is high and muddy from recent rain. We paddle across the turgid river, turn the canoe over on the rocks, and put on our daypacks. Mushrooms are already popping up, and blueberries—although small and sour from the cold spring—are ripening. We follow an old river course, avenues of stony ground framed in shimmering poplar, and emerge from the willows close to the water. The Blackhearts and their three fledglings set up a clamor on a bar across the river and a bald eagle takes to the air. I scan the area and see the velvet antlers of a recently killed caribou. The herd does not summer in the mountains, but often a lone animal remains until the wolves find it.

"Look there!" I whisper. Tom and I sink to the ground behind a fringe of willows.

Downstream at Pike Slough, White Wolf is descending the escarpment, bright as a snowdrift on a summer day. He slips into the churning water and swims strongly across, disappearing with a shake into the brush. We crouch in the bushes and take turns with the binoculars. A few minutes later, the wolf steps from the thicket directly across from us. Cautiously, he approaches the kill and begins tugging off a sizable portion, throwing his weight into the effort. He looks thin in his summer coat, breeze playing with his long tail. He carries the meat to the water's edge and lies down to eat with his back to the friendly river and eyes on the bushes. The five ravens settle companionably close by. They are sated and not interested in feeding. Ravens are called "wolf birds," for they spot prey for the wolves to bring down and open. A raven's bill cannot penetrate thick hide.

Quietly we back into the poplars and continued on to Pike Slough, crossing the rivulet to climb the bluff by an ancient game path marked by wolf, bear, and hoofed feet. A hundred feet below, the valley spreads like a picture as we crawl out to the edge. The wolf glimmers white on the exposed bar, still eating in the company of his five friends.

"Over there!" Tom breathes. "Goldie! He's headed for the kill."

I catch the coppery glint of muscled shoulder as the grizzly slips through forest a hundred yards inland. Goldie descends into the young poplar grove and disappears, his movements effortless. The old bear is wise and cautious. He does not approach the carcass directly, but circles downwind, checking. Like Don Juan, he never forgets Death. It is a daily dance for both him and the wolf, this measuring of food and danger. White Wolf lifts his head frequently. He continues to feed, but remains alert.

It is several minutes before Goldilocks emerges on the bar. As he appears, White Wolf rises and approaches stiffly to within a few yards of the bear to claim what he has torn from the kill. They are old acquaintances, nodding politely, neither underestimating the other nor desiring conflict. White Wolf hoists a weighty chunk and departs downstream, meat swinging between his front legs as he disappears into the bushes. His ravens lift on the breeze and follow him. Goldie watches them go then ambles down to check where the wolf has been feeding. The bear goes over the area carefully, nose down. He is the boss, yet still he scans the scene, taking his time. Finding a large strip of hide and part of a front quarter, Goldie lifts it in his jaws and carries it high and swinging into the bushes. In a few minutes he returns to the kill. He bites into the caribou's head, antlers twining around his big shoulders, and throws his considerable weight into hauling the remaining carcass back into the willows. He does not trust the open, but seeks the privacy of bushes before he eats.

"They may be competitors," Tom says as we descend the steep path from the bluff, "but they have a relationship. Notice how we always see wolf and bear tracks together?"

Relationships are the deeper narrative. I think of ravens and wolves, of moose and ducks feeding together in the shallows. It takes years to see the threads. A forest is a prolonged conversation of life with place, a sculpting by consensus. After nearly two decades at our cabin, I am suddenly aware of the intricate dance of insects. Reappearing at the same place each year, they—like the larger animals—have a curious relationship with us: the bumblebees that tend our patch of fireweed, dragonflies that hover about us catching gnats, spiders gathering on our screens for mosquitoes, wasps building paper nests under our eaves. These tiny sparks of life are easy to overlook. Collecting data can deceive us into thinking that we know their story.

This is the last time we will see our elusive old friend, Goldie: a decade and more of coexistence, respect, and curiosity. Perhaps he understands that not all humans are his enemies, yet he is right to remain wary.

Rude toasting sausage for lunch at Wandering Slough in 2009.

Rude and I set off to clean trails.

Chapter 30

Playing at Life

Summer 2008

This summer, my restlessness is gone. I am deeply contented with a cup of tea, the movement of my fingers plucking berries, the shifting sunlight. Tom and I move into our old rhythm, quiet and compatible. Far from tiring of yearly solitude, I fall deeper into it—the stillness a portal. The "other world," as Laurie once called it, recedes. After a lifetime of trying to change it, my only power seems to be in my attention. This entails nothing monumental: gratitude and compassion. I am not wise enough to know what is right for anyone else, but I can bless each person in my life.

Lucas's continuing struggle is the one hook that still snags me. Each Saturday my anxiety builds as we dial the satellite phone to hear his gentle voice across the miles. He is slowly wading through a long summer with no response to his queries about college, drifting in limbo without a face to recognize him. Somehow I can never get beyond my fears for him. He seems so vulnerable—this young eagle learning to fly in the city.

"Is it really worth bringing in a gas washing machine?" I ask Tom. He has finished plumbing the "laundry room" and installing a drain pipe beneath our floor for bathwater to flow into a leach field of sawdust off the edge of the bench. Willows will easily absorb the amount he hauls in buckets.

"I'm not certain they even make wringer-washers anymore, at least in the United States," he says.

"Once we're too old to live here, it'll just be another piece of trash to take out." We are committed to not leaving the mess that most old cabins become.

He nods. We study our new six-by-eight foot addition; the thick log walls are chinked with moss and the clerestory windows are in place. The floor is made of two inch-thick planks, chain-sawn from dead trees. Tom has fashioned a solid plank door.

"It would make a good toolshed," he observes. "Bear-resistant. We could stop lugging things in and out of the cache, and find them easily."

"Anything except food," I agree. "I suppose burning our filthy work clothes after a summer would be a better use of resources than washing them." Disposable clothes had been Tom's idea. Ours were already past prime when they came north. "We can wash the bedding in Fairbanks and still do some hand laundry."

With that, we finish our new "toolshed" with shelves and a raised porch. Once the tools, totes of books, and Tom's widgets are moved inside, we cast about for a summer project. I design a diminutive smokehouse-and-bakery—a work of art with complex angles that will engage us for two summers. There will be a covered porch with rails where we can set up our extra stove for baking in hot weather. We erect a small solar panel on the cabin roof, which I use for writing. I type away on this manuscript one more summer. I don't know why I feel so compelled and I don't know how the story will end. Tom has also brought in a battery-powered drill. It makes me happy to borrow the sunlight.

"People will say our structures got smaller as we aged," I tease.

Despite my joke, our focus is artistic proportion rather than log weight. *The key*, I decide, *is to choose what one creates*. Rumi says that our intentions have children: nothing is without consequence.

We spend the morning felling dead trees and lunch along a mossy bank by a small fire. To our backs, the old spruce forest wraps us in dappled shade and birdsong; ten feet below, the smoky-jade river whispers of power. The ground is spongy and deep with sphagnum moss, lichen, and blueberry bushes. An urgent peeping pulls our attention skyward where three large birds circle. An immature bald eagle is calling to its parent while an osprey, more agile, repeatedly climbs and dives. The three spiral up and drift north. "The eagle screams," I grin. Our national bird has a call not unlike a baby chick. It's such an unlikely sound that movies dub in the cry of red-tailed hawk.

"We can still haul logs," Tom states with satisfaction. A neat pile of skinned poles is stacked at the edge of the cutbank. Mosquitoes waver about his head in a fine veil. He is roasting a slice of summer sausage with cheese balanced on top, melting them together on a stick. I have folded my sausage and cheese into a tortilla and am toasting the packet.

"I'm pleased we're taking time to clean up," I say. Clearing bark and branches from felled trees takes much of our time. The summer that I was twenty-one, I had worked with an all-girl crew cleaning up "slash" after loggers. Neatness, I now understand, is not what the forest needs. Tom and I work for a balance between returning nutrients and freeing the new growth.

"The river has really shifted this year," Tom says. "There's a whole new bar growing up along that bend. I can't get over how much it changes."

"I get lost in it," I add. "Memories, printed over year by year. Once it changes, it's hard to remember the past. Geologic time is not that long." We eat in watchful silence. "As a young person, I was always seeking that ephemeral quality of Being that seemed to shimmer beyond the next ridge. I wanted to migrate through the snows like a caribou. I thought if I could just walk far enough, I'd see God."

"You always seemed so impatient with our little place." Tom's voice is soft. "You weren't content to hike with me to Horseshoe Lake. You wanted the Continental Divide."

I shrug. "I'm finding my way, discovering that it's not about distance. I could crawl from here to Luke's Creek and never see it all. The land is so alive. Even the rocks!" I push the end of a burnt stick into the dying fire. We are silent with our thoughts—comfortable in stillness. "If I die first, will you come back?"

"Oh, probably."

"You wouldn't be lonely?"

"No more than anyplace else. I hope you'd come back too."

I try to picture myself setting up the cabin: hauling supplies in, climbing onto the roof to erect the solar panel, putting in the windows, making my little meals. Going for a hike. I shake my head.

Tom is watching me. "You have friends you could ask. Rude, for one. I'd encourage you to keep doing things that bring you joy and to ask for help."

Wind tickles the river and a cat's-paw of dimples skips toward us. Tom is studying the cumulus darkening to the south. He seems so complete without trying. *How does he do that?* His eyes are gentle; I can warm myself before them like the fire. I notice a new topography of wrinkles overprinting the old, his face softening like a candle left too close to the stove. I touch my throat where Winnie's neck ropes are gaining definition. While we have played by the river, time has indeed carried us invisibly downstream.

"Life seems to have taken us in a spiral," I say. "I thought we were going somewhere, but it seems to be an eddy."

That night I dream of a golden maiden running with wild horses. She becomes brighter until she turns into flame. There is also something about receiving assistance from an old man. I awake happy to the querulous voices of gray jays and sunlight streaming through our loft windows. It's as close to home as I've ever been.

JULY CONTINUES WET AND COLD. Along our path to the river, the little mound of blueberry bushes that Luke planted when he was nine is still hanging on, though it has yet to produce a berry. I clear it of debris deposited by logs being lugged home. *Why didn't I help him instead of saying, "Berries won't grow there"?*

Lucas is spending a hot summer in exile, waiting for word from the College of Nursing. On our brief Saturday conversations, he picks up on the first ring, sounding weary and scared. Eve is focused on completing her degree while he twists in the wind. Even his childhood dog is gone. He recounts holding Lucy on his lap as Eve drove them to the vet: advanced cancer, squeezing her heart. I think sadly of the brave little Corgi mix who staunchly guarded his sleep these many years. We had chosen her at the pound when Luke was seven, just returned from our first year at Kernwood. After seeing his parents attacked by a bear, he was afraid to sleep alone. He tells of cradling Lucy in his arms, her gray muzzle trustingly on his shoulder as the needle is inserted. Her ashes are on his dresser next to the block of cement that carries their combined paw and hand prints.

Tom and I commiserate over the satellite phone at a dollar a minute, standing in the rain and angling it to keep the tenuous connection. I think of our son's gentleness. He tells of being present in ICU when a vastly obese young man is removed from life support, organs failing. Insulated behind uniforms and clipboards, the students watched the final rhythms on a cardiac monitor as the big man's heart faltered and stopped. *Surely,* Lucas ponders, *there is more to dying that this. Something profound is occurring, yet no one seems affected.* After his class in Critical Care, he writes a short story from the patient's perspective. His version is surprisingly peaceful. A kindly nurse holds the man's hand and speaks softly as he relinquishes his ungainly body for the Light.

I recall 1978, when I lost my way. Phil was gone and I had failed to gain entrance to medical school. I wandered back to the University of Arizona—the only thing I knew to do—and into Donald Sayner's class in scientific illustration. Like other forlorn students, I was drawn there because Sayner really cared about kids. He was a modest and unlikely college teacher, portly and unkempt with tufts of gray hair and two-day bristles, yet his face lit up with the smallest of our wins. His lab was a big sunny room full of quirky treasures not unlike the pockets of a small boy. It was the one place on the university campus where students always felt welcomed and valued.

That year I also enrolled in honors English. Humanities was only a required hoop on my way to medical school, but I was nominated for the honors program and vanity (more than interest) caused me to accept. Six of us met with a professor three times a week for a year, sitting around a table to discuss ideas from Plato to Faulkner. We got to know one another very well as we delved into the meaning of life. My grandmother's deep water had cycled back—another importance piece of my journey. Science without ethics, I would come to realize, is enhanced barbarism. The Nazis proved that.

The irony to this story is that one morning our small group was abruptly diminished. Stuart Timberlake, a tall young man with gray eyes and light brown hair, was gone. He had been about twenty-one, quiet and self-possessed, a person who thought before he spoke. We were told Stuart had died in a car accident over the weekend. Following a moment of shocked silence, the group took up the day's topic. I sat stunned until I suddenly burst out, "Why are we discussing Aristotle? I want to talk about Stuart. What's the point? Why bother with the pain and struggle just to lose it all so young?"

Six pairs of eyes shifted uncomfortably, gazing everywhere except at me. Silence weighted the room until the discussion again found its feet, as if I hadn't spoken.

CLASSES ARE ALREADY UNDERWAY IN August when Lucas is finally permitted to return to school. There are no textbooks available, but he again has a seat among his classmates. Everyone gets the message: students have no power here.

Autumn paints our mountains in heartbreaking colors and the river drops, clearing. Sandhill cranes come winging low, filling the valley with their loud music. Swallows chitter high over the water as their young learn to feed on swarms of mating insects. Little birds flock up, making trial runs through the trees. A full moon silvers frost on the scarlet fireweed. The last of the bumblebees dies despite my gift of honey. Our pair of great gray owls *hoo-hoo* in the twilight and we hear the occasional wolf howl as families range afar. Goldilocks makes a few statements, tipping over our windsock and sniffing where we dip water from the spring, but generally detouring the cabin. His great tracks add mystery to our lives—a ghostly bear whose journey weaves about our own. I am no longer afraid. If he wanted to harm me he could have done so long ago.

It's a good year for spruce cones and the current owner of Squirrel Hall above Trickle Creek litters the ground with clumps of them. If the old saying about animal behavior foretelling winter is true, this one will be long and hard. I've never seen a more diligent red squirrel. He practically runs across our feet with his mouth crammed. Working deep into twilight, he flings cones from the trees and lugs them back to the ancient labyrinth of tunnels. Squirrels are fiercely territorial and although we sometimes spot an intruder quietly scouting the area, ours is too busy to think of anything beyond his wealth. Early one dawn we hear the scrabble of feet against the cabin and an ominous thump. Peering suspiciously out—we are always cautious of noises when darkness returns—I can just make out the form of a great gray owl perched in a nearby tree. Within a week, the intruding squirrel has moved in to Squirrel Hall. He is careful and not nearly so ambitious.

Nights are freezing when a weasel moves in to our area. Winston is about six inches long, excluding his tail—which seems to take control at times, jerking him around in circles. An amazing athlete, he somersaults off objects and twists into impossible shapes for the sheer joy of play. He is everywhere, curious and interested, appearing suddenly inside the cabin or following us down to the bluff. He is turning white, becoming an ermine for winter, when we make him a little bed in the corner. He wriggles and pulls up the covers with dexterous paws, but is never still for long, coming and going by holes beneath the floor.

Darkness is rapidly reclaiming the land. Evening finds us inside, warmed by the stove, often laughing at the antics of our weasel. Tom and I again play cards by lantern and climb down the ladder in darkness to venture out together and pee under the aurora. Dawn arrives later each day, streaming through the eastern windows or slinking in under a blanket of wet clouds. Mist rises from the river as the ground freezes. The sun rolls lower along the flank of Mount Laurie until September 12 when it can no longer climb over the peak. An hour later it emerges, pale and tepid, south of the mountain on its shrinking daily trek.

"Do you think living here is really a good plan for two old folks?" I ask. We are having morning coffee inside, heated on a little propane stove—another recent luxury. Sunlight pools on the table and splashes in gold onto the log walls.

Tom doesn't answer. He looks content, rhythmically slurping scalding coffee and pulling on white whiskers with his gnarled hand, a sure sign he's lost in his own thoughts. I smile at the balding top of his head, which is marred from the latest collision.

Except for the tick of the woodstove, the stillness is complete. I can hear my heart beating. Choosing another home is proving as difficult as letting go of our Sonoran desert oasis. *How long can we keep hauling firewood and buckets of water?* I wonder. Tom is down to about one hundred fifty-five pounds, all ribs and shoulder blades despite blueberry pies. Tough as old leather, his muscles nevertheless have a soft feel when I hold him at night. Then there's me—I never drop weight unless I diet, no matter the logs I drag. By fall I outweighed him by ten pounds, not altogether muscle, and my old spine remembers the miles. My gaze travels out the window to our sturdy "smokehouse-bakery" only head-high in an early snow. The proposed porch remains an odd-shaped foundation of logs. *Next year.*

MOOSE SEASON AGAIN HERALDS AN influx of planes. The cover of the 2008 hunting manual shows a man with "his" brown bear, holding a huge paw up with both hands to show the twelve-inch spread of claws. The man seems a decent fellow: reddish beard, eyes squinted against November sunlight. His rifle with scope rests on the shoulder of the dead animal. The bear lies in the snow beside a river running ice, its eyes glassy. It looks to be in good shape, back padded with fat that no one will eat. The man will probably take only the required hide, claws, and skull.

Selling wilderness has become big business and there is little incentive for restraint. The might of modern technology—snow machines, four-wheelers, airplanes, satellite tracking, night-vision goggles, sonar, radios, and automatic weapons—is pitted against whisker, paw, and beating heart. With the lobby for "predator control," grizzlies and wolves receive less protection each year. Officials bait and snare bears, machine-gun animals from helicopters, destroy whole packs, and kill cubs in the den to please a vocal minority.

The word "frontier" implies a land to be conquered. It is time to examine this assumption about wildness. By viewing our kin as possessions, products, and vermin, we miss something crucial about our own humanity. These forgotten others hold a sacred part of us. We are members, not owners of this vast community.

The land stills. There is a watchful tenor. Hundreds of grayling school in the lower creek, massing for a dash to the river ahead of freeze-up. Winter is rolling down from the north as we remove the windows and door, pack everything out of reach of bears, and call Dirk on the satellite phone. Color has vanished with the leaves and the valley looks stark as we wait on the rock bar with our few possessions. An icy wind trickles off Flattop where lenticular clouds hang smooth and silky along the ridge line like standing waves in the river of air. *Fractal geometry, the language of nature.* I smile, thinking of Lucas.

It's noon when the Beaver growls out of the low sunlight. This year we take only our camera, laptop, sleeping bags, tent, and rifles. Hardly noting our small load, the plane lifts in slow motion—bar dropping below us, cabin gliding past. As always, I crane for one last look at the familiar landscape, receding.

Dirk chats with me over the headphones as we slip low above the trees, curving over snowy passes and above freezing rivers. A proliferation of roads heralds the Dalton. In the back seat, Tom is silent, gazing out the window. In Coldfoot we pull the tarp from the truck and reconnect the battery. Pretty Boy starts right up. Bumping south over the muddy Dalton, we soon catch up with autumn. By the time we arrive in Fairbanks, gold hills flame brightly in the dusk. We are in no hurry to pick up the great affairs of the world. Our thoughts are still infused with the smell of poplar leaves and water the color of sky. Tom wears his wilderness clothing until I accuse him of smelling like smoked pike. When the bank manager agrees, he finally changes into town clothes and the aroma begins to fade from his beard.

∼

"I can't reach anyone at my agency," I complained. "Kelly is off for a long weekend and no one returns my calls. I feel like an orphan!" It was the same old problem. We were again ensconced in Mark and Denise's welcoming home.

Next morning I received a call from another agency. "I want to work in Alaska," I told a recruiter named Tammy. "I've had my Alaskan nursing license for years, but my agency tells me that jobs here are scarce."

"There's an OB opening in Sitka and one in Homer," Tammy said.

"Put me in for both. I'll go with the first agency that finds me a position."

Tammy did most of the paperwork of signing me up with her company, and I used the Wartses' Internet to complete my resume that afternoon.

Homer called first. "You want to come to Homer?" The nurse manager sounded surprised. With my credentials in high-risk OB, I was overqualified.

"Days," I stated. "I only work days."

"Not even an occasional night?" she wheedled.

"I'll put in a very occasional night," I conceded. "I've paid my dues."

"Oh, by the way," she said as we concluded the interview, "we're a small hospital and you might have to work on Acute Care when no one is in labor. Can you do that?"

"I worked a year in orthopedics as a new nurse, otherwise I've always been in maternal-child. I've never even catheterized a man. I know they have something different down there but…" I paused, but she didn't laugh. "I can learn," I finished.

Homer lies six hundred miles south of Fairbanks on the Kenai Peninsula, below Anchorage. In the week we tarried in Fairbanks, the hills tarnished to brown, and impending cold was written on the faces of people hurrying by in the stores. We pulled out of town in freezing sleet and climbed in four-wheel-drive through snow and fog, where bleached trunks of birch trees leaned against a faded sky. Spruce and the bare sticks of deciduous trees were rimed in hoarfrost, appearing like wraiths through the scurrying clouds.

I had called ahead, wanting to visit my father and stepmother in Wasilla, where they were now settled in the modern house Jeff had built for them. By afternoon, Tom and I drove back into autumn. The hills north of Anchorage billowed golden against a calendar backdrop of rugged white peaks as we pulled into the new subdivision.

Martha looked harried and too thin when she opened the door. The house was warm, clean, and well-furnished with a uniform expanse of green lawn. Her flowers still bloomed along the walk. She was dressed in a rose pantsuit with off-white lace collar, her damaged feet in matching shoes. The house smelled of roasting meat and she limped about the cluttered kitchen preparing a large standing rib roast, salad, asparagus, and fresh rolls. She had obviously gone to a great deal of trouble.

My father was bundled in a recliner, his hands icy despite the warm room. Although he said little, his eyes followed me with the old intensity, the tight little smile back on his smoothly shaven face. When dinner was placed on the table, he crept painfully to his chair, where he sat pushing food about on his plate, but ate little.

"You know, Connie never was part of Takahula," he announced.

Martha stared at him as one would at a stubborn child, willing him to desist. She passed the rolls and said, "Have another piece of meat." The three of us smiled politely, trying to think of something to say.

"It's done perfectly," Tom said, forking off a sliver of prime rib.

"I built the cabin after she left," Bud persisted. "She really had no part in it at all." He was staring at me, eyes intense and challenging.

It doesn't matter. I gazed beyond the window and perfect lawn, where icy peaks whispered of grandeur. Up there, clouds were shredding in the wind and snow plumed hundreds of feet off the lee sides like eddies in a rapids.

"She was never there." Bud kept pushing for battle or agreement.

"Really?" Tom said mildly. "So where were those *LIFE Magazine* pictures taken?"

In each of our minds arose the iconic photo: little Jeanie feeding popcorn to her young parents. In Kodachrome (and now in digital) the little family remains throughout the decades, smiling on a polar-bear rug before the cozy fireplace, at home on Takahula Lake.

Anger flickered across my father's face and he withdrew to study me. I felt a sinking disappointment. He seemed determined to reclaim his cold supremacy, choosing control over love. *Sad,* I thought, *for one whose very body would soon be reduced to a shoebox of ashes.*

I studied my dinner plate while Martha said something pleasant about her cat or one of Jeff's new planes—I forget now.

There are moments when we move beyond our definitions, when the universe opens, vast and laughing with possibility—like a banquet. Then the door seems to close. Easy to forget our majestic visions, to discount them as some fancied dream. Nevertheless, they are reality. And the other parts? Only illusion.

That was the last time I was to see my father. Early the next morning, Tom and I continued south after a goodbye of no particular note.

Chapter 31

HOMER BOUND

September 2008

The lowering sun came warm through our truck windows the next afternoon as we topped the hill above Homer—end of the road. Below us opened the panorama of Kachemak Bay, backdropped in glaciers and mountains. The Homer Spit, an old glacial moraine, fingered into the ocean halfway across the inlet as if pointing toward mysterious fjords and islands. Light glimmered off the ocean in shifting blue-gray layers as wind toyed with the surface. Out in the open Pacific we could see living volcanoes, a reminder of life's ephemeral quality. Ahead the road dropped into a village that climbed the hillside, with homes all facing the bay like flowers tracking sunlight.

I'm not certain if I knew then that our wanderings were over. It may have been a month or two later as I watched a cow and calf moose browse the fading bushes below our kitchen window that the punchline of a cosmic joke hit me: all those nights in Milwaukee watching *Northern Exposure* on our laptop had drawn us here! As usual, I had failed to recognize it. Thinking back over these six decades, I again see how each moment has been woven into my fabric in some inexplicable way. *Who am I to say what is relevant?*

Our lovely furnished apartment nested above a law office. As the year dwindled and life slept deep beneath the snows, I too retreated into quiet, drinking in the muted colors and hushed stillness. From our high vantage we celebrated the changing skies over Kachemak Bay. Below us on Pioneer Road, busy folk traveled by foot and bicycles, and in dented vehicles rigged with snowplows with headlights on stalks like the eyes of insects.

"It's the ice you have to watch out for," nurses warned me. The little hospital had given me ice cleats for walking to my truck.

"We have four-wheel-drive and good tires," I assured them. "My commute is short and I never get out of second gear."

"I finally bought studs after I smashed my third car," someone said. Most vehicles looked like wrecks and they all had studs.

"You can buy quite a few taxi rides for the price of studded tires," Tom reminded me. He laid a pile of bills next to the phone. Taxi rides cost $5 for any in-town destination.

By November I could have shoved the truck sideways (provided I could stand up). One night I sailed right past our driveway at five miles an hour, all four wheels merrily going their own and individual directions. The next day we bought studded tires.

"Good thing our old truck gave out," I told Tom as we peered through blowing snow and the flick of wiper blades. We were driving out of town for dinner with new friends and the highway—clear moments before—was now inches deep in powder. We followed the tracks and taillights of someone just in front. There would be no view of Mount Redoubt as we climbed around the bend toward Anchor Point. "Aren't you glad we have four-wheel-drive?" *And now studded tires.* Bit by bit we were committing our lives to Alaska.

In December, Janet's flame lost its heat and flickered out. None who loved her wished a prolonged departure. Uncle Bert summed it up by saying, "It is a blessing that we don't have to keep going forever." Nevertheless, my world seemed impoverished—not dismal, but somehow appropriately pensive. I could no longer call her or ever again see that radiant and loving smile. I wasn't able to travel to Phoenix for the memorial, but I was caring for another gracious woman in Homer who reminded me touchingly of my aunt. They breathed their last within a day of one another. Supporting my patient helped me cross the chasm of my grief for Janet.

When I called Annie, she said, "Now we are the matriarchs."

Janet Chittenden Cutler: June 10, 1922 ~ December 19, 2008

ON CHRISTMAS EVE, SIX INCHES of sparkling fluff fell during my shift. I had put in almost fourteen hours, but a baby girl had arrived safely—beginning her own long journey. I emerged into the cold night, my solitary footprints punctuating an unbroken blanket across the small parking lot. After scraping my windows free, I started the truck and inched off the hill through falling snow. The pickup glided down through billowing white, wheels seeming not to rotate. I imagined reindeer hitched to the front bumper. I turned east on Pioneer Road at ten miles an hour, snow whispering off the cab in a sparkling mist. There were no other vehicles, but people were out walking. A couple waved and smiled. Modest Christmas lights reflected off the snow from little shops and homes. The one blinking stoplight looked cheerful. Despite my tired back and feet, I grinned fondly. *Yes*, I decided, *I will renew my contract in January, even though it means working nights.* I was certainly not driving the Alcan in midwinter.

Next morning Tom and I headed out on foot, leaning into a biting wind as we walked to the library. The sky was clearing at twenty degrees and powder snow danced across sparkling dunes. Down on Beluga Lake, pickups were plowing a great oval racetrack above fifteen inches of ice. At the end of Main Street the ocean was pounding and on a whim we turned downhill where three cars were parked, facing out from the bluff. The passengers seemed to be peering intently at great waves. Then we heard a cheer. Below the icy overlook, little dots were lifted onto the dark swells—surfers! We stood transfixed as one caught a wave, silhouetted for a moment against a backdrop of glaciers and frozen volcanoes in a triumphant statement of human imagination and resilience.

"I think life washed us up in exactly the right eddy," I said as we put the wind to our backs and climbed the hill.

"I don't have a clear image of us moving here," Tom admitted. He looked a bit troubled, face shrouded in his hood. His nose was red. "I'll have to trust your sense of things."

"Even if Homer isn't it," I reasoned "we seem to have chosen Alaska. I'll stay here and work while you fly to Arizona to sell Sylvia House. You can put Lucas in an apartment until he finishes school." Our son was repeating psychology—the final credits for his baccalaureate degree. Had he not stumbled, he and Eve would have graduated together. Lucas had taken it hard and had withdrawn into his own thoughts. When Eve completed her associate degree and passed the national exam, she moved into a place of her own. Although they remained close and he often took care of Megan after school, he was again alone in the house.

"What about the economy? We won't get as much as we planned," Tom stated.

"It could take years to recover," I said, "and we don't want to be absentee landlords. If we get what we put into the place, we'll be able move on with our lives. I think it will be good for Lucas too. Sylvia has served its purpose and put several kids through college."

We smiled at one another. Our path was decided.

I WAS FALLING IN LOVE with Homer and with the little hospital where I did everything from cradle-to-grave (more hospice than birth). Stocking laundry in the labor rooms—neatly folded baby clothes, sheets, and under-pads—made me feel like a guest in somebody's home. Dr. Wise's mother told me how women in town used to take turns cooking and washing when the hospital had only three beds. The community had created this resource and everyone was rightfully proud of it.

In Homer they said, "You eat the view." Life wasn't easy at the end of the road, but it was authentic. People found ingenious ways of living, working various jobs depending on the season. Some had arrived by choice; others wandered until they ran out of road and couldn't seem to find their way back. It was the sort of place you brought your own candle and shared the light. I liked that. There were nurses who didn't have indoor plumbing and showered at work. Some walked the last mile to a remote cabin if they couldn't make it up the driveway. The hospital had cots in case a blizzard closed the roads. If a disaster came, we would need one another. I kept revisiting that from different levels. It left me feeling compassionate and humble.

A small and isolated town makes everything personal. I was beginning to understand how someone could work so many hours for decades and not burn out: this was their town; these were their friends and neighbors. Mary Lou Kelsey delivered the babies of women she had delivered. Ancient Doc Sayer, one of two general surgeons, was a gold prospector who had broken his back. He was cantankerous, opinionated, crude, and he didn't believe in pain medication. He was known to take stitches out with his pocketknife and didn't carry malpractice insurance—but his patients loved him. He was there when an appendix ruptured in the night or a car overturned. Hardly a family didn't owe him a life or limb.

TOM FLEW TO ARIZONA THAT January and helped Lucas move his few possessions into an apartment. As always, we were operating on a shoestring, and Tom even shared the old car as they worked together cleaning up Sylvia House and giving things away. I visualized our son taking to the air—free as a young hawk—while Tom and I settled from the skies to roost in Alaska. It all seemed to be coming together.

"A Realtor told me we'll never sell in this market unless we put another fifteen thousand dollars into finishing the backyard," Tom said when he called. "What should I do?" His voice sounded plaintive and far away. The housing bubble had just dissolved and nobody was buying.

"Just sell it," I told him. "It only takes one buyer. Life brought us this far."

I hung up and sat in the snug comfort of our apartment, watching dawn climb over the southern mountains. Beyond the big windows, spruce trees drifted darkly in blue snow. We had been given the best accommodation in town: heated floors and three hundred sixty degrees of view. I closed my eyes and pictured the shabby little Tucson home that we had loved back to life. It had been a sturdy refuge where Lucas and numerous other young people had transitioned into adulthood. I imagined it passing to new owners and I blessed them. I thanked each special corner—the gardens and artistry—and imagined someone stepping through the front door.

"This is just what I want!" she would say. "This room will make an office, and I will sit here in the mornings with my coffee. It is perfect!"

Yes, it will be perfect for that right person, I decided. *Everyone will win.*

Within a day Tom called—elated—to report that he had sold the house. "I put a 'For Sale by Owner' sign in the front yard and a woman walked in this morning. She had watched us restore it! She said, 'What's your asking price?' and I told her, 'I don't have an asking price. I have a sale price: the amount I need after escrow.' I gave her the remaining furniture and garden tables. We are getting all our money back!"

"We'll recreate what we need here. It all feels right." *Yes*, I let out my breath. *We're in the flow. This is where we commit to the rapids and dig in our paddles!*

"She really liked our win-win attitude," he told me. "Now my friends are telling me that if it sold so quickly, I didn't ask enough."

We both laughed. The year before we could have doubled the price, but that was then. The only cards you can play are in your hand today.

"Next you need to get safely home," I said, recalling the long cold miles. I thought of Tom riding the crest of change—again—with all our possessions. It felt like breakup on a river—all the pieces in motion. Nevertheless, the current was strong. There was excitement in Tom's voice and a lightness in my heart. *Enthusiasm*, I thought. *Yes.*

"I plan to rent a U-Haul van and give away everything that won't fit. Do I have your permission to decide?"

"Yes. You know what I value. Mostly it is personal things and a few books."

"There's a whole room full of books! I don't know which ones you value."

"Just choose. It's still cold and dark," I said. "I've driven the Alcan in winter and I wouldn't recommend it. Why don't you take a couple of weeks to visit your family in Ohio and let spring advance. How's Lucas doing?"

"He's excited about finishing up. I think he's relieved to not have the responsibility of the house. We've had some good talks. I'll tell you when I get home."

MEANWHILE, A FEW HUNDRED MILES south of Homer, the Pacific Plate continued its relentless dive under Alaska—buckling the planet's crust in one of the most geographically active areas on Earth. Out of fire, this land is born. Homer had been shaking and grumbling for weeks, and across Cook Inlet, 10,197-foot Mount Redoubt was getting ready to blow. The hospital gave employees masks for the ash that fell sporadically; people were buying tarps to cover cars and electronics. *Those who live on a moving planet consent to change*, I told myself.

Tom's journey back was long, cold, and expensive. It was early March when he finally pulled the big van into to Homer. The afternoon was bright with returning sun, and ice glazed the snowdrifts like taffy. We unloaded our remaining possessions into a small storage space and waited to see where life would carry us.

"This is it?" I asked as we stuffed scuffed boxes into the rented shed. I was discouraged at how dingy and worthless our earthly belongings now appeared.

"We have each other," Tom reminded me.

The next morning ash was again falling, mixed with snow. I brushed fairy flakes with trapped layers of grit from our truck. The local car wash had been busy, people working quickly to give those in line behind them a chance. At the hospital, a secretary had come out to hose down cars so that employees could drive home.

I had expected that Tom's arrival would bring closure and renewed purpose to my heart, but instead it laid bare my fears. Perhaps it was the extra shifts and working nights again; maybe it was seeing the remnants of furniture Tom had built crammed into a frozen shed on East End Road. The image of being a lost waif arose from some dark recess in my mind and blew up like Mount Redoubt. All my mantras and meditations were blasted away, revealing unexpected calderas of lava. I wasn't at all sure we had climbed out on the right limb.

I awoke before daylight and plugged in the coffee pot. I still couldn't sleep on my days off and my mind was already gnawing on questions that hung like a cloud over our spring. As the aroma permeated our cozy living room, I was surprised to have Tom join me on the sofa. He usually slept in.

"When we began this quest we had five beautiful acres, a business, a home and a community of friends," I told him as I gazed out at the gray and uncertain world. "I've lost track of our purpose. I said I would work anywhere, but it had to be days and with moms and babies. Now I'm working nights and most of my patients are old people on heart monitors. Shoving those boxes into the shed really hit me. Is that my life? I thought there was more to it! With the plummeting stock market, the only thing of value we own is a pickup covered in volcanic ash."

Tom lifted my feet into his lap and worked his thumbs along one arch. "Remember my mother?" he asked. "And yours? Everybody's life ends up in dusty boxes."

This didn't help. "I'm not ready! I thought there would be another chapter. I miss friends. People are good to me at work, but it takes a long time to make solid friendships—someone who will show up with chicken soup when you get sick." I gazed pensively out the window where a pale yellow sky silhouetted the black mountains to the east, reflecting off the bay and glazed snowdrifts.

"That's one way to hold it," Tom said. "Another is that we're on the verge of a new life. Remember how we maneuvered and planned to be here? Years ago we set out to get Lucas through school, find a new community, and move our lives somewhere beautiful and green? Well… here we are!"

He had a point. I thought of what Lydette, a coworker, had said: "People don't come here expecting an easy or structured life. They're here because they value freedom, beauty, and individual responsibility."

Suddenly my ears perked. "Is that thunder? In the snow?"

Tom opened a window and we stood listening into the frosty air. There it came again—like a thunderstorm looming in the distance. Lightening walked across the sky. A dense blackness seemed to be crawling over the mountains, obliterating the canary streak of dawn.

"Maybe it's old Mount Redoubt," I whispered.

The sky was growing rapidly darker. Tom switched on his computer to check the Alaskan volcano web page; indeed, a sizable eruption was underway.

Ash was already falling as we scurried to cover our electronics and truck windows. Tom called downstairs to the landlords, who turned off the air-exchange. An eerie blackness descended with bursts of grit raking Pioneer Road like silent rain. Clouds of ash billowed with each passing car; soon we could not see the nearest building. We watched in awe while the world was eerily transformed.

This is Life, I thought: *raw, magnificent, unpredictable—wonderful.*

A few hours later, the sun came out and the sky cleared. Beyond our windows lay a strangely gray world; dusty vehicles coming down Pioneer were caked with colorless ash. People emerged to clear away the gray snow and hose down cars and walks. Tom and I drove up to the hospital and washed cars. This was home.

SPRING BARRELED DOWN ON ALASKA, bleaching away several minutes of darkness each sunrise. Cranes returned, filling the sky with their wonderful songs, and eagles courted in fierce aerial ballets. The woods were suddenly alive with small birds—thick as blowing leaves: juncos, finches, redpolls, and any number of anonymous tiny pilgrims who had made the heroic journey one more season. Yearling moose wandered forlornly through town, newly outcast as their mothers prepared to give birth. Snowblades were put away and big boats—emerging from hibernation like bloated groundhogs—shoved dented pickups down toward the bay. Shorts and skateboards appeared, and figures dotted the surf behind parachute kites. The town dusted off and opened up for another season. Soon the run of tourists would be on like the salmon: lifeblood of the community. Meanwhile, old Redoubt was building another lava dome.

Tom and I turned our focus to finding a home and I dug out the list we had carried all these miles. It should be well-built, easy to maintain, not too big, thermally efficient, one story, and full of sunlight. I revised our list to include a view of the bay, garage for the truck, and a stream. Tom's original requirement had been fish that we could eat. Now that world-class fishing was handled, he revised his list to include a shop.

Homer had little in the way of building codes, and many houses had no foundation or were built on pilings that gradually tilted in the wet clay. We spent days driving and walking local roads in all weather. This was a different landscape for us. There was frost heave and drainage to consider. The whole hill, we were told, was gradually sliding into the bay. Kathy, our landlady, was invaluable as Realtor and guide. Walking acreage east of town, we fantasized about where we would build the house and place the garden. Of course there would be a garden. Snow was melting back and water gushed between birch and spruce trees as we studied our potential land.

"By the time we put in a road, utilities, foundation, and a bridge," Tom pointed to the creek, "we'll have enough money left for a blue tarp."

Reluctantly, I had to agree. Beautiful as the spot was, I was not up for that old Alaskan standby—the unfinished house moldering beneath a blue tarp. "Another lifetime," I agreed, "when we are young and enthusiastic. Maybe we should live close to town and not have to plow a mile of driveway when we're eighty. I don't want to navigate the hill in the icy dark to work, either. We have Kernwood for wilderness. Let's be part of this community."

Then one day we chose a house within walking distance of the hospital—committing our future to this quirky little town. It was more expensive than we had planned, but exactly what we needed. We hadn't recognized it at first because it had an upstairs, was almost new, and was located near a subdivision; yet as the ground thawed, I discovered that it even had a creek. The house was well-built—bright and airy—with lofted living room, two bedrooms, two bathrooms, and five-star energy rating. There was even a detached and heated double garage that Tom could use for his shop.

"We'll live upstairs as long as we can climb them," I decided. "Then we can move to the lower bedroom and invite some young person to share our home."

We needed to buy everything: washer, dryer, refrigerator, sofa, bed, chairs, vacuum, table, lawnmower, freezer, rugs. "I didn't realize they'd take the refrigerator and curtains." My voice echoed in the vacant structure. The place felt sterile and empty.

"It's just waiting for us to love it." Tom put his arm about my shoulders. "We have a home now." He watched to see if I would relax, but I was still on edge.

It was almost June before the property closed. We drove ninety miles north to the larger town of Kenai and—in one whirlwind day—furnished the whole house. Still, it remained foreign to me. Next, we unloaded the storage shed and placed our homely belongings. They looked familiar, though slightly embarrassed, in the opulent new surroundings.

"We may as well stay in the apartment," I decided. I was sitting tentatively on our new sofa in our strange new house. "We're settled there and it's paid for, and we'll be going to the cabin soon." I was having what I once described to Lucas as "post-purchase depression." We knew little about caring for a real house in this land of ice, and the hefty mortgage made me jittery. We had always survived by limiting expenses.

"I think we need to make this our home," Tom said.

"Maybe you're right. It doesn't seem much like home yet."

"It needs us," he answered. "Can't you feel it? Let's have a housewarming. You can invite everyone from work and we'll walk around the neighborhood knocking on doors. This is our home and it's time to start putting down roots."

"Let's fly Lucas up and show him our new place!" I said suddenly. "It's been two years since I've seen him. I want him to know that we're okay and to see our new community. Maybe he'll even want to settle here. Eventually. After he gets his skills at a big hospital." My voice trailed down, wistful.

Tom smiled. "We'll make it a graduation party too. With his classmates already gone, he isn't planning to attend graduation, but we can acknowledge him for achieving his goal—despite setbacks. That's no small thing."

"Oh, Tom!" I threw my arms about him. "It's going to be okay."

He held me close, and I could hear the steady beating of his heart. *Day by day. Here and now. The gift.*

～

TOM AND I WATCHED LUCAS climb from the Navajo onto wet tarmac. He was talking with a young woman. She looked happy and flattered as he lifted her bag from the tail compartment and then picked up his own with an effortless swing. He seemed mature and at ease. For a moment I saw him, not as my son—a kid who lived down to his last pair of socks—but as a remarkable young man. He had always been his own being; now I glimpsed a larger reality where our roles were only the briefest of games.

As he stepped inside, Lucas gathered us both into his arms for a long hug. "Gosh, it's good to be back in Alaska!" he said and smiled with his whole face.

He was clean-shaven again with a gentle hint of double chin and not much heavier than when I had last seen him. The glossy dark hair was longer now and he was neatly dressed. His large features had matured into a handsome and striking presence. He had wide-set and thoughtful brown eyes that seemed to reserve judgement from a depth of comfortable silence. Although only twenty-three, I would have guessed him to be about twenty-eight—a man of confidence and principle. I felt suddenly shy, like a girl with a crush.

"You made it! Congratulations! We are so pleased for you!" I snuggled warmly beneath Lucas's arm as we trailed toward the small parking lot. "Did you ask friends to go over your psych paper before you turned it in like I suggested?"

"No," he glanced down at me impishly. "I just turned in the same one I wrote last year. I had to iron it because it got wrinkled." His eyes sparkled as he watched me.

"Ahggg! With your whole life in the balance, you didn't think it worth rewriting?"

"There was nothing wrong with the paper." There was a hint of warning in his tone. "I knew there wasn't."

"We're looking forward to showing you our new house and community," Tom said as we got into the silver pickup. I had climbed behind the seat. "Your Mom has an itinerary mapped out."

"Good old Mom." Lucas turned his lovely head to shower me with an affectionate grin.

"We're still living in the apartment until our party." I rested my hand on his shoulder, soaking him in. "I hope you don't mind sleeping on the floor or sofa. Tomorrow a wonderful old man offered to take us out on his boat. Wait until you see Gull Island! It's like God breathing! Birds come down in waves—gulls, kittiwakes, murres—by the thousands! I have so wanted to share this all with you!"

About thirty folks showed up to our housewarming that Sunday bearing home-canned salmon, garden salads, plants, and a variety of handmade treats. The day was warm as our new home filled with light and friendship. Mike and Maka, two gnomes who lived in a tiny cottage in the nearby woods, came with crab salad and guitar. Mike dedicated songs to Lucas, who sat with his arm around me on the sofa, his Buddha smile lighting my heart. Though he laughed and smiled, seeming at ease with everyone, he listened more than he spoke, and I seemed to catch an undercurrent of melancholy. Still, he had graduated and easily passed the national exam, and for that I was grateful.

As the guests departed, we prepared for a first night in our new home. I made a nest on a thick pad in the downstairs bedroom for Lucas. He kissed each of us fondly goodnight and then went out alone to explore the town. I saw him head for the beach, where I could hear the surf from our window.

Enlightenment, I thought, isn't about living without problems. Life is an obstacle course where strength and beauty emerge from the improbable: mud and ash, fire and ice. These are blessings. How else do we experience our true mettle?

Rude gazes out over our valley from Annie's Peak, 2009.

Rude crafted a rocking chair for Tom, 2009.

Chapter 32

NEVERLAND

Summer 2009

I heard Tom whistling as I approached the garage where he was building me a dresser. The double door was up and our silver pickup stood in the driveway. Alders were leafing out along the road and a pair of bald eagles circled in blue overhead, cheeping their courtship.

"Rude's been on my mind," I said. "I'd like to invite him to the cabin this year."

"I miss him too," Tom admitted. He twisted a clamp and looked up. "But don't you think it's a bit late to ask?"

"He'll understand. I'm gonna call him."

Rude answered on the third ring. We spoke every few weeks, long conversations on philosophy and our lives. He was curious about Homer and I sent him our local paper. He always asked about Luke, whom he called by the old name.

"It's interesting you caught me," he said. "I haven't been in here all morning." He was living in his unfinished house, but his phone was still in the garage.

"Come play with us in Alaska this summer."

"Funny you should ask." He sounded pensive, his Minnesota accent so familiar. "I've been dreaming about that."

"Come," I pleaded. "It's time."

"I have to be honest with you, Jeanie. I don't have much money. There's been almost no work here and I need surgery again on my other shoulder."

"It won't cost you much beyond a ticket to Fairbanks. We have plenty of rice and beans from 2004, and we're already paying for the charter. Next fall you can drive back with us and see Homer for yourself. How 'bout it?"

"I've changed." He sounded embarrassed. "I'm wearing out."

"We all are. It's the process. Aging has gifts—like patience and forgiveness—you might miss if you were always young and strong."

"I wish you could've seen me when I was young and strong. Man! I was a powerhouse! I'd take them dogs and disappear for days. My life is pretty complicated right now…"

"Yes, life is that way. There are always things." I took a breath. "You're the only one who knows what's best, Rude. Just remember that life keeps going by and then one day it's gone. Don't let circumstances make your choices. Ask your heart where you belong this summer."

The next day he called. "Jeanie, I couldn't sleep last night. Pick me up in Fairbanks on your way north. I'm in!"

∼

RUDE STILL LOOKED FERAL STANDING with his knapsack in the Fairbanks airport. Nevertheless, like a child, he had made friends with half the people on his flight. When I hugged him, the tight little shoulders bunched as before, but the muscles of his arms seemed delicate, and I could sense that years of brutal pounding were catching up. He was dressed in jeans, good leather boots, and a soft flannel shirt with the cuffs rolled up. His silver hair was tied with a leather thong at the nape beneath the familiar felt hat. My eyes were drawn to a black feather woven into the hatband.

He grinned. "You remember that feather, do you? It's the raven feather you gave me on the river. I thought it should come back. Feathers are an Indian blessing, a symbol of moving lightly on the wind." He reached into his shirt pocket and handed Tom a delicate bit of fluff. "I made this for the two of you." It was the breast feather of an owl carefully held by a soft ribbon of buckskin.

Rude tossed his rucksack into the truck bed and hopped onto the small bench behind the seat as we set off for last-minute shopping. He didn't look much changed. He still moved with wild grace, his golden eyes as curious and wary as a fox.

"Let's meet over near the exit," I said as we split up at the entrance of a big store. Tom and I started for the pharmacy. I could see Rude near the exit, watching us with the intensity of a dog left in the car.

"He's like a butterfly," I said. "He looks big and bright, but he's fragile. We need to look after him this summer."

Tom gave me a doubtful glance that said, "Nobody 'looks after' Rude."

Next morning we set out on the long and dusty drive to Coldfoot. Rude and I took turns riding behind the seat while Tom drove. To our surprise, Dirk was able to fly us to the cabin that afternoon. He hadn't flown over our place since breakup and didn't know if he could land. *That's always the gamble.*

THE BEAVER GRUMBLES BACK INTO the sky, sliding away like a stick in the current until there is no sound except flowing water. Mist dampens the stones as I start a small fire to announce our arrival to bears and to deter the mosquitoes. I begin lugging totes down to the river as Tom and Rude set off to get the canoe. Tom's gait is solid, head swiveling, hips canted left by the weight of his pistol; beside him, Rude is gripping his rifle with one hand. Even from a distance, Rude appears coiled and ready to spring. Two trips with the canoe and all the supplies are freighted home. Traces of Goldilocks are significantly absent this spring. After a decade of his presence, the bar is strangely blank of big tracks, the cabin empty of his curiosity.

We work to set up the cabin: door on, windows in, floor cleaned, loft emptied of totes, kitchen readied, and bedding laid out. Rude makes a neat bed for himself on the far side of the loft. After a simple dinner around our campfire, we crawl up separate ladders to sleep.

"Goodnight, Tom. Goodnight, Rude." My voice is soft. A varied thrush is calling, notes drifting like leaves down the stillness. A faint whisper of the creek brushes through the screens. The cabin absorbs sounds like a cave—solid and still.

"Goodnight, Jeanie. Goodnight, Tom." Rude sounds content.

"Goodnight, Rude," Tom says. "It's good to be home."

It's a summer of play. Like three aging children, we spend much of our waking time outdoors. Rude slips easily into our rituals. He and I rise early and are usually on our second pot of coffee before Tom joins us at the fire. During these mornings alone, we often explore philosophy. Rude is trying to reconcile a Catholic upbringing with his experience. He is angry with the church for gluing a devil to his back, but seems unable to shake it off. I too am working through the dichotomies of life. Tom seems content with whatever the day brings. He and Rude compile their skills, trading ideas like boys building a fort. It's freeing to release one's art to the wind and bears: it takes the ego out of it. Rude understands. They work on the smoke-bakehouse while I write.

"He's teaching me how to use a chainsaw," Tom tells me. "No one ever taught me and he's a real master."

Only once does a misunderstanding arise. They are positioning a heavy log when Rude snaps, "You don't have to protect me!" His fists ball up, and he looks dangerous. Injured or not, Rude wants nothing less than a full load.

Tom speaks gently and the moment passes. When we are alone Tom says, "Pain is what Rude is fighting. I think he got mad because he hurt his shoulder again. It's not going to be easy for him to get old."

Rude and I are by the campfire next morning when I say, "Tom loves you. He's not competitive and will never make you wrong."

"I just gotta do things my way sometimes."

"You don't have to give up doing things, just learn to treat your body like an old friend. Life brings the same lessons back—each time louder."

After that, Rude accepts that we mean him no harm. Despite a fierce show of stamina, I can see that it costs him to cover the miles now. Within the safety of our cabin, he relaxes and sleeps deeply, at times snoring softly. He no longer flinches when I touch him; the lone wolf begins to accept and offer hugs to both of us. In the evenings, Rude pours out the story of his life in meticulous detail. *Witness*, I think, *is a gift of long friendships.* Then I wonder how the Facebook youth of today fill the need for witness.

"Explain this to me, Jeanie," Rude's voice inflects down on the last syllable of my name. "Why do you say we 'create our experience'?" He is probing for pieces to his own puzzle as we sit by our morning fire. Herringbone clouds ripple across the sky like an anaconda.

Where to begin. "Everything is connected," I finally say. "On a quantum level, matter doesn't exist in the way we see it and neither do we. At that level, there is no separation. Your energy is broadcast throughout time and space. You experience what you focus on."

Rude puzzles over this and then says, "I sometimes know things that I shouldn't. I mean thoughts come to me that turn out to be true."

"That doesn't surprise me. Intuition is normal; most of us just don't listen."

"It's spooky." He is feeding cornbread to a gray jay, stroking the downy breast with his other hand as it balances on his finger.

"It's natural," I reiterate. "How do you think polar bears congregate from hundreds of miles when a whale dies? How do animals know to move away from shore before a tsunami? We limit our experience with our beliefs. If you believe in evil, the world looks dark and scary."

"How do we get out of that?"

"I'm not certain," I admit, "but thought is creative. If you focus on pulling weeds, you just get more weeds."

"If we always see things through our beliefs, how do we know what's true?"

I shrug. "On one level, it doesn't matter. I choose to see purpose, because it makes my life more fun and interesting. Belief in evil just makes it scary or pointless."

The cabin door opens. "How's the river look?" Tom ask as he joins us. He pours hot coffee through the sieve and sits in the chair Rude places for him by the fire.

"It's still dropping," I say. "Would you guys like a day of play? We could take the canoe downriver and drag it over to Long Lake."

"I've always wondered if there are fish in there," Tom says.

ON OUR HIKES, RUDE IS the wild man—alert and stealthy—communicating with the lift of his eyebrow or tilt of his head. We three spend days exploring, cooking lunch over a fire in some wild spot and returning with berries, fish, and sore feet. Like wolves we fan out, silent and watchful, trusting one another. It feels right to travel in a little band, like a memory from the Pleistocene.

Tom and I also take Rude by turns. I hike with him to the top of Annie's Peak when the fireweed reddens and mushrooms erupt through the moss. Tom goes fishing with him at Wandering Slough, pulling the canoe upstream where they spot three bull caribou—antlers in velvet—swimming the river. Sometimes Rude wanders alone. I ask where he is headed, but he will not say. I don't think he knows. He returns exhausted, eyes smoldering. Sometimes we catch his sign on a far ridge, where a shed antler or a feather has been placed carefully in a tree. I think about how we fall in love with a unicorn because it is wild and mysterious, and then want to tame it. If we do manage to collar what is illusive and wild, the magic disappears. Domestication is poisonous—but oh! so seductive.

When Rude and I hike alone, he steps silently behind me, protective and watchful. Always his rifle is in his hand, never slung over the shoulder.

"You know, I am capable of looking after myself," I say. "I really don't need a bodyguard." Rude is working on the trail with me, a chore I'm used to doing alone. We take a break, and I sit by the creek. Rude squats nearby, rifle across his knee.

"Little One," he addresses me—although he is only a year older and I have him by twenty pounds—"do you understand what I mean by 'Friend'?" His eyes are intense.

"I know it isn't trivial to you."

He places a hand over my heart. "It means I will protect you with my life. I promised Tom that I would take care of you. That is my word."

"What happened to the silent man of the woods?" Tom grumbles. Rude is off on a solo trek. "Evenings used to be our time to read."

"Patience," I counsel. "He'll run down in time."

But Rude doesn't. The years, people and events flow out of him; in turn, he wants to hear our stories. It's like a transfusion of one another's lives. Rude's memory is astounding. He talks of his brutal childhood, his days in North Africa with the military, volunteer work in Guatemala, of going through the ice with his dogs, of camps and bears, friendships and old injuries, of life in the trenches as a plumber. Always he speaks with compassion for the disenfranchised and of his love for his children.

"I gotta find my own place," Rude confides to me at our morning fire.

"There's plenty of room here," I tell him.

He shakes his head. "I'm too used to living alone."

"What about the smokehouse?" I joke. It's only five-by-eight feet inside. "We'll call it 'Rude's Little House.' It'll be kinda tight, but there'll be the porch with a view."

"I've been thinkin' about that. I don't need much space." He sounds half serious.

One day Tom returns from Kernwood Forest with news that he has found a great white spruce, perhaps two hundred fifty years old and recently dead. Big trees are unusual, and we do not cut living ones. If it's solid, they can rip floorboards for the bakehouse and for lowering the cabin floor.

Tom and Rude go to appraise it. "I'm really surprised Rude didn't put up a fight when I said I wanted to fell it alone," Tom confides. "He seemed almost relieved."

"He probably doesn't want to be the one to mess up your best tree," I say.

Rude and I remain at the cabin, listening. Sometimes a tree will hang up or shear off; it can split and twist, or a gust of wind can take control. The distant snarl of Tom's little sixteen-inch saw is followed by a crack and the soft crunch of the tree hitting moss. The saw resumes as Tom levels the stump even with the ground. Rude and I glance at one another and breathe. *It's down, and Tom is safe.* When he returns for us, we set off together. The "Grandmother Tree" is a beauty: solid and reasonably straight, measuring twenty-two by sixteen inches at the butt and seventy-five feet tall. It's the biggest one we've ever cut.

Rude rips the boards—a precision task that takes several days. He cuts them in place, slicing the tree into sections and carving boards freehand. He uses the little chainsaw with the dexterity of his pocket knife. The lumber is beautifully straight and uniform. We clean up the site and haul the boards home together, except for a big section that Rude trusses up and sneaks back by himself. He is grinning like a kid who's gotten away with something when he climbs out of Trickle Creek with a three-hundred-pound log strapped to his back.

By midsummer the men have completed a charming structure of curious angles and cantilevered supports. On the west is the "bakehouse," a covered porch enclosed by two split-log puncheon rails; the east side forms the small smokehouse. The ceiling is of split logs covered with a roof of living sod, hauled from a cutbank that the river is taking. Artistic process with nature is our purpose. Rude spends several days crafting the door. The smokehouse chimney is hollowed from a log with a sculpted cap like a mushroom. Tom makes holders for coffee mugs and pie plates. I do an ink drawing of gray jays and our names above the door.

The men set up our spare stove and stovepipe oven, and each evening they retire to stumps on the porch for a taste of bourbon. Rude whittles as they talk, sunlight splashing low through the trees. The western sky lights and Annie's Peak glows like flame. I hear their quiet voices as I bathe in the cabin. Rude has carried home a curious section of a dead tree, shaped like a trident. After studying it for several days, he rips the twisting trunks in half. Ants have tunneled along the grain where his pocket knife enters a conversation with the old tree. Gradually it is transformed into a rocking chair with arm rests made from the top of the Grandmother Tree—each piece deliberate and imbued with meaning. When it is finished he gives it to Tom. Now Tom rocks in the chair, while Rude perches on his stump for their evening talk.

I join them, my hair still damp. The fire in the cookhouse stove pops warmly. A fine mist falls through slanting sunlight, backlit like descending stars.

"Here, take the chair," Tom insists. He moves to another stump on the bakehouse porch. The chair is warm from his back and wraps around me like a shawl. From downstream comes the guttural "*calk*" of a raven.

"How did you start in hospice?" Rude resumes their conversation.

Tom ponders the question. "When we got home from our summer here in 1995, I became depressed. I needed out of my head, so I called the Tucson home for neglected children, but they didn't want volunteers. Next I phoned hospice and they did."

I turn my head to study Tom. *Depressed? Did I miss something?*

"Then when Jeanie started nursing school, I had to get a job. She couldn't keep working in glass. I could've made a good living in construction, but I didn't want us to grow apart, so I became a certified nursing assistant and studied to be an EMT. That's when I went to work in hospice. They only paid seven dollars an hour, but taking care of dying people is a remarkable privilege."

I'm silent, realizing that Tom worked nights as a nursing assistant to stay connected with me. He hadn't told me. *I wonder what else I fail to notice.*

"I'm not certain I could do it," Rude says.

"Dying is part of life," Tom replies. "Our culture turns it into something scary. We always talked to Lucas about death like we talked of sex. We treated both as natural."

"How would you die?" I ask no one in particular. "If you had a choice?"

Rude gazes down at the log bridge across Trickle Creek. The land is ablaze in autumn colors and suddenly I remember that he's color-blind and sees only yellow and blue.

"I suppose I'd like to die suddenly," Tom says, "and without pain. With dignity. I don't want someone wiping my butt."

"You've wiped a lotta butts," I remind him. "You just called it a privilege."

"Not mine." Tom's advanced directives have been in place for decades. No resuscitation.

Rude nods in silent agreement. He has told us of coming out of anesthesia like a grizzly bear, yanking tubes and fighting. *No, Rude wouldn't like the hospital exit.*

"I always believed dying suddenly would be best," I say, "but now I think a little warning might be good—tie things up and say goodbye."

Rude looks thoughtful. "I don't wanna die in a hole. Plumbers—at least where I come from—spend a lotta time in wet, heavy ground." He shivers. "I've saved myself more than once by bailing out of a trench when I got the creeps. Somehow, I always know."

"It's good to pay attention to those feelings," Tom says.

"Do you want to be cremated?" I ask.

"I don't want to be in a hole," he repeats, "but being burned seems worse. I think the Indians had it right. Put me up on a platform and let the birds pick my bones."

"I have a photo my parents took of me as a toddler, playing on the tundra with Inuit skulls," I say. "The early people used to leave their dead open to the sky. Of course, with frozen ground and no trees to burn, they didn't have much choice."

We are silent, listening to the land and the popping stove. Brilliance fades to violet; Annie's Peak turns to rust with a nimbus of yellow where the sun has vanished. "I don't want people crying over me," Rude says. "Let them teach the children to love the Earth in memory. That's what I've tried to do…" He freezes, staring.

Tom and I follow his gaze. A few yards away, White Wolf stands watching, a milky ghost in the soft light. For a moment he holds us in his wild gaze and then shape-shifts back into the trees.

～

"There's a new grizzly moving in," Rude tells us one evening. "I seen fresh claw marks on a tree along the bench trail. I peed on it and now the tree's been shredded."

"I'm so pleased!" I say. "You get to name it."

"Cocoa, maybe. It's got dark fur." Rude pulls a tuft from his shirt pocket.

Tom and I finger it by turns, seeing the gloss as we twist it in the lantern light. "I know it's late in the year," I say, "especially with a new bear out after dark, but I've been thinking about backpacking up King Mountain." Luke named the peak when he was six because its long ridge reminded him of a crown.

Rude's eyes light up. Tom shakes his head and settles back. "You two go ahead. I'll keep the home fires burning."

It takes me a day to put an outfit together. It might be cold up there: raining or even snowing. For now, the sky is sharp as glass and the burgundy mountain looks close enough to touch. Rude has a good set of all-weather hiking boots, but mine are less than ideal. I rub beeswax into the leather and set them in a warm oven.

Morning dawns clear. I lead, with Rude—rifle in hand—just behind. We follow our trail up Luke's Creek and then choose a route inland. Returning later to the creek, we pause to eat beneath the cliffs at the base of Annie's Peak. Rude has named the spot "Yellow Stone" after a boulder in the tumbling creek. I notice a shed caribou antler set in a tree. Climbing away from the creek, we circle up the ridge above Janet's Creek—a side drainage. The ground becomes progressively wetter and more brushy as we ascend. I am tired when we crest a rocky knoll that forms a gorge, almost blocking the canyon. On the other side, a wet amphitheater climbs treeless into late sunlight. Eighty feet above the swift brook, this knob is protected by a few ancient spruce trees. The lichen-covered cliff of decomposed shale overlooks the amphitheater, while behind us, the valley falls away in splendor.

I start a fire while Rude descends to the creek for water and breaks up a pile of firewood. He strings his tarp and lays out sleeping bags in the shelter of twin trees that have split at their base and fallen at right angles. These great spruce shared three centuries and died in the same storm. Rude squats contentedly beside the fire as I stir the little blackened pot. He is whittling a pot-grabber for me.

"Jeanie… what do you think happens when we die?" Rude gazes across the distance where an eagle circles to gain elevation in the cooling air. The bowl of peaks turn bronze as the sun drifts down the ridge, shafting between trees as it settles into the forest.

"I don't think we die and I don't believe in a happy-land where we sit in white all day."

"Would be boring," he agrees.

"I decided against heaven when I was six. Anyplace you can't get dirty or bring your dog wasn't for me." I pause to gather my thoughts. "I don't know, but I trust the trees. Listen to them." Beyond the crackle of our fire and rush of water, comes the song of wind through forest—the breath of our planet. Spruce tops nod like undersea plants. "They do it so gracefully, this transformation we call death. They tell me there is nothing to fear."

Rude looks at me quizzically.

"It's like a ripple where the current goes over a rock. Once the rock is gone, the water creates something new. Did you ever think, 'being' is a verb? We are humans 'being'—a process. The energy that animates us is universal. Land, sea, this planet. Stars. Nothing is ever lost. Whether my personality goes on really isn't important. I'm just happy to be with you, part of this current. Now."

"I'd like to be laid out here," he says, spreading his arms to the breeze. "This is my place."

I can almost see him flying. In the distance, the eagle circles, growing smaller and disappearing at last against the encircling peaks.

During the night the wind drops. There is no moon and it's very dark. I feel Rude awake and hear him sniff like a fox. I can see the silhouette of his head. "It's gonna snow," I say.

"Yeah, I'm afraid you're right." His wool cap bobs darkly under the tarp.

We are late getting up. No point in an early start with the curtain of falling flakes. I reach over and pinch through his sleeping bag, making him squeal indignantly.

"No one has ever pinched my bottom!"

"Up, lazy bones, and make the fire," I command. "It's not gonna stop snowing."

By the time I join him, Rude has a fire going. He has moved our kitchen into the shelter of the twin trees off the shoulder of the knob. The mountain above is hidden in shifting white. "We can't go up there," I speak for us both. "It'll be dangerous, and we won't see anything. It'd be really easy to get lost too."

Rude squats by the fire while I cook. I hand him a hot cup of instant coffee. He nods. "I'm not sure we can find our way home in this," he says.

"Yes, we can. If I die, just keep the sound of Janet's Creek on your left. This ridge will take you back to Luke's Creek and that will take you home. You can't get lost if you don't leave the sound of water."

It's a long trip back down the mountain and we take our time. My feet are cold and wet. Rude wants to give me his boots, but I decline. Three times we stop while he builds a fire, warming us with hot drinks. The land is transformed under snow, the rivulets making dark runnels, bushes bending and wet. Bog lemmings appear, erupting like chocolate popcorn as we tramp into their hidden cities. Rude spots ten for every one I glimpse. As we descend, the snow turns to sleet and then rain. By the time we hit the home trail below Birch Bench, the sun is out and we can see old King Mountain basking frostily in the golden afternoon. Tom has dinner waiting. He is not surprised to see us.

SEPTEMBER PEACE IS AGAIN SHATTERED when the Kenai planes return to comb the valley for moose. We stand on the bluff while the two Cessna 170s circle and land across from our cabin. "I'm going to talk with them," Tom says. "Alone. I don't want a fight."

Rude helps him launch the canoe and then stands with me. Tom looks small and vulnerable as he beaches the canoe and starts toward the planes, but seeing the feral gleam in Rude's eye, I understand why he chose to go alone. The men wait, allowing Tom to close the distance. No one extends a hand in greeting. One speaks with him while the other continues unloading mounds of gear. A few minutes later, Tom walks back to the canoe and slides it into the glassy current. Rude is down on the river to catch the bow and help him carry it into the trees, moving in easy step. They join me on the overlook where we can see Dennis and Terry in conversation.

"I asked them not to camp here this year," Tom tells us. "I said it disturbs my wife to have them flying and shooting so close. Terry said, 'We can camp wherever we want.' I agreed, but said that since they had planes they could go anywhere and that I was asking. He wanted to know why you were always photographing them and I said we give the pictures to the State Troopers."

Across the bar the men erect a tent but load the gear back into the planes. Within a few minutes, both planes roar towards us, making a low pass over the cabin. They circle north and we hear them land upstream near Wandering Slough.

"Do you think they plan to come back?" I wonder.

"Hard to tell," Tom says. "Maybe they're claiming this area from other hunters. I imagine they'll be back for the tent before they go." For the next ten days we hear their ruthless aerial pursuit of animals in the distance. Once a day Terry buzzes the cabin, but for the most part we enjoy September unmolested.

AFTER COMPLETING THE SMOKEHOUSE, WE decide to hunt for the first time since we overwintered in 1999. Tom carries his pre-1964 Winchester .30-30 carbine with open sights; I have my mother's ancient Winchester bolt-action .30-06 with a peep sight. Rude isn't hunting—just guarding me.

"If we get one," I say, "we'll make jerky for next summer. To climb King Mountain." Rude is very fond of our old moose jerky, which is almost gone.

"We only shoot a small bull, in the morning, and close to home," Tom insists. "We aren't packing miles or sleeping out on a pile of meat with the bears."

"A moose is huge," I tell Rude. "You have no idea how much work it is to pack home."

"You have no idea how hard I can work," he answers. His eyes have the glint of a carnivore who has lived on rice and beans for three months.

Tom hunts alone while Rude dogs my steps, an almost invisible companion. I pause and find him flattened against a tree, motionless as bark. "You have to think like a deer," he instructs me. "They don't just walk, they step-step-pause-step." He demonstrates, gliding between the trees. Even the inclination of his head says "deer" as if he has become one. "Stop with a shadow across you to break up your silhouette."

I try it, feeling clumsy at the irregular pattern that looks so natural for Rude. He drifts like smoke over the country. We get close to more than one cow, but no bulls. Rude is disappointed when I put away my rifle. "Not this year," I tell him.

"When I was young," Rude says, "I could stay out in the woods all day if I kept my feet dry. My mother gave us two pairs of old socks and a set of plastic bread bags for the snow. I learned to walk very carefully and not tear the bags."

Snow comes early, inch after inch carpeting the land while we wait for an opening in the weather. "We may not get out until November," I warn. The freezing river is an Ansel Adams's photograph in black and white. Grayling school up in the creek and make their rush for deep pools in the river. Life is slowing for the long cold sleep. Ice forms in the shallows, bobbing on twigs in the rapids. I pull snowshoes from the cache and begin stamping trails. Rude is still fishing, his back matted white as he casts into the dark river between pans of slush. The cabin seems stark by kerosene light; most of our things are packed away and the windows replaced by thin plastic.

I'm heating beans in the oven one evening when the growl of a Beaver breaks the silence. Mount Laurie is invisible in falling flakes, and spruce trees drift in mist. Out of the blue-gray twilight, the plane suddenly appears—low through the trees. Tom grabs the radio. "I'm here to help you pack," Dirk's voice crackles cheerfully. He lands without a pass, swinging around and taxiing up to the creek before I get my boots on. Up the path he comes bounding.

I greet him with a hug. "I thought we might have to get a plane on skis out of Fairbanks in midwinter."

"I wouldn't leave you." His beard, now graying, sparkles with snow. His blue eyes are laughing.

Within twenty minutes we have the cabin door off, stove dismantled, everything stashed in the cache, and the trapdoor wired tight. Dirk stows our gear aboard as fast as the men heave it up. We climb in and the plane lifts into violet, shifting sky.

"Let's not try to drive to Fairbanks tonight," I say as we debark in gathering darkness onto the airstrip in Coldfoot. Tom and Rude nod in agreement.

We sleep one last night together in the warm office-cabin of Coyote Air. Tom and Rude roll out their sleeping bags on the floor, leaving the sofa for me. Runway lights flash through the windows. Dirk and Danielle invite us into their quarters for an unforgettable meal of caribou backstrap. Outside, temperatures plunge. I am grateful to be safe and warm one more night, and aware that my life is about to shift gears again.

Chapter 33

MEANDERS

October 2009

Back in the "other world," obligations flooded in. Like entering the freeway from a country lane, there was no contemplative drifting—even in Homer. Issues that had managed without us all summer now clutched at our skirts like whiny children.

"I may have to go travel-nursing while you stay here," I told Tom. We were having morning coffee on a love seat in the cozy loft of our new home. "Maybe I can get an in-state contract and commute back occasionally." It was the dilemma I had foreseen: as a resident, I couldn't work here as a travel nurse, yet if I signed with the hospital we'd have to give up summers at the cabin. Our new home was an expensive acquisition—everything was expensive here—and unlike houses in warmer climates, couldn't be left unheated. The strange logic was that to live in Homer, it seemed that I had to work elsewhere.

"You could take a job here and quit next spring," Tom suggested. We looked at one another then shook our heads. "Nah... lacks integrity."

Beyond our window, autumn rested under a milky drizzle and the sky was as soft as feathers. Shafts of sun arrowed down like searchlights onto the shifting, gray ocean. A wedge of cranes ribboned overhead, their musical calls muted by distance. I sat pensively biting my lip while ideas bounced like ping-pong balls inside my head.

"Why not write your own contract?" Tom reiterated.

I shook my head. "The hospital can't do anything outside the union."

We sat quietly, thighs touching, while my eyes traced the luminous glaciers and sky. "I love this town," I said at length. "We didn't buy a home for me to work somewhere else. I'll try working per diem and see if we can make it. It'll be bottom-level pay with no benefits, but I've spent most of my life without insurance. We'll be together through the winter and go north next spring." I smiled and relaxed. Tom nodded.

Lucas was still on our tab. After more than half a year of searching, Eve finally had a position and was flying strong. With the "economic downturn," many hospitals were simply not investing in new grads. Employees across the country were being pushed to work harder for less and even seasoned nurses expressed concern. Travel contracts, so abundant months before, had dried up.

"I have friends who've given up on nursing and taken whatever job they can get," Lucas told me during one of our frequent calls. "Most new grads are deeply in debt and have to work. I'm so lucky to have parents who helped."

"You must work in nursing or all your education is for nothing," I stated. "You have a license to learn. Work will be your real education and the longer you wait, the harder it'll be to find. Hold out for hospital nursing."

"I don't know what to do. I keep sending out applications and spending your money. I want to pull the wagon, not ride it."

"You will," I assured him, though I too was anxious. The impact of so many expenses had left us with little resiliency and our new house was a constant drain.

"You've done a lot more than you signed up for." His deep voice was soft.

"Eve and Megan were a good investment," I told him. "What you plant comes back in unpredictable ways. You have to trust that. It isn't tit-for-tat and you can't do it for that reason. You give like an apple tree—because that is what you do. You trust in the sunshine and the rain. The nursing shortage hasn't gone away. It might be pushed underground, but it will emerge with greater urgency as old nurses break down and our population ages. Hang in there, kiddo. What about Alaska? I always hoped you'd come north."

"I've been thinking of that too."

"You have ties up here. Friends and family make a difference. But you'll need to choose soon. It takes time to get a nursing license, and I hate to see you drive the Alcan in winter. Sitting there without a job just digs a hole. Sometimes you have to jump."

THE SPRING THAT LUKE TURNED twelve, he and I had set out to hike down the backside of Mount Lemmon, north of Tucson, a trek I'd first made with my mother when I was four. The road snaked into a clear sky as Tom drove our Civic up the familiar turns. Summer was rapidly taking the lowland, but here above nine thousand feet, snow still crusted the trunks of great ponderosas. We had planned to drive to the trailhead, however the last steep mile was chained off by Mount Lemmon Ski Valley company: *Closed for the Season.* It was becoming increasingly difficult, I noticed, to access public lands. At the other end of our trek, we would need to bushwhack out of Canada del Oro and up an eight-hundred-foot rocky slope clothed in Spanish dagger and cholla cactus. Here too the public road was now in private hands.

"Are you sure?" Luke asked, eying the barrier. He was already taller than me, his upper lip fuzzed in dark hair. Red as a fox, but far heavier, his dog Lucy strained against her leash while Tom unloaded backpacks from the car. Luke had wanted to bring her and, against my judgment, I had agreed.

"It's public land," I stated. "That's us. Companies do not own our planet—but let's get moving before someone comes to argue that point." Like Connie, I preferred stealth to confrontation.

"You have Joyce's cell phone?" Tom asked. I nodded, fingering the pocket of the Kelty backpack I had carried since I was fifteen. Tom hugged each of us goodbye. "Call me when you get to the road."

"I'm sure there's no reception in the canyon," I said as he helped us into our packs. "Don't expect to hear from us until Sunday afternoon."

"Have a wonderful trip and be safe." Tom climbed into the car and was soon out of sight.

Luke and I skirted the barrier and trudged up the steep asphalt. At first Lucy dashed ahead, but by the time we reached the mountaintop, our six-year-old Corgi mutt was ambling sedately. We rested on a great log amid pinecone scales left by a squirrel and shared a snack in the bright sunlight. Below us the world expanded into haze. An icy breeze leaked from the forest, whispering through the pines at our back. Luke's face was happy. Lucy watched us eat with the undisguised attention of a short, fat dog.

"We need to get down into the canyon before dark or we'll have no water," I said. "It'll take much of the day." The old trail traversed a ridge before it dropped into the canyon. I traced it for him on our topo map.

At first we threaded between lofty trees on a trail banked in blue shadows with snow crusted halfway to our knees, but soon we emerged along a rocky and bleached spine where sun gleamed bright on crystals of rotten granite. A forest fire had passed over this ridge and the old track was an overgrown mess of blackened and fallen trunks. Torpid ladybugs clustered in the bushes awaiting spring winds to disperse them. We paused occasionally to sip our hoarded water under the flat sky. I recalled when hikers and the Forest Service had maintained backcountry trails and wondered aloud what had happened. It seemed that human activities that didn't generate cash were now forbidden.

By the time we dropped into the steep beginnings of Canada del Oro, the sun had wallowed into bluing mountains. Down we switchbacked between giant ponderosa and Douglas fir until at last I heard the reassuring trickle of water in a rocky cleft below. Uphill from an ancient fir tree whose bark was scarred by fires, we spread our sleeping bags on a carpet of needles. Black night and frost settled early into the canyon. After a supper of chicken roasted in foil, we snuggled our tired little dog between us and slept to the sough of wind in tall trees.

It had been a very dry spring, and as we descended into piñon, scrub oak, and manzanita the next day, the dancing brook began to dry up. In past years it had run strongly onto the desert floor and I had counted on this. The following afternoon found us amid yucca, cholla, and mesquite in a thirsty canyon where heat reflected from granite and sweat ran down our sun-browned faces. Suddenly our wild trek was jarred by an onslaught of off-road vehicles, pounding down the canyon and muddying the last puddles of water as they passed in a plume of exhaust, dust, and noise. The old trail through Charlou Gap—a ten-mile route over the ridge to our west—had become a mechanized playground for a new generation.

We camped that night near a last fetid pothole. It was a deep cup worn into the bedrock by the Ancient Ones who had ground mesquite beans here over the centuries. Peccary, raccoon, and deer had preceded us, and the precious water was murky and wriggling with life. Mesquite smoke from our small fire ascended the cliffs in a rosy glow of dusk. Nearly full, a waxing moon climbed the eastern sky, while daylight bled yellow into lavender along the western ridge. Faint pricks of stars appeared overhead—light from the beginning of time.

I pulled our little enamel pot of boiled water off the coals and poked at the fire. Luke and I sat in comfortable silence eating cups of rice with canned tuna and listening to the evening song of the canyon awakening from the day's heat. "Tomorrow we'll follow the road over Charlou Gap and call Dad," I said. "The track will take us down to the Oracle Highway, though I don't know where it comes out. I hate to quit early, but we can't make it without water. If Dad can get his truck a little way up the mountain, it'll help. Tomorrow is going to be a scorcher."

"I'm worried about Lucy." Luke was running a gentle hand over the exhausted dog's head. "I shouldn't have brought her. Maybe I can carry her." She was curled on his sleeping bag, too tired to eat. Her short legs were wearing down, yet at thirty-five pounds she would not be an easy load. In addition, she had a justifiable Humpty-Dumpty fear of height.

"We'll sterilize enough water to fill everything we have, even our cooking pot and plastic bags. It's at least ten miles, and the first four are uphill. Let's start before dawn." I paused a moment. "I'm sorry, this wasn't quite the trip I envisioned."

"I'm glad we came. I forget what it's like to be out here. I think the hardest part of coming back to civilization from the Arctic is the constant noise. You get numbed to it after a while, like a headache, but it's always there."

"Maybe next year we'll overwinter at the cabin. How would you like that?"

"I don't know…" He was silent a long moment. "There are so many things I want to do, I hate to waste time repeating anything."

"You'd be a major partner this trip, not a little kid. It wouldn't be the same adventure. Well, it never is, but at twelve you begin to have personal volition. That's the significance of bar mitzvah. Each of us has a unique soul journey, things we come here to remember and experience. Your parents shelter you until you're ready to take the wheel, but it's your journey."

Luke leaned into the water-smoothed granite and gazed up at the deep pool of sky where ancient stars drifted toward the fading horizon. Night was transforming the broad canyon under the magic of moonlight. Snow on the mountain behind us glinted silver-blue. An owl called. "I've always loved the moon." His voice was dreamy.

"Moon Boy," I said. "I think you were conceived under a full moon; certainly, you were born on one. 'Moon' was one of your first words. Do you remember?"

He shook his head.

"When you were little, you sometimes had 'night terrors.' You'd wake up screaming and nothing would calm you. It was like you couldn't see us. Dad would carry you outside under the open night sky. That's how we called you back."

"I've been playing with dreams," he said. "Sometimes I can stay conscious and direct my dreams. It's exciting, but also a little scary. I think I could wander off and forget to return."

"Ask for guidance in your heart. Your soul knows the way. It's always there, if you listen."

I awoke to the cold edge of dawn. The fat moon, pale as winter butter, was settling into the western ridge. We broke camp in the dark and hoisted packs, heavy with water. Three hours later, we topped Charlou Gap just as the great sun erupted from beyond the mountains at our backs. Before us, the rough track dropped over a series of ridges and descended out of sight into the smudged distance of Oro Valley, three thousand feet below. Our map did not extend to the valley floor and familiar landmarks had vanished under new construction. I stood there, trying to identify roads.

Luke took out the borrowed phone and called Tom. When he finally connected, we couldn't tell him how to locate the jeep trail. "Call Pete Cowgill," I finally said. "He'll know."

We rested only a moment before starting down. The track was steep and unbelievably rough. The sun's warmth, so pleasant at first, was a growing enemy. "Dad can't make it up here and Lucy is already looking fatigued." I said as we stood waiting for her to catch up. The little dog's head was down, her fat sides heaving.

"She can't go any faster." Luke stooped to cradle her in his arms, trying to carry her, but Lucy struggled and he soon had to put her down.

We stopped repeatedly to sip water and wet Lucy's thick fur as a white sun climbed a blank sky. The dog was slowing, lagging. She wobbled onward, tongue lolling. Birds had disappeared and even lizards lay hidden in the scant shade of palo verde. The track continued: undulating over hills, climbing and descending endlessly into the shimmering heat. One place known as "The Wall" was a smooth surface of crumbling granite not unlike an eighty-foot rampart. I couldn't believe any vehicle could climb it. We had walked perhaps six miles, yet the valley seemed no closer.

"There he is! There he is!" Luke cried out in sudden joy.

I squinted through the heat waves. Far below, I could just make out Little Red wending over boulders, jerking and spinning as Tom worked his way up the mountain. On we trudged, occasionally catching sight of him. Within half an hour, we began to hear the laboring engine—the sound growing and receding on the still air. Then suddenly the truck hove into view directly below us and we scrambled off the road, giving Tom room to maneuver on the steep mountain. Lucy collapsed, her tongue like a quivering slug in the hot sand, eyes pinched shut. Tom fought to turn the truck on the incline, racing at the hill and letting it drop back until he had it angled toward the valley. He had loaded the bed with heavy stones, which bounced and tumbled as he turned. He pulled on the parking brake and jumped out to block the tires before hugging both of us. Then he gently lifted the little dog onto the truck seat.

Luke's eyes were swimming with pride. "I knew you would find a way to get us, Dad! You saved Lucy's life."

Lucas applied for his Alaskan nursing license, but winter of 2009 was encroaching before he had it in hand. He had eaten heavily into his credit cards, but refused our offered money. In late October, he gave away everything that wouldn't fit in his Honda and prepared to move north.

"It's okay," Tom assured me. "He knows we're here if he gets in over his head."

"The Alcan, in his ancient car, at this time of year…" I thought of the battered vehicle, a window and dash lights broken from the recent theft of his prized stereo.

"It's an adventure and he's young." Tom smiled. "Remember?"

"He'll be close to us again. That makes me happy."

Lucas sounded excited when he next called. "I'm ready to leave Tucson!"

"If you don't find a job, you can spend the winter here," I said. "There's no work for new grads in Homer, but you'll have a place out of the snow—better than many."

"You have no idea. There are so many abandoned kids who never had parents like you and Dad. They've been on the streets since they were young teens."

"How's Eve doing with this?" I asked.

There was a thoughtful pause. "I'm hoping we'll reconnect in a couple of years, after we both have careers and I've grown up some. She wants marriage, a baby. I'm just not ready."

"The old biological clock," I said. "She's ten years older."

"What do you do when you meet the right one at the wrong stage of life?" His voice was soft, serious.

"Follow your heart. You have an inner compass. Trust it."

He was silent. "Gotta go, Mama. I love you. I'll call you from the road."

"Take care, Son," Tom said from the other phone. "We're here if you run into trouble."

"Buy some winter boots before you get to Canada," I advised.

"My shoes are fine." His tone was irritated. "I'm headed out tomorrow."

A few days later, Lucas called from Oregon. "Mom, I can't find my passport." His carefree tone was gone. I could hear rain drumming on the roof of his car. "What should I do?"

I tried to think. "Stop over with Laurie in Washington and go through your whole car. You can't get into Canada without a passport."

"I'll get another one over the Internet." He had ignored my suggestions about maps and used his computer to access Internet as he drove through towns. He slaved his hard drive to a reconditioned laptop and plugged it into the mangled dashboard, but it kept blowing fuses. *My impractical genius, you make your mother nuts.* I was sure he hadn't bought boots or coat. "Hey!" he said cheerfully, "I think my sunroof is leaking. Either that or my breath is condensing and dripping down. Think I ought to open it and find out?"

"No. Call us from Laurie's."

In Laurie's driveway, Lucas unpacked his treasures from the disheveled little car: teddy bears, mementos from friends, books, the forty-pound block of cement with his small handprints next to Lucy's paw prints, and the box of her ashes.

"No passport," he said. "I've checked everywhere. I did find Megan's birth certificate under my spare tire and a paycheck I forgot to cash. I ought to go through my car more often."

"Where did you last see your passport?" I asked.

"On the pile of clothes I gave to the Goodwill," he sounded proud, goading his old mom, "or maybe the homeless kid I paid to help me clean out the apartment..."

Alarm bells were jangling in my head. Lucas could tease me about his sloppiness, but this was no laughing matter. I had nagged him about preserving important papers and even bought him an oak file cabinet, yet try as I might, I could not persuade him to be cautious.

"Why don't you check out Everett, Washington?" I suggested. "It's a couple of hours north. I really liked it. Do you want me to make some calls? It's hard to get an interview unless you know somebody."

"Tell me about it. I've spent months doing online resumes and not hearing back."

THE FATE OF NATIONS CAN indeed hinge on a horseshoe nail: you miss your flight, forget to mail a letter, slip on the ice, look into the eyes of a stranger—and are swept down a different channel. That's what makes life so difficult: choosing when to strive and when to surrender. Does God, as Einstein so adamantly denied, play dice with the universe? Or does the capricious soul, knowing our immortality and caring not a whit for our comfort and security, lead us to the cliff and push us over? For four years Tom and I had cautiously ridden updrafts around the nation like a pair of migrating cranes in search of a place to land. We had maintained a nest for our only chick and plotted a safe route for him. Yet when the moment arrived, Lucas flung himself into the sky with the exuberance of a dandelion seed.

And so it came to pass through a series of near misses—or in his case near hits—that Lucas landed in Washington. The Everett hospital was building an eight-story tower and would need to staff it. They had almost completed hiring when he walked in cold and asked for his first nursing position. The manager who interviewed him said, "I'll call you." To which he replied, "I need to know by tomorrow or I'm driving on."

They hired him in orthopedics (the specialty where I started), which would give him a broad grounding in medical and surgical skills. Typical of Lucas, he was the last new grad hired, yet he could not start orientation without a Washington nursing license. He leased a set of empty rooms in the basement of an old house and moved in with his wrinkled treasures.

"Mom, you'd love it!" he told me with enthusiasm. "My apartment is within a mile of the hospital, and the street is lined with big trees! They are beautiful with fall leaves. I've been exploring everywhere—down on the docks, up in the mountains, eating new foods, walking everywhere. I'm really going to enjoy living in this city! I'll post a picture of a crab I ate in a bowl of bread. It looks creepy with the legs hanging out."

His basement had one high window for light. He called to ask his father what to do about the water oozing down the walls over the bare electrical wires.

"Pay the extra hundred a month for a safe apartment," Tom advised.

Lucas moved his few things up the steps to rooms that overlooked the ocean. His voice radiated excitement and he posted photos on the Internet of his old teddy, Oliver, dining with him along the docks or seated in his bay window like a small furry monk, gazing at the Pacific. Meanwhile, Lucas slept on a nest of rumpled clothes on the floor as rain drenched the coast and November darkened the skies. The day before Thanksgiving—and the final round of orientation for new employees—our son received his Washington nursing license and was finally employed.

That December, he wrote:

> *I give thanks to all of you in my life who have continued to cheer and encourage me. I am truly blessed to be surrounded by such an enormous community of love, support, and friendship. Because of you, I can now set my sights as high as I want. I give my heartfelt thanks to all of you and I hope you continue to bless my life with your presence.*
>
> *Lucas Irons is filled with joy, excitement, and gratitude. Standing outside in the cool night air, listening to running water in a beautiful part of the country (and with a full tummy), I am filled with contentment. I have achieved everything (down to the last detail) that I set out to do those many long years ago when I started down this path.*

OUR LIVES WERE ALSO FINDING a strong cadence in Homer. I was getting as many hours per diem as I wanted on the day shift, and we were settling into the community.

Early in the new year my brother Jeff called to tell me that our father was in hospice. Jeff had flown the old folks south in one of his larger planes for another winter in Salome, for Bud could no longer tolerate a road trip, even in a motor home. He had been moved into the impersonal care of an expensive Arizona nursing home and wouldn't be coming back to Alaska.

I phoned my father just before his death and repeated my words about stepping beyond our histories and discovering purpose in the larger journey. His whispered voice was as faint and scratchy as the flutter of a moth, but again he seemed to reach for me beyond the discord of our lives. It was a completion we both needed. He had just turned ninety-three.

Harmon Robert Helmericks: January 18, 1917 ~ January 28, 2010

TOM AND I FINALLY TURNED our attention to completing our orphaned documentary, hiring a local editor—Brian George Smith. He was a handsome man in his early fifties, tall and lean with cautious green eyes, thin graying hair, and quick, urbane humor. A talented artist, Brian had written, directed, filmed, edited, and produced two independent movies using local talent and no money. He was a reclusive fourth-generation Alaskan who still hated winter. Like Lucas, Brian seemed to live perennially on the brink. Passionate about his art, sailing, and stray cats, he spent every spare moment and dollar volunteering at the Homer Animal Shelter. His forearms were always scratched and his laptop was linty with fur.

The three of us soon formed a strong team. Brian would come bounding distastefully up our driveway through snowdrifts, arriving on the steps like some great, malnourished panther. After kicking off sodden tennis shoes, he would hunch over to give each of us a hug, and then lope up the steps to the warm loft with a mug of coffee. He was a perfectionist, prepared for creative battle, and was surprised at the depth of our footage and our ability to collaborate—a skill Tom and I had developed during our years creating glass art. We in turn were impressed with his skill and sensitivity. "Kill your darlings," Brian would say as we poured over scenes on his smudged screen. The student work was good, but voluminous, and cutting it became an act of love. There were also maddening challenges from material that had evolved through changing technology and several editing programs.

We focused on telling our authentic story. By spring, the rambling footage was honed into a layered two-and-a-half-hour documentary with music. It was still too long (and we would later cut a shorter version with special features), but in April 2010, *Arctic Son: Fulfilling the Dream* debuted at the Homer Theatre. It played as a split fundraiser for Hospice of Homer (where Tom was involved) and the Homer Animal Shelter.

Lucas flew up for a long weekend and did a radio interview with me. He was heavier now, clean-shaven and neatly trimmed, his face open though subdued. It was sleeting the night of our show, yet the theater was packed and some folks were turned away. Most in the audience remained after the presentation while Brian, Tom, Lucas, and I sat on the edge of the stage fielding questions.

"What's it like seeing yourself as a six-year-old?" someone asked Lucas.

"I'm surprised how much I'd forgotten," he said into the microphone. "I think that little boy holds a key for me. I see him as a mentor, someone to guide me back to myself."

At home we continued a quick exchange of lives. "How's Everett?" Tom asked.

"I love my apartment. I bought a quality queen-sized bed, a sofa, chair, and a set of new sheets—black like my dishes. The sofa and carpet are gray. I know you'll be happy to hear, Mama, that I'm off the floor and sleeping better."

I nodded. "I worry about your snoring. How's work?"

"I'm becoming a good nurse. I love my patients. I'm really quick on the computer, so when I get done, I've started helping others. Nobody did that before, but now I have a couple of others doing it. I say, 'Give me a five-minute chore.' If you just ask, 'Can I help?' you get a long story. Oh!" he interrupted himself, "let me show you the April Fool's joke one of the nurses played on me! I feel really honored that he cared enough to organize such an elaborate joke. He called me into the room to help him 'fix' his IV. Here, look at this!"

He pulled his phone out. He had upgraded to the newest model, loaded with medical references that even the doctors didn't have. I watched as he thumbed up a picture. He was posing beside an IV drip, looking young. He had on black scrubs and a radiant smile. At first I couldn't see the joke, then I saw the goldfish swimming in the liter of solution!

"People have been good to me," he continued, "but it's just not that easy to make close friends. They assume you have the same goals. There's a unit assistant who's very motherly. She thinks what I need is to settle down, get a house, marry. She can't understand my dreams of exploring the world. She means well and cares about me.

"I never really fit in anywhere, I guess. I have to admit I hadn't realized what it means to live in a university town. Everett is working class: bar fights and dumb behavior. I miss the intellect." He laughed. "Last week there was a guy who pulled off his clothes and hid behind parked cars, darting out to scare drivers—typical canine behavior! I get plenty of off-the-clock experience in my own neighborhood. People call me when they get hurt or do something stupid. I leave my phone on."

"You should work in ER and get paid," I said. "You don't have to live it."

"I live in downtown Everett," he answered, as if that explained everything. "Besides, I like being the go-to guy. It's not Guatemala, but it's close. Remember, Dad, when you came to get us at Charlou Gap? I like being the friend people can count on. You taught me that."

"We've had some good times," Tom said. They exchanged warm smiles.

"Meet any pretty girls?" I asked.

"Pretty is not important to me." His tone was patient. "No, Mom, there's no particular girl. Mostly, I hang with kids at the bar and listen. They don't say much of value, but it's fun. I walk into the Alligator Soul restaurant and someone calls out, 'Hey, it's Lucas!' and the band plays my song, *Ain't No Sunshine*. They serve me half a pig with beans. They take me into the kitchen, treat me like one of them. It's like a big family."

"Wow!" Tom said. "You've only been in town a few months and already you're making friends. That's really cool."

I kept quiet with my opinion about eating half a pig. Tom, with his gentle and positive words, brought out the sparkle in Lucas's generous face. I was tired of hearing my own advice.

Lucas grinned happily. "This is the first thing I've really created for myself. I arrived in town knowing no one and I've made it mine."

THAT SPRING UNCLE BERT FOLLOWED his beloved Janet in a dignified passage. I spoke with him a couple of weeks before his old heart gave out. He was as clear and centered as ever, and plainly looked forward to whatever lay next. Neither of them had been religious, yet they had faced mortality with calm acceptance. I was going to Arizona in June to support Faith during the birth of her first baby and the family agreed to schedule Bert's memorial around my plans. I was traveling, as always, with little money.

"I planned to stop in Everett, but it's just too complicated and expensive," I told Lucas when he called. "I'll visit you when we get back from the cabin next fall."

"I want to show you my place," he said. He was walking to work, striding the mile up tree-lined streets. I could hear occasional traffic and a slight wheeze when he laughed. He had just finished relating a comic tale of a recent misadventure. "I hear that Megan wants to go north with you this summer."

"Yes. She called last week. If she's serious, I'll bring her back from Arizona."

He was silent a moment. "I wish I could see her. Truthfully, I'm a bit jealous. I wish I could come too."

"Your turn will come again," I told him. "Finish your two-year commitment, and you can go anywhere."

"I'm walking into the hospital, Mama. Gotta go. I love you."

My trip to Arizona was an exercise in serendipitous living. Bert-Son and Nadine picked me up at the Phoenix airport and drove into the mountains where our loosely connected clan gathered from several states at Standwell, the little cabin we had all helped to build. We were a diverse group, bonded by our love for two remarkable people. We shed tears, told stories, ate, and laughed around a fire under the old ponderosas, and then we took turns sprinkling Bert's ashes into a shallow hole next to Janet's. I thought of my two families and their legacies: my father with his "thousand-year trust," which had spawned bitterness and lawsuits, and Bert and Janet who celebrated everyone with open hearts.

Albert B. Cutler, Jr.: December 12, 1920 ~ March 23, 2010

∼

I RECALLED THE WORDS OF Phil Gordon, a Homer friend: "People say, 'You're born alone and you die alone.' Well, that's not the story I want. I wasn't born alone—I know at least Mom was there—and I don't plan on dying alone." Then Phil, who loves adventure and whose little home perches on a crumbling cliff above the ocean, had grinned. "I'll probably take some of you with me!" *That wouldn't be a bad way to go*, I decided. *Over the cliff, down in the sea—with friends.*

After Standwell, Bert and Nadine dropped me off at a gas station on the Black Canyon Freeway where Stan and Ruthie picked me up for the next leg of my casual journey. From Prescott, I took the bus to Phoenix—being passed along in a chain of friendship. Faith's son Kody had been born by the time I arrived in Tucson, but Annie was there to welcome her first grandchild. *What would happen*, I wondered, *if I simply live the day that arrives? Maybe all my plans and lists are unnecessary.*

Driving around Tucson in my rental car was oddly completing: a time warp of remembered events viewed through the perspective of sixty years. I caught unexpected glimpses of myself, mostly struggling and uncertain, as I drove about town.

At Roskruge Elementary, seven-year-old Jeanie comes out of the candy store wearing a blue-and-black plaid dress, sash untied. Her knees are scuffed from gathering "sand rubies" at recess and her blonde hair is pulled back in skimpy braids. She has on dusty saddle shoes and carries a metal lunch pail with milk leaking from a broken glass thermos. Crumpled tin foil inside is saved to make a halter for her invisible horse. It smells of tuna and whole wheat. Popular kids eat peanut butter and jelly on white bread. There are freckles across her nose and her two front teeth seem large and new. She trudges past, engrossed in some fantasy, and I smile fondly. She seems to pause a moment and look up. The traffic light turns green. "It's going to be okay," I whisper as I drive on. "You will turn out, and life will be good. Trust yourself."

At the corner of Speedway and Fourth Avenue, four-year-old Jeanie is coming home from nursery school. She's in the front seat of a brown station wagon loaded with kids. Little Annie is in back, wedged against the door. As the car turns, the door swings open and Annie tumbles into traffic. An older woman, her face ashen, comes running between the cars with Annie clutched in her arms. My sister's mouth is open, screaming. She looks small and terrified. *I wasn't paying attention*, Little Jeanie thinks. My future life is built upon that four-year-old's decision: *I must be vigilant.* Perhaps it is time to choose again.

Along Sixth Street, I catch sight of teenage Jeanie, angry and hurt, walking miles home from her boyfriend's house in the dark after some disagreement. Phil Beisel will become her first husband and they will have wonderful adventures in the Arctic. I know this, but all she sees is a blank wall. *The river moves. Nothing that is real can be lost, yet nothing remains unchanged.* Again I surround this anxious teenager with affection.

Maybe we are the ones who save ourselves. "Here I am," we reassure those younger selves. "Enjoy your short ride through this magical kingdom. It's going to be okay."

Tom teaches Megan, age twelve, to fish, Kernwood 2010.

Tom and I start up King Mountain, fall 2011.

Chapter 34

SONG OF FRIENDSHIP

September 2010

Megan is seated beside me on the plane back from Arizona. She's almost thirteen, an awkward and ponderous adolescent who seems to steer rather than inhabit her young body. Eve hopes our simple life will help her daughter recover balance on the path through puberty.

"Is this your idea or your mother's?" I had asked Megan before we agreed to the summer.

"Mine."

"You know that once we get there, you'll be stuck for three months?"

"Yeah…" She's still not much of a conversationalist.

Lucas is wistful, yet pleased when I call him. "It'll be so good for her," he says.

"Maybe you can get a leave of absence next summer," I suggest.

The old Beaver sets the three of us down on our familiar sandbar at Kernwood. Megan helps me haul supplies up from the swollen river, then climbs into the sleeping loft to fashion a nest of bedding, clothes, and books in Rude's old corner. Here she roosts the first few days. She is appalled by the mosquitoes and seems to view her sojourn as an endless sentence. Sequestered from media and peers, she goes through withdrawal—as Luke had at thirteen. Eve has paid for two hundred satellite phone minutes and Megan lives for these brief calls. Tom and I are gentle and undemanding, inviting her to join in our projects. This summer we plan to enlarge the west windows and lower the cabin floor using the boards Rude made from the Grandmother Tree.

"You're pupating," I tell Megan one sun-streaked evening. "Like a butterfly." I stroke her dark hair and she leans against me on the padded wooden sofa built into the logs along the west wall. Big, brown eyes peer up through curly lashes. "Everyone goes through it—times of transformation. You have to trust the process. You'll turn out better than you can imagine."

"Stuck in the Arctic with a couple of old trolls," she says wryly. It is only half in jest.

I too wonder why she is here. I sense no deep yearning for wilderness. Still she is slowly evolving: opening, slimming down, and cautiously moving into her body. A generation that leaps virtual buildings with the click of a mouse has no gauge for jumping a puddle. She gets lost within yards of the cabin. She is frustrated with herself.

"I want to hike up Mount Laurie," she tells us. I realize that she wants to try everything Luke did. Perhaps that is why she's here—a quest for connection.

"That's a fourteen-hour hike," I caution. "It looks closer because the air is so clear. Why don't we try Annie's Peak first?" I have yet to see her walk a mile.

Megan studies the ancient humans who share this scary land with her. If we can do it, she can too. "Okay."

But she's not up to it. She is angry and withdrawn when I pause along Luke's Creek and build a lunch fire. The bugs and country have beaten her. "Would you like to turn back?" I ask.

She won't look at me but swings her arms at mosquitos. I cut a willow twig and show her how to swish around her shoulders. "It's okay," I assure her. "You're getting stronger every day."

Megan remains in the cabin playing endless rounds of solitaire at our hand-hewn table, but gradually she begins to speak of her life: the pressures for sex, drugs, gangs in school. It's a dangerous and complex world our young ones navigate behind their plastic surfaces. I try to listen like Janet would and help her assess consequences. She reads through her collection of teen romances and begins to pick more thoughtful books from our stored totes. Tom brings in old favorites—Mary Stewart's four books on Merlin, John Irving's *A Prayer for Owen Meany*—and reads them aloud. He's an excellent reader, making her laugh with Owen's scratchy voice.

"You can write your own script," I tell her. "You don't have to color within the lines. Don't follow someone who's unhappy or mean. My grandmother used to say, 'The proof of the pudding is in the eating.' "

She turns thirteen in August and we name Mount Megan for her, visible from the bluff. It's another wet summer and again there's an abundance of mushrooms. They erupt in myriad shapes and colors from the deep moss and from between scarlet and butter-yellow leaves. There are fleshy fungi the size of dinner plates with knurled edges—sensual as the lips of giant clams—on stems like broom handles, and villages of rounded pagodas the color of brass. Some are gray and fluted; others are like lacy parasols, no bigger than peppercorns. There are translucent mushrooms and ones that appear as solid as rock, mushrooms of ivory, hairy mushrooms, black ones, and great reptilian platters.

One day as Megan dutifully follows us on a short walk, she is drawn into the fairyland of lichen, moss, autumn colors, and mushrooms. For two hours she impishly leads us on a winding exploration through the diminutive kingdom of Kernwood Forest, weaving between the trees and hopping across Trickle Creek. There is new grace and confidence in her stride. *Seeds take time to sprout*, I remind myself. That's my lesson—don't keep pulling them up to check their roots.

Megan chooses to work with me on Creek Trail and is learning to swing an ax. It's cool now, and the bugs are mostly gone. "Jeanie," she says. I straighten, breathing in the ripe smells of autumn. The river has turned to emerald and the creek is a friendly clear presence. I wait while Megan searches for words. Suddenly she blurts, "If you hadn't helped Mom and me, I don't know what would have happened to us. We owe you everything!" She starts to cry.

This is so unexpected! I put my arms around her. "You are so worth it," I say. Her simple words make the whole summer worthwhile for me.

The Kenai gang arrive in the valley, two planes roaring low over the cabin to see if the old guardians are still here. As before, they camp upriver and do not trouble us much. A few floating hunters stop in for coffee and to admire our cabin. We make them welcome, feeding them blueberry pie. I think of Peace Pilgrim saying that when we treat others as inherently good, they glimpse goodness in themselves.

Freezing temperatures arrive on a gusting north wind. The scarlet and gold leaves turn to rust, wither, and blow away. Spruce trees stand silhouetted against a colorless sky and morning fog blankets the river. Geese are leaving early, great phalanxes splitting the clouds in determined wedges, their excited voices reminding me of tenacity and adventure. I recall how they travel together, a bonded community, encouraging and supporting each another.

"Do you want to hunt?" I ask. We haven't killed a moose in eleven years. "We could dry most of the meat for hiking next summer." Rude has assured us he will come, and I'm hoping Lucas can join us. *Maybe we can hike to the Divide.*

"I'd like that," Megan says. Her voice is excited.

"It's a big responsibility, taking life," I tell her. "We have to haul it all home and dry it."

"The only way we can realistically do it," Tom reiterates, "is to take a small bull, close to home, early in the day. We can't carry that weight any distance and I don't want to be out on a kill with the bears after dark."

"The jerky would serve us for several years," I decide. "It would be a good experience for Megan too." I have a license, but I don't even fish. I cringe at violence and yet I eat some meat—a contradiction in values.

She nods eagerly. "I'll help."

Early one morning out on the delta, I glimpse a young bull. My mother's old rifle rests comfortably in my hand. I have carried it hundreds of miles, though I haven't fired it in a decade. It has open sights and I must move in close through the willows. After all my mental deliberation, a deep and silent place within me makes the heart shot. The moose lies on his side in the sand as Tom and Megan arrive. Dawn is clear and cool, the sun still behind Mount Laurie. We stand quietly together and thank the great animal for his life. I am saddened that a chance encounter has turns a vibrant life into steaks and roasts. I am grateful too for the gift of food and for his clean death. *That's what we all hope for, is it not? A quick death.*

We build a fire, claiming the bar. True to her word, Megan helps skin and gut the moose, and we all work to get the meat safely stashed in the cool storehouse. Off comes the slippery weight of hide. "Careful not to kick sand!" Out comes the great pile of guts. He was still feeding, and the cooling carcass smells sweet and good, not "rutty" as it would in a few days—during breeding season. Heavy and slick, the quarters are heaved onto tarps and covered from the birds. Our jays are hauling away tidbits as fast as they can fly. Ravens sit patiently across the river and sing. A lone seagull rides at anchor just off shore. Word carries down the wind. Food!

"Let's try using the log-hauling wheel," Tom decides. We slice the animal into nine pieces: neck, spine, pelvis, two rib sections, four legs. Some weigh close to a hundred fifty pounds. The moose becomes unrecognizable except for the severed head, now divested of its modest antlers. Megan sits in the sand next to it, stroking his soft nose and peering into large glassy eyes, the color of her own.

"Taking life is no small thing." I kneel in the sand beside her. "This is no different from the hamburger you eat in Tucson, except you get to see this animal. Whenever you eat meat, an animal has died. You can thank that life or you can choose to be a vegetarian. Now you know."

She doesn't answer.

"Our job is to make sure none of it goes to waste and that we don't endanger other animals. Come, let's haul the guts, hide, and head back into the willows so that bears and wolves won't be shot by floating hunters. Other animals will celebrate too. Listen to the ravens!" From the forest comes a musical "*plunk!*" like falling water.

Obediently, Megan stands, cradling the great head in her arms, and follows me. By evening, the bar is empty and the meat is safely hung. The next ten days are spent smoking, slicing, drying, and sorting jerky. Megan joins in the endless cutting, stringing, and turning of meat. I am ready to become a vegetarian. Little is wasted. We boil sinewy parts and dry the cooked and shredded meat as "machaca," which will keep years and can be rehydrated for cooking. We keep two hundred pounds of fresh meat to transport back to Homer. Wolves, bears, and ravens discover our gift in the willows. Ravens come by to sing to us and White Wolf climbs our trail to leave a large "thank you" scat packed with moose hair near the cabin.

One evening a floating hunter stops in with a strange tale. Two years before, he and another man had pulled their raft ashore below a cutbank just downstream from our cabin. They were eating when they spotted a great, golden bear across the river. They shot and the bear fell thrashing into the brush. Suddenly, it rose, looked straight at them, and struck out across the river toward them. The current was swift, but the bear was determined.

"In all my years hunting bears, I never saw one do that," the hunter says. "We both emptied our rifles into that swimming bear." Just before it reached shore, the blond head sank into the fast, muddy current. Our guest tells how he ran along the bank and plunged into the river. "That bear rolled over and reached up for me! It wasn't a muscle spasm—he really wanted me! I jumped back and ran along the shore. The second time I went in, his movements were weaker, and then they ceased. He really had it in for us!"

Goldie, I think, my heart suddenly cold as muddy water. *Why?*

THE YOUNG PERSON THAT WE put on the plane in Fairbanks in late September was a very different girl from the one who had arrived only three months earlier. There were tears in Megan's eyes as she hugged her "old trolls" goodbye at the boarding gate.

"Do you think she'll call?" Tom asked wistfully as we watched the jet taxi out.

"Probably not," I said, looping my arm about his waist. "That doesn't mean anything."

Lucas sounded harried when I reached him on the Wartses' phone. "I'm working double shifts," he told me, "seventeen hours a day. There's always something—car insurance, a broken tooth, paying off my credit cards, rent." We were silent a moment. I knew he didn't want my advice. "I don't know who I am anymore," he said at last, sounding discouraged. "I eat too much, I drink too much. I started smoking..."

"You're smoking!" *My kid with asthma?!*

"Oh, just sometimes. I don't know... what happened."

"Not-knowing is a powerful place," I said, tentatively. "Most of us spend the first half of our lives wearing shoes that don't fit." I thought of Lucas, so eager to leave home at seventeen, not as certain now at twenty-three. It was my hardest lesson too—watching him go through pain. I remembered Bert-Son saying, "I care and I don't care. Perhaps failure is the experience they need."

"I plan to visit you once I get settled back at home," I said. "We can talk."

"I'd like that." His voice was gentle. "I'd love to show you my town and introduce you to the people I work with. And Mom..." he hesitated, "I've been thinking about the Arctic Continental Divide."

I felt the wind whisper between his words, and saw an eagle riding high over snowy peaks. "Yes," I answered quietly. "Whenever you are ready."

Stars hung bright in the frosted dawn above Kachemak Bay when I called Annie. "What can I do to help Lucas?" I asked her. She had worried over her own children, watching them struggle for footing.

"There is nothing wrong with Lucas," she told me. "He's luminous and beautiful! I know you think he's fat, but he's like a big Buddha. People love him and he loves them. He doesn't have any judgments and they know they can trust him. Jeanie, it's his life now. You need to celebrate him and let him live it."

Gazing from my loft window at the changing light on the bay, I knew that despite my fears, life continued to turn out better than planned. *The universe wishes us joy*, I realized. *Life is supposed to be fun.* That's the part we forget. I sat in the growing dawn and wondered: *Was it possible I'd been so intent on helping my son that I failed to see him? Who could he ask for advice that was perhaps less critical?* Closing my eyes, I imagined him on our love seat, his arms extended along the back. He was smiling that gentle Buddha smile. Then I saw a little boy of about four walk up and lean on his knee. The child laughed and Lucas lifted him into his big lap. With a start, I realized it was young Luke. Out of the shadows came another one, this time about twelve. Soon there were perhaps ten of them, all ages happily encircled in his big arms. One was even holding baby Luke. *My son*, I realized, *is complete. He has all the wisdom he needs.*

When I called Lucas to tell him of my vision, he said, "Thank you, Mama. I appreciate your Golden Light. There are times that I really need it. I don't need your good ideas or advice, but your Light is always welcome."

Next to my bed I kept a little pewter figure he had given me: a mama koala with a baby on her back. Around the baby, I placed the child's diamond ring that Luke bought me when he was about eight. These I draped with a little necklace that said, "Mom." Each night I looked at them, surrounding him with Golden Light. As I studied the small figures, I suddenly wondered if I wasn't the little one on the back, and he the bigger one. *Who is the master and who the student? Do we ever know?*

Rude called in October for one of his long talks. I had tried to reach him all week, a quiet urgency tugging at my mind. Tom took the call and then dialed Rude right back to save him money. I could hear them laughing. They talked for half an hour before Tom handed the phone to me. I settled back on the love seat in our loft with a cup of tea.

Rude was somehow gentler, smoother. "It's funny," he confessed, "but ever since summer at your cabin—especially when someone's been visiting—I get lonesome. I never felt that way before. I've called most of my friends this summer. I'm almost becoming social."

"You can phone us any time. I have plenty of minutes on my calling card."

"I really appreciate that. I've had no work all summer."

"You can always live here," I teased. I pictured the three of us playing together along Kachemak Bay, turning over rocks in the tide pools, catching fish, cutting firewood. "You're coming north with us next summer? We have jerky now, as much as you can eat. I'll send you some. We'll climb King Mountain early in the season and find your knife." It was unlike Rude to lose something, but he had set his pocketknife down in our camp that snowy morning.

"I've been thinkin' hard about coming. I told Tom where to find that knife."

"We'll find it together. With jerky. How's your house coming?"

"Ah, Jeanie, I'm slowin' down, but I'm getting it done. It's a lot more comfortable than when you were here. You could move right in." We both laughed. It was that old question: who was going to move so we could play together in the woods?

"Are you learning to use your body like a friend?" I asked.

"It ain't that easy, you know."

"Different journeys for different times of life," I reminded him. He'd heard it before.

"You should have seen me when I was young." I'd heard that before.

"The Rude I see is perfect right now." There was a pause. "How are your dogs?"

"I'm down to just one old dog. You would laugh: I let him stay in the house until he gets too hot. He goes for walks with me like an old friend."

I smiled, thinking: *You never know where the river will take you, but when you arrive, you say, "Of course! This is where I was headed all along."*

"Jeanie," his tone became serious, inflecting down on the last syllable, "I know you won't laugh at me, so I have to tell you something. I had the strangest experience. A friend told me about feeling the energy of the planet. I went out in the woods and just stood, pressing my back against a big tree with my eyes closed. I could really feel it! Like a powerful current coming up from the Earth through my whole body with each breath. I stood there a long time. I don't know if I believe that stuff," there was wonder in his voice, "but when I opened my eyes—for several minutes—everything was the deepest shade of blue I've ever seen. Cobalt, I think they call it."

"Experience is always real," I said quietly.

He was silent for a moment. "I tried to call Luke."

"Yeah. It's not easy with his schedule." Lucas worked evenings and slept much of each day. *That, and he sometimes disregards his phone.*

"Well, when you talk with him, give him 'two beats' from Old Rude." I heard him thump his chest, just over his heart.

THE NEXT DAY, RUDE WAS gone, vanished like a flame dropped into the sea—though no one knew it. He was alone in the forest, cutting firewood for a friend, when the rotten heart of a great tree gave way. It shattered up the trunk, twisted down, and drove him into the ground. As agile as he was, it must have happened very fast.

His wife Marge phoned to tell us. Rude had failed to visit her as planned. Though they had long been separated, they remained friends. She must have spent a lifetime awaiting his call, knowing he was out somewhere on the edge. It was getting dark by the time she arrived at his place. She knew something was wrong when she found his dog locked in the kennel with an empty water bowl. It would have bothered Rude that his last old dog went unfed while he lay in the woods for two days. Marge phoned a neighbor and they located his truck. At first they walked around calling, but then she remembered how Rude, so deliberate in everything, always left a trail of bent twigs—just in case. She found him by following those twigs.

Rude was lying in a sandy hollow that was filled with colorful, autumn leaves. "It was a beautiful spot," she told us. "The kind of place he would have chosen to curl up and take a nap. He would have called it 'just his size.'"

It seemed a perfect departure for Rude—alone in the woods that he loved. He never wanted to grow old and feeble, and he wouldn't have appreciated any deathbed scenario. How like him to slip out the backdoor and die privately beneath the forest sky while those of us who loved him were gathered around the front. He was far away before any of us could pull at him with our grief, our expectations, our pleas for one more hour, for one more blessed day. I try to visualize him, not lying like a broken butterfly in the drifting autumn leaves, but moving forward curiously, with that slight crouch, his hazel eyes intent on the mysterious blue Light. In one hand he carries a feather; the other is open and forward, palm down—like a dancer or a fighter—the way I often saw him move. His face is shining with wonder as he steps silently into this grand new adventure.

It was a huge funeral, people coming for miles. The lone wolf had made a difference in ways that he never realized. Perhaps that's always true. Flowers germinate in our footsteps, though we do not look back. Only when a flame among us goes out, do we pause to notice how beautiful we are—angels in common clothing. Tom, Lucas, and I were not alone in seeing Rude as special, but I like to think we had a special place in his life. Maybe he made each person feel that way. I had hoped we would age together like wrinkled children with no one to make us stay inside on rainy days. I miss that future. I'm not the only one. I think of Marge and how she waited, and of his beloved children and grandchildren. He cherished each of us and yet eluded us all, the unicorn who refused domestication. I imagine him far away, maybe up on King Mountain or camped above the gorge with the wild creek below. I see him spreading his arms gracefully into the wind. Flying.

Losing Rude tinted the autumn of 2010 in sepia tones for me. I missed his thoughtful observations and the way he made Tom laugh. There seemed a shadow across my path. It didn't incapacitate me and yet the light was diminished, as if the moon had vanished from the night sky. To be honest, my world without Rude seemed scarier too. I had trusted him to quietly guard my back, knowing that if I ever needed my Friend, he would be there. I caught myself reaching for the phone, longing to speak with him. As a child, I knew that I could fly—but I couldn't quite remember how. In the same way, I now searched for Rude—an achingly one-way conversation. Nevertheless, if I listened into the rosy dawn, I could almost hear his voice.

"Tell me, Jeanie…" that familiar, downward inflection at the end of my name.

Timothy Amerud: April 18, 1949 ~ October 10, 2010

OUR LIFE SETTLED DOWN WITH friendships and stability. The hospital needed me and our documentary was selling modestly. I finally extricated Takahula Lake from Bud's trust, freeing Annie and me. I sold my share to pay off our home and buy an adjoining lot. All but a small copse of spruce and birch had been cleared, but the land was rapidly regrowing high in alders and I was again planting trees. I was grateful for this gift from my mother, as from my window I watched a mamma moose bedding down with her twins.

Tom was putting a beautiful meal on the table: halibut caught with his old friend, Guy Rosie, potatoes grown in our garden, blueberry pie from Kernwood, and the last of our summer kale. Late evening sun flooded the bank of southern windows, illuminating our home. Sixty miles southwest, the frozen volcanic island of Saint Augustine floated on a placid, orange sea. A sliver of moon hung low over the snowy mountains across the bay. The house was ours now in more than title, for Tom's handmade furniture filled the corners—warm and real. The woodstove Bert-Son had given us was installed in the center of our lofted living room.

"It's time to visit Lucas," I said.

Tom considered a moment. "I think you should go alone. You can stay in his small place and two is a good number."

I nodded. "Maybe you can ride the ferry north with him next spring."

"I always love traveling with him."

Lucas was dressed in sea-green scrubs when his decrepit Honda pulled up to the curb outside SeaTac Airport. He hopped out to envelop me in a hug and then tossed my luggage into his trunk where the cement block with Lucy's paw prints was wedged next to his spare tire. Wires still protruded from his cracked dashboard, but he had plugged his cell phone into the speakers for music.

"I am so glad you came!" His shaved face was beaming, cowlick defying a new haircut. "I cleaned out my room and washed the sheets for you." November drifted golden through the open window as he accelerated onto the freeway.

"Where are you gonna sleep? I don't wanna take your bed. You're over six feet tall." He was also quite heavy now, a sight that made me sad.

"Over six foot one," he corrected. "It seems I'm still growing." He rested a big hand on my knee. "It's okay. I'll sleep on the sofa. I work night shift and tend to stay awake at night. I'll be fine on the sofa."

"Maybe we can hot-bunk it," I suggested. "I'll get the bed at night and you can have it in the daytime. I know you're working Sunday, so I'll take the shuttle back and let you sleep in."

"We'll see," he waved away my concerns. "I really don't need much sleep. I want you to meet my friends. My girlfriend Misty is nervous, so you probably won't see her. I tell all my friends to contact you with their problems. I say, 'My mom is like Gandhi. She'll know what to say.'"

I coughed. "No wonder she's worried! As if meeting 'the mother' isn't hard enough! Seriously? Gandhi!"

His eyes flicked over at me, impishly. "Well, it's true."

"Tell me about this girlfriend."

"Oh, we haven't much in common, but you'll like her. She's twenty-one, shy—kinda a lost kid who's had a rough time. She came to Everett with her sister last year, then her sister died of swine flu. Her car was totaled on the freeway, she lost her job, and her little dog got sick. I spent a thousand dollars on vet bills, but he died. I hope you can talk to her."

"Certainly, if she wants to." *A thousand dollars?*

"I'm excited about showing you my town. I'm really proud of pulling it all together by myself!" He showered me with another smile. "I'm taking you to dinner at Alligator Soul tonight and then we'll go by Tailgaters, where I hang out. I want to walk in the woods. I'd like to drive you into the mountains, but we probably don't have time. I almost got stuck in the snow there last week. Misty thought I was nuts for making snow angels, but I did get her to play. I love the snow!"

"I see you got the shoes I sent. You're not mad?"

"Mad? No, they're great! I really don't use my car much anymore. It needs work and insurance is expensive. Walking is better for me anyway. I'm thinking of letting my insurance lapse. I can always put it back on with a call. Sorry I had to take you off my cell plan, but was too expensive, so I switched programs."

"That's okay. I only used it to talk to you. Do you read my emails? I wrote all those essays for you, you know."

"Oh, they're on my computer. I will someday." Again the impish grin.

"I'm writing about you in my next book. I hope you don't mind."

"Naw. My life's open. Anyway, I trust you."

"Did you ever read my last book?"

"Seriously, yes. Don't look surprised. Sometimes I reread it, just to remind myself, and I lend it to people if I want them to really know me."

We dropped my luggage at his apartment. The place was messy, though the bedroom had been cleaned for my visit. Oliver, Pooh Bear, and a host of familiar faces, along with some new teddy bears were arranged on the stack of pillows. Large framed photos of our family and Luke as a child lined the mantle in the living room next to the box of Lucy's ashes.

Lucas took my hand as we walked the mile to Providence Hospital, where he proudly showed me the orthopedics unit and introduced me to his coworkers. Faces lit up when they saw him—and not just nurses. He was friends with the cleaning staff and kitchen workers. We stopped at the nurse's station and he introduced me to a tall young man.

"Lucas will try anything," the other nurse told me. To my astonishment, he took a step, pitched forward, tucked and rolled onto his shoulder, and ended lightly on his feet. "I've spent years in martial arts. So Lucas sees me do that entering a patient's room and says, 'Cool!' The next thing I hear is 'BAM!' and he's down like a brick! Dude!"

"Ow…" Lucas whined. They were both laughing.

We stopped next in the break room, where his locker was pasted with notes of acknowledgment from staff and patients. "That's really impressive!" I said. Lucas grinned and opened the locker. Inside, a flurry of thank-you notes drifted in the sudden breeze.

"You should keep those in a folder," I advised, "build your resume and get trained in Advance Cardiac Life Support. You'd be great in emergency or intensive-care nursing. You have the brains for it. Now that you have your footing, get a specialty."

"Ah, Mama. You know I'm too lazy." He stretched and yawned broadly, furry belly peeking out from beneath his scrubs. "Besides, I'm committed to my unit," he said in a serious tone. "Remember me telling you how I offer to do a 'five minute chore' for other nurses when I'm caught up? Well, everyone is doing it now. Besides, see the new tower?" he pointed through a window. "We're moving next spring. All new!"

"Are you still thinking about a few weeks at the cabin this summer?" I asked.

He didn't answer immediately. We were walking toward the cafeteria, where he would treat me to lunch on his badge. "Maybe the summer after. I'll be free to negotiate a leave of absence or quit after my two years. They took me in when no one else was hiring. I owe them."

Alligator Soul was packed that night, but the waiter cleared a place for us close to the stage. Lucas ordered for us both, with a seafood Creole dish for me. He wanted everything to be perfect for my visit. The music was excellent—a soul-blues-folk group led by a black man who looked to be in his seventies and was so lively that I feared for his heart.

The old man stepped to the microphone and announced to the crowd, "This is for Lucas and his Mama tonight, who came down here to visit him from Alaska!" Then the band struck up *Ain't No Sunshine*. Lucas beamed at me and cocked his head, watching my reaction. I thought suddenly of Connie's last outing to Sunset House, of how I wanted her to know that she didn't have to worry about me. She could die knowing that I was launched and flying strongly in my own life.

Jeanie and Tom, Kernwood, 2015.

Lucas at age twenty-three.

Chapter 35

Straight on 'til Morning

Spring 2011

Lucas's shy girlfriend Misty was a heavy girl with enormous, hurt blue eyes. I soon opened a discussion about the losses in her short life. Within a week of my return to Homer, Misty emailed.

"Lucas warned me that you could be kind of intense," she wrote. "I was joking with him after you left and asked if you knew how to make small talk. Of course he said, 'No,' which is a bit intimidating. My sister was always the focus in my life and I'm not ready to see her death as a blessing. She was supposed to be with me until we were old and gray. I lost a part of myself along with her. I have lost sight in many things in my life since I moved to Everett. You put that seed back in my mind."

I wrote back. "I didn't say her death was 'a blessing,' just that resisting doesn't change it. You are the only one who can find meaning in any event. Freedom comes in being willing to experience whatever happens. Be present. Feel the pain until it burns away. When you love completely, knowing this moment is temporary and nothing will hold it still, even pain becomes a gift—which is also temporary. At the core we are One, which is what you might call God. I don't use that word often, for it evokes too many different images. Your sister has her own path. Her gift to you might be to experience that you are complete and that she never left. Sit quietly sometime, close your eyes, and have a conversation with her. Try it."

During the months that followed we deepened this dialogue, and gradually Misty began to look up. We never discussed Lucas, for I did not want to pry, but I did ask her to call me if ever there was a serious need. I doubted anyone else in Everett had our number.

Lucas phoned early in the year. "My patient last night was an old woman who was found down after two days with a broken hip. I've never seen anyone so skinny. No one cares about her. There were orders to place a feeding tube, but I just couldn't do it! Mama, she was crying, and all I could do was hold and rock her. I promised her that I wouldn't force her. I spent my whole shift feeding her three spoonfuls of pudding. What should I do?"

"Contact the ethics committee. Speak to the chaplain. Go up the chain of command. She has a right to refuse treatment. There are worse things than dying."

He called me a few days later. "I did what you suggested. They put her on comfort care and she died last night, but she didn't die alone or unloved!" I could hear tears in his voice.

"You did the right thing, Son." We were quiet for a moment. "This is hard to ask, but will you serve as second after Dad as my Power of Attorney? We're updating our medical directives."

"Yes, of course."

"You know, I don't want any heroic measures."

"I watched the sun come up last week with a beautiful woman of ninety-four, who was sharp as a tack. She enjoyed her morning coffee with me. You can be old and still have a quality life."

"I don't want to be turned and changed every two hours…"

"Mama," he stopped me. "You may not know when it's time, but I will. You can trust me."

"Thank you." Again we paused and I could feel his warm smile.

"I often volunteer to take care of bariatric patients," he said. Those that are morbidly obese. "No one wants them. Everything is harder and of course they're sicker. Wounds don't heal and they can't ambulate. Toileting. You can really hurt yourself caring for a five-hundred-pound person."

"Don't you hurt yourself! You could end up injured for life if you're not careful."

"I am careful," he said in a neutral tone that warned me not to nag. "I take good care of them. The lives of these people are the definition of 'living hell.' I always start my shift by introducing myself. 'I'm Lucas and I will be your nurse and advocate tonight,' I tell them. 'I'll be rounding on you every hour, but you can always call me for anything.'"

"You're a good man, Lucas, and a good nurse. You're also a good writer. Maybe we'll write a book together someday."

"I'm beginning to write again, did I tell you? It helps me sort out my feelings. I'm so glad I can talk to you. Other people have no idea of our work."

"You should marry a nurse. Dad worked as an aide when I was in nursing school so that we would stay connected. It's a tough profession—the things we see."

"I don't think I'll ever marry." He sounded sad. "Eve has a boyfriend now, did you know?"

"No, but I'm not surprised. It's time."

"Gotta go, Mama. I'll call on my walk to work tomorrow. Oooh! It's snowing again!"

APRIL 2, 2011. IT'S COLD and dark. I bolt from bed at the explosion of a phone and find myself standing in the loft. A new moon gives no light, and stars gleam dimly on the crusted snow. It must be an emergency at the hospital—they wouldn't call me otherwise, not after a day of work. I am fatigued and disoriented. The connection is poor, but in the background I hear a heart monitor and alarms—that unmistakable *Beep! Beep!* Someone's heart, performing badly.

"I can't hear you!" I say. I am naked, shivering. The woodstove in the living room below has gone out and the heater is set to sixty-two degrees to conserve fuel oil. "Step away from the heart telemetry! It's interfering with reception." *All hell must be breaking loose up there.* "Move away from the tele monitor!" Finally, I hang up and then dial the hospital.

The place is serene. "No," Donna says in surprise. "Nothing unusual going on here."

I slide back into the high captain's bed that Tom built. He opens the warmth of his abdomen to my chilled back and legs. "What was it?" He mumbles.

"I don't know." *Maybe a time warp. A bad dream?* "I thought it was the hospital, but there's no trouble up there." I drift into his warmth, but my brain is coming awake. *Maybe a wrong number… what else? Lucas!*

I slip from bed and pad across the carpet into the office, pulling on my robe. The phone lights and I punch the numbers. Misty answers—her voice shaky and shrill. "Lucas just passed out! We were eating with friends, and he just turned white and slumped over! I did CPR and they called 911. When the ambulance came, they wouldn't let me go with him!"

"You did CPR? Chest compressions? His heart stopped?"

"Yes! All I could think was to grab his phone when they took him!"

I am awake now, but strangely quiet inside, like when the bear charged Tom, or a baby is stuck in the pelvis—hundreds of trial runs for responding to emergencies. I take a breath and reach out to calm Misty. "I'm very glad you were there. Thank you for calling. Do you think he might have choked on something?"

"I don't think so. I don't know what happened! What do I do now?"

"Can you get a friend to drive you to the hospital? Or a taxi? You'll have to insist or they won't let you into his room. Call me from the hospital if you need backup. I will get you in!"

I hang up, my mind working. I switch on a lamp and boot up my computer. *Everett Hospital. Dial the switchboard. Call the Emergency Department.*

"Yes, he came in a few minutes ago," says a bright young woman's voice. "He's talking now. He seems fine."

Talking. Seems fine. No brain damage. Misty is a big girl, but Lucas is big too. Probably no broken ribs. "Nothing on the EKG?"

"No, all seems fine now. We'll keep him overnight on tele, just in case."

I recall when Luke was nine and suddenly couldn't breathe. We had calmed him until whatever it was passed. Doctors found nothing. I thank the woman and crawl back into bed. Tom and I talk gently for a few minutes. I surround our son with Golden Light and slowly drift back to sleep.

"You must have been very frightened," Lucas says when he calls the next day.

"Yes."

"What did you do?"

"After I spoke with the ER nurse, I went back to sleep. What else could I do?" In the silence of my soul I hear the softest click of a door closing—or opening. *Which?* I don't want him to withdraw from my worry. *How should I respond?*

∽

June was in brilliant leaf when I boarded a plane to Seattle for the ferry trip north with our son. It would be just a short vacation this year. Again, Tom offered it to me. Lucas had given his unused car to the mother of a friend, an older woman with little money, so I caught the airport shuttle to his place. He owned little of value and walked everywhere now, but it didn't seem to bother him. His shoes were worn and his clothing wrinkled.

"You take the bed," I insisted as he carried my bag inside. His apartment was long and narrow with a back view dropping steeply into the ocean. I pushed pizza boxes and random clothing off the sofa and sat down. "I'll sleep here."

"I made the bed up fresh for you. I'm going out tonight. You sure I won't disturb you?"

"You need the rest. I'll be comfortable." I had earplugs and was determined not to spend our nights together listening to his snores or worrying about him.

The next morning was sunny and the backstreets of Everett were decked in flowers. Lucas and I chatted happily as we walked, hand in hand, the mile to a store to buy groceries for our trip. These we packed into the big tote he used for a laundry hamper. We also took one of his two towels and his can opener. Misty and her best friend Katie drove us to the Bellingham ferry terminal in Katie's old car, where I treated everyone to lunch and paid for the gas. Lucas folded both girls into his arms before we lugged our tote, his backpack, and my travel bag onto the deck of the MV *Kennicott*.

Tom had reserved a small cabin for us, perhaps seven feet square, with a porthole and folding top bunk. It served as a secluded place to sleep and store our belongings; toilets and showers were down the hall. Many passengers slept in lawn chairs on the sheltered top deck and most brought food to eat in the ship's cafeteria. We settled amicably into the warm atmosphere of the little floating community that would share this space for most of a week.

For the next few days we chugged north—two old friends. We spent much of the trip at the rail watching the magic islands drift past or seated near the big windows in the cafeteria, where we splurged on hot dinners and occasional snacks. Like Megan, Lucas never complained at the repetitive crackers, cheese, tuna, and peanut butter from our tote. Sometimes he overflowed with light and joy; at others he seemed distant and somber. I tried to visualize him like Annie saw him, as a great Buddha, but foreboding clouded my heart. Occasionally, I saw him smoking at the rail, concealing it from me out of deference. He looked old in his glasses and flapping coat. Even his hairline was beginning to recede.

"Next summer I want to hike to the Divide," Lucas said as we stood at the rail, "but I need to get my bills paid off first." Eighty yards away, the cliffs stood bright in late evening sunlight. An eagle's disheveled nest hung reflected in the painted water as tide flowed like a river between the islands. Lucas's face was lit from within and he smiled down on me. It wasn't hard to see him then as a Buddha.

"Why not let us help?" I offered.

He turned steady eyes on me. "I need to do this myself."

"I think a summer off the treadmill will help you remember your path. Life works in cycles—ebb and flow—periods of growth followed by quiescence. Dad and I don't care if you stay in nursing, we just want you to be excited about life. Follow your heart."

"I'd like to try being homeless," he said. "I was going to live out of my car, but that's gone. People say it was foolish to let the car go, but I wasn't using it. She shows up occasionally and pays me a few dollars."

I raised an eyebrow. "Homeless?" I couldn't tell if he was serious.

"You'd be surprised how many people are homeless. I just wonder what it would be like. Remember the kids in Guatemala? I sometimes let street kids stay with me. They steal my stuff, but you can't blame them… and it's just stuff."

"Like I told you in Guatemala, you need to have your life handled to be an asset to others. Being homeless doesn't give you much resiliency."

"I just want to experience everything," he answered. His eyes were on the ocean.

Tom was waiting on the dock in Whittier where snowy mountains cascaded into the ocean. Beside him stood Monica Ford, a friend Lucas had made on his last trip to Homer. She had driven the hour from Anchorage just to greet him. It continued to surprise me how many people were moved by Lucas. The two hugged and laughed until the Whittier tunnel opened for traffic going west under the mountain. Then she drove back to Anchorage and we headed for Homer.

TWO DAYS LATER, I DROVE Lucas to Anchorage to catch his flight back. We stayed over a day so that he could research employment options. I suggested he call ahead, but he preferred to walk in cold, leaving me to read in hospital cafeterias. An hour later he would return with job offers.

"Let's scout for nearby housing," he said over lunch.

We spent the afternoon driving the streets, looking at apartments that were close enough for him to walk. We also discovered a maze of trails and connecting woods around the hospitals. "You might have to use skis or snowshoes," I said.

"I can do that. It will be good to live in a college town again."

That night, Lucas's cousin Derek Helmericks treated us and some of his friends to dinner at a Japanese restaurant. As the young folk laughed and talked, I breathed a contented sigh.

Morning light filtered through the hotel curtains as I read. In the other room, Lucas was snoring deeply and occasionally forgetting to breathe. I had arranged for a quick sleep study and the news was disturbing. He promised me he would pass the report along to his physician. Someday. "Sleep apnea will hurt your heart," I had nagged.

Now in the morning quiet, I turned within as I had long counseled others to do. There is a part of us beyond the talking mind that knows our answers. Our soul, that boundless connection to the Whole, directs the journey when we listen. It was obvious I could not make decisions for my son, and agonizing over him was doing neither of us any good. Pulling out my journal, I cleared my mind and began to write—first my question and then the words that came:

Lucas is asleep. He snores so deeply that his oxygen desaturates into the 70s. He makes repeated choices that pull him toward physical disaster and pain my heart. What do I do?

> *You hold this beloved child of the Infinite gently in your heart while releasing him to his own path. He has greater support than you can know. He is not lost or forgotten. Be not saddened or dismayed at appearances! This journey has not gone as you envisioned, however it has been pivotal in his shift, a trim tab that will have profound ramifications some ways down the line. Come only from love—not from disappointment or pain—to make the greatest difference and create the least amount of turbulence.*

Will Lucas survive?

> *This is not for you to know. He is not yours. He knows his choices are other than yours for him, and protects you. Do not pry. He needs to explore these darker passages and find his own way.*

Why did he come through me then? I am not an easy energy to ignore.

> *Do not underestimate your influence upon him! You are the center of his storm. He is not who you see. Know this about the*

one you call 'your son': great is his soul. Bright burns his light. His reasons are his own. Know only that the gift he brings you is the opportunity to move beyond appearances. He dances with you here. Hold that vision of perfection and stop trying to fix what is not broken!

~

Tom and I are alone when we head north to Kernwood in early July. The months have washed away the sharp edges of Rude's death, polishing it like a stone to wear as an amulet close to my heart. Far from being gone, his memory has crystalized into something precious, a jewel that changes with the light. It is a reminder to pay attention and to cherish each moment. Often as I descend the path or step through a doorway, I try not to saunter, but to move with deliberation—the way Rude would. On the bakehouse porch, his empty chair seems to glow in the afternoon light. Sometimes I sit there of an evening, talking to him. I notice that Tom does too. The loss is a deep ache in my chest, one I don't really want to heal, because to lose touch with it feels like finally losing Rude.

"There's hardly a foot of this land that doesn't speak of him," Tom says. "He's always out there, pointing out curious trees or stones. I want to hike up King Mountain and see if I can find his knife. He said I would know the place, that it would feel natural when I saw it."

It's already autumn and stars have returned when we hoist our backpacks and set off for Rude's Camp on the knees of King Mountain. It seems fitting that birch trees again blaze yellow between the olive spruce along the bench, and the moss is sequined in red lingonberries. The creek rushes clear as glass below the path that Rude helped to build. "Rude's Trail" (as we call it) makes the early journey easy, but beyond it we must pick our way through a swale tangled in high brush. I am in the lead when I suddenly hesitate. An inner voice is trying to get my attention—I have the strange impression of smelling bacon! The thought flits through my head, *Someone is here!*

As I pause, Tom pivots toward a large, dark grizzly—intensely present a few yards away. Tom's reaction is faster than I can think. He lunges forward to put himself between me and the bear. There's no time to grab the pistol from its holster; I don't think he even tries. The bear's charge is unbelievably fast! Tom challenges the animal with a menacing bark, and the grizzly smoothly reverses course, disappearing like a phantom in the high brush. The whole event is over in seconds.

"Well, we've met Rude's bear," I say. It is strange how invigorated I feel. Glad to be alive one more minute.

We are walking again. "Keep your eyes open," Tom orders. "Let's trend uphill and see if we can't pick up the second bench. I'll feel better when we get clear of these bushes."

"Let's extend Rude's Trail up to Second Bench next summer."

"Rude would have been excited running into that bear," Tom says. He sounds happy.

Gradually, thin clouds knit across the open sky. On Second Bench, the going is easier, and we soon hit a game trail that tiptoes along the edge, dropping back to the creek at Yellow Stone. Animals also prefer the easy walking and good view. Rude's bright boulder has washed downstream a hundred yards, but still gleams from the foaming current near the cliffs. Tom and I stop for a snack beside the shed caribou antler placed in a tree.

Evening chill descends on the narrowing cleft, and I am footsore by the time we climb to Rude's Camp. I start a fire while Tom hauls water and then searches for the knife. It's windy on the knob and we hunker in the lee where Rude built our morning fire. He had carefully scattered the rocks, but Tom rebuilds the little platform. I pull off wet tennis shoes and put on camp moccasins. I'm not wearing boots because of an inflamed Achilles tendon. Late sun sneaks in under the clouds, painting the highland in brilliant autumn: fawn, wine, and russet. Cold wind eddies from the heights, gusting the blaze.

I scrounge for firewood, limping on my injured Achilles and opposite knee. I have nursed them all summer. I think of how Rude never complained or allowed pain to show. Tom is setting up the tent, rolling out our bags where Rude and I slept. *It will be cold tonight.* My hand reaches for a small stick. It's about as long as my forearm and the size of my finger with a slight upward curve at the tip—just the sort Rude would have carved into a pot-lifter. It feels warm and natural in my hand. I turn it curiously. One edge is whittled where an extra branch was carefully removed. The cut looks surprisingly fresh. I hold the bit of spruce in my cold hands, fingering the smoothed area.

"It's got to be around here somewhere," Tom says. For two years he has wanted to find that knife. The place it should have been is obvious—a level spot along the trunk of one of the fallen twin trees—but the knife is not there. Tom squats, picking through the thick layer of bark, moss, and twigs on the ground.

Through my mind flashes the image of a raven, dark wings shushing down the wind, a pocketknife in his beak. I smile. *The old trickster.* "Maybe we aren't supposed to find it."

I lift the boiling pot with the magical stick, comforting in my hand. "He said he wanted his body placed here for the birds." I gaze across the wild view of tree line and rushing creek. It isn't a cozy place, more like an aerie—exposed and magnificent. I hand Tom a spoon and his enamel mug, steam drifting on the cold wind. Dinner is rice and moose meat dried in Rude's smokehouse. There doesn't seem to be a way around it: Rude is everywhere. Tom has carried a shed caribou antler the last mile up the gorge and now places it in the big tree next to our tent. *We will have to bring Lucas here next summer*, I think.

I pull out a small flask of whisky, sequestered in my pack. Tom raises an eyebrow. "I thought we were only packing essentials."

"Let's drink to Rude." I pour a bit into my cup and hand him the little bottle.

"To Rude. Truest of friends," Tom toasts. His eyes glisten with tears. He smiles at me, unashamed.

"Thank you, beloved friend, for reminding me that the journey is brief and that every day is a gift. Go lightly upon the breeze." I raise my cup. "Until we meet again, I shall miss you!"

Two days later, we awaken on the crenelated ridge to steady rain. The land of shelter and firewood lies tantalizingly below. We emerge from our small, dripping tent and I hunker in a crevice trying to build a fire with the few hoarded sticks we have carried up and sequestered in the rocks.

"I don't think we should go on," Tom insists. "Not with your knee and ankle."

"We can save it for Lucas next summer," I agree. "It doesn't matter if we make it to the Divide. I just want to see him balanced and happy." *Maybe we need an unattainable goal.*

We squat between the ancient rocks, sipping coffee by the feeble warmth of our fire and gazing down upon the scudding clouds, swamps and forest that stand between us and home. I am reluctant to turn back, but I am limping badly. "We covered the hard part," I say. "It seems a shame to quit now that we're on the ridge."

"We'll come up that promontory next summer," Tom points. "It looks easier."

"It's been a good hike. Let's head home and I can finish a first draft of my book. Sometimes it feels like I wrote it a long time ago, that I'm just waiting to see how it ends. Life keeps turning out and at some point, I'll simply have to call it done."

"You can always write another."

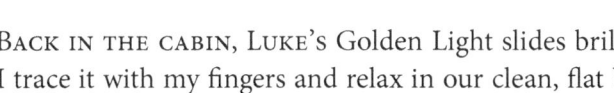

Back in the cabin, Luke's Golden Light slides brilliant across the loft wall. I trace it with my fingers and relax in our clean, flat bed. The sun only makes this transit in spring and fall. *Maybe it's the ephemeral quality that makes life so precious. Perhaps that's why we cherish flowers and babies and snowflakes.* "It worries me so when we can't reach him." I say. "He lives so close to the edge." We haven't talked with Lucas for two weeks, our Saturday noon calls going to voicemail.

"He probably lost his phone again," Tom reassures me.

"Carlos Castaneda writes that we each have a 'luminous egg,' an energy body around our physical one. He says that becoming a parent creates a hole in your luminous egg, and at some point you have to heal it. I feel like I hold Lucas up with my love. When he was little, he was like an eaglet nestled into my feathers. As he began to explore outward, it felt like my energy was pulled into an elliptical bubble. I know it's time to let go."

We try to call Lucas again at noon the next day. Tom plugs our satellite phone into the aerial we now have on the roof. Again our call defaults to voicemail. With satellite, you pay for every second—even the time it takes to ring. I am restless. At twenty-five, Lucas still looks to us for stability. Without that touchstone, he wanders off path. I know this about him.

"Sometimes I feel like I'm trying to hold him up against a current, like he's sliding downstream. If only we can get him up here for a summer, he'll find his bearings. The wilderness is a powerful friend."

Ten minutes later I try again. Lucas answers on the last ring. His voice is hard to recognize, a weak whisper filled with emotion. "Oh, Mama! I missed your call!" He is crying. "I've been standing here with the phone in my hand hoping you would try again! My phone doesn't ring anymore, and sometimes it doesn't vibrate. I missed your calls, and I've been so sick. I was hospitalized for a week, but I'm getting better now."

He had developed a raging, multi-organism pneumonia at work one night. "I started to walk home, then decided that I couldn't make it. When I went to the ER, I had a temperature of 104 and they admitted me. I was practically unconscious for days. If I had walked home, I would have died."

"Do you have anyone who can look in on you?" I ask. "To bring you food?"

"Misty comes by sometimes when she can get a ride. Most of my friends don't have cars. Don't worry, I have some food."

We strain to make out his hoarse whispers. Tom takes the phone. "We'll call you every day at noon, Son. We'll be home in a few weeks. If you need money or help, call Denise. You have friends beyond Everett." Tom holds the phone so I can hear. Our heads are touching as we cradle our son between us.

"I hate to use up your minutes." His voice is sounding stronger as we speak. I can feel the wind catching beneath his wings. Knowing we are here makes that difference.

"Don't worry, we can buy more minutes over the phone," Tom tells him. "You just get well."

"Everyone needs support sometimes," I put in. "That's what community is about. You need to receive as well as give. That's a hard lesson for me too."

Ice was crinkling over puddles at night when we departed Kernwood. Snow dribbled down the browning mountains, and the quieting land lay golden under a pale sun.

In Homer, I was offered the full-time position of OB Coordinator. They had worked hard to craft a contract that would allow me three months at Kernwood. My first thought was to decline. I wanted to finish my book, work on a cleaner draft of our documentary, and explore the peninsula. We had lived here three years and had yet to go hiking. And then I thought, *Perhaps I can make a difference*, and accepted the position.

Winter settled on our little town and the moon slid through its cycles: bathing the snow in surreal white and then dimming to a sliver in the orange glow over the cliffs and ocean. From our loft, we watched the changing landscape. Moose browsed the alders where pheasants roosted and snowshoe hares wafted like ghosts in the fading light. Life was good.

Lucas was back at work. His had sworn off cigarettes and was proudly losing weight as he walked the streets of Everett. He called one night to tell us of saving a friend's life. The cook at Alligator Soul had gotten into an argument. A gang was waiting when he stepped outside and had beaten him unconscious. Someone called for Lucas.

"I stopped the bleeding and opened his airway," he told Tom. "The ambulance crew had me ride with them to the hospital. He's still unconscious in ICU, but they think he'll pull through. I've been talking with his mother. They've been estranged for years and she doesn't know how to reach him. I feel honored that this fifty-year-old woman trusts me to help communicate with her son."

"You make a difference," I said.

"Mama, I really want you and Dad to know how much I love you. This experience brought home to me how important that is to tell you. My friend's mother has suffered deeply—feeling unvalued by her son. Well, I cherish you! I am so fortunate to have you as parents. I just need to tell you that."

Christmas came and then a new year dawned. Homer had yet to see much snow. Light began trickling back, growing daily in the sky over Kachemak Bay. Gentle waves emerged like magic from beneath a pan of ice, tossing lacy ribbons of slush onto the frozen sand. I walked the beach in the chill wind while bright sun streamed low over southern peaks. My nose was red and my hands were deep in the pockets of a warm coat that Annie had sent to me.

Tom had walked down the hill to play Tuesday night poker with friends, leaving the truck parked for me at the hospital. A last tint of yellow fingered the sky as I drove down the hill. Snow glistened in skimpy patches on lawns and a fingernail new moon trailed the vanished sun into the ocean as stars hung low in the frosty night sky.

"Lucas called," Tom had written next to the phone. "We had a good long talk."

Dinner waited for me: salmon, squash, sweet potato, and a bowl of salad—lovely and conscious as a flower arrangement. I ate and then settled comfortably in bed to dial Lucas.

He answered on the first ring. "I'm getting excited about going to Tucson." He would represent us at a screening of our documentary at Greenfields, his old school. "I put in my resignation here. It's hard to leave Everett, but this feels right."

"I hope you've given up thoughts of travel-nursing in Tucson," I said.

"I think you're right," he agreed. "I'll come to Homer this spring and then go to the cabin with you. I still have my Alaska nursing license. I might get on as a traveler in Anchorage."

"You'll have enough time for one travel assignment before summer. When we come out of the wilderness, you can sign on in Anchorage if you want. Our offer still stands to help you get a used vehicle—something dependable for winter. Anchorage is only a five-hour drive from here. You can spend holidays with us and still have your own world."

"I've been reconsidering your offer about a vehicle," he conceded, "but

I will pay you back. It's just all the medical bills right now. I am so looking forward to my tax refund! You'll be proud: I'm filing early this year. I'm getting to be more like you all the time. By the way, I've lost thirty-four pounds. I love the new shoes you sent, Mama. The soles on my old ones were flapping."

"The red ones too? It's hard to find them in your size. They're not too flashy?"

"Heck, no! You kidding? Especially the red ones. They've got tread that separates and rolls when I walk—like being barefooted with support. I love 'em!"

"Should I get you a ticket from Tucson, then?"

"Yeah, go ahead and buy it. Give me a week in Tucson to connect with old friends. Then I'm coming north."

"Hey, maybe we'll finally make it to the Divide. If your old parents are up to it."

"Gotta go, Mama. I love you!"

Chapter 36

Across the Great Divide

January 2012

It's gone away – in yesterday
and I find myself on the mountainside
Where the rivers change direction
Across the Great Divide

—Kate Wolf

At some point, one must set the pen down. There will be other books, of this I am now certain. What began as a silver thread connecting us to Lucas when Tom and I set off in search of a new home has evolved into this book. With a start of surprise, I now discover that I wrote it for myself—a lantern to raise to the shadows. Coming full circle, I understand that any light

I hold for another illuminates my path as well.

When darkness wavers through the forest it is easy to say, "This too shall pass," and yet everything I cherish is also temporary. The Buddhists understand this: our sacred task is to see the glory in each moment, no matter how painful, and to rejoice in the sea, though it washes our castles away.

I began by saying that it takes two logs to keep a fire burning. For over three decades, Tom has been my other log. I wrote the Preface first, reassuringly. Like Bilbo Baggins, my memoir would conclude happily—nothing left to stitch but a satisfied border. Indeed, we are safely cupped in the palm of community, our seasons predictable. The shy faces of children in the grocery store are often babies I helped deliver. Lucas was coming north. In time, he might settle on the land abutting ours, picking up tasks as we laid them down. Finally, I could cease my striving.

The caterpillar, however, can only imagine growing larger, while transformation requires death and rebirth. *I should have remembered.* The Dalai Lama speaks of "Clear Light," of moments beyond time and thought. That is what I've always sought: a way out of the busyness of my mind. One can also be knocked out of it like a planet hit by an asteroid. "Be careful," my grandmother Winnie used to say, "of what you pray for." All thoughts are creative.

"I'm a hypocrite," I tell Tom, "writing about trusting a river that I never trusted. I want to wear a life preserver and carry waterproof matches." The river doesn't care. It laughs at our fears, knowing the ultimate truth: physical life is a remarkable journey, a house of mirrors where everything is temporary. Eventually, all come home to the Sea.

Modest and gentle, Tom listens and says nothing.

There are events that forever fracture one's world, branding it undeniably *Before* and *After*. Luke's birth had been such a moment—a blazing Son that altered our course and gravitational pull as he circled my heart and Tom's. February 25, 1986, 5:05 P.M.

The last words I speak before the sky explodes are, "Look at my beautiful view. They gave me the best office in the hospital." January 25, 2012, 9:48 A.M.

THERE ARE NO LABOR PATIENTS this morning and I am dressed professionally as Obstetrical Coordinator instead of in nursing scrubs. The hospital is quiet and warm beneath the feathers of winter dawn. Still groggy from his night at poker, Tom drives me the short distance up the hill to work. Below the hospital, the bay awakens softly in muted grays.

I see Becky in the bright hallway and stop to share my news. "Lucas is coming to Homer next week. I'm buying his ticket today." She's the first person I've told, holding my hopes close.

"Will he apply here?"

"Only as a casual. He's coming to the cabin with us next summer and then maybe travel-nursing or Anchorage."

"Yes," she agrees, "he should get more experience." Becky has a lifetime of experience. She's been generous in advising Lucas.

Suddenly, Tom and Lydette are coming down the hall. I am surprised to see him at work. *Good news or bad*, I think.

"I need to speak with you. Alone." His face is a closed book, energy flashing in shards—light off a diamond.

Good news, I hope. I lead him into the locked OB unit and back to my secluded office with its magical vista of glaciers and bay. Nevertheless, I postpone the moment. *This is it. The end of my world.* I stall for one more breath. "Look at my beautiful view. They gave me the best office in the hospital." A ray of sunlight spills low through the clouds and puddles like molten silver on a pewter sea. It is a moment out of time, perfection hanging on a word.

Slowly, I bring my eyes to Tom's familiar face. As I look, it twists and melts like wax, energy flying past me in a spray of fragmented glass.

"It's Lucas… he's… dead!" His voice is a wailing sound, muffled and far away like a man falling down a well.

For years we have surrounded our son with Golden Light, cradling him between our hearts. Lucas is our comet, swinging wide into the blackness of space and then flashing brilliantly past. We are twin stars—his center—pulled like an oscillating dumbbell by his playful arcs through the heavens. When he drifts afar, I feel cold and stretched thin; as he comes singing by, I am warm and glowing like the full moon. Instinctively I reach for that connection—my lifeline in free fall—and hear a silent "*pop!*" in my chest, an abrupt amputation as the cord snaps off. A great solar wind blasts icy through a cavern the size of a basketball that opens between my breasts. Then comes a soundless explosion that shatters my world, blowing slivers of me to the furthest galaxies. Curiously detached, I watch the dust spin away as I cling to my broken mate. *Clear Light. This is It.*

Phil Gordon is waiting at the hospital entrance. We three huddle into the suddenly falling snow for the drive home—new territory. Free fall. Drifting. White Space. I am blowing past the Milky Way. Wordlessly, Tom and I climb our stairs, strip away clothes, and curl into bed trying to sense Lucas warm and safe between our hearts. I remember how he liked to burrow between us when he was a child. Our beautiful Son is nowhere.

A gentle whisper ripples through my frozen heart, "Mama, I'm all right."

It was an easy death. There are so many ghastly ways to go. Lucas had simply stopped breathing in his sleep. A homeless friend asleep on the sofa had been disturbed by his snoring and turned him onto his side. Misty had found him when she came by in the morning. After nearly twenty-six years, Lucas's big heart had stilled, and he drifted beyond our gravitational reach.

Snow continues to fall, piling over the house as if to bury us. Tom fights the snowblower in the icy wind and I feel fresh waves of grief. *Lucas would love this snow.* I picture him making snow angels in front of his Everett apartment in soggy, worn shoes, his face red and laughing. Sifting powder undulates in dunes across our long driveway.

Phil arrives in the dark next morning to accompany Tom on his journey into sorrow. I am frozen in place, too numb to go. *Tom always does the hard duty for me.* I break trail out to the road where our friend Ela waits to take them to the airport. I can't see through the blowing snow. Taillights disappear and I flounder back toward the warmth of our home. Soon I find myself whining like a puppy, pacing the empty house. The noise rises (*Is that me?*), an animal howl of agony. I crumple onto the floor and sob until the carpet is soggy and my nose full of snot and lint.

Dark wind buffets the house and the drifts accumulate. Friends come by to plow our driveway, haul in firewood, bring food, and tell me to eat. In Everett, Laurie and Phil help pack up Lucas's few things and clean his apartment. Tom stands rigid in the mortuary, hugging the cold form of his only son. He cannot look beneath the blanket. It is soft and clean—mercifully not a body bag. I think of Lucas's big feet, now icy and pale, the dark hair on his toes. The toe tag. No stranger to this pain, Phil stands guard while Tom sobs and strokes the great shadow beneath the blanket. Together they witness Lucas's final journey into the flames. I sit rocking, rocking before our woodstove, my eyes fixed on the fire through the glass doors. We rocked our son to sleep until he was too big to fit in our laps.

"Sing me a song, Mama." I clutch the little pewter sculpture, the koala with a baby on her back. "I tell everyone I'm a mama's boy." The little fake diamond ring around the koala sparkles in the candlelight.

Losing a child is a profound experience. One loses heart in Life. Everything is washed away in a vast tsunami. Sometimes grief shakes me like a volcano with great sobs, and I groan in bottomless agony. Mostly I drift in the falling snow: winter shadows and firelight. Dreamscape. *What will I do with the rest of my life?* I don't want his last paycheck! I don't want his tax return or his insurance! He was so looking forward to paying off his bills.

"I'm all right, Mama," gently, out of nowhere. "I don't need it."

I pull out my meditation journal and write:

My only child. Why? What am I supposed to get from this? Was his life's purpose fulfilled?

> *Do not name an experience "good" or "bad," for you cannot see all the ramifications. Because of his shift, your lives and those of others will evolve differently. Do not let that gift go unnoticed.*

What am I to do with my own life?

> *Do not discount ANY potential future and do not choose today. Let this great wind blow away all that you think you are. Like breakup upon the river, it is not what you can imagine from the deep of winter; like water turning to steam, it is a process you can neither anticipate nor control. Great change has been set into motion by this event, but the pressure has been building. Ride the flood, surrender to its power, embrace its current, and let go. Enjoy the ride over the cataract. There IS NO DEATH!*

I stand naked, a skeleton. I would have given everything to see him become a leader and a healer.

> *What makes you think he's not? Know this, Mama: your son has learned you well. Do not grieve, for he loves the Light and understands the Dark. See him now as he is: not broken or confused, but a warrior of the Light, a healer of the planet, encompassing the polarities so that he may transcend and so unite them.*

I have not dreamed of him or felt his presence beyond an occasional whisper. I haven't reached out because I didn't want to hold him back.

> *You couldn't hold him back! No one could. He is vast and magnificent. He goes where he needs to go and rides the wings you gave him. Do not regret anything. You and your mate were perfect, are perfect. He cherishes you and uses your Light well!*

~

WE LEARN ABOUT LUCAS FROM others: he is loved by hundreds of people! They come forward with stories and grief—these coworkers, street kids, business men, and shop girls. He was not alone those two years in Everett, but the friend that people called when things got tough. I wanted him safe and warm, but he shared all that I gave him.

"It's okay, Mama. I don't need it," whispers through my heart.

In Washington, Tom attends the first of three memorials organized by Lucas's diverse friends—a potluck at a local tavern. "They came to me in waves for hours," Tom writes, "hugging me and telling me how much they loved and admired him. 'He was so smart, funny, loving, generous, talented, wise, honest, and fearless. You could tell him anything. He stopped fights and saved lives. He always seemed to know what to do. He jumped in to help, and people followed him.' He was still giving away teddy bears! At the hospital, I learned that nursing students vied for his time. One nurse told me of seeing him in bright, red scrubs at the end of the hall with all the nursing students gathered about him 'like a great, red flower surrounded by bees!' Jeanie, he was so very special! And he was loved!"

Tom returns home with our son's few possessions, the cement block with hand and paw prints, and two boxes of ashes: Lucas's and Lucy's. His box is heavy—those big bones. *So final.* I think of how upset he was when he broke a tooth. For me, Tom brings a lock of hair, Oliver, Lucas's writings, and a shirt that still smells of him. I can't touch them yet—only his ancient teddy. *Why?* I ask the enigmatic little face.

"I think you should attend the ceremonies in Arizona and then Everett," Tom tells me. Greenfields still plans to show the documentary—now as a tribute to Lucas. A scholarship is started in his name. I think of travel, of money, of talking with people. My flame gutters low.

"It will inspire you," Tom encourages.

I sleep fitfully, curled against him. His skin is cool. In the darkness of another blizzard morning, I put my request on the Internet. "Air miles," I ask.

Denise donates miles. Coworkers arrange the flights and donate their paid time off. *People are so generous and kind!* Snow swirls endlessly out of the heaving Pacific. *Luke's snow.* Tom pushes the snowblower down our long driveway, his small figure drifting as snow accumulates in his tracks. *Lucas would love that machine, the plume of crystals blowing back into his rosy face.* I start to cry—weeping so easily—empty, yet leaking. Hunched against the cold, Tom looks vulnerable, our future reduced to two old people shoveling snow. Alone.

Alone? With all of Homer? Unasked, the gifts and help continue to pour in. My trip south is borne on the wings of love. Everywhere, I am gently handled. Remote and strangely peaceful, I float as planes and friends carry me through the days and meetings with five hundred people who love our remarkable son. I am astonished and moved. Each has stories of how he helped them or saw good in them when no one else did. In Everett, a coworker takes me up to the deck of the new tower to watch a great moon rise golden over the city lights. I never knew he was so valued. *Did he know?* Without darkness would we see the light? Each of us a Buddha unawares.

"What do you learn when your world explodes?" I ask Tom. "When you've done everything right: prayed, paid your taxes, sent your kids to good schools—and the river wipes it all away? 'Life sucks and then you die?' Is that it?"

He listens patiently, aware that I'm not asking him for answers.

"There has to be more. I look at the moose, so complete. The Arctic hare. They don't seem anxious. 'Hey, little bunny, your life will be short and hard. You were born to feed predators.' They don't personalize it. They're alert, alive, engaged. What do they know that I have forgotten?"

I don't know what death is. I don't understand life either. Mystery beyond mystery, says the Tao. A lifetime of preparing for this moment—and still, I do not know. Sixty-two years lie in rubble. Devastation? Freedom? I'm in no hurry to cobble together fragments of old dreams. In my chrysalis, I await a spring I do not expect to see. I wake each morning and the void is still there. Space. A white page. Pain that sears everything away. Without pain, would we know joy? I weep easily with both now, raw—pared to this moment. It's as close to God as I've ever been.

"The whole left side of my body feels blackened and shriveled," Tom whispers. "I'm crippled and unable to stand straight. I may never be whole again." He is crying, holding me. "I didn't sign up for this!"

There is nothing to say. I place my palm to his cheek and he holds it there. "Do you want arms?" I ask. We used to say that to little-boy Luke when he was hurt. Come into my arms. Let me heal you with my love. Tom and I curl close in bed, old hearts giving off a dim light. I forget to breathe. I am sinking into the sea. So easy to slip off the edge of the world.

"When my brother Fred's son died," Tom says, "I thought he handled it well. I didn't know! You never get over it."

"Are you going through the stages of grief they talk about?" Annie asks over the phone.

I don't think so. Bargaining? *What more could I offer?* Anger? *At who?* Denial? No… just that split second of brightness when the phone rings, or in the numinous landscape between sleep and waking—before I remember. I circle around and around, but it's always there.

"Half the people who lose a child get divorced," I tell her.

"They can't bear to see their pain in the mirror," she says.

Maybe. I have no answers anymore. Sharing sorrow with Tom keeps me from sliding beneath the waves. I can't imagine starting over with someone who never laughed at Lucas's humor. Do memories cripple me or are they keys?

I go back to work because the hospital needs me. I run my body by remote control, unpredictable and numb. Perhaps I look normal—I can't tell from here. A doctor stops me in the hall and says, "How are you doing?" pauses a moment, then adds, "You know, I have a theory about grief." For the first time in my life, I'm out of words. Like the doctor, I had believed that my education meant something. *God, I was so arrogant!* I didn't know that I didn't know. Awareness cannot be achieved from the eyebrows up! Brain is no good in this milky twilight, where physics and metaphysics merge, where sperm wiggles into egg or a last breath sighs out and stars explode in the infinite space between ribs and throat.

"I'm glad I'll never have to go through this," says a friend with no children.

I don't believe him. Never to have loved a radiant son? Our only egg, dropped into the sea. Fell off the edge of the world. I think about that too. Had we ten children, none would be spares: ten chances for disaster, ten potential holes in my heart. There is no insurance against grief. *What will I do with the rest of my life?* I run across my old trail, so sweet and ordinary it knifes through my heart. An email, an appointment—footprints of someone else wending along the top of an invisible cliff. I am jealous of that other me. *Look where she plunged into the surf! What was she thinking?* Pictures of *Before* without the scar across my eyeballs.

"It makes dying easier," Tom says.

Indeed it does. How fortunate to be old. It's only a short ways. We can travel there hand in hand. "You stay because of me," I say in wonder.

Tom's eyes are swimming in anguish. He nods. "I always have."

"I would have leapt into the water after him—if I thought I could grab his ankle," I say, "but I don't think it works that way." I recall Tom jumping between me and the bear. Either of us would gladly have taken Lucas's place.

Tom nods dumbly. "I like to think he's with Rude, building the cabin for us."

Comforting image, that. Powerful to choose our images. "It's as if he lived his whole life on fast-forward. Maybe twenty-six years is all he needed."

Grief is not an exclusive club. I never knew. They wear no brand on their foreheads, no T-shirt saying, "I lost my child." They approach me carefully, like crossing a winter river in falling snow. "You never recover, but you go on," they tell me. Limping. Amputated. Forever changed. How had I missed seeing them? *You too?* I whisper. A nod. My eighteen-year-old committed suicide. My only baby was stillborn. My sixteen-year-old died of brain cancer. My toddler was snatched from my arms one ordinary afternoon by a tornado. We found only his shoe. I didn't know what to do with it! My three-year-old drowned. My son was murdered. Mine was killed in a hunting accident by his best friend who then shot himself. Mine by a drunk driver. Mine disappeared into that beautiful bay. *How do they breathe, all these lost parents? Who tucks them in at night?* I am humbled. How can I judge anyone, each so fatally wounded? You never know who hemorrhages from a terrible gash beneath everyday clothes.

Those who stand beyond the glass peer down and ask, "How did he die?" They want to name the unnamable, to swim without getting wet. They are curious, safe in that other dimension. Some are embarrassed or perhaps afraid that grief is contagious. Most hold out a helpless hand. Those who have slipped in, had the flesh washed clean from their white bones, they do not pry. It doesn't matter, you see. Lost in the dark, eaten by a monster under the bed, thrown out with the bathwater, stepped on by a dream, drowned in our culture: gone from our sight. Vanished with our hearts.

"How old?" they might ask. How many days did you have? When did time stop for you? Four years or fifty-two, they were our children. We remember teddy bears and school plays. We have saved the baby teeth they left under their pillows.

I am strangely quiet inside, deep and liquid. My river has emptied into a white ocean, and from the vantage of my little canoe, there is only mist and water as far as I can see. Words are a useless blueprint here. Tears wash the pastel surface easily and unexpectedly. Newborn, I am conscious only of a great emptiness that seems to stretch to the end of my life. I keep paddling, reflexively. Some days are stormy, some calm and clear. Empty space. What I feared has come upon me. All my lists could not keep him safe. No preparation, no pleading, could prevent the world from dissolving beneath me. And yet, if I had it to do over—knowing all that was to come—I would still choose this magnificent journey.

I am sad to the bone. I can't seem to get over it, around it, through it—this bottomless grief. I navigate each day from a great distance and when I pause, a piercing sorrow overtakes me. It would be so easy to flicker out. Where once I was enthralled to the future, I now risk losing this sacred moment by peering back over my shoulder, like Lot's wife. I pretend—smile, talk, eat, work. Skating over thin ice, I despair of finding a shoreline. I haven't the heart to create a miracle or pray for one. I am lost on the White Sea, treading water. Grief is also chiseling away all that is not true, teaching me. But did it have to cost so dearly? Might I have learned humility without losing so much blood? Worth pondering, you who still hold hands with the living.

DAYS AT SEA BECOME WEEKS. My mind returns timidly—servant rather than master. That's a relief. The ego I strove for years to tame is nowhere in sight. From one perspective, our grand adventure upon this planet is a litany of loss. In trickling sand or roaring cataclysm, everything is inevitably washed away. Whole forests gone in a breakup, riverbanks scoured clean. I have defined myself by those I love. *Without them, who am I?*

Out of the silence comes an unexpected answer: love is not something I have, but my very fiber. Without an object to pour myself into, I still Am! Before me the path divides. One trail drops into a bottomless abyss. I peer into the blackness, flirting with the edge. There's nothing wholesome down there, no answers. The other path climbs into the light of gratitude. It's not the easiest way, but it's certainly the more interesting. Slowly, I turn and blink at the Light. I am tearfully grateful for every day of Luke's 9,464 sunrises. *There are no ordinary moments.*

Sunlight grows and eagles begin their mating dance. It's been a record winter for snow: Lucas's joke. Within my cocoon, I stir timidly. Moments of grace shimmer through the rising mist: delicate and fragile minutes—and then whole mornings—without agony. I am afraid to look down, almost frightened to breathe. *Is it possible?*

"I'm okay this morning," I whisper to Tom, fearing to leave him behind in the dark, yet wanting him to believe in the possibility. My dreams have been kind these three months, holding me tenderly. For the first time I dream of Lucas—an innocent moment of childhood. It's also the first night Tom dreams about him.

One day we find ourselves singing to an old favorite on the truck stereo.

"What if we tend the seeds that Lucas planted," we ask one another, "and inspire those wild and frightened children to live their dreams? They are all our sons and daughters." Half full? Half empty? Tom and I begin to recut our documentary as tribute to Lucas and as a way of reaching out. We buy a high-definition camcorder to take to Kernwood. Life is a creation—you can't get away from that. The only choice is what we create. *May I be a channel for good.*

"I can't be the OB Coordinator," I tell Tom. "It's as if there's a great bird on my left shoulder—fierce and disheveled. I've kept it caged for years, but now it's loose and I can't force it to do tricks anymore. It's dangerous and unpredictable."

"Remember the girl who walked into Sunset studio thirty years ago?" Tom's eyes glisten with tears. "I know that wild bird."

I pause, listening. There seems the faintest tinkle of wind chimes, a shimmer of light between dimensions. "Where have I been these last decades? How did I get so lost?"

"You didn't get lost. You just explored a side channel."

"You are bedrock for me." I melt into his hazel eyes. He is so beautiful—this balding man with glasses and white beard. "When did you learn to stay so centered?"

"I learned it from you."

"That picture of us you hung in the kitchen, I've never much cared for it. It doesn't show you well, but I look beautiful. Yesterday, I realized that you are the frame. That's what you were saying! You stand in the background, holding me up to shine."

Tears splash down Tom's cheeks. They spill so easily now. "Of course! It has always been my greatest joy. What would my life have been without you to support? I never wanted to be the flower, only the vase," he brings his gnarled wrists together and allows his fingers to open like a petals, "that holds it."

"These years—they weren't wasted," I say. "They were the nest that cradled Lucas! Always he was central. I am so grateful that he knew. It was only twenty-six years, but God, they were magnificent! Toward the end, in all the pictures, he is smiling fondly down, cradling us in his love."

"Now we get to transform, again."

"When you are not afraid to die, you are free to live. That is his parting gift."

∽

FRIENDS EXPRESS CONCERN THAT WE will vanish at Kernwood, die together out in our beloved wilderness. Yet it is here that we can finally dive into our grief—spending the summer in personal ceremonies to honor Lucas and release him. Birds alight on us as we sit before the fire, and mushrooms erupt between the berries. Trees speak in calming whispers, while the wind breathes warmth into my veins and thaws the ice around my heart. In dawning wonder, I feel an immense love from this sacred Planet. I am her child, bone of this soil, blood of this river. She knows me—even when I lose myself. Rocked in ancient lullabies, I watch my old skin peel away, revealing a new pink glow. Setting our camera on a tripod, we speak candidly and the wilderness listens. At last, I dare to look down.

"I've been soft and without bones these six months. If I had cobbled my life back together from the wreckage, I would have remained broken." I pause to find words for something beyond words. "I need some form, but nothing solid. Sometimes I am powerful and rushing; at others, deep and still beneath the snow. I am becoming the River."

Form. Reform. I gaze into the dancing current, seeing whorls like tightly curled embryos of possibility. In one future a gentle and defeated old woman is sitting. Her image appears like a tintype out of an antique book: solid, heavy-footed, and limping. She reminds me of my mother. Across her shoulders she carries the death of her only child like a worn and faded shawl. Her eyes are quiet as she rocks by the window in falling snow. Dawn illuminates her wrinkled face, but she doesn't look up. I do not easily dismiss her: she has learned a great deal, and perhaps has a right to her pain. No one blames her.

I pull back, eyeing the spectrum of potential futures. My attention is arrested by the violet glow of a fledgling possibility. Leaning close, I notice movement—a living cameo of a woman, neither young nor old. Her hair is silver, but her body is supple and strong. Her bare feet travel lightly through the grass. She is clothed in shimmering colors that seem to shift in the breeze. Over her left arm she carries the beauty of her years like a basket of flowers, and with her right hand she offers them to passing travelers. She laughs easily and loves everything.

I suddenly remember Lucas's vision of me at the end of the world. "Look at the beautiful flowers," he whispers across the dimensions.

Which future shall I choose? That, of course, is always the question.

Supernova
For Jeanie, Tom, and Lucas Irons

You've lived your lives not knowing that you know:
the shocking news that split your world today
in truth already happened long ago.

Gaze fixed on his high wire, you, down below,
stretched nets between you to anticipate
his leaps—you've lived, not knowing that you know.

A dying star with massive light explodes,
but years elapse before we see the flame,
and then the void, that opened long ago.

So, time's a borrowing. While light moves slow
we clasp beloved forms in its delay.
You've lived your lives. Not knowing, you yet know
that time tracks more dimensions than we're shown.

Already you've made efforts to reframe
a void that truly opened long ago.

In void's wide openness, you're letting grow
new purpose, based in love, to light your days.
You've lived your lives not knowing that you know:
this supernova happened long ago.

—Ela Harrison

Other Works by Jean Aspen

Arctic Daughter: A Wilderness Journey, 1988, 2015

A Child of Air (a novel), 2008

Arctic Son: Fulfilling the Dream, 1995, 2014

Documentaries filmed and produced by Jean Aspen and Tom Irons

Arctic Son: Fulfilling the Dream, 2012

Desert Glass: A Love Story, 2017

Books by Constance Helmericks

Down the Wild River North, 1968, 1989, Epicenter Press 2017

Flight of the Arctic Tern, 1952, Epicenter Press 2018

Our Alaskan Winter, 1950, Epicenter Press 2018

Our Summer with the Eskimos, 1949, Epicenter Press 2018

We Live in Alaska, 1944, Epicenter Press 2019

We Live in the Arctic, 1947, Epicenter Press 2019

Hunting in North America, 1956

Australian Adventure, 1972

A note from Jean: Tom and I have come to believe that our highest legacy is intact wilderness. In 2016 we began three years of carefully dismantling and removing all traces of our lives at Kernwood except for Lucas's memorial garden. Watch for our two final documentaries, *Arctic Daughter: A Wilderness Lifetime* and *Rewilding Kernwood*. For photographs and updates, visit:

www.JeanAspen.com

www.ingramcontent.com/pod-product-compliance
Lightning Source LLC
Chambersburg PA
CBHW071724080526
44588CB00013B/1886